POOR RECEPTION

COMMUNICATION

A series of volumes edited by:
Dolf Zillmann and Jennings Bryant

POOR RECEPTION

Misunderstanding and Forgetting Broadcast News

Barrie Gunter
Independent Broadcasting Authority

1987

LAWRENCE ERLBAUM ASSOCIATES, PUBLISHERS
Hillsdale, New Jersey　　　　　Hove and London

Lawrence Erlbaum Associates, Inc., Publishers
365 Broadway
Hillsdale, New Jersey 07642

Library of Congress Cataloging-in-Publication Data
Gunter, Barrie.
    Poor reception.

    (Communication)
    Bibliography: p.
    Includes index.
    1. Television broadcasting of news. 2. Television
audiences. I. Title. II. Series: Communication
(Hillsdale, N.J.)
PN4784.T4G86   1987   070.1'9   87-468
ISBN 0-89859-597-5

Printed in the United States of America
10 9 8 7 6 5 4 3 2 1

Contents

Preface

This book is about learning from television news. It considers the significance of news on television as a source of regular public affairs information, not only from the standpoint of what people themselves claim about
its importance for them but also from the more objective, empirically
verifiable perspective of how much their knowledge of domestic and
world affairs benefits as a consequence of exposure to it.

The news is a prominent and routine feature of daily television schedules in the modern world. In recent years, there has been a marked
expansion in the amount of news broadcast on television. The quantity of
news on long-established television channels has steadily increased from
their earliest years to the present day, and brand-new channels have in
some cases devoted most of their airtime (or cable time) to the provision
of information. Annual surveys of public opinion towards broadcast or
other media services provide further testament to the importance people
attach to the news on television. Most people today claim that television
is their major and most trusted source of news about the world.

The provision and purpose of news have been discussed in terms of the
rights of individuals living in democratic societies to know what is going
on around them. In a democracy, the populace are required to be informed so that they can form their own opinions about events and issues
on which those opinions could eventually be sought, such as during
political elections or referenda. As a right, people in a democracy are
entitled to make up their own minds about how society should be run and
to comment on that. But they need to have access to the relevant facts in

order to do this. Television, as a public service medium, is one source of such information.

Although people say that television is the most significant news source in their lives, behavioural research concerning the use of different mass media and also cognitive research concerning information uptake from the media together provide evidence that often contradicts that personal claim. In the first place, is television the most used source of news? This must surely be one crucial measure of its importance to the public. Figures for Britain indicate that television may not be as extensively used, however, as other media news sources. Recent combined audiences for the two main weekday evening television news programmes, for example, rarely exceed 45% of all adults, and in the summer months may often fall below 35%. Compare these figures with regular daily readership of a morning newspaper of about 70% of the adult population in Britain, plus a further 10 to 20% who do not read a morning newspaper but do read one in the evening, and the total far outstretches the television news audience sizes just described.

Newspaper readership outstrips news viewing for the major evening television bulletins not only in terms of numbers of people using each news source but also in terms of the amount of time people spend with each medium. The average weekday time spent reading a daily newspaper is around 30 minutes. Contrast this with the length of the main evening news programmes, which is usually less than 30 minutes, and the knowledge that only about one third of the audience for these programmes will watch them all the way through, and it becomes clear that for most people exposure to television news each day may be less than that to a newspaper.

People not only spend more time reading newspapers than they do watching news on television, they also consume more information in the same time when reading than when viewing. Newspapers carry more information than do television news broadcasts. As we see in this book, there is reliable evidence that information sticks much better after reading than after seeing it on television.

People in public opinion survey samples often claim that they learn a great deal about the world from watching the news on television, and that television is more important to them for acquiring the news than are other sources. However, how does learning from television news compare with that from other media? As we will see, research on recall of broadcast news has repeatedly indicated that much of what is presented seems to be quickly forgotten. It may even be, as evidence strongly suggests, that information under certain conditions of presentation in television newscasts is not learned properly in the first place—in other words, it never attains a state of settled storage in memory. And even when information is remembered, much of it will be misunderstood. Why should this happen? The answer is extremely complex and lies with the characteristics of audiences, the way in which they watch television, the techniques of television news broadcasting, and the way the news is presented on screen. In this book, we explore these factors and their influence on remembering and understanding news on television.

There is evidence that people do not concentrate as hard when watching television as when they are reading. Indeed, many people, it seems, do not believe they need to try very hard to learn from television as compared with reading a newspaper, book, or magazine. In consequence, information uptake from television news may be poorer than from a newspaper because of the relative amount of mental effort invested in each medium by the individuals who use them.

Another audience-related factor that may account for the relative ineffectiveness of television as a news medium is that television news attracts a disproportionate number of older people. Younger people watch less television in general and are less likely to be at home to see news programmes. Or, if they are at home, younger and middle-aged adults may be distracted by domestic and family matters that coincide with the times when news programmes typically are broadcast.

Cognitive psychologists have found that certain mental capacities and processes, including aspects of memory functioning, may deteriorate significantly among older adults. Difficulties are especially likely to be experienced with the processing of new information when one is faced with a succession of rapidly presented items of information concerning many different unrelated, and unfamiliar topics.

Another significant set of factors that are important in the context of the impact of television news on its audience, regardless of the character of the audience, concerns the nature of the production itself. The production of television news is of necessity a highly routinised and selective process. Bulletins are scheduled to fill regular slots and are constructed and ready to run at specific times each day. Newscasts are limited in the amount of airtime allocated to them each day, which also means they are restricted in the numbers of stories they can carry and in the depth to which each story can be elaborated and discussed. The few stories eventually transmitted are selected from many hundreds that reach the newsroom from various sources every day. The net result of this selection process is that through watching television, the public can become aware only of those few stories that news editors choose to present in their programmes. This has led to questions being raised about how representative televised news is of all available stories each day, and of how comprehensive the accounts are for particular stories presented in television bulletins. These are issues that have been discussed at length by sociological studies of the inner workings of television newsrooms and is not a subject that will be dwelled upon here. Instead, the focus of this book is on the significance of particular features of news structures and presentation that affect or are related to the intake, retention, and comprehension of televised news.

As we will see, routine styles of presenting the news do not always promote ease of retention and comprehension of news programme content. A great deal of attention is paid to programme format by news broadcasters, often chiefly for reasons of boosting programme popularity. The use of attractive presenters and dramatic, realistic, or "eyewitness" reporting on film are all features designed to build large, loyal audiences. Even when the news concerns serious topics such as politics, the economy, or foreign affairs, presentation frequently emphasises the drama of the event at the expense of explaining clearly the reasons why it occurred. As we will see in later sections of this book, videotape or film, although a popular format with producers, can create particular difficulties often because what is shown does not match or even bear any real relevance to what is being said by the reporter.

In summary, the production of television news is a well-established routinised process designed to create a stylized product whose contents and format meet the professional requirements of television journalism, attract large audiences, and can be achieved well within the time and space constraints imposed by tight deadlines of daily production and restrictions of scheduling. What this book explores is the extent to which the professional intuition of journalists about the information-processing capabilities of audiences as reflected in the ways they routinely present the news, are reinforced by empirical research into the informational effectiveness of their programmes.

Although journalists have long been suspicious of research intervention, just lately it seems as if some of the challenges research into news comprehension has thrown at them have begun to filter through to a group very guarded against outside intervention in their profession. Broadcasting Magazine in 1985 quoted NBC News President Larry Grossman as saying:

If we have any single priority for every one of our news shows in the months to come, it will be to clarify, to explain, to write our scripts and file our reports in a style that makes what is happening as fully understandable as we can possibly make it to every one of our viewers. That, I believe, is the single most important improvement we must now make in the vital service that NBC News provides.

In this book we examine some ways in which, through a better understanding of the ways audiences approach and cognitively process the news, the production of more informative and comprehensible television news broadcasts may be accomplished.

Acknowledgments

The author would like to express his thanks to the following for permission to reproduce data and reprint tables and figures orginally published elsewhere:

George Gerbner of the Annenberg School of Communications, University of Pennsylvania for Table 1.10 from A. Rubin "Ritualised and instrumental television viewing", *Journal of Communication*, 1984, *34*, 67-77

William Belson for Tables 4.11 and 7.1 from his book, *The Impact of Television*, Crosby Lockwood & Son, Ltd., London, 1967

Colin Berry and Carfax Publishing Company, Abingdon, Oxfordshire, UK for Figure 9.1 from C. Berry "A dual effect of pictorial enrichment in learning from television news: Gunter's data revisited", *Journal of Educational Television*, 1983, *9*, 171-174

Frans Kempers, Chief Editor, Gazette, Institute of the Science of the Press, Amsterdam for Tables 6.1, 6.2, and 6.3 from V.M. Sparkes and J.P. Winter "Public interest in foreign news" *Gazette*, 1980, *20*, 149-170

Winfried Schulz for Tables 6.6 and 6.7 from the latter's paper "News structures and people's awareness of political events" *Gazette*, 1982, *30*, 139-153

Beverly Bergerson and the Association for Education in Journalism and Mass Communication, Columbia, South Carolina for Figure 8.1 from P. Tannenbaum "Effect of serial position on recall of radio news stories" *Journalism Quarterly*, 154, *31*, 319-232

Tables 4.7, 4.8, 6.5 and 9.3 from E. Katz, H. Adoni, and P. Parness "Remembering the news: what the picture adds to recall", *Journalism Quarterly*, 1977, *54*, 231-239

Table 9.1 from J. Stauffer, R. Frost and W. Rybolt "Recall and comprehension of radio news in Kenya" *Journalism Quarterly*, 1980, *57*, 612-617

Table 5.6 from M. Levy "The audience experience with television news" *Journalism Monographs*, 1978, No. 55

Olle Findahl of the Swedish Broadcasting Corporation to use Figures 7.1, 7.2, 9.2,

9.3A-D, 9.4A-B, 10.1A-D, 10.2A-B and Tables 7.6 and 7.7 from O. Findahl and B. Hoijer "Man as a receiver of information: repetitions and reformulations in a news programme" Stockholm: Swedish Broadcasting Corporation, 1972
O. Findahl and B. Hoijer "Fragments of reality: an experiment with news and TV-visuals" Stockholm: Swedish Broadcasting Corporation, 1976
O. Findahl and B. Hoijer "Comprehension analysis: a review of the research and an application to radio and television news", Lund: Studentlitteratur
Steen Folke Larsen for Tables 7.2, 7.3, 7.4, and 7.5 from his report "Knowledge updating: three papers on news memory, background knowledge and text processing", *Psychological Reports*, 1981, vol. 6, no. 4, Aarhus: University of Aarhus, Institute of Psychology
John Robinson for Tables 4.1, 4.10, 5.3, 5.4, and 6.8 from J. Robinson and H. Sahin "Audience comprehension of television news: results from some exploratory research", London: British Broadcasting Corporation, 1984
Elsevier Science Publishing Co., Inc., for Tables 4.5, 4.6, 5.5 and 6.4 from W.R. Neuman "Patterns of recall among television news viewers", *Public Opinion Quarterly*, 1976, *40*, 115-123
A.C. Nielsen for Table 1.1 and Figure 11.1 derived from "Television viewing to network news programming", Nielsen Television Index, New York, A.C. Nielsen Company, 1984
The Roper Organisation for Tables 1.2, 1.3, 1.5, 1.6, 1.7, 1.8, and 1.9 from "trends in attitudes towards television and other media: a twenty-year review", New York, Television Information Office, 1983.

POOR RECEPTION

1 The Growth of Television News

THE GROWTH OF NEWS ON TELEVISION

Television news is the most pervasive source of public affairs information in western industrialized societies today. The provision of news has come to be regarded by broadcasters and audiences alike as one of the most important functions carried out by television, a fact that is illustrated by the amount of air time routinely occupied by news programmes in the schedules of major networks and local TV stations, and by the behaviour of many millions of people who have their sets tuned in to television news bulletins every day.

The news has been an important part of the development of network television from the very beginning. Today, news programmes constitute a large segment of total programme output for major television networks. In the United States, for example, network television news programming expanded from 2.5 hours a week in 1950 to over 70 hours a week by the early 1980s, or from about 3% to 21% of regularly scheduled programming (Nielsen, 1984) (see Table 1.1). In 1950, U.S. television audiences had a choice of just two 15-minute programmes transmitted at one time, whereas nowadays they have 28 network programmes to choose from, spread across all times of the day.

Regularly scheduled news programming on U.S. network television increased in amount substantially during the first half of the 1950s. During the early days of television news, the style of presentation changed too. By the middle of the decade, news "personalities" began to emerge, adding a more friendly and human touch to the news. The news continued

1

TABLE 1.1
The Growth of Network News in the US

	1950	1955	1960	1965	1970	1975	1980	1982
Total TV Hours	85	160	174	230	231	257	266	345
Total TV News Hours	2.5	12	9	19	18	26	36	73
News Share %	3	8	5	8	8	10	14	21

Source: Nielsen Television Index Ratings reports, 1984. Reprinted by permission of A.C. Nielsen, Inc.
Note: Excludes specials and programmes under 5 minutes duration.

to be broadcast in 15-minute prime-time segments throughout the 1950s but by 1955 had already begun to establish itself in its now traditional early evening time slot. By this time also, NBC's *Today Show* had expanded regular news coverage into weekday mornings.

Between 1955 and 1960, the networks continued the development of their main early evening news broadcasts. Weekend reporting in 30-minute bulletins was introduced in a move which set the stage for extended news formats on weekdays. During the 1960s news personalities became firmly established and were an important ingredient of a show's success with the audience. The main evening news shows were expanded to 30 minutes, and direct or "head-to-head" competition between simultaneously presented programmes became a feature of the schedules.

During weekdays, there was an increase in the number of 5-minute news briefs and updates, and weekend news became a familiar part of the network schedules. In 1967, CBS introduced its *Morning News* programme to provide a competitor for NBC's *Today Show*. With this continued expansion of network news, news "anchors" came to be supplemented more and more by correspondents and reporters who contributed on special news topics.

The 1970s saw further developments in network news. By 1975, early evening news was broadcast on all networks at 6:30 to 7:00pm, and this format (with different "anchors") was also used on Saturday and Sunday. Early morning news became available on all networks during the same year, with the introduction of *Good Morning America* by ABC. Short-duration news shows designed especially for children also appeared.

Although by 1980 all main news programmes were of 30 minutes duration or longer, the next couple of years witnessed an unprecedented rate of growth of news on television with the expansion of news into previously unscheduled late night or very early morning time periods. During the first 2 years of the decade, network news coverage in the U.S. doubled (see Table 1.1). News growth during this period, however, has

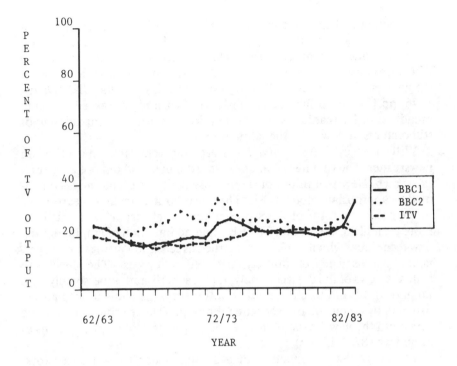

FIG. 1.1 TV network news output in the UK. Percentage of Total Output on Each Channel Devoted to News and Current Affairs Programmes

not been restricted to the networks. With cable television, subscribers across America gained access to continuous 24-hours-a-day, 7-days-a-week news and weather information services.

In the United Kingdom, television began as a regular high-definition service on 2 November 1936. At that time it showed Gaumont-British and British Movitone newsreels such as those shown in the cinema. There were only 2 hours of television a day then, one in the afternoon and one in the evening, and only 400 sets in the London area could receive the service. Television closed down on 1 September 1939 for the duration of the war. It returned on 7 June 1946 and spread slowly across the country. But until 1954, there were no television news programmes, other than outside broadcasts of major events and newsreels.

In 1948, the British Broadcasting Corporation progressed to making its own newsreels, which, from weekly editions with repeats, became bi-weekly and eventually nightly. In those days, radio was the principal medium people turned to for the most up-to-date news. No efforts were made to speed up the news process on television.

The situation began to change in 1953 when, following the Coronation coverage, the demand for television sets grew. In 1954, with the promise of a new Independent Television channel providing competition, the BBC introduced *Television News and Newsreel*, heralded as "a service of the greatest significance in the progress of television in the UK" (Davis, 1976, pp.12–13). In fact, all it consisted of each night was a 10-minute broadcast with a reading of the latest radio news to an accompaniment of still pictures, followed by the familiar newsreel.

With *Television News and Newsreel* however, came the television newsreader. The first newsreaders were radio men and did not appear on the screen. Newsreel film footage in those days was silent and accompanied by appropriate mood music. There was no attempt at this early stage to create a new form of news presentation—television news was little more than illustrated radio. The BBC had no intention of employing any new techniques which might be construed as sensationalising or personalising the news. The Corporation's declared policy was: "The object is to state the news of the day accurately, fairly, soberly and impersonally. It is no part of the aim to induce either optimism or pessimism or to attract listeners by colourful and sensational reports. The legitimate urge to be 'first with the news' must invariably be subjugated to the prior claims of accuracy" (BBC, 1976b).

Following the introduction of a second major television network, Independent Television News (ITN) began on September 22, 1955. According to ITN, the emphasis of television news should be visual and should interest the greatest number of people. The style ITN adopted was in contrast to the BBC's illustrated radio format and was inspired to some extent by American television news broadcasting. Rather than simply using news*readers,* ITN opted for news*casters,* who were trained journalists who provided their own input into the writing and compilation of the news programme. These individuals were chosen not simply for their professional experience in journalism, however, but also for their personalities. The policy adopted at ITN was to make the news more human and friendly than it had hitherto been. In the beginning, ITN broadcast three news programmes each weekday, at noon, 7:00 pm, and 10:00 pm, and two daily on weekends. The new newscasters were seen by viewers not only presenting the news and introducing stories on film but also interviewing and reporting their own stories. For the first time on British television reporters put direct and pointed questions to politicians and persisted until they answered. Film crews and reporters also went out and sought and recorded the views of the men and women in the street—"vox pop," as they became known in the profession. Often these early film reports featuring interviews with the ordinary working folk involved in social or industrial disputes had tremendous impact.

With the birth of ITN, for the first time the news also contained elements of humour, usually delivered by the newscaster as the final item in the programme. Davis (1976) quotes one early amusing example: "In Israel a car taking an expectant mother to a maternity hospital collided with a stork. An hour later the mother gave birth to a healthy boy. The stork was stunned and slightly injured. Latest reports say that it is doing as well as can be expected" (p. 18).

Following ITN's lead, the BBC introduced a 15-minute illustrated news bulletin in which newsreaders were shown on camera, though at first anonymously and only during the headlines. During the late 1950s, the BBC's news became more human and more personable as its newscasters too were finally named and took on a friendlier style.

For historians of television news in Britain, the next major turning point is identified with the Cuban missile crisis of 1962, when the United States secured evidence of the establishment of Russian rocket bases on Cuba, 90 miles away from the Southeast coast of the United States. President John F. Kennedy appeared on U.S. television and warned that any nuclear attack launched from Cuba against any nation in the western hemisphere would be met with a full retaliatory response against the Soviet Union. As U.S. forces were put on full alert and the world waited for a week on the brink of nuclear war, it was only broadcast news via radio and television, and not newspapers, that was immediate enough to provide news of the latest developments. With two television channels by now serving the British nation as a whole, it was television that the public turned to. At the same time, television became, for the first time in Britain, the chief mass media source for news.

During the second half of the 1960s, television news in the United Kingdom expanded further with the introduction on both major channels (BBC1 and ITV) of main half-hour news programmes on weekdays. Once again, America had shown the way, with CBS's *Evening News with Walter Cronkite*, which began in September 1963, followed by NBC's *Huntley-Brinkley Report*. Although BBC2, the third channel, included a half-hour news programme when it began in April 1964, the audience for this transmission was very small. Half-hour news first came to a major channel in the United Kingdom on 3 July 1967, when ITN introduced *News at Ten*. This move was regarded as one not simply of lengthening the news but of providing room for greater flexibility. Until then, the news had been delivered in short bulletins, whereas in-depth coverage had been confined to current affairs programmes. This new extended news programme was aired at 10:00 pm. The independent companies were reluctant to transmit it any earlier because they believed it would be unacceptable to the mass audience interested primarily in entertainment programming. Even at this fairly late hour, there was some anxiety about the effect of the programme on the independent channel's audience. Many ITV executives feared it would drive people away from the channel.

ITN, however, was confident that the programme would make good viewing. There was enough interesting news available each day that people would want to know about to make an attractive half-hour news programme. The programme would be able to hold an audience and would become an integral part of everyone's viewing, and not just a brief respite from entertainment programming.

The underlying idea was that the programme would not have a fixed format every night. Some nights it would feature a variety of hard news items; on other nights it might focus for most of the time on a single story. More time would also be available for and allotted to human interest stories and fuller coverage of sports. A new presentation style was introduced for *News at Ten*: The programme was presented by two studio anchorpersons. This served the dual purpose of offering visual variety and allowing for up-to-the-minute changes to the news while the programme was on-air, as one newscaster could be freshly briefed while out of camera shot.

During the early 1970s, the BBC decided to experiment with the two-anchor format as well but soon returned to a single anchorperson. Weekday news broadcasting on the two main channels on settled down to three main bulletins a day at lunchtime for about 15 minutes, in the early evening for the same duration, and in the late evening for around half an hour. These programmes were supplemented by national and regional news magazines and summaries throughout each day. By the middle of the decade, news on the BBC took up 426 hours or 5% total programme time, added to which were 1,700 hours or 20% of total time devoted to current affairs, features, and documentaries. A quarter of total television broadcast hours on the two BBC channels was thus devoted to news and other information programming of various kinds (BBC, 1976a).

From the early 1950s to the present day in the United Kingdom, the choice of television news has increased from a single television channel's weekly newsreel seen in only certain parts of the country to 11 nationally broadcast news programmes available each weekday on four channels plus a further 10 bulletins on weekends. It is worth noting that the growth in amount of news shown on television in the United Kingdom has been due largely to the introduction of new television channels rather than to sudden substantial increases in news programming on any particular channel. As Fig. 1.1 shows, the percentage of transmission time devoted to news and current affairs programmes over the 20 or so years leading up to the mid-1980s on the three channels in operation during this period has remained fairly constant, averaging around 25% of total output in each case.

As in the United States, the first half of the 1980s saw a marked expansion in the amount of news broadcast on television in the United Kingdom. The manifestations of this sudden news growth were, firstly, the introduction in November 1982 of a new hour-long weekday news programme at 7:00 pm on the new fourth channel, and, secondly, the introduction in February 1983 of two early morning television programmes, on BBC1 and ITV, each with a focus on news and informational features. Although in the face of stiff competition from entertainment programming on the major television channels, *Channel Four News* has attracted only a small selective news audience of around one million viewers, the audiences for the breakfast programmes have grown steadily, so that after just two years, some 25% of the U.K. viewing population were watching at least some breakfast television every week.

As news programmes have come to occur more frequently and to occupy more time on television, so the medium's importance to the public as a major source of up-to-date and reliable news information about domestic and world affairs has increased substantially. Today, for most people, television is identified as the most significant news source in their lives.

THE GROWTH OF PUBLIC ACCEPTANCE OF TV NEWS

Between the mid-1950s and mid-1980s, television evolved as the primary news medium. On average, around two thirds of the mass publics in modern industrialised societies claim that television is their main source of national and international news (IBA 1985; Roper, 1983). It has long been recognised, however, that the ability of different media to transmit information varies and that the communication effectiveness of a particular programme may depend upon the way it is approached and used and on the kind of content it is presenting to its audience. Certain media are better than others at communicating certain kinds of information content.

Public opinion surveys over the years have indicated varying attitudes over time towards different news media. In a comparison of public response to television and newspapers, a Gallup Poll in 1979 found that only a minority of the U.S. population expressed "a great deal of confidence" in either of these media. Among younger people, indeed, rather more (22%) expressed confidence in newspapers than in television (14%). Among older individuals, the proportions—19% for newspapers and 18% for television—were about equal. One important point to note, however, is that the question referred to television and not specifically to news on television (Bogart, 1981).

Public attitudes towards television news and newspapers have been tracked continuously for many years by surveys in the United States and the United Kingdom. In answer to the critical question of where they usually get most of their news about what's going on in the world today, the first Roper survey among the U.S. public (in 1959) found that 57% said newspapers, 51% said television, and 34% mentioned radio. By 1963, television and newspapers were about even, and in 1967, television was ahead and has stayed there ever since.

Summarising the results of these surveys, Tables 1.2, and 1.3 show that in the United States since 1963 television has led all other media as the source from which people say they get most of their news. The overall pattern is that over the last 20 years television has steadily increased the margin of its lead over newspapers.

Since 1975, a similar question has been asked of national samples in the United Kingdom in the Independent Broadcasting Authority's annual survey of public attitudes towards broadcasting. Table 1.4 shows that, as in the United States, television has in recent years consistently received the greater number of first mentions as the most important source of news about the world among the British public.

The public's perceptions of the effectiveness and informativeness of television as a principal or best news source is not constant across all kinds of news, however. Although television is commonly endorsed most

TABLE 1.2
Major Source of World News: United States

Source of most news:	1959 %	1961 %	1963 %	1964 %	1967 %	1968 %	1971 %	1972 %	1974 %	1976 %	1978 %	1980 %	1982 %
Television	51	52	55	58	64	59	60	64	65	64	67	64	65
Newspapers	57	57	53	56	55	49	48	50	47	49	49	44	44
Radio	34	34	29	26	28	25	23	21	21	19	20	18	18
People	4	5	4	5	4	5	4	4	4	5	5	4	4

Source: Roper Organisation, 1983. Reprinted by permission of author.

TABLE 1.3
Share of Audience Among Major News Sources

Source of most news:	1959 %	1961 %	1963 %	1964 %	1967 %	1968 %	1971 %	1972 %	1974 %	1976 %	1978 %	1980 %	1982 %
Television	33	33	37	38	40	41	43	44	46	44	46	47	48
Newspapers	37	36	36	37	35	34	34	34	33	34	34	33	32
All others	30	31	27	25	25	25	23	22	21	22	20	20	20

Source: Roper Organisation, 1983. Reprinted by permission of author.

TABLE 1.4
Major Source of World News: United Kingdom

	1975 %	1976 %	1977 %	1979 %	1980 %	1981 %	1982 %
Television	62	54	56	59	52	53	58
Newspapers	26	33	31	29	33	34	27
Radio	11	11	12	11	14	11	12
People	1	2	1	1	1	1	1

Source: IBA, 1975–1982.

often as the main source for world news, the picture changes for local news. On a local or regional level, newspapers are typically rated as far more important sources of news than either television or radio. In a survey of national public opinion concerning broadcasting in Britain in 1982, 58% of people said they got most of their world news from television, 27% first mentioned newspapers, and 12% gave first mention to radio; but when asked about sources of local news, newspapers came out on top, being given first mention over television and radio by 58% of the population, while television and radio were each mentioned first in this context by just 12% (IBA, 1982).

The respective positions of television and newspapers in public opinion as first sources of information at national and local levels were further illustrated by attitude trend data concerning the mass media reported for the United States by Roper (1983). Throughout the 1970s and early 1980s, people were asked questions about their sources of information on candidates running in local, state, or national elections. With the exception of 1980, in all surveys since 1971 newspapers led television in acquainting people with local candidates, although television was named increasingly as a news source. In 1980, television, for the first time, moved into the lead, but lost it again very narrowly in 1982. (see Table 1.5) In Congressional elections and statewide elections, television consistently showed a clear lead over newspapers as a source of information about candidates (see Tables 1.6 and 1.7).

NEWS SOURCES FOR NEWS TOPICS

There is evidence that people can make even more refined judgements about which news sources are best for finding out about particular kinds of news. Bogart (1981) reported a 1966 survey in which respondents were presented with one-sentence summaries of 120 news stories and asked what was the "best way" to find out about each. These brief distillations of

TABLE 1.5

Major Sources of Information About Candidates in Local Elections

	1971 %	1972 %	1974 %	1976 %	1978 %	1980 %	1982 %
Newspapers	41	41	41	44	45	36	39
Television	27	31	30	34	39	44	37
Radio	6	7	8	7	10	6	6
People	19	23	14	12	15	11	15
Magazines	1	1	1	2	1	2	1
Other	5	5	5	6	7	5	7
Total Mentions	99	108	99	105	117	104	105

Source: Roper Organisation, 1983. Reprinted by permission of author.

TABLE 1.6

Major Sources of Information About Candidates in Congressional Elections

	1974 %	1978 %	1982 %
Television	40	48	46
Newspapers	35	38	31
Radio	6	8	5
People	8	10	9
Magazines	1	2	2
other	5	6	7
Total Mentions	95	112	100

Source: Roper Organisation, 1983. Reprinted by permission of author.

TABLE 1.7

Major Sources of Information About Candidates in State-Wide Elections

	1971 %	1972 %	1974 %	1976 %	1978 %	1982 %
Television	51	49	48	53	55	53
Newspapers	19	39	33	35	39	29
Radio	6	7	6	5	8	6
People	10	9	6	6	8	7
Magazines	2	1	1	1	2	1
Other	4	3	3	3	5	5
Total Mentions	102	108	97	103	117	101

Source: Roper Organisation, 1983. Reprinted by permission of author.

10

originally much longer news stories were designed so that they could have come from any medium and were not characterised by the flavour of a newspaper or a television news story.

Newspapers were considered the best way to find out for 59% of the statements, television for 29% magazines for 8%, and radio for 4%. Looked at from another angle, the results showed that for the average item, newspapers were named as "the best way" of finding out by 37% of those interviewed, television by 26%, radio by 14%, and magazines by 7%. Bogart contended that the general preeminence of newspapers may have derived from the fact that they normally cover a greater variety of stories than other media and hence are regarded as a good source of information with respect to a greater array of news material. For a handful of special-interest stories of the sort often reported on television, however, television was nominated as the best news source.

Television was the most favoured medium on stories about disasters, freak weather phenomena, and space and science, items that were likely to feature a strong visual component. Newspapers, on the other hand, were favoured in particular for less obviously "visual" stories about domestic legal and political matters. On a local level, newspapers featured strongly as the best way to find out about subjects such as community affairs, local personalities, and crime. Any stories likely to be reported in the medium of film, even if footage did not depict the actual reported events, were ones for which people would turn to television for information.

In a recent survey, Roper (1983) included several new questions about how well television covers the news. The first of these asked people to rate the kind of job television is doing covering eight different kinds of news: national news, local news, major national events, news about the economic situation, business news, major sports events, major international events, and general news about what's going on in foreign countries. A large majority of people rated television's coverage of all eight kinds of news as "excellent" or "good." Highest marks were given to coverage of major national events, national news, and major sports events, closely followed by major international events and local news (See Table 1.8).

National surveys on both sides of the Atlantic have shown that people trust televised news and rate its coverage of events highly. In their *Annual Review of Audience Research Findings*, the BBC (1977) reported that when asked to name the "best things" about television, 41% of a United Kingdom national sample said that "it provides reliable, up-to-date information about what is going on in the world." Periodic nationwide surveys of attitudes towards various news sources in the United States have revealed increasing public trust in television news over the years (See Table 1.9).

TABLE 1.8
How Well Television Covers the News

Percent considering the job television does covering it as:	Excellent or good	Not very good or poor
	%	%
Major national events	93	5
National news	91	7
Major sports events	90	4
Major international events	87	8
Local news	80	17
News about economy	75	20
Business news	65	26

Source: Roper Organisation, 1983. Reprinted by permission of author.

Q. If you got conflicting or different reports of the same news story from radio, television, the magazines and the newspapers, which of the four versions would you be most inclined to believe—the one on radio or television or magazines or newspapers?

A follow-up question asked: "In terms of meeting your overall needs for news, would you say television is doing an excellent, good, not very good, or poor job?" One fifth of respondents said that television was doing an excellent job. Only one in 10 said that television was a "not very good" or "poor" provider of news.

A third question asked people how fair investigative news shows on television are in their presentations. Nearly three-quarters of respondents said that the reporters who conduct the investigations on such shows are usually careful and fair in what they put on the air. Fewer than one in five said they are often unfair.

Television is believed to report events accurately by many more people than believe that newspapers, radio, or magazines do so. In 1980, if they received "conflicting or different reports of the same news story" from different media, 51% of Americans said they would be most inclined to believe the television version, whereas only 22% would believe the newspaper version (Roper, 1983). This pattern of results has been confirmed by smaller academic studies done in the United States. In a study among Seattle residents, Bush (1969) compared print and broadcast media as sources of foreign news and found newspapers preferred over broadcasting, which was considered inadequate in foreign news coverage. On the other hand, Lee (1975) found television was preferred when he asked respondents which medium they would believe in the event of conflicting reports, over television and in the newspaper, on the same national or

12

TABLE 1.9
The Relative Credibility of Media

Most believable:	1959 %	1961 %	1963 %	1964 %	1967 %	1968 %	1971 %	1972 %	1974 %	1976 %	1978 %	1980 %	1982 %
Television	29	39	36	41	41	44	49	48	51	51	47	51	53
Newspapers	32	24	24	23	24	21	20	21	20	22	23	22	22
Radio	12	12	12	8	7	8	10	8	8	7	9	8	6
Magazines	10	10	10	10	8	11	9	10	8	9	9	9	8

Source: Roper Organisation, 1983. Reprinted by permission of author.

international event. Seventy-six percent said they would believe television, and 24% said newspapers. On other scales (honest, trustworthy, reliable, expert, and substantive), television was judged significantly better than newspapers. Only on the matter of accuracy was the newspaper judged slightly better, but both media were on the low end of the scale.

In some respects the news seems to lend to an ever-changing world an element of certainty and security. Bulletins occur routinely at the same times daily. Whereas other parts of the television schedule may vary considerably from one day to the next, only under exceptional circumstances does the position of the news change. Together with one or two long-running soap operas, television newcasts are the only truly enduring features of the schedules. As a consequence, viewers may develop powerful learned expectancies to see them at certain times.

These expectancies, together with the impression of actuality given by film may form an important ingredient of the reliability and trust worthiness which so many people say they perceive as essential characteristics of television news.

THE PERCEIVED BENEFITS OF NEWS WATCHING

Not only is television perceived by mass publics as the most important source of news about what is happening in the world, but one of the main reasons people give for watching television at all is to obtain information. When questioned about their television viewing, the reasons people give for watching may vary widely. But recent studies have indicated that these can be boiled down to a manageable number of readily interpretable factors. This is especially true in the particular case of watching the news, which seems to be associated with fairly specific motives.

In a study of the audience for the popular U.S. television programme "Sixty Minutes," Rubin (1981) identified two types of viewers—a time-consuming (habitual) information seeker who is a more frequent general user of television, and a non-time-consuming (non habitual) entertainment-information seeker who exhibits an affinity with the programme. Subsequently, Rubin and Rubin (1982), in an investigation of older persons' television viewing motives, identified motivations associated with these two types of television viewers: an habitual viewer who watches to fill time and for companionship, relaxation, arousal, and escape, who views a great deal of television, and who displays a definite affinity with the medium, and a selective viewer who seeks information and watches news, talk, and magazine programmes. Rubin (1983), in an analysis of adult television use, confirmed these two types of viewers.

In the most recent study in the series, Rubin (1984) once again examined the motives for watching television. On this occasion he investigated the ways in which particular sets of motives are related to perferences for particular categories of television programmes. Respondents were asked to rare 14 statements as to how they reflected their own feelings as to why they watched television. From Table 1.10 it can be seen that "Information/learning" was the most powerfully endorsed reason for watching television.

In all, about 70% of Rubin's 300 respondents from two midwestern U.S. communities agreed that they watched television to learn about people or events. The other main reasons given in rank order, were: because it is entertaining and enjoyable (55%), is convenient (46%), is less expensive than other activities (45%), enables one to relax (43%), keeps one company (31%), at helps to pass the time of day (27%). Each of the remaining listed reasons were endorsed by fewer than 20% of the sample.

More significant in the context of the current discussion, however, was the way in which these motives were associated with the extent to which different types of programmes were watched. Motives of using television for companionship, out of habit, to pass the time, for economic reasons, and for entertainment, relaxation, and arousal were associated positively with viewing action adventure, game, music/variety, drama, and general comedy programmes. On the other hand, watching television to learn

TABLE 1.10
Motives for Watching Television

Motive	Mean Score
Information/learning	3.77
Entertainment	3.53
Relaxation	3.22
Convenience	3.17
Economics/inexpensive	3.13
Companionship	2.79
Pass time	2.65
Arousal/excitement	2.63
Escape/forget	2.33
Habit	2.27
Topic for conversation	2.25
Behavioural guidance	2.02
Social interaction	1.79
Product advertising	1.73

Source: Rubin, 1984. Reprinted by permission of publisher.
Note: Each item was endorsed along a 5-point scale from strongly disagree (1 point) to strongly agree (5 points).

about events, to acquire topics for subsequent conversation, and to seek behavioural guidance were positively correlated with watching news, magazine/documentary, and talk/interview programmes.

Research elsewhere has shown that television audiences may give a variety of reasons for watching even highly specialised current affairs programmes, but the most prominent reasons relate to the cognitive benefits viewers subjectively perceive they gain from tuning in. Levy (1978) investigated the social and attitudinal characteristics of audiences for television news interview programmes. These programmes which included *Meet the Press, Face the Action*, and *Issues and Answers*, were broadcast each Sunday and attracted small audiences of around 3 to 5 million, but numbered among these were known to be individuals in important political positions.

Levy conducted focus group discussions with two dozen adults and a personal interview survey with a further 240 people. Respondents who watched these interview programmes were asked to indicate their reasons for watching. Table 1.11 is reprinted from Levy and shows the extent to which ten "subjective orientation propositions" were supported by viewers of interview programmes. It is clear that prominent among viewers' motivations and experience with these programmes were perceive cognitive gains. Almost all viewers believed that the interview programmes gave them food for thought and taught them about public issues. It is also clear, however, that viewers enjoyed seeing how leading public figures performed under the pressure of being interviewed on television and found the programmes provided an opportunity to evaluate politicians' abilities.

Although well received by the public as an important and reliable news source relative to other major news media, to what extent is the high public regard for television news and the level of knowledge about public affairs it is believed to communicate reflected in actual knowledge gained from the medium? Even though people believe they know a lot about various current issues, are able to understand much of what television tells them, and learn extensively from it, research has often shown this to be far from true.

For instance, people say they value weather forecast information on television. They claim that weather bulletins are important to them and that they generally find these forecasts easy to follow and understand. Such subjective feelings do not, however, tally with objective measures of comprehension, which indicate that few people understand the meanings of the symbols shown on weather charts or the terms used by weather forecasters (Wober & Gunter, 1981). Furthermore, although highly valued, broadcast weather information is usually only poorly recalled (Wober & Gunter, 1981; Wagenaar, 1978).

TABLE 1.11
Respondent Support for Subjective Orientation
Propositions

	Strongly Agree %	Agree %	Not Sure %	Disagree Strongly Disagree* %
1 Interview programmes give me food for thought	15.4	75.0	3.8	5.8
2 I learn new things about public issues from interview programmes	19.2	75.0	3.7	2.0
3 By watching, I can compare my own ideas with those of people in the news	15.4	67.3	11.5	5.8
4 By hearing, an interview, you find out what the person being interviewed really thinks	5.8	50.8	28.8	14.6
5 It gives me a chance to see how well people in the news do under pressure	15.4	61.5	11.5	11.6
6 It's like watching a contest of brains between the reporters and the person being interviewed	7.7	57.7	11.5	23.1
7 I like it when the reporters ask tough questions	26.9	55.8	11.5	5.8
8 You see news actually being made on the interview programme	9.6	48.1	25.0	17.3
9 Sometimes interview programmes are dull and boring	3.8	59.7	7.7	28.8
10 The reporters do not always ask hard or important questions	7.7	57.7	15.4	19.2

Source: Levy, 1978. Reprinted by permission of publisher.
*Fewer than 4% of respondents "strongly disagreed" with any one proposition, and none chose this response for Propositions 1, 2, 3, 4, 5, 6, 7, or 8.

Another subject matter covered extensively by television news programming is the economy. Do people really understand this subject, however, and is their understanding enhanced by television news coverage of economic news? Again, the available evidence suggests that understanding is poor. In one Israeli study, concepts such as balance of payments, gross national product, value-added tax, and cost-of-living index were found to be properly understood only by one third of the population (Adoni & Cohen, 1978). Regardless of how much they actually knew, people tended to feel that television was helping them to understand. But there was only weak evidence that television actually contributed towards better understanding and then only among women.

So is knowledge about political, economic, social, and environmental happenings communicated effectively by television? Does the public actually gain as much information about major news stories from television as it believes? Is television a good news medium? These are questions to which we turn in the next chapter.

2 The Reception of Television News

Although news programmes occupy prominent positions in the daily television schedules and are watched by millions of people, how effectively do they impart information about the world? We have seen that viewers believe that one of the most important functions of television watching, from a personal point of view, is to provide them with information about social, economic, political, and world affairs. Those who watch particular news programmes believe they actually do learn from them and that their knowledge of current affairs is enhanced as a result of the experience. But is what viewers *believe* the same as what actually happens? Contrary to what the claims audiences make for news programmes might lead one to expect, research on the retention of television news has indicated frequent miscomprehension or even wholesale forgetting of information presented by these programmes.

In this chapter we examine evidence for learning from news broadcasts. How effectively does the nightly (or daily) news impart information to the audience? To what extent are viewers and listeners able to recollect stories from the news after initial or repeated exposure? There is accumulating research evidence to indicate that extensive losses of information among audiences commonly occur within a relatively short period after exposure to a broadcast news presentation. These findings signal what appears to be an ineffectiveness on the part of standard news broadcasts to communicate information about public affairs in a manner that viewers and listeners can comfortably grasp and absorb.

Although systematic theory-driven research into the cognitive impact of television news has much to achieve, already researchers have identified a complex array of factors that mediate learning and memory of broadcast news, and that in some instances may account for the apparently common breakdown in the learning process. In the next chapter we turn our attention to some of the cognitive phenomena that may be involved in the processing of news and may provide explanations as to why failure to remember and understand the content of news broadcasts occurs.

LEARNING THROUGH DIFFERENT MEDIA

One major concern of this chapter is to establish the efficacy of television compared with other media as a surveyor of memorable news. How does television compare with, say, newspapers as a medium through which the public actually obtains news about the world? We have seen already in the first chapter that people make different claims about the value of each of these media as news sources. But just as in the context of measuring attention to the news what people say they have watched and what they have actually watched may be quite different, so, with learning from television, what people think they have learned and the knowledge they have in fact gained may not be the same.

It was observed quite early in the comparison of diffusion of knowledge about a major news story that television and newspapers played different parts in the diffusion process. Television can play a major role in delivering important news flashes quickly and concisely to large numbers of people, whereas newspapers tend primarily to supplement or embellish brief broadcast news shots with details about the stories in question (Deutschmann & Danielson, 1960; see also Harvey & Stone, 1969).

Since then, other studies (many of which are reported in this chapter) have shown that both newspapers and television news programmes can convey information and increase the salience of various topics, but information loss seems to be greater from television than from newspapers. There may be substantial information loss even from newspapers, but in general research has shown that printed stories result in more information retention than do televised stories (e.g., Dommermuth, 1974; Wilson, 1974).

Should we expect differences in the extent to which individuals learn from newspapers and television news programmes? To some extent, the answer is "yes." The reason is that by their very nature the two media are different. And by this is meant not simply that they differ in the way they present news information. It is a well-known and often cited fact that the script of an average television news programme would fill only two columns of most broadsheet newspapers. Newspapers provide more detail, whereas television provides more immediacy, or at least a feeling of actuality through its filmed or "eyewitness" news reports. But there are also important differences in the way individuals cognitively process information while reading or while listening and watching.

It is at this point that conflicting arguments and evidence begin to emerge. Some researchers have argued that reading requires more cognitive effort than does listening or watching (Greenfield, 1985). Television viewing, for instance, has been labeled as a cognitively passive experience. This being so, one would predict that if the same news narrative is presented both on television and in news print, readers will be likely to retain more of its content than viewers. Experiments reported later in this chapter have yielded support for this prediction. There is also evidence, however, that sections of the public who are uninterested in, for example, political news, will actually learn more about politics over time if they are exposed to television programming about political matters than if they are uninterested users of other news media but have not seen this television fare.

In connection with this last phenomenon, Wamsley and Pride (1972) talk about the "relatively unavoidable nature of TV news" (p. 438) as a significant quality that sets it apart from other media. Essentially, with newspapers, the subscriber has great deal more control over the way he or she takes in the news compared with the television news viewers. Readers can work through a newspaper at their own pace and choose which parts to read or ignore. The television news viewer can control whether to turn the set on or off, whether to watch a particular programme, and the level of attention he or she pays to the screen when the programme is on. Viewers, however, have little control over how to consume the news once the decision has been taken to watch a news programme. The pace of the programme and the order in which stories are presented are determined by the producer. Unless the viewer is able and takes the trouble to video-record the programme, there is no opportunity to go back over the news again.

Although there is greater cognitive effort involved in reading than in viewing, and although the former also affords the consumer greater personal control over the rate at which information is taken in, there is some survey evidence that incidental learning about topical issues may be greater from television than from newspapers. In their study of television's impact during the 1964 General Election in Britain, Blumler and McQuail (1969) found that although a large portion of British viewers were not highly motivated by political interest to view political programmes during the election campaign, these "unselective viewers" were in the end significantly more knowledgeable and more interested in the upcoming election than indifferent nonviewers. Wamsley and Pride (1972) argue from this finding that, assuming there are similarities between political programmes and television news, and that the news in other media, such as newspapers and magazines, can be avoided by the audience, then Blumler and McQuail seem to have found political information acquisition by the uninterested in part possible because of the "unavoidable nature" of television news.

There are several reasons why print might yield better retention and better comprehension as compared to audio-visual or televised presentation of the same material. For one thing, the visual and vocal cues on a television communication may actually "distract" the receiver from paying attention to message contents, thereby reducing the effectiveness of a televised communication relative to a written one (Baron, Baron, & Miller, 1973; Haaland & Venkatesan, 1968; Insko, Turnbull, and Yandell, 1974). There is a growing literature that indicates the significance of nonverbal features of news presentations for audience response to news programmes. Shosteck (1974), for example, found that voice quality and manner of speech were of central importance to the popularity of television presenters. Julian (1977) reported that a newscaster's perceived credibility was influenced by amount of eye contact with the camera, facial expression while reading the news, and physical appearance and dress. And Baggaley (1980) reported that viewers' impressions of a newscaster could be affected by the amount or kind of visual detail inserted as background behind him or her.

On the other side of the coin, there have been reasons put forward as to why a television presentation ought to be superior to print presentation of the same material. One reason, suggest Jacoby, Hoyer and Zimmer (1981), is the old saying that "seeing is believing," which suggests that audio-visual presentation ought to be better understood, especially when what is being presented is complex and unfamiliar. Another reason is that television offers multichannel presentation. Content conveyed verbally and visually allows for more variable encoding of information and increases the likelihood of effective communication of at least some part of the message. The problem with this argument is that the data conveyed by different (verbal and visual) channels in a televisual presentation often are mutually distracting. Another argument offered by the same authors for the superiority of television over print stems from the finding that people are more critical of, and perceive as less varied, material that is written as opposed to material presented via audio-only or audio-visual modalities (e.g., Maier & Thurber, 1968; Barrett & Sklar, 1980).

On the question of the relative effectiveness of television and radio, there are two reasons, at least, why one might suppose radio to be better. First, an audio-only presentation contains fewer source and background factors to distract the audience's attention from the essential message content. Second, from a McLuhanian perspective, an audio-only presentation such as radio provides a much more intense and involving (or "hot") experience than does a "cool" medium such as television.

THE EVIDENCE FOR LEARNING (OR FAILURE TO DO SO) FROM TELEVISION NEWS

That people can and do learn from the mass media, and from television in particular, cannot really be doubted. Television brings into the homes of individuals, day after day, a wealth of information about the world in which they live. Much of this information concerns people, places, and events they have never seen or may never be likely to meet or experience firsthand. Research has demonstrated, however, that learning from television (and other mass media) is not a consistent phenomenon, or one that can always be readily predicted.

Television drama is designed principally to entertain, though research has indicated that it may also inform. Audiences may assimilate drama content into existing knowledge and belief structures that are altered in the process. In this way, some writers have argued, television drama can influence public conceptions of the world around them (Gerbner & Gross, 1976; Gerbner et al., 1977; Gerbner, Gross, Jackson-Beeck, Jeffries-Fox, & Signorielli, 1978; Gerbner, Gross, Signorielli, Morgan, & Jackson-Bleeck, 1979; Gerbner, Gross, Morgan, & Signorielli, 1980.

Television news, on the other hand, is defined both by broadcast institutional structures and by the audience as programming principally designed to inform. Research has shown, however, that large sections of the public often display poor memory for news broadcast on television, even though, as we saw earlier, surveys of public opinion have indicated that subjectively people feel that the televised news provides well for their news needs.

What then is the evidence for the informational impact of television news? A number of research models can be distinguished that provide empirical tests of the effects of television news broadcasts on levels of news and current affairs knowledge among the mass public or certain sections of it:

1. Research on the impact of television news coverage during elections on public knowledge of campaign issues and candidates' and parties' policy positions.
2. Research on the role of television news in the political socialisation of young people.

3. Research into the role of television news in setting the public's agenda of issues and events to think about as the most significant of the day.

4. Research on relationships between exposure to television news and knowledge about recent or current news events.

5. Research on retention of information from individual television news broadcasts shortly after transmission.

Learning from the News During Political Campaigns

The focus of much of the news presented on television concerns political issues and affairs. Although news programmes are quite understandably full of political stories during election campaign periods, politics is a prominent source of news at any time. Content analyses of television news have revealed that at least one of the two or three lead items in any network news bulletin invariably will concern political or government matters. The earliest research on the impact of the news also focused on its political influence, in particular on the persuasive effects of media communications on political allegiance and affiliation.

In the context of information broadcasts on television, research has indicated that the main political functions of television may be to stimulate interest and to provide information about political affairs, rather than to persuade viewers to vote for a particular political candidate or party. Early American research on the effects of exposure to the principal informational mass media of the time (newspapers and radio) about the 1948 presidential campaign indicated that those individuals who used the media most showed the greatest gain in knowledge throughout the duration of the campaign. Although knowledge gain was greater for those individuals who had good knowledge already than for those who had poor knowledge at the beginning of the campaign, substantial use of the media resulted in a marked growth of knowledge for all types of media consumer (Berelson, Lazarsfeld, & MacPhee, 1954).

Since this early political communications research, evidence has emerged from both the United States and United Kingdom that indicates the public's reliance on television for information about political campaigns. Increasingly, electorates have come to nominate television as the best medium for helping them to evaluate political leaders (e.g., Blumler & McQuail, 1968).

More recently, in a three-wave national survey study of political knowledge, opinions, and voting intentions and behaviour of people in Britain, Gunter, Svennevig, and Wober (1984, 1986) found that respondents themselves felt they had learned more about the major political parties contesting the 1983 General Election through television than

through any other medium. Furthermore, the perceived value of television as an information source increased across the campaign weeks
leading up to polling day.

Overall though, research on the political impact of television has
provided mixed support for the informational effectiveness of the medium's news output, regardless of how television is perceived by voters.
Some studies of the role of television during political campaigns have
indicated that viewing contributes in a positive way to public knowledge
of the issues, whereas others have found that exposure to news programmes relates far less well to campaign information gain than does
exposure to political spot advertising.

In their study of the first extensively televised General Election in
Britain in 1959, Trenaman and McQuail (1961) reported that voters with
the greatest amount of exposure to television during the election campaign were most likely to know where candidates stood on different
issues. This finding was subsequently confirmed by Blumler and McQuail
(1968) in their investigation of television's influence during the 1964
General Election in Britain.

In a more recent British General Election study, Gunter and others
(1986) assessed the informativeness of the media during the 1983 campaign by relating reported use of each mass medium to independent
subjective and objective measures of political knowledge. Relationships
between subjective and objective estimates of political knowledge and
claimed consumption of and interest in news and politics in the mass
media indicated that interest was more strongly associated with knowledge than was consumption. Claimed frequencies of newspaper reading
and of numbers of party broadcasts seen on television were not related to
any measures of political knowledge. Claimed listening to radio news was
significantly related to subjective knowledge estimates only; that is, those
who said they knew about the issue were also likely to claim frequent
listening to the news on radio. Claimed viewing of television news was
significantly related to claimed knowledge, and to objective knowledge of
party policies. Those who claimed or had better knowledge were also
likely to say they watched television news a lot. Much more powerfully
related to both subjective and objective party policy knowledge was
claimed level of interest in political discussions programming on radio
and television. Those who were more knowledgeable were also the more
interested.

Gunter and Others' (1986) findings in part reinforced earlier British
election research results, although previously reported relationships between viewing of party election broadcasts and issue awareness (Blumler
& Mc Quail, 1968) were not confirmed. But whereas these British surveys
suggested an influence of television news on political campaign informa-

tion gain, U.S. research has produced less convincing evidence that people learn much about political campaigns from news programmes on television.

Television can function importantly as an image-builder during political campaigns. It can convey better than any other medium the flavour of a candidate's personality—certainly more so than do any print media (Kraus, 1962; Patterson, 1980). Extensive studies of debates between presidential candidates have shown that these broadcasts can raise the level of information in the population about candidates' stands on different issues quite substantially (Kraus, 1962; Bishop, Meadow, & Jackson-Beeck, 1978; Kraus, 1979). One survey study reported an 18% increase in the proportion of the population aware of Jimmy Carter's stand on unemployment among viewers of the 1976 Carter–Ford debates. The researchers also observed a smaller, though still substantial increase in knowledge among nonviewers, who may have obtained their information from reading newspapers or talking with other people (Becker, Sobowale, Cobbey & Eyal, 1978).

Studies such as these have indicated that certain types of television can have a powerful impact in conveying to the public the flavour of a personality, and to some superficial extent information about candidates' positions on various issues. On the other hand, television news programmes seem to be much less efficient when it comes to conveying information about the qualifications of political candidates and about the major issues on which campaigns are fought (Quarles, 1979). Indeed, some researchers have argued that television news causes more confusion than clarity over political issues (M. J. Robinson, 1975).

In research on the Senate Watergate hearings, Robinson (1976) found that television-dependent persons were less knowledgeable about the scandal than were newspaper-dependent persons. Robinson attributed the superiority of print to the fact that newspaper stories contained more hard data and information about procedures than did television news stories.

Newspaper readers appear to absorb more facts about political candidates and issues than do television news viewers. When people interviewed in a number of states that were having senatorial elections were asked to explain their candidate preferences, researchers found that individuals who relied mainly on newspapers were more likely to be able to give reasons for favouring or rejecting a particular candidate than were individuals who relied on television (Clarke & Fredin, 1978). In this study, it was not just the amount of newspaper reading or television news viewing that proved to be important, however. Respondents' opinions about political candidates were also related to the extent to which they were aware of campaign stories in each mass medium. Discriminating campaign messages in the press as well as having a general interest in public affairs were positively correlated with knowledge about senatorial contenders, whereas discriminating stories on television news was negatively correlated with knowledge levels. On this evidence, Clarke and Fredin concluded that newspapers enhance information gain about election campaign issues, but television news viewing appears to have an inhibiting effect. People who watched television for political news were less informed than individuals of similar education and public affairs interests who did not.

Becker and Whitney (1980) studied the effectiveness of newspapers and television in informing residents of central Ohio about political news. They divided their sample into those dependent on newspapers and those who relied on television. Newspaper-dependent persons knew more about local issues and politics. These people were also more likely to think they understood local affairs, to trust local government officials, and to be knowledgeable about national affairs. Television-dependent people, on the other hand, exhibited less knowledge and understanding of national and local affairs and less trust in local officials, thus reinforcing Robinson's earlier findings.

In a study of television effects during the 1972 U.S. presidential election campaign, McClure and Patterson (1973) examined the content of weeknight network newscasts and conducted a three-wave panel survey over a 2-month period. McClure and Patterson found that issues emphasised on television did not become more salient to heavy television viewers than to light viewers, but that newspaper-emphasised issues did become more salient to heavy readers than to light readers. These researchers then went on to examine further the impact of one medium on political agenda-setting during the campaign, with the use of the other controlled. In the presence of controls for exposure to network news, increases in the salience of voter issues were higher for heavy news readers than for light news readers. On the other hand, in the presence of controls for newspaper reading, heavy news viewing was only somewhat likely to increase the salience of these issues relative to light news viewing.

Similarly, voters in the 1976 presidential election who followed newspapers regularly knew more about each of the candidates at the end of the primary campaign than did those who watched television evening news regularly as their main source of information (Patterson, 1980). One of the reasons why political knowledge is greater among those people who rely mainly on newspapers for political information than among those who rely on television may be because information from print media seems to be recalled better than that from broadcast news. Patterson (1980), for example, reported that 57% of a survey sample were able to recall in fairly complete terms news stories they had read about in newspapers during the previous 24 hours, whereas only 45% could recall stories seen on television equally well.

Although many people may attend exclusively to television for news and political information, there is some reason to doubt that television can transmit political information effectively. Wamsley and Pride (1972) identified the chaotic nature typical of many television bulletins as one reason why this is so. News broadcasts focus too much on dramatic, visually exciting events that may distract the viewer's attention from the essential ingredients of a political story and convey none of its meaning themselves. Television news not unusually also tends to condense much information into a very short period of time so that the viewer becomes cognitively overloaded and unable to stay with the pace of the programme and properly assimilate its content.

In another study of learning during political campaign information, Patterson and McClure (1976) found no difference in knowledge of candidates stands on issues among voters in New York between those who watched evening network news and those who did not during the 1972 presidential campaign. But they did find that regular viewing of TV campaign commercials produced a significant growth in awareness of candidates' positions on major campaign issues.

Patterson and McClure offer a number of reasons for the differential impact of television news and television political advertising on viewers' information gain about the campaign. For one thing, they suggest, in network news programmes political stories about the presidential contenders stood out far less than did political advertisements about the same individuals. In television newscasts, campaign news stories were surrounded by other news stories, creating what Patterson and McClure called a "montage effect", whereby one news story is pretty much like another. Campaign commercials, on the other hand, were typically shown adjacent to peak-time entertainment programming and stood out from these programmes to have greater attentional impact. The authors reported further that in response to open-ended survey questions "many respondents could not recall what they had seen on the previous evening's news, explaining that the stories had run together in their minds" (McClure and Patterson, 1974, p.23). Clearly, much of the information presented in television newscasts was forgotten by viewers or, alternatively, was irretrievable in any meaningful fashion.

Another reason put forward for the relative ineffectiveness of television news as a purveyor of information on campaign issues is its frequent use of irrelevant and distracting film footage. Frequently running in parallel with the commentary on the issues discussed at the day's campaign rally would be film depicting enthusiastic crowds greeting the speaker or reacting to his speech. Although considerable air time on television news shows was devoted to campaign events, film of the crowds at one rally on one day looked much the same as film of the crowds at a different rally the next day. When asked to recall details of the day's campaign events, respondents often reported having seen large gatherings at rallies, but said little about candidates' remarks.

The Role of TV News in Political Socialisation

Political socialisation is a developmental process by which children and adolescents acquire knowledge about their political environment. Several societal agents, particularly parents and schools, have been identified as transmitters of political orientations from generation to generation. The political socialisation process has been observed to begin typically with abstract emotional attachments and identification with political figures and institutions during elementary school years. These vague affective allegiances are supplemented with specific knowledge during adolescence when that child develops a more rational understanding of the political world (Greenstein, 1968). The family has been recognised as playing an important role in the development of certain types of political variables such as party identification and political knowledge and involvement (Chaffee, McLeod, Wackman, 1973; Greenstein, 1968).

Results of studies conducted since the early 1970s have also shown that political knowledge levels among children and adolescents vary with their use of the mass media and interests in news and current affairs content in the media. Research indicating that watching the news on television may play an important role in the political education of young people provides yet further evidence of the informational impact of television news broadcasts. So far, however, the findings have not consistently pointed to a powerful effect of television news in this context.

Writers have differed in their endorsement of the mass media as important sources of information in the development of political knowledge in children. Some have regarded the media as having secondary socialising properties, reinforcing attitudes, beliefs, and values learned from other sources (Klapper, 1960). Others, however, have pointed out that children usually have few political views to be reinforced (Chaffee, Ward, & Tipton, 1970).

There is little doubt about the considerable potential of the mass media, especially television, to impart at least some information about government and political affairs. Such topics are covered by news and current affairs programmes nightly at times when millions of young people are likely to be watching. Those young viewers who take a special interest in watching these programmes might be expected to develop a far greater knowledge about governmental structures and procedures and about political leaders than those who do not pay much attention to them.

In one sample of U.S. children studied by Dominick (1972), over half said they received most of their information about the president and vice-president from television. Thirty percent listed television as the most important source of information about Congress, and 21% for information about the Supreme Court. However, newspapers and magazines were listed as more important sources of information about elections, and about candidates and issues, with television running a fairly distant second. About 20% named television as the best information source in this regard.

In a subsequent study, Conway, Stevens, and Smith (1975) compared the contribution of newspapers and television news to the political social-isation of nearly 300 fourth-, fifth-, and sixth-grade school children from Maryland. The children were questioned about their identification with a political party, which party they would vote for, awareness of party interests, and laws and the role of government in making laws. Partisan identification and perceptions of party policy among children varied significantly with levels of consumption of television news and newspapers, but not with higher levels of total television viewing. A similar pattern was found in party voting choice. Relationships between television news viewing or newspaper reading and party preferences were dependent, however, on political interest. Only those children with a high level of political interest showed significant relationships here. Perception of parental political interest was also important in the same way. Knowledge about other political and legal processes was significantly related to viewing of television news and reading of newspapers; more frequent consumers of news possessed greater knowledge. In the case of legal processes, however, relationships with news media use disappeared in the presence of statistical controls for political interest levels.

In summary, the findings of Conway et al. indicate that the mass media (both television news and newspapers) can play an important role in political socialisation, especially in relation to knowledge about more personalised objects, such as political parties, to which a close attachment may be formed. However, more abstract politico-legal knowledge about the perceived importance of political parties and the passing of new laws tended not to be significantly associated with media use.

Furnham and Gunter (1983) produced further weak evidence that television news viewing was related to political knowledge levels among a small sample of adolescents. These authors distributed political knowledge questionnaires to 200 teenagers aged 16 to 18 years based on an instrument used in an earlier nationwide study of British school children's political awareness (Stradling, 1977). Respondents were required to specify their interest in politics, economics, and current affairs, and their use of television, radio, and newspapers. Political knowledge questions fell into five different areas: (a) identification of party policies; (b) identification of prominent political leaders; (c) identification of local political leaders; (d) knowledge of parliamentary and local political issues; and (e) knowledge of who was responsible for various public services.

Multivariate statistical analyses revealed that interest in politics was the best indicator of political knowledge, with sex of respondent, claimed viewing of television news, and talking about politics with adults emerging as weaker indicators.

All the studies described so far employed a cross-sectional survey design demonstrating relationships between media use and political awareness at one time. This design is not appropriate for demonstrating that television news or use of other media for information purposes enhances political knowledge. Correlational relationships as such can be reinterpreted differently to show that those individuals with greater political knowledge to start with also consume more news. A more effective method for identifying the direction of causality is a longitudinal design whereby media usage patterns and political knowledge growth are monitored over time with the same people.

Atkin and Gantz (1978) conducted a longitudinal study to examine the possible role of television news in the political socialisation of groups of children from kindergarten to fifth grade. Two waves of questionnaires that measured political knowledge were administered one year apart and asked whether the children discussed news events with parents or friends, whether they had any interest in particular kinds of news topics, and whether they ever tried to find out more about a news issue after seeing it reported in the news. The children were also asked whether they viewed evening network television newscasts for adults or the special news slots designed for their own age group on Saturday mornings. (At the time of this study the CBS network in the United States produced specially designed 2-minute spot news broadcasts for children every half hour during Saturday and Sunday mornings' children's entertainment programming.)

Among the older (fourth-and fifth-grade) children, results showed significant correlations between viewing of both weekend children's spot news and evening (adults') news and political knowledge levels, interest in presidential affairs, and the tendency to discuss the news with others. Among the younger children (third-grade and below), news viewing correlated significantly with political knowledge on the second (but not the first) wave of interviews and also with interest in governmental affairs and discussion of the news with others. On all ten political knowledge items used in this study, a greater percentage of heavy than of light news viewers had some awareness.

The findings showed that more than half of the children occasionally or frequently watched television news programming and that reported news viewing contributed to political knowledge, interest, and information seeking. Causal analyses with panel data over time indicated that influence flowed primarily from news viewing to political knowledge; young viewers became more informed about political matters, whereas previously knowledgeable children did not necessarily seek out news programming.

Children with different characteristics acquired varying amounts of knowledge from the news programming they viewed. The findings showed quite clearly that older children, in the fourth and fifth grades, were more affected by the news than those in early elementary school, although the younger group did display limited learning from the simplified Saturday morning mini-newscasts. This developmental difference was probably due to older children's more sophisticated ability for processing, structuring, and storing incoming information; thus, they have a greater capacity for learning from news messages. The exposure-knowledge relationship was also stronger for middle-class than for working-class children and among those who were interested in news as against those who were not. Thus news programming can have a much greater impact under certain conditions relating to the capacities and predispositions of audiences.

Television News and the Public News Agenda

Within the conceptual framework labeled *agenda-setting* it is posited that the mass media function through their informational communications to draw public attention to certain personalities, issues, and events. News headlines focus on particular stories that at the time of their media coverage became the most salient news events to the public.

Agenda-setting research investigates the relationship between issues and subjects given prominence in the news media ("media agenda") and the salience of such topics in the minds of the public ("public agenda"). Conflicting findings have emerged on the potency of television news to set the agenda. It has been argued by some commentators that television news coverage may structure our world for us by directing our attention towards certain social objects and issues rather than others (Glasgow University Media Group, 1976, 1980).

This assumption concerning the supposed "impact" of television news was only inferential, however, being based on analyses of the content profiles of U.K. network news programmes rather than from direct audience research. Survey and laboratory studies (reported in this section) have since indicated that the effects of television news watching on the significance of issues for viewers may be only skin-deep. Although there may be some influence of television coverage of issues on "feelings" towards those matters, comprehension of what they mean and why they occurred is not significantly enhanced by television news.

One hypothesis of agenda-setting research is that when the media emphasise an event, they influence the audience to see it as important. During the course of television news production, editors and producers have to decide which topics out of many available stories should be included in the day's bulletins and which are to be rejected because they are not significantly "newsworthy". Audiences learn which issues are most important from the stories that survive the editorial selection procedure and finally appear in bulletins (McCombs & Shaw, 1972).

In an empirical test of agenda-setting, McCombs and Shaw (1972) found strong correlations between key election campaign issues covered by the media and those named as the most important issues by people who had not yet decided for whom to vote. Although these data were not offered by the authors as proof of the agenda-setting capability of the media, the findings did seem to indicate some influence of the extent of media coverage on the placement of issues in voters' priorities.

One of the interesting questions of agenda-setting research, and one that is important in the context of the current discussion, concerns the relative efficacy of television and newspapers in influencing personal agendas. The original McCombs and Shaw study found no significant difference between the influence of the two news media. Subsequent research reported by McCombs, Shaw, and Shaw (1972), however, noted that personal news agendas appear to be more strongly related to television viewing. This finding was reinforced by McCombs (1976), who reported a stronger influence of newspapers than of television on voter agendas during the months preceding the 1972 U.S. presidential election.

Further comparative evidence on the agenda-setting function of television news and newspapers has indicated that if television has any impact at all, it is only at a relatively superficial level of learning and understanding. Benton and Frazier (1976) conceptualized three levels of agenda-setting. At Level One is a set of broad issues or topics; for example, the state of the economy. At Level Two are sub-issues, including specific problems, causes, and proposed solutions, which, relating to the foregoing example, might include matters such as inflation, unemployment, taxation, and oil prices. Finally, at Level Three is specific and detailed information about these sub-issues, including analysis of the reasons for inflation or unemployment, arguments for and against ways of solving these problems, and the people or parties connected with the latter arguments.

Benton and Frazier classified their respondents according to which medium, television or newspapers, was their most important source of information about the economy. At both Levels Two and Three, they found strong correlations between the issues of which the public were most aware and newspaper coverage among those people for whom newspapers were the primary source of current affairs information, but only weak relationships between television news coverage and the agenda of those for whom television was the main claimed source of news information. These results imply that television news may be less effective than newspapers at enhancing public awareness of *detailed* information about specific economic issues. To a large degree, however, the validity of this conclusion hangs on the assumption that the agenda-setting framework is a useful one in which to measure information uptake from the media. But is agenda-setting a good measure of the informational effectiveness of broadcast news?

There has been some indication that even those people who pay relatively little attention to the news media may adopt the same news agenda as that endorsed by heavy consumers, as a result of conversations with others (E. Shaw, 1977). A number of writers have questioned whether agenda-setting research has demonstrated media effects at all—and opinions are divided over the causal direction of the relationship between the public's judgements about the importance of issues and their media priorities (Becker, McCombs, & McLeod, 1975; Erbring, Goldenberg, & Miller, 1980). Although these are important questions, even more critical in the context of *learning* from the news is a finding that agenda-setting appears not to be mediated by information recall from the news at all (Iyenger, Peters, & Kinder, 1982).

In an experimental study, Iyenger et al. tested the effects of evening news bulletins on the perceived importance respondents attributed to different news issues. Respondents agreed to attend a viewing location over a spell of four days to view evening news bulletins, the content of which had been systematically manipulated by the experimenters. On the day before seeing the first newscast, participants completed a questionnaire that covered a wide range of political topics, including the importance of various national problems. On the sixth day, 24 hours after the last broadcast, participants completed another questionnaire that again included measures of problem importance.

Although respondents' perceptions of which news stories that week were of greatest current importance reflected the degree of coverage given to those items in the bulletins to which they were exposed, there was little indication that enhanced salience was accompanied by increased understanding of the issues. No significant correlations emerged between how important a story was rated and how much information could be recalled about it. Instead, Iyengar et al. found that agenda-setting was probably mediated more by covert evaluations triggered by the news stories. Experimental social psychological research on the dynamics of persuasion has revealed that the impact of a persuasive message is predicted powerfully by the intensity and direction of favourable or unfavourable reactions to it on the part of the receiver (see Petty, Ostrom, & Brock, 1980). The greater the level of unfavourable reaction to the message, the less persuasive it becomes. In their second experiment, Iyengar and his colleagues asked participants to list "any thoughts, reactions or feelings" they had about each news story they recalled. Participants were then scored for the number of counterarguments they produced to each story. Results showed that counterarguing was significantly and negatively related to increase in problem salience.

Television News and Knowledge
About Recent News Events

Studies of public awareness of recent news stories have provided further evidence of television's role as a supplier of information. This perspective has typically examined correlations between respondents' claimed viewing of television news and levels of knowledge about recent events in the news. In the presence of controls for other variables, equivocal evidence for the informational effects of television news has emerged.

Edelstein (1974) asked respondents in one part of the United States to identify the local and world problems that they regarded as highly important to them. Their answers were then related statistically to their claimed usage levels for various major news sources. The press were identified most often as the most useful source of information about both local problems and world problems, followed in each case by television news (more closely so in relation to world problems). Far behind in third place came radio.

In an extremely detailed study on news exposure and learning, Graber (1984) interviewed a small panel of 21 people individually 10 times during 1976. Graber investigated the sources to which her respondents turned for news and the information they had absorbed from the news stories they had experienced during the time of the study. Eighteen panelists also kept diaries of the news stories to which they had become exposed. These panelists noted more than 10,000 news stories and were considered through interviews to have acquired reasonable knowledge about over 1,500 of them. In a comparison of the role of news sources, newspapers were found to be much more important sources of information about those stories for which a reasonable knowledge had been acquired than was television.

Sparkes and Winter (1980) reported that with respect to foreign news, television was judged to be more "on top of current developments" and to offer more accurate reporting than newspapers. Newspapers, on the other hand, were believed to provide more in-depth understanding. Sparkes and Winter found that even though frequency of newspaper use was higher for their sample than was frequency of television news viewing, television emerged as the more important medium for foreign news per se. In one part of their study they asked respondents to recall what they thought had been the major news stories from the preceding few weeks. Then for each story recalled, respondents were asked to identify the source from which they heard about it. Two findings emerged of most significance. First, there was a higher level of recall for international news than for local or national news. Second, television was cited as the source of most recalled stories, followed distantly by newspapers. In a separate line of questioning, Sparkes and Winter asked their respondents about their frequency of media use. Foreign news story recall was also found to be associated more closely with claimed network television news viewing than with claimed frequency of newspaper reading, thus reinforcing the claims that television was the main source of recalled foreign news.

Further insights relating to the differential impact of broadcast and print media on public affairs knowledge have emerged from a recent British survey of news awareness (Gunter, 1984). Telephone interviews were carried out with over 500 residents of London who were asked a series of questions about eight political figures and three stories prominent in the news during the previous week.[1]

For all political figures respondents were asked to say *who* they were and, with respect to four of them, *why* they had been in the news in the last week. For each news story, questions probed for knowledge of where events had occurred, who was involved, and why events had happened. Information was also obtained from respondents concerning their use of different sources of news. They were asked to estimate subjectively the number of days on which they had read a newspaper in the last week and to say what type of newspaper they usually read—"hard news" broadsheets or more largely "soft news" tabloids. Subjective estimates were obtained of the numbers of radio news broadcasts, radio political discussion programmes, network TV newscasts, and local TV news programmes they had heard or seen over the last seven days. Respondents were also asked if they talked about news with others and if so how often.

Relationships were examined between news awareness and claimed use of different media and nonmedia news sources. Respondents scored an average 23 points out of a possible 46, or a 50% correct response rate. Differences in news awareness associated with different claimed levels of use of different news sources are schematically presented in Figs. 2.1A-G.

---

[1]The political figures were Mr. Yuri Andropov, Mr. Yasser Arafat, Mr. Nigel Lawson, Monsignor Bruce Kent (*who* and *why* questions), Mr. Michael Heseltine, Mr. Roy Hattersley, Mr. Spyros Kyprianou, Mr. Rauf Denktash (*who* questions only). The three news stories concerned the Middle East conflict, political rift between Turks and Greeks in Cyprus, and deployment of U.S. nuclear missiles in Britain.

The overall pattern of relationships that can be observed here is that the more respondents said they had used different sources of news during the previous week, the higher were their news awareness scores. It is clear from the figure, however, that increased use of certain news sources was associated with greater increases in news awareness than was use of others. Claimed frequency of newspaper reading and viewing of local television news were apparently most weakly related to enhanced news awareness, whereas claimed frequency of talking about the news and type of newspaper commonly read were related to the most substantial variations in news awareness.

Table 2.1 shows fourth-order partial correlations between news awareness and use of different sources of news in which joint effects of sex, age, class, and education were statistically controlled. Two news sources stand out as most powerfully and consistently related to awareness of news overall and across different categories or elements of news.: personal discussions with others about news and claimed frequency of watching network or nationally broadcast television news. The greater their frequency of talking with others about news or of watching network television news, the more respondents knew about recent news stories. In addition, overall news awareness was significantly, though more weakly, related to type of newspaper read and claimed frequency of listening to radio newscasts or radio political discussion programmes. However, none of these news sources was related consistently with knowledge levels across all categories or elements of news.

The type of newspaper read was significantly associated with knowledge of three major news stories, but there was no significant correlation between this variable and knowledge of prominent political figures in the news. Radio news listening was significantly associated with identifica-

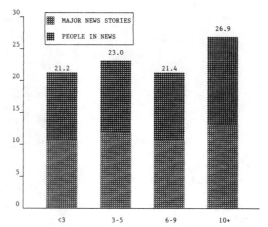

FIG. 2.1A Reported network television news viewing and knowledge of news from the previous week (Gunter, 1984). Frequencies represent number of programmes seen or heard over previous 7 Days.

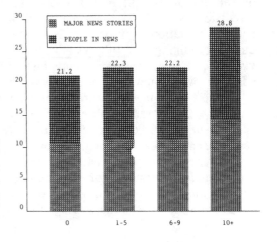

FIG. 2.1B Reported local television news viewing and knowledge of news from the previous week (Gunter, 1984). Frequencies represent number of programmes seen or heard over previous 7 Days.

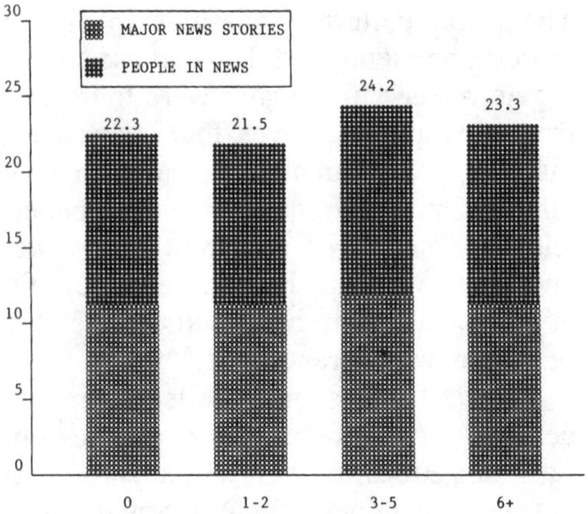

FIG. 2.1C Reported Radio News Listening and Knowledge of News from the Previous Week (Gunter, 1984). Frequencies represent number of programmes seen or heard over previous 7 Days.

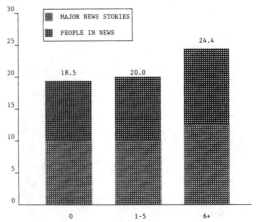

FIG. 2.1D Reported radio discussion listening and knowledge of news from the previous week (Gunter, 1984). Frequencies represent number of days on which newspaper was read during previous week.

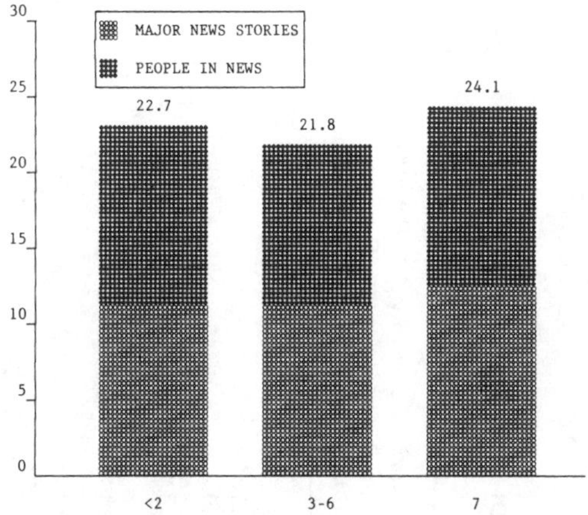

FIG. 2.1E Reported newspaper reading and knowledge of news from the previous week (Gunter, 1984). Frequencies represent number of days on which newspaper was read during previous week.

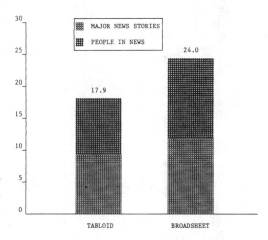

FIG. 2.1F Reported type of newspaper read and knowledge of news from the previous week (Gunter, 1984).

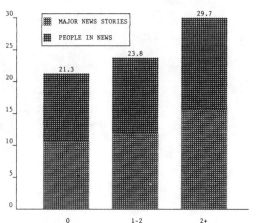

FIG. 2.1G Reported frequency of talking about news with others and knowledge of news from the previous week (Gunter, 1984). Frequencies represent number of conversations in last week.

39

TABLE 2.1
Partial Correlations Between News Awareness and Use of Different Sources of News

News Category	Frequency Newspaper Reading	Type Newspaper Read	Radio News Listening	Radio Discussions Listening	Network TV News Viewing	Local TV News Viewing	Personal Discussions of News
People in News							
Who	.04	.07	.12*	.07	.13*	.06	.23**
Why	.04	.05	.07	.09	.11*	.02	.18**
Total	.05	.07	.11*	.09	.13*	.05	.23**
Major News Stories							
1 Middle East Conflict	.04	.11*	.04	.11*	.11*	.03	.16**
2 Cyprus	.07	.15**	.08	.08	.10*	.03	.11*
3 Nuclear Missiles in Britain	.04	.04	.04	.03	.08	.05	.08
Total	.01	.13**	.07	.10*	.12*	.02	.15**
Overall News Awareness	.03	.11**	.10*	.10*	.14**	.04	.21**

Source: Source: Gunter, 1984.
Note: Fourth-order partial correlations with sex, age, class, and education controlled.
** p < 0.001
* p < 0.01

tion of prominent people, though not with better knowledge of why they had recently been in the news. Listening to radio political discussions, on the other hand, was related to knowledge of the more concrete—who, what, where—elements of major news stories, though not with awareness of why certain events had occurred.

Among the major news media the type of newspaper read and claimed frequency of watching network television news were most powerfully related to news awareness. They were, however, related principally to knowledge levels for different aspects of news. Type of newspaper read was particularly closely related to knowledge of major news stories. Readers of the more serious, broadsheet dailies, which offer greater depth of story coverage than the tabloids, exhibited greater knowledge about major news stories. Network television news was also related to knowledge of main news stories from the previous, week though less robustly. In addition, however, television news viewing was related more powerfully to identification of prominent people in the news. Television news apparently had greater impact—if indeed impact can be inferred from these findings—on awareness of personalities than of story details. This finding is consistent with the results of political communications studies indicating that television stories seem to produce better awareness of candidates' personalities than understanding of the campaign issues on which they stand (Patterson, 1980). It is also supported by experimental work showing that information concerning people involved in the news is usually much better learned and retained than that about the underlying causes of events (based on simulated television bulletins) (Findahl & Hoijer, 1972, 1976; Gunter, Jarrett, & Furnham, 1983; Gunter, Furnham, & Jarrett, 1984).

Retention of Individual TV Bulletin Content

Some researchers have tested learning from television news broadcasts more directly by asking respondents to recall bulletin content soon after they have seen it. These investigations have generally been one of two categories. The first are field surveys in which respondents are contacted in their own homes either in a face-to-face or telephone interview and without prior warning are asked questions about stories reported in a news programme they may have seen just a short time before. The second are experimental studies in which participants are invited to watch either a live or specially prepared television news programme in a central viewing location or, occasionally, at home, and are tested for retention of its content shortly afterwards.

Although test conditions have varied to some extent, studies conducted so far, in a number of different countries around the world, have produced fairly consistent findings. Typically, memory for broadcast news tends to be poor even though viewers are tested just a short time after exposure.

Field Surveys. Several telephone surveys conducted with samples in the United States have indicated poor memory for the content of network television news bulletins among the general public. Stern (1971) put together a study testing what people in the San Francisco area remembered from the evening news on television. Every evening Stern and his co-workers monitored the main newcasts on all three major networks. They listed the stories carried by each newscast, including details of each story's length and whether or not it was on film. Respondents were telephoned shortly after these news broadcasts had finished and were asked if they watched any of the programmes. Those viewers who claimed to have watched a particular broadcast were first asked which stories, if any, they remembered. After this, they were read a list of stories and asked to indicate which they could remember from the programme. If they identified a particular story, they were probed in more detail about it. Each respondent was rated for his or her amount and level of recall.

When asked, "What do you recall from tonight's broadcast?", 51% said they could not recall any stories. Those who did remember usually recalled more than one story. On average, though, people remembered just 1 story out of the usual 19 stories per newscast, or just over 6% of the programme. When given a list of headlines to aid memory, recall usually improved. People, on average, recalled four stories without any factual details, plus four more stories with some details.

In another American survey in which viewers were questioned at home by telephone about a television news bulletin they had watched earlier in the same evening, spontaneous or unaided recall reached little over 5% of the reported news topics (Neuman, 1976). Even after receiving topic-related cues to aid recall, few respondents were able to give details of more than 20% of the items from a 20-item bulletin less than an hour after the programme had been broadcast. In a later field study in which news recall was tested immediately after each newscast on several consecutive evenings, but on this occasion via face-to-face interviews in the respondents' homes rather than by telephone, Robinson, Davis, Sahin, and O'Toole (1980) reported somewhat better overall memory performance. Tests of free recall of the 12 to 20 major news items typically presented per broadcast were followed by brief descriptive labels referring to the actors or locations of news events. These were provided to trigger respondents' further recall of the salient content of individual news stories. Viewers here recalled some element of about half the bulletin items on average. However, this fairly creditable memory performance was offset by frequent distortion or misunderstanding of important details of news stories. One finding was that viewers sometimes confused the content from two stories, so that elements of one story became merged with elements from another. This finding corresponds with the "montage effect" observed by McClure and Patterson (1980) during recall of political campaign items from television news broadcasts. Robinson and his colleagues refer to it as "meltdown."

Even when viewers know in advance that they will be tested on their memory for the content of an evening's television news, most of the stories are quickly forgotten. Stauffer, Frost, and Rybolt (1983) recruited a sample of nearly 600 people from suburban Boston to take part in a television news recall study at home. Some people were forewarned about the test and were asked to pay particular attention to the following evening's network news. Others were not notified in advance. Over four consecutive evenings, telephone interviews were conducted with these individuals within three hours of that evening's major television news broadcast. Respondents were asked to provide a brief description of all the news items they could recall from that night's programme. After a story was identified, interviewers requested additional details about the item.

The four evening newscasts contained a range of 10 to 18 news items, with an average of 13.3. The average number recalled unaided by respondents overall was 2.3. There was a significant difference between cued and noncued respondents. Those who had been asked to pay attention to the news recalled on average 58% more news than those who had not been forewarned. Even so, cued respondents still managed to recall only 3 items out of 13, on average. Those who were called unexpectedly remembered only 1.9.

This American evidence has been corroborated by research done in other parts of the world. The Finnish Broadcasting Company studied the effectiveness of their television newscasts and found that people could remember little of the content of these programmes when asked about it immediately after transmission. They also noted that any details that are retained tend to be confused and inaccurate. Even when given help by interviewers, half the respondents were still unable to recall anything from a news broadcast just seen (Nordenstreng, 1970).

Following another Scandinavian study, Linne and Veirup (1974) of the Danish Radio Training Department reported that even when tested immediately after a broadcast news bulletin, listeners and viewers typically remembered only 2-5 stories out of 12. In Israel, researchers found that 34% of radio listeners and 21% of television viewers could not recall even a single news items within an hour of a news broadcast. Overall, the average number of news items remembered was two (Katz, Adoni, & Parness, 1977).

Experimental Studies.   Although field surveys have the advantage of testing memory and comprehension of broadcast news in audience members' normal viewing and listening environments, there is no guarantee that respondents paid careful attention to news programmes as they were being broadcast. Consequently, poor memory performance may have resulted from the fact that respondents were doing other things, such as eating, reading, or talking to members of the family, while the news was on, which distracted their attention away from the programme for a considerable portion of it.

However, even under laboratory-based experimental conditions, corroborative evidence has emerged that individuals are unable effectively to remember the content of news programmes to which they have paid careful attention.

In one early study in the United Kingdom, the Opinion Research Centre (1972) was commissioned by the Independent Television Authority to examine audience learning from the weekday ITV programme *News at Ten* Viewers, all recruited in London, tended to be younger and better educated than the overall U.K. population. "Before" and "after" tests were carried out in theatre conditions on the contents of *News at Ten* bulletins, which viewers saw as they went out live. The postviewing questionnaire was actually written while the news was being broadcast. The researchers found that viewers could significantly recall an average of 3 items out of 15 per bulletin, and in only a few instances were any details mentioned. Apart from a few unrelated idiosyncratic answers, viewers could describe in only broad, general terms what they had seen. The items most recalled were ones that at the time were causing the most public interest, but even on these, recall accounts tended to be thin and vague. This evidence indicated that even under alternative viewing conditions, recall of detail fades after the initial stimulus of the news.

These results were reinforced by further work of the Swedish Broadcasting Corporation, which found that more than half of a sample of Stockholm residents who took part in a laboratory study of memory for televised news either failed to recall or misconstrued the content of nearly all items of a 7-minute bulletin of 13 items (Findahl and Hoijer, 1975).

Stauffer and his colleagues conducted a series of experimental studies during the late 1970s in Africa and the United States that indicated not only that the ability to recall broadcast news deteriorates rapidly after initial presentation but also that this deterioration is worse among some segments of the audience than others. Although audience differences in memory and comprehension of broadcast news are the subject of more detailed discussion in a later chapter, the results of these studies, because relevant to the present discussion, are described briefly here.

Stauffer, Frost, and Rybolt (1978) tested literates and adult nonreaders recruited in two locations around Boston and Philadelphia. Participants were shown a videotaped television news programme that had been recorded some 6 months earlier. They watched the programme and then immediately afterwards made a list of all the news stories they could recall. At this stage, a brief verbal description of each item was all the experimenters required. After this unaided recall test, participants completed a 23-item, multiple-choice questionnaire administered orally to nonreaders. Some questions tested for memory of factual knowledge; others tested visual recall (e.g., what was the colour of the newscaster's dress), and others tested for knowledge that could reasonably be inferred from programme content. Across the total sample, an average of 6 items out of 12 were recalled spontaneously. Recall was significantly better among the college group, who managed to recall 7.3 items on average, than among the adult basic education group of nonreaders, who managed just 4.7 items on average. Performance on the multiple-choice test was somewhat better. Overall, participants scored 13.8 out of 23 (or 60% correct). Once again, though, the college group did considerably better than the adult illiterate group (17.1 against 10.5 out of 23).

In a subsequent study, Stauffer, Frost, and Rybolt (1980) recruited nearly 400 people for a broadcast news recall test in Nairobi, Kenya. Among these individuals were adult illiterates, college students, tenth-grade schoolchildren, and out-of-school adults. Respondents were required to listen to a 5-month-old radio news broadcast that was about 15 minutes long and contained 13 items. All participants were told to listen carefully to the bulletin but were not informed that they would be questioned about it later.

Immediately following the newscast, respondents were asked to make a list of news stories they could recall, as in the previous experiment. After this, they completed a multiple-choice test, on which questions tested for recall of names of persons, place names, numbers, and knowledge that could be inferred from the programme's content. Average recall over the total sample was 3.9 items out of 13, or 30% of the bulletin's items. Reinforcing earlier findings, recall was best among the college educated (6 items) and worst among the illiterates (2.8 items). On the multiple-choice test, the average score over all participants was 31%. College students scored 42% while illiterates scored just 23%.

IS TELEVISION A GOOD MEDIUM FROM WHICH TO LEARN NEWS?

This chapter has considered the effectiveness of television as an information medium. Can the rapid and extensive forgetting of information from television news broadcasts that is often observed in studies of memory for the news be due to some inherent inability of this medium to communicate informational material to its audience in a readily comprehensible way? Some writers have argued that television has severe limitations as an information medium, whereas others have demonstrated that its effectiveness in getting information across to the audience depends significantly on the cognitive framework with which viewers approach television.

Research on children's learning from television, radio, and print has indicated a number of factors inherent in the television medium and the way viewers approach television that affect learning from it relative to other media. Salomon (1979) suggested that the crucial difference underlying different patterns of learning the same narrative material presented via different media arises from the symbol systems presented by different media rather than from the media themselves. The symbol systems, not the media, vary in their ability to represent certain types of information. Experience with symbol systems in media leads to the reciprocal enhancement of general cognitive skills and media-specific skills. General skills are necessary prerequisites of learning from whatever source, whereas media-specific skills aid learning from particular media.

Television conveys dynamic visual images as a symbol system in addition to language and sounds or music, which are also conveyed by radio. Print, on the other hand, conveys information simply via the symbol system of language. Television's symbol system therefore is able to represent the shape and form of objects and events visually, whereas radio and print can present only verbal descriptions.

Research with children has shown that structural differences between the media in the way they represent information can influence which content is conveyed most effectively by television, radio, or print. Meringoff (1980) compared children's learning of an unfamiliar story either read to them from an illustrated book or presented as a comparable televised film. She looked at recall of story content and inferences about characters and events. Children who saw the televised story remembered more story actions and relied more on visual content as a basis for inferences. Children who were read the story in picture-book form recalled more story vocabulary and based more of their inferences on textual content and background knowledge. It was clear, in other words, the structural differences in these media influenced which content was conveyed most effectively. The film's provision of more visual information may well have brought this content to the foreground of children's attention, inasmuch as they apparently relied more on visually provided information in their responses about the programme. The less pronounced visual information offered in the book seemed to permit greater attention to the verbal text. Children who were read the story remembered more figurative language, which (having no visual counterpart) relies solely on being heard.

In a subsequent experiment with young children, Beagle-Roos and Gat (1983) compared story learning from audio-visual (television) and audio-only (radio) presentations of a common narrative soundtrack. Recall of explicit story content was about the same from both media, but there were differences in the kinds of details recalled. Recognition of expressive language was facilitated by audio-only presentation, whereas picture sequencing was augmented by the audio-visual presentation. Once again, the use of general knowledge in forming inferences was more common following audio-only (radio) presentation. The audio-visual (television) version enhanced inferences based on actions. In sum, the radio version promoted the use of verbal content, whereas in the television version, although verbal content was not totally ignored, more attention was given to visually presented material.

Other recent work with youngsters has revealed that it is not only the symbol structures of the media and level of development of appropriate media-specific cognitive skills that mediate learning but also the amount of mental effort typically invested in learning from different media.

Singer (1980) argued that inherent in the power of television to attract viewers lies its limitations as an information medium. Fundamental to the appeal of television is its constant sensory bombardment in sound and in vision. But the pace at which television typically presents material is such that it leaves insufficient time for effective cognitive processing. According to Singer, "*The [TV] set trains us merely to watch it. It does not provide us as a rule with a psychological situation that permits us to process the information presented in a manner that will allow us the most efficient use of what we have seen*" (p. 51).

Singer refers to television commercials when illustrating how cognitive overload can occur when watching television. The parallel presentation of information in voice-overs, on film, and in captions may be simply too much for us to deal with. To some extent, the same principle may apply in the context of learning from the news on television.

News programmes do not have the same objectives as advertisements, nor do they move as quickly in their presentation of information. However, there are certain significant similarities, insofar as information may be presented via several channels—narrative, film footage, maps, graphics, and captions—simultaneously or in rapid serial progression. The problem fundamental to television (and this includes television news) as an information medium is that it constantly introduces new material before the viewer has been given a chance to grasp properly the visual and auditory material that has just been presented.

Salomon (1983) reported a series of studies in which children's preconceptions concerning television and print were investigated in relation to levels of learning the same materials from each medium. In particular, Salomon wanted to know what the effect would be on actual learning of knowing one's own ability and the amount of effort required to process information from a particular medium. If someone believes he or she is good at doing something, and that a particular task is very easy, then they may invest less effort in performing it, and the quality of performance may suffer as a consequence.

In one study, Salomon presented 12-year-old children a television film or the equivalent story in print. When asked about their ability with each medium, children generally believed themselves to be capable of learning more effectively from television than from print. Salomon also asked the children to explain success or failure in learning from each medium. He found that there were clear differences in the kinds of explanations they gave. Success in comprehending television was attributed by most children to the ease of the medium, whereas success in understanding print was attributed mainly to the reader's smartness. On the other hand, failure to comprehend television was blamed on the viewer's stupidity, whereas failure to comprehend print was seen to be a function of the medium's difficulty.

The children reported different amounts of effort with television and print. Less effort investment was reported by viewers than by readers. Comparing learning scores for each medium, there was no difference on simple memory, but print produced significantly better inference generation. It was the print group that reported investing more effort in comprehending the story that generated on average most inferences.

There were interactions also between perceived self-efficacy and learning from different media. Those who believed they were good readers made more effort and learned more. However, those who believed they were good televiewers and that television was easy for them invested less effort consequently and learned less.

In a further study, comparisons were made between more and less able children and their learning from television. This study was conducted by Leigh (reported by Salomon, 1983). More than 90 12-year-olds were questioned about the amount of effort they generally expended in watching television and in reading, and about how worthwhile they thought effort is for each medium. They were then asked to estimate their own abilities to generate inferences and remember from television and from print.

Next the children were divided into three groups to watch television or read an easy or difficult passage based on the same film soundtrack. Afterwards, recall and inference generation, along with effort expenditure, were tested. Results showed that children reported more effort expenditure in reading the difficult text than in reading the easy text or watching television. Ability correlated higher with information processing with the difficult text than with the easy text or television film. Ability was associated also with perceptions of how worthwhile it would be investing effort in reading or viewing. More able children thought it more worthwhile investing effort in the difficult text than in the easy text or television film. In terms of learning, high-ability children performed best in the two print group and least well in the television group, whereas low-ability children performed best with television and worst with the difficult text. It would seem that the more able children perceive television to be less demanding than the less intelligent ones, and report less effort investment in viewing than their less able peers. Abler children look down on television. Another interesting result was that children's belief in their ability to remember details correlated negatively with reported investment of mental effort, and in turn with actual learning. The conclusion one is led to draw from these findings is that because abler children enter the viewing situation with the preconception that television is an undemanding medium, they are inclined not to try very hard to process its contents, and hence don't.

Are these preconceptions sufficient to explain the shallower processing of material from television than from print? Singer (1980) suggested a range of inherent characteristics of television itself and the way it presents information that may also be significant factors. Television's pace is fast, facts are often crowded together, and its pictorial, mosaic–like qualities impede information uptake. Salomon accepts that television can be processed shallowly and still be enjoyed, unlike print. But this does not mean that television cannot be processed deeply if the preconceptual context of the viewer has been adjusted appropriately.

If information from television is not processed effectively because viewers do not believe the medium itself demands or is worth much careful attention or cognitive effort, then perhaps its educational or informational benefits can be enhanced by requiring viewers to invest more energy in their viewing.

In a third study reported by Salomon (1983), an attempt was made experimentally to change children's perceptions of the task to be accomplished by watching a television programme. Children from the same age-group as in the previous studies were divided into groups who either watched a television programme or read the text of the show. These groups were further subdivided into those who were told that the material they were presented with was "for fun" (low demand) and those who were told to see how much they could learn from it (high demand).

As expected, the high-demand instruction produced reports of greater cognitive effort than the low-demand condition. In addition to this, however, the instruction had certain important effects on learning. In reading, the instruction had little effect; apparently effort is high when one is reading, regardless of pretext. Task demands, however, had especially strong effects on learning from television. High demand produced better learning from television than did low demand. Furthermore, the instruction worked particularly well for more able children. More intelligent children learned considerably more than less intelligent children when told to make more effort.

CONCLUDING REMARKS

This chapter introduced discussion on the efficacy of television as an information medium in terms of how well audiences remember and comprehend information from news broadcasts on television. This subject is the principal theme of this book, and some attempt is made to seek out factors within audiences for the news and within news programmes that contribute to the learning process or its breakdown.

We have begun with an examination of research evidence from a number of different perspectives. These included research on the role of television news during political campaigns, in the political socialisation process, and in setting an agenda of events for the public to think about. We have also included more direct tests of the impact of television news on knowledge levels for recently covered news stories and on retention of bulletin content shortly after transmission.

Taking all these research perspectives together, on balance the evidence to emerge from them has provided equivocal support for the informational effectiveness of television news. And certainly, the strength of television's unique cognitive impact as indicated here does not measure up to the strength of claims concerning its importance and reliability made by the public in some oft-quoted national surveys of public opinion about broadcasting or, more specifically, broadcast news.

There is some evidence that television may have some impact on issue knowledge during election campaigns, but its significance may be overshadowed by levels of public interest or involvement in politics. Likewise, youngsters who claim to watch television news fairly often have been found to have better political knowledge than others who say they rarely if ever watch the news. Yet it is often difficult to separate the unique contribution of television from the influence of other important factors linked to family and social background. Although television may indeed have some influence on political socialisation, this effect may be mediated by or dependent upon the nature of other factors concerning the individual's personal make-up and upbringing.

Events covered extensively by the media may often be the ones uppermost in the minds of members of the public. And television may contribute to this agenda-setting process. However, careful analysis of the nature of television's impact has indicated that awareness may only scratch the surface of the full meaning of news stories. Furthermore, agenda-setting measures may be poor indicators of knowledge gain, indicating changes at the level of feelings about events rather than at the level of comprehension.

More direct tests of the cognitive impact of television news in which reported use of television news is related to knowledge about recent news stories have yielded evidence consistent with a television impact. Once again, though, specific kinds of information seem to be getting through to the audience for television news better than others. So, learning about the people who have recently been in the news may be substantially boosted by watching television broadcasts, whereas learning about why certain events occurred and what their repercussions were or are likely to be does not seem to be so effectively enhanced by television news.

It also seems that time is not necessarily to blame for this lack of comprehension (perhaps through some long-term forgetting process.) Even when tested soon after watching a television news broadcast, individuals retention of programme content has typically been found to be very poor.

This chapter concluded by asking if television is a good medium from which to learn. It has been suggested by some researchers that the pace and rapid changes of presentation format that characterise television and represent essential ingredients of the medium's inherent attractivenes may also be largely responsible for impaired learning from it. At the same time, viewers may approach television believing that it is an easy medium to learn from, which it is not. This frame of mind may also contribute significantly to failure to learn effectively from television. Already, then, we see that there are emerging factors within the audience and within the medium that are important determinants of the learning process and need to be carefully investigated for their independent and interdependent effects on information acquisition from television.

3 Locating the Sources of Bad Reception: A Cognitive Research Perspective

The sources of poor reception of broadcast news, where reception is measured in terms of memory and comprehension, have a number of loci. Failure to learn from news broadcasts on television may be a function of characteristics of the audience and the way they watch television, or characteristics of the medium itself, or characteristics of the structure and format of its news programmes. It is a central argument of this book that the cognitive impact of television news can perhaps most effectively be measured within a cognitive information-processing paradigm. This is not to say that other theories of communication are totally useless and uninformative. But a cognitive model is probably the best equipped perspective conceptually and methodologically to study communication problems involving measures of human memory and comprehension performance.

It has often been assumed that extensive forgetting and miscomprehension of broadcast news information is largely due to factors residing within audiences and the way they use and pay attention to the news. Conceptualisations about human cognitive functioning have typically been fairly simple, however. Although audience factors may well be fundamental to effective information uptake from the news media, mass communications researchers need to improve the sophistication of their models of human learning and memory if they are to achieve a better understanding of the types of audience factors that are most significant in this learning context.

Rather less emphasis has been placed on the role of factors residing within the television medium that may affect learning from the news. The findings of public opinion surveys indicating that most people in the western world today say that television is the most important and most reliable source of information are largely taken for granted. The fact is, though, that people may not generally get most of their information about the world from television but may learn a great deal more from newspapers and magazines, or from simply talking to other people (Robinson & Levy, 1985; Tunstall, 1983). The reasons for this are manifold. Perhaps people learn less from television than from newspapers because the former usually provides less information than the latter. Or maybe television, as a medium of communication, is simply less effective than print. To some extent our understanding of why one medium is better than another must rely on some notion about the cognitive information-processing styles demanded or required by each medium. There is some evidence, for example, that people try less when learning from television than when reading because they do not believe television is a medium demanding of cognitive effort (Salomon, 1983). As will be explained, this idea is wrong. Although learning from television may require different styles of information processing from reading, in neither case will much learning occur without a certain amount of effort, especially when the information being learned is new to the learner.

Even if it is shown that television can effectively transmit information, special styles of presentation may be necessary for this to be achieved successfully. It has been observed by some researchers, for example, that television news programmes often exhibit stereotyped profiles and formats. Assumptions are made by journalists concerning the information needs and processing abilities of audiences on the basis of professional intuition rather than empirical verification. Sometimes these assumptions are wrong. It is important to ask whether news programmes often fail to get the news across to their audiences because their style of presentation is not conducive to learning.

It is pertinent to question also the value of the research done so far on memory and comprehension of news information from the broadcast media. Surveys of public news awareness have indicated that rapid and extensive forgetting of news stories can occur soon after watching the news on television. But what can we infer from these findings? Have researchers themselves been guilty of using over simplistic measures of learning that stem from ill-defined or inaccurate theoretical assumptions about human memory processes? For instance, concepts such as *memory* and *comprehension* have distinct meanings and refer to different cognitive processes, but many mass communications researchers have failed to distinguish clearly between them. Measures of memory are often assumed to be sufficient to reflect understanding. Sometimes they are, but on other occasions they may not be. Furthermore, experimental psychologists have shown that memory can be measured in different ways. Some methods may be more useful than others under particular learning conditions to measure the full extent of learning. It is possible therefore that some part of poor retention or understanding of broadcast news identified in some studies may be due to inappropriate methods of probing for information uptake and interpretation among members of the audience.

These problems of method, however, stem from a lack of conceptual sophistication in mass communications research when dealing with problems of human cognitive functioning. More consideration needs to be given to cognitive concepts familiar to cognitive psychologists who study human learning and memory. In this chapter an overview of contemporary ideas about memory structures and processes is presented as an essential theoretical base on which to build research leading, hopefully, to a more complete understanding of the way audiences understand the news.

A COGNITIVE PERSPECTIVE

The dominant contemporary views of memory stem from cognitive information-processing models that envisage memory as the result of an active process of acquiring information from the environment. Cognitive information-processing models could provide a useful theoretical basis for research into retention and comprehension of broadcast news. Up to now, there has been little attempt to find some common theoretical ground on which to work in this field, or even to base research in theory at all (Kellermann, 1985; Woodall, Davis, & Sahin, 1983).

Yet a fundamental question that needs to be asked about the informational impact of broadcast news is how viewers and listeners actually process the content of news programmes. What sense do audience members make of the news as it is customarily presented to them on television, and what are the determinants of how effectively news is cognitively processed? Associated with these theoretical considerations are practical questions, such as how best to operationally define and measure the uptake of broadcast news. Different kinds of cognitive structures and control processes are involved in the learning and understanding of news information and require distinct measurement techniques. As Woodall et al. (1983) have pointed out, it is questionable whether the most appropriate techniques have always been used by researchers in this field to measure what is purportedly being measured. In a subsequent paper, Berry (1983b) pointed out that different methods of probing for information uptake from television news can give rise to quite different indications of memory and comprehension performance. Some measures are more sensitive indicators of news retention than others.

AN INFORMATION-PROCESSING APPROACH TO MEMORY

The information-processing approach to human learning and memory and cognitive functioning is relatively new, emerging during the 1960s. It is based on the idea that human beings are processors of information. Within this general perspective, two important distinctions are made. The first is the distinction between different memory *structures* and memory *stores*; and the second is the distinction between memory *structures* as such (the "hardware" of memory) and memory *processes* (the "software" of memory). We begin by considering the structure of memory. Cognitive researchers have proposed various separate storage models that divide the memory system typically into two or three separate and distinct memory stores, each with specific characteristics and each with its own control processes. Then we turn to examine memory processes, which are classified broadly into three types: encoding, storage, and retrieval.

MEMORY STRUCTURES

A relatively simple conception of memory was proposed by Waugh and Norman (1965), who distinguished two separate stores that they called *primary memory* (PM) and *secondary memory* (SM). It was assumed within this model that every stimulus item that is perceived enters PM. Once there either the item is maintained through rehearsal or it is fairly quickly forgotten. If an item is rehearsed and remains in PM, it may eventually enter SM, which was considered to be a more permanent store. Once in SM, an item need no longer be rehearsed to be retained. The capacity of PM was believed to be limited, whereas SM was believed to provide more storage capacity than an individual would need in a lifetime.

Although many more models of memory have been proposed since this one, Waugh and Norman's (1965) model set the scene for subsequent information-processing theories, which continued to distinguish between two memory stores, one in which information is kept for short periods of time and another in which information can be retained permanently. The dichotomy between a short-term store and a long-term store (or PM and SM) has become the focal characteristic of many modern models of memory.

A more widely accepted conception of the structure of memory is a model that distinguishes three cognitive systems. Atkinson and Shiffrin (1965, 1968, 1971) produced a memory model that distinguished between a short-term memory store and a long-term memory store, and introduced a new store that they called the *sensory register*. This third component of memory, which has been variously referred to as the *sensory buffer* (Hastie & Carlston, 1980) and the *short-term sensory store* (STSS) (Tarpy & Mayer, 1978), was seen as preceding the short-term memory store (STM).

The three-component model of memory runs as follows. Environmental stimuli or information that impinges on the sense receptors (e.g., eyes and ears) is first entered into a short-term sensory store (STSS). This sensory buffer or register holds "very basic, unelaborated impressions of the external environment" (Houston, 1981, p. 341) for very brief durations (½ to 1 second), which decay rapidly unless attended to, processed further, and entered into the short-term memory store (or eventually into long-term memory).

The next memory store is short-term memory (STM). STM represents the stream of current consciousness and is where information from immediate experience is first interpreted. This store has a limited capacity of seven plus or minus two items of information (Miller, 1956), and information is forgotten within half a minute unless it is acted upon or rehearsed (Brown, 1958; Peterson & Peterson, 1959).

Experiments in which cognitive tasks have involved a mixture of processes believed to characterise both STM and long-term memory (LTM) have led some writers to introduce a fourth memory store called *working memory* (or WM) (Feigenbaum, 1970). Like STM, WM has a limited capacity. In it, information from STM and LTM is combined and manipulated. Information may be transferred to and from it and STM and LTM. The concept of working memory has become especially important in research on complex forms of human learning and problem solving, where knowledge from LTM is accessed to guide the processing of new information held in STM (Tarpy & Mayer, 1978).

The final memory store is long-term memory (LTM), which technically is assumed to have an infinite capacity but is different from the other memory stores in that information is represented in a meaningful, organized, and abstract way. LTM is assumed to be a permanent store, and it is assumed that when information is "lost" it is because of interference from other information at recall or due to failure to access it effectively.

The long-term memory system has been differentiated into two major components: *episodic* memory and *semantic* memory (Tulving, 1972). Episodic memory is assumed to store information about temporally arranged or dated events and episodes. It is the memory of personal experiences. Semantic memory, on the other hand, refers to memory for the meaning of words, concepts, and facts. Information stored in semantic memory is not temporally ordered or related to time of experience. Semantic memory is akin to a library of general factual and linguistic knowledge.

Tulving (1972) does point out that although conceptually distinguished, the two long-term memory systems often interact with one another during information processing. However, they can function independently and may well differ from each other in terms of the nature of their cognitive processes (encoding, storage, and retrieval), which control the flow of information into and out of them. If this is true, it carries important implications, as we will see, for mass communications researchers studying memory and comprehension of television news.

Although a fairly new idea, the distinction between episodic and semantic memory has been recognised by cognitive psychologists as heuristically useful (Houston, 1981). There have not been many experimental comparisons of the two systems, however. Indeed, most memory studies—and this is also true of research on memory for broadcast news—have been concerned essentially with episodic memory functions and phenomena.

Recent experiments on broadcast news retention have shown, however, that semantic memory factors, operationalised in terms of relevant background knowledge about particular news topics, may be highly predictive of comprehension and memory of televised news content (Berry, 1985). Consequently, some consideration of theories concerning the structure and Organization of semantic memory could provide useful conceptual insights into the way broadcast news information may be stored in memory and could offer reasons why memory for news appears so often to break down.

Semantic Memory

Three general models of the structure and Organization of semantic memory can be identified: *network* models, *set-theoretic* models, and *feature-comparison* models.

Network models assume that semantic memory consists of a great network of associations between concepts that are hierarchically arranged into logically nested subordinate-superordinate relations. Each concept or item of factual knowledge occupies a "node" in this branchlike system, with the "links" between concepts or nodes representing semantic associations (Collins & Quillian, 1969). For example, "Boeing 747" is a subordinate to "airplane," which in turn is a subordinate to "mode of transport." In Britain, "Parliament" subsumes two houses, the "House of Lords" and the "House of Commons." The "House of Commons" in turn contains the "government" and "opposition" parties.

Other hierarchical models of semantic memory followed that proposed by Collins and Quillian (e.g., Anderson & Bower, 1973; Kintsch, 1974; Norman & Rumelhart, 1975), many of which were far more detailed than the original. The latter models have generated a great deal of research but have not been universally accepted. Some of the assumptions network models have made about the way knowledge is organised have not been supported by research. One alternative to the network models of semantic memory has been termed the set-theoretic model because it treats semantic memory as if it consisted of a large number of sets of elements.

A two-stage model proposed by Meyer (1970), called the *predicate-intersections* model, assumed that semantic memory consists of sets of attributes. Thus, to take one common sphere of news as an example, the economy may be represented by a set of defining attributes that includes inflation and the balance of payments. The latter themselves may be further defined in terms of overseas trade, industrial productivity, management-union disputes over pay, rising costs of certain commodities or services, and so forth. In deciding whether news about inflation is also news about the state of the economy, the individual must compare the defining attributes of each concept to see if they match.

The third model of semantic memory has been represented in the *feature-comparison* model. The model proposed by Smith, Shoben, and Rips (1974) assumes that the meaning of any item in semantic memory can be represented as a set of semantic features. Among these are features that are central or essential to the meaning of the item, and these are known as *defining features*. In addition to these, there are nonessential features that are nevertheless descriptive of the item. These are referred to as *characteristic features*.

When someone is required to decide if an object or event or issue, *X*, is a member of a particular category of objects, events, or issues, the feature-comparison model assumes that the sets of features corresponding to the example and category are partitioned into two subsets corresponding to the defining and characteristic features. If all the defining features of the category are also defining features of the example, then the latter is judged to be a member of that category. If all the defining features do not match, the example is judged to be not of that category.

Although these models differ in their explanations of the structure and Organization of knowledge in semantic memory, and each has specific strengths and weaknesses, together they provide useful ideas about the way information is kept in long-term memory from which mass communications researchers involved in the study of news comprehension could learn. Before elaborating further on just how useful semantic memory models could be to such researchers, memory processes, or the "software" that controls the flow of information to and from memory, will be considered.

LEVELS OF PROCESSING

The level-of-processing framework was presented by Craik and Lockhart (1972) as an alternative to the view that there is more than one type of memory. A primary argument for the separation of memory stores has been that information might be stored in a different format in each case; specifically, information in STM was presumed to be stored in a sensory (auditory or visual) format, whereas information in LTM was presumably encoded in a sematic format. However, there is now good reason to believe that short-term retention also involves semantic information and that LTM may involve sensory information as well.

The levels- or depth-of-processing approach is a general framework for investigating memory. It divides memory into various stages that correspond to various processes rather than to distinct storage structures. The characteristics of the memory trace are due to the type of perceptual analyses imposed upon the structures, rather than to the storage compartment in which the trace resides.

Craik and Lockhart (1972) suggested that memory is determined by the depth or level to which a stimulus is analysed. The perceptual analysis of the stimulus may concentrate solely upon the physical features of the stimulus—the shape of the letters in a word or the sound of the word. This represents a low-level, superficial processing that leads to an unstable memory trace.

More persistent traces are formed with deeper processing that involves analysis of semantic characteristics of the stimulus. In the case of verbal material this may involve elaboration of the meaning of words, sentences, passages, and so forth. There is evidence that the more elaborately individuals are required to interpret verbal materials, the better those materials are learned and subsequently remembered (Craik & Tulving, 1975).

MEMORY PROCESSES

Cognitive psychologists working within an information-processing perspective have distinguished three broad categories of processes that control the flow of information through the human cognitive system: encoding, storage, and retrieval. Mass communications researchers concerned with audience comprehension of information broadcasts on television have usually investigated how much information can be recalled or retrieved. Before recall can occur, however, information has to pass successfully and unhindered through various stages of cognitive processing. First of all, the information is taken into the short-term sensory store

(STSS), from which it may then be selected into short-term memory (STM). Attention is the control process that determines whether information will be transferred from STSS to STM. If the information represented in the visual or auditory images of STSS is attended to before they rapidly fade away, then some of it can be transferred to STM. Once it is in STM, two basic control processes operate on the information to determine whether it reaches the permanent long-term memory (LTM) store. These are encoding and rehearsal (storage). Rehearsal serves to maintain information in STM, whereas encoding involves trying to integrate the information into the existing knowledge structures in LTM, where it can be retained permanently.

In LTM, the flow of information is controlled by retrieval processes, which refers to the accessing and utilization of stored information (Murdock, 1974). Although LTM is regarded as an essentially permanent storage house for knowledge, and therefore a stored item of information should always be *available*, this does not mean that it is always readily *accessible*. Thus, although a viewer may have understood from a news broadcast the reasons why the President announced trade sanctions against foreign trading partners, he or she may not necessarily be able to recount the details for a researcher who telephones to ask about the bulletin a few hours after transmission.

Encoding

Encoding refers to the formation or acquisition of memory traces: that is, to the entering of information into memory. Environmental stimuli impinging on the sense receptors must be transformed into a format compatible with the "hardware" (or structure) and "software" (or processual features) of memory. Although we are constantly encoding new information during conscious waking hours, the effectiveness of encoding varies. Some experiences are remembered better than others because they have been better encoded, whereas certain kinds of information may prove to be especially difficult to learn. Cognitive researchers have identified a number of factors that are involved in encoding information into memory. Examples of encoding operations include transforming a visual form into a verbal label or concept, selecting only a portion of the incoming information for storage, or elaborating it by processing it in the context of knowledge that is already held in memory.

Arousal. How well events are remembered depends on a person's level of alertness or physiological arousal at the time the event occurs. Experimental evidence suggests that the effect of arousal on memory usually occurs at encoding, although arousal level is also known to influence ability to retrieve stored information. The precise effect of arousal on memory often depends on the nature and complexity of cognitive processing required. Learning of relatively simple information can be facilitated by arousal, whereas acquisition of complex and unfamiliar information may be inhibited severaly by too much arousal. This notion that the optimal level of arousal is inversely related to information difficulty was formulated as an early "law" of learning by Yerkes and Dodson (1908) and has received support more recently (Spence & Spence, 1966).

Arousal and learning ability are known to fluctuate in a cyclical fashion during each 24-hour period. Even in the last century, Ebbinghaus (1885) found in learning experiments with himself as subject that his ability to remember lists of simple items varied across the day. Immediate memory for material was best in the morning between 11:00 a.m. and noon and at its poorest in the evening between 6:00 and 8:00 p.m.

This finding has been replicated in modern times by cognitive researchers (Blake, 1967; Folkard, 1979; Folkard & Monk, 1978). More importantly, as we see in Chapter 11, the same time-of-day effects occur with regard to memory for broadcast news (Gunter, Jarrett, & Furnham, 1983; Gunter, Furnham, & Jarrett, 1984).

Selective Attention.   Another important encoding operation not unrelated to arousal is that of attention. Such is the volume of information impinging on us from the environment that much of it is simply not encoded. Faced with a complex, informationally dense communication, for example, we find that only certain features will be selectively entered into memory.

Broadbent (1958) proposed that selective attention acts like a filter, blocking out one communication channel and allowing another channel to receive attention. Attention can be influenced in two general ways. Firstly, it can be influenced by features of the message itself, such as its intensity or novelty, that may determine what is attended to. Secondly, the person may control what features of the message are attended to—an operation determined among other things possibly by the meaning or relevance different parts of the message have for the receiver. Broadbent's original model proposed that while attention was focused on information in one channel, the other channel remained unattended to. This model was later revised by Treisman (1969), who replaced the all-or-non property of the filter with an attenuator model that assumed that the flow of information could be weakened, though not necessarily completely blocked, in the low-priority channel.

The implications of selective attention hypotheses for remembering news presented in television broadcasts relate in particular to the relative salience of information presented in the visual channel (e.g., film footage, still photographs, characteristics of newscaster) and information presented in the audio channel (story narrative) and to the relative amount of audience attention each receives during the course of the programme. Visuals are designed to be and often are attention-grabbing. Yet, at the same time, research has indicated that visuals and narrative do not always convey mutually supportive information or tell the same story. In consequence, attention predominantly directed towards the visuals in a programme can produce poor retention and comprehension of news stories (e.g., Berry, 1983a, 1985: Findahl & Hoijer, 1976; Gunter, 1980a).

Spacing Effect. The way stimulus items are spaced also affects encoding of information. Items that are massed together are recalled less well (when recall is tested immediately) than are items that are distributed throughout other material (Underwood, 1961; Underwood, Kapelak, & Malmi, 1976). Improved learning due to spacing of items is often reported in tests of memory for long lists of verbal items, for verbal materials under fast rates of presentation, and for unfamiliar verbal materials (Underwood, 1961).

In a typical experiment on the spacing effect, individuals are presented with a long list of words. In the list, some words occur only once, whereas others are presented twice. The number of words separating repeated presentations of the same item varies from 0 to 16. Afterwards, individuals are asked to recall the words. Invariably, repeated words are recalled better than singly presented words, but the likelihood of recall of repeated words increases with the lag between their two occurrences in the list.

Various explanations have been put forward for this effect. One theory is that the second presentation of an item immediately following the first disrupts consolidation of the memory trace of the first presentation (Hebb, 1949, 1958). This effect does not happen when the gap between presentations allows sufficient time for the first trace to be laid down. Another theory is that the amount of rehearsal an item receives is increased as the space between its repeated presentations grows. The amount of rehearsal aids the transfer of information from STM to LTM (Rundus, 1971).

A third explanation has been offered in terms of *encoding variability* (Martin, 1968; 1972; Melton, 1970). The basic idea here is that spacing allows learners to encode new material into different contexts, thus providing more chance of retrieval at a later time. Essentially, it is hypothesised that the same item may be perceived differently with different presentations. A different memory trace may therefore be formed for that item each time. This is more likely to occur, however, when repeated occurrences of the item are spaced apart than when they are close together (see Madigan, 1969; Underwood, 1970).

Organization. Encoding has been described as the transformation of information into a form suitable for storage. The contents of the long-term memory store are assumed to be highly organised to make efficient use of the available storage capacity and to facilitate the search for stored information. As a means of maintaining efficient storage, once information has been selectively encoded into STM, the encoding operation continues by chunking information. This procedure allows complex informational units to be integrated into higher-level single ideas. The aim is to systematically alter or rearrange information to a form that is compatible with the existing organization of LTM.

The operation of subjective organization of information during encoding has been inferred from measured discrepancies between experimenter-defined input and the way individuals order the same material during recall. One finding from the study of free recall of word lists is that individuals may group together a randomly mixed array according to conceptual categories (Bousfield, 1951, 1953; Wood & Underwood, 1967).

Although research has indicated that the provision of conceptual labels as cues at recall can aid structuring of lists of words, it has also been found that in the absence of such memory aids, individuals provide their own structure to unstructured verbal materials. This phenomenon has been called *subjective Organization* (Tulving, 1962, 1968). Organizational processes, self-generated by individuals, are inferred from the consistent order in which lists of items are recalled, even though the order in which they are presented is varied across study sessions.

Constructive Processes in Memory

Information that has been encoded into short-term memory may be not simply maintained through rehearsal but operated on by constructive and elaborative processes directed by knowledge structures that exist in long-term memory. These processes may modify or distort the original information while integrating it into a coherent form in readiness for storage in LTM.

The best-known demonstrations of the role of constructive processes during the encoding and storage of information are Bartlett's (1932) studies of story recollection. When individuals who had read a folk tale were required to retell it afterwards, much of the original story was lost or changed in the paraphrases that were typically produced. Interestingly, however, the central theme of the story was usually retained.

More recently it has been observed that individuals tend to persist with distorted or mistaken reproductions when retelling stories, even when they have been given the chance to hear the original correct versions repeatedly (Howe, 1977). It seems that when we hear a story we do not typically register the contents word for word but instead construct our own memory representation that may depart in structure and detail from the original. We impose on stories our own ready-made organizers, which may sometimes depend on existing knowledge about the subject matter of the story or about the usual way stories of that type are told. Sometimes prior knowledge of the subject of a story can make all the difference to how much of that story is subsequently remembered (e.g., Bransford & McCarrell, 1974). Similarly, Ausubel (1968) demonstrated the effectiveness in teaching of "advance organizers," which activate memories of what is already known and aid the understanding, integration, and acquisition of new related information.

Cognitive theorists have recently conceptualised these directive knowledge structures in terms of the notion of schemata or scripts. These entities represent conceptual frames of reference that provide organizational guidelines for newly encoded information about people and social or behavioural roles and events (Taylor & Crocker, 1981).

In one schema theory, Schank and Abelson (1977) proposed the concept of "scripts" as schemata concerned specifically with the organization of information about events. These researchers argued that many event scenarios take on a repetitive, stereotyped format that can be learned. Our understanding of many events is therefore governed by sets of expectations that lead us to anticipate certain chains of occurrences if events are to follow their normal course (or "script"). One commonly cited example is the "restaurant script". Normally, when we go to a restaurant we would expect to find a certain cast of characters, (e.g., other customers, waiters/waitresses, a chef, and possibly a cashier). We would also expect to experience a certain sequence of events, perhaps running something as follows: enter the restaurant, select and be shown to a table, sit down and receive menu, order food, wait for first course to arrive, eat meal, receive bill, and finally pay and leave, possibly leaving a tip for the waiter. For social events as such, therefore, we construct a script that serves as a ready-made organizational framework in which the set of experiences are made sense of.

Schemata have been found to play an important role in guiding information processing when reading texts. In order to make sense of a text, we must be able to see how successive sentences that make up the text connect and eventually to form an overall concept of the meaning or major ideas they convey. Cognitive psychologists have found that knowledge of the type of text can be useful in organizing our internal representation of it. Often, when reading, readers not only work out the connectedness between sentences in the text but also integrate the new information with previous knowledge they have about the usual structure of texts of this sort, forming what has been termed by one theorist a "text base" (Kintsch, 1976). Thus, according to some cognitive researchers, when faced with a story from a familiar genre (e.g., a detective drama), readers may utilize a pre-existing conception or schema of how the story is likely to evolve. This schema serves to organize the "text base" and aids information processing and understanding.

From work on the interpretation of simple stories, one typical story format that has been identified has shown that a story tends to include a scene-setting stage in which main characters are introduced, a theme-elaborating stage telling what the story is going to be about, a set of episodes featuring actions involving the main characters, and a resolution sequence in which loose ends are tied up. Put more simply, typical stories have a beginning, middle, and end.

The premise of applying schema theory or script theory to news is that the structure of news events recurs to some extent. This is more obvious in the case of some events than in others. For instance, different accidents and catastrophes may have similar ingredients, but diplomatic, political, and industrial events can often appear stereotyped or even ritualised.

How useful are schemata? The answer seems to be that they can be very useful devices and may often serve as an effective way of reducing information-processing demands in familiar situations or with familiar materials individuals have encountered many times before (Eysenck, 1984). Schemata may be involved in guiding encoding, organizing information during storage, and aiding retrieval. During immediate processing, for example, a schema may direct attention to certain elements within a story. It may organize or interpret different ideas into higher-order units, thus reducing the memory load. A schema might also aid in the selection of information from the text base during retrieval. Schemata may influence not simply how much is remembered from a text but also what kinds of things are remembered. Individuals recall ideas critical to the story, its theme, principal actions, and resolution with greater accuracy than subordinate details (Bower, 1976; Mandler & Johnson, 1977), and produce such ideas more frequently in summaries of stories (Kintsch, 1976). Such selectivity disappears, however, in the absence of a thematic sequence (Thorndyke, 1977).

Retrieval

Remembering information depends not only on encoding and storage but also on retrieval processes. The fact that information has been successfully stored in LTM does not mean that it is always readily accessible.

The problem of retrieval is considered by some psychologists to be the major one in memory. Efficient retrieval may depend on the drawing up of effective retrieval strategies and plans (see Miller, Galanter, & Pribram, 1960). Miller et al. drew an analogy between an individual in a memory experiment and a librarian. Books are stored in the library, and the efficiency with which they can be retrieved by the librarian depends on the use of a systematic code for storing the books. Failure to find a book does not mean it is not in the library, merely that it cannot presently be located. Similarly, items "forgotten" by the individual may still be in memory storage but cannot be found and reproduced. Retrieval encompasses the search processes necessary for accessing information that is stored in long-term memory. Given the enormous amount of material stored in LTM, search processes are most likely to be effective if directed or guided in some way.

Memory can be evaluated by simply asking a person to reproduce the material that was studied. This may often produce only limited memory performance, however. Sometimes respondents may fail completely to mention certain items presented to them (for example, on the news), or they may manage only partially to retrieve them. In some experiments, therefore, researchers present additional information to guide the retrieval operation, known as a *retrieval cue*. This cues functions to direct the search to appropriate locations in the memory store.

The importance of retrieval cues has been clearly demonstrated by Tulving and his colleagues. In comparisons of recall in the presence and absence of retrieval cues, Tulving and Patterson (1968) and Tulving and Osler (1968) reported a considerable advantage for cued recall. Cues are most effective when presented with the material for which they are guiding retrieval, and when they bear some meaningful relationship to the material being retrieved (Thompson & Tulving, 1970, 1973).

The effectiveness of retrieval also depends on the context in which information was learned. One of the prime causes of forgetting identified by psychologists is confusion of tested information with other information presented either just before or just after it. Two types of interference effects have been distinguished. Information learned before the information under test may cause *proactive interference* (PI), whereas information learned after the tested information may cause *retroactive interference* (RI).

Interference is likely to be especially severe between items of similar meaning or with many attributes in common (McGeoch & MacDonald, 1931; Wickens, 1972).

IMPLICATIONS FOR NEWS COMPREHENSION RESEARCH

Memory and comprehension of broadcast news are mediated and affected by the components and processes of the cognitive information-processing system described previously. A proper understanding of the ways in which audiences are able to learn from broadcast news depends importantly on a sound knowledge of the way the human cognitive system works. This knowledge may not only enhance the quality of research and academic understanding but may also give rise to useful practical implications for the production of more memorable and comprehensible news programmes. Routine procedures for the selection, telling, packaging, illustrating, and pacing of news stories in television news bulletins give rise to programmes with stereotyped structures and profiles. Research on the way individuals cognitively process verbal information would lead one to expect that memory and comprehension of news will be affected in different ways by these production features of television news broadcasts.

PRODUCTION VARIABLES AND NEWS COMPREHENSION

Interesting Stories.   At the forefront of news broadcasters' considerations each day are the selection of "newsworthy" stories and how to create an interesting and stimulating programme that will attract and retain a large audience. The criteria of newsworthiness that determine which stories out of the hundreds that are available every day will eventually be chosen for the programme often embody assumptions about the cognitive and affective impact of the programme on its audience (see Galtung & Ruge, 1965; Schulz, 1982; Sparkes & Winter, 1980).

The introduction of the *Eyewitness News* format on U.S. network television news in the early 1970s resulted in greater emphasis on violence, humour, and human interest stories in the news (Dominick, Wurtzel, & Lometti, 1975). In other words, there was more emphasis on stories likely to have an affective impact. To what extent would one expect this change in content and style in news programmes to have an effect on the cognitive impact of the news, and in what direction—good or bad?

Cognitive research has indicated that effective memory and comprehension of information may depend on the level at which it is processed (Craik & Lockhart, 1972). Memory is best following cognitive processing at a relatively deep level that focuses on the essential meaning of a message. Highly arousing content, however, has been found to impair encoding at a semantic level and instead causes attention to shift to more superficial physical characteristics of verbal material (Schwartz, 1975). Emotionally arousing news items may therefore leave the viewer with a strong affectively toned impression but may not impart much information or meaning about the reasons why certain events occurred.

What does seem to be important, in those cases in which affectively toned content is used, is the way it connects with and supports the meaning of the story. Arousing content (e.g., humour) can affect attention to information and, when related directly to the central concepts of a presentation, can also improve learning (Kaplan & Pascoe, 1977). In contrast, highly arousing materials (e.g. violent film footage) that is used merely for effect, and that does not support information in the story narrative, may impair memory and comprehension (Berry, 1985; Furnham & Gunter, 1985; Gunter, Furnham, & Gietson, 1984).

It may be important to be careful in presenting a highly arousing item among a number of adjacent affectively neutral items. Von Restorff (1933) found that under such circumstances, although the outstanding item is well remembered, memory for others around it may be substantially impaired.

Telling the Story. During encoding and storage, new information may be acted upon by constructive processes that organize and integrate the information to make it compatible with long-term memory structures. Cognitive psychologists have found that learning from story narratives can be significantly influenced by cognitive frames of reference, variously known as schemata or scripts, which individuals utilize during learning. Understanding of events and memory for stories can be substantially enhanced when individuals have appropriate schemata available to aid information processing (Chiesi, Spilich, & Voss, 1979; Thorndyke, 1979). Research on children's comprehension of television has shown that as young viewers become familiar with the narrative structures of television dramas, they are better able to remember events from these programmes afterwards (Collins, 1979). One study found that before the development of appropriate "scripts" there was little difference in children's recall from versions of a programme in which the actions were in the correct story sequence or randomly mixed up. Following "script" development, however, recall was far better when events were placed in their proper order (Collins, Wellman, Keniston, & Westby, 1978).

Schemata may be important mediators of learning from broadcast news. Graber (1984) has argued that schemata may determine what information is stored and available for retrieval from news programmes, may aid in the organization of new information in long-term storage so that it fits in with existing knowledge, and may thus enable people to go beyond the information given. Cognitive researchers have found that although the presence of structure can aid memory for a text, the absence of structure may contribute to poor comprehension and rapid forgetting. In the context of broadcast news information, this last point has been illustrated in Dutch research on memory for weather and traffic reports on radio. When interviewed shortly after the morning weather report, for example, although most people claimed to be interested in the information, it was found that recall from weather bulletins was generally very poor (Wagenaar, 1978; Wagenaar & Visser, 1979). The researchers suggested that this low recall was probably a function of the typical structure of these broadcast messages. An analysis of their narratives revealed that weather reports lacked any real grammatical structure. Instead, a typical forecast consisted of an unstructured list of some 32 idea units, which required the listener to process them in the same way as nonsense materials are.

On average, respondents recalled a maximum seven plus or minus two idea units per forecast, which marks the upper limit of short-term memory capacity (Miller, 1956).

The lack of narrative structure that typifies weather forecasts is not characteristic of television news bulletins in which narrative structures are employed to create interest and enhance comprehension (Golding & Elliott, 1979). The question remains, however, as to whether the story-telling formats used in television news programmes necessarily enhance comprehension. Recent work done by cognitive psychologists has challenged the efficacy of narrative structures arising out of the naive psychologising of television journalists. (Berry, 1985; Findahl & Hoijer, 1985; Larsen, 1981). More is said on this in Chapter 7.

Packaging the News.   A news programme consists of more than a set of haphazardly arranged, disparate news stories. Underlying the structure and order of events is a concept of what a professionally produced and constructed news programme should look like. In an attempt to shape the miscellany of news items into a news programme, one method commonly employed by news editors is to link together disparate news stories by theme or topic. Grouping together thematically similar news items often produces clusters of quite distinct issues under a common label, sometimes with the implication that they are all aspects of a general problem (Glasgow University Media Group, 1976; Golding & Elliott, 1979).

Cognitive research has demonstrated that how well a particular item of information can be remembered can depend to a significant extent on the context in which it is learned. One important contextual feature is the nature of any other informational material that occurs with the to-be-remembered item at presentation. Memory for an item can be impaired, for example, by interference from preceding and subsequent items in a sequence. And the level of interference is positively correlated with the degree of similarity between the items. If a verbal item is preceded by other verbal items that are thematically similar, its retention may be seriously impaired (Blumenthal & Robbins, 1977; Gunter, 1979; Wickens, Born, & Allen, 1963). This proactive interference effect has been found more recently to occur across thematically similar television news items (Gunter, 1983; Gunter, Clifford, & Berry, 1980; Gunter, Berry, &

Clifford, 1981). The implications of this research are that topically similar news stories may be confused either at encoding or at retrieval and that by packaging such stories together, memory and comprehension may be adversely affected. In Chapter 8 we examine these findings and their implications for broadcast news production in more detail.

Picturing the News. Television news editors try to use the visual potential of the medium to the fullest possible extent. The most favoured visual input is film, which lends an element of immediacy to the news that is regarded by newsmen as important to good-quality news reporting. The availability of film footage may often determine how much time is devoted to a story, where it occurs in the programme, and whether it is included at all (Golding & Elliott, 1979; Schlesinger, 1978). In the absence of suitable film, an editor may decide to visually enhance a news item with still photographs, graphs, diagrams, or maps. Sometimes a combination of moving and still visual materials may be used to embellish a single story.

A crucial issue in the production of news programmes from which audiences' knowledge and understanding of current events will grow is the question of how visuals are deployed. This is important especially in the light of what is known from cognitive psychology about memory for pictures. Depending on how they are used in news programmes alongside accompanying news narratives, pictures may enhance or impair memory and comprehension.

The meaning of a news story is carried in the narrative. News comprehension therefore depends on effective processing of the story text. Cognitive research has shown, however, that memory for pictures tends to be better than memory for words (Shephard, 1967). Furthermore, pictures tend to be well remembered even long after presentation (Nickerson, 1965). There is evidence, also, that because they are more readily processed than words, pictures may "drown out" the verbal content in television news. Dhawan and Pellegrino (1977) found that pictures are encoded to a deep semantic level of processing faster than verbal materials. For content presented at short, fixed intervals, this indicates that pictorial information can be processed more deeply than verbal information and retained longer due to unequal learning.

There is evidence that pictures and pictorial representations in broadcasts can enhance memory and comprehension of information, however. Some writers have argued that imagery has an important role in memory. Words that readily evoke images are better remembered than more abstract ones, because they provide better conceptual pegs on which information can be hung and more readily retrieved (Bower, 1970; Paivio, 1969).

The dual-code hypothesis proposes that two kinds of representation of information can occur in memory. Imaginal representations consist effectively of "pictures in the head"—a direct representation of the physical appearance of an object. Then there are verbal or propositional representations that do not evoke images but consist of descriptions of an object's properties (Bower, 1972).

More recently, an alternative hypothesis to the dual-code notion has been proposed that argues that both pictures and words are represented in memory in the same way, as logical propositions (e.g., Kosslyn, 1980). The propositional representation position has now become widely accepted and may provide a more adequate theoretical framework in which to assess the cognitive processing and representation of visual and narrative content in broadcast news. The extreme form of the propositional representation hypothesis argues that there is essentially no difference in the way pictorial and verbal information is represented in memory. However, evidence that people encode information about modality of input and about pictorial material in pictorial forms would suggest that the extreme notion of this hypothesis may be wrong (see Hopkins, Edwards, & Gavelek, 1971; Kroll, Bee, & Gurski, 1973; Wells, 1973). In a modified form of this hypothesis, however, it has been suggested that although both types of information are stored as propositions, there are distinct representations of linguistic and pictorial material at the propositional level (Kieras, 1978).

Whichever theory one accepts, research findings have pointed to an advantage of using readily visualisable ("concrete") terminology over more abstract, less easily pictured terms. Comprehension of the meaning or substance of sentences is much more likely when they consist of concrete information for which visual as well as verbal encodings are possible (Begg & Paivio, 1969; Kuiper & Paivio, 1977; Pezdek & Royer, 1974). Likewise, with extended narratives, concrete passages are remembered and understood better than are ones filled with abstract terminology (Philipchalk, 1972; Yuille & Paivio, 1969). There are indications that concreteness enhances the degree of semantic integration among sentence words compared with abstractness (Rosenberg, 1977).

Pictures may enhance memory for texts by illustrating more clearly the theme of a story and therefore providing a contextual framework in which the verbal content can be more effectively processed. Bransford and Johnson (1972) found that learning a difficult or ambiguous passage could be enhanced if prerequisite knowledge in the form of a picture that provided information about the context underlying the passage was presented beforehand.

The effectiveness of visual illustrations, however, depends crucially on the extent to which they support and are relevant in some way to the accompanying narrative content. Bransford and Johnson also found that when the pictures did not match the verbal description of a scene, comprehension was no better than if no pictures at all had been shown.

The Main Points of the News.   Another feature of news broadcasts on television is that programmes usually begin and end with summaries of the main news stories of the day. Sometimes these headlines are simple verbal descriptions of the central or most dramatic elements of stories, and sometimes they are accompanied by brief clips of film or other visual embellishments. Opening headlines and closing summaries are taken for granted by the practitioners as a routine feature of telling the news. The headlines at the beginning of the programme function as hooks to attract and retain the audience.

Although a standard element in news presentation, the effect of headlines and summaries on memory and comprehension of the news is not something that has been studied in much detail. Yet evidence from cognitive psychology would suggest that the nature of these opening and closing statements may have a significant effect on news comprehension.

Research on memory for texts has shown that use of thematic titles can affect how much is learned and what is learned for narrative materials. Dooling and Lachman (1971) found that by presenting titles immediately before a passage, they could produce a significant improvement in readers' recall of a prose passage, compared to a condition in which no title was presented.

In a subsequent study, Dooling and Mullet (1973) found that thematic titles presented before narratives were more effective in enhancing memory than titles presented afterwards. This finding is corroborated by the work of Bransford and Johnson (1972).

Some cognitive theorists believe that use of titles can alter the comprehension of a text by affecting the selection of information from it and influencing the way the information is organized in memory (Kozminsky, 1977). Headlines or titles may help the reader or listener to make sense of a text, but they can also bias comprehension by focusing an individual's attention on those elements in the text that were emphasised in the headline summary (Niegeman, 1982). In research with broadcast news materials, it has been found that emphasis placed on personalities in the news or on dramatic descriptions of events, rather than on the underlying causes and meaning of stories, can severely limit audience understanding (Findahl & Hoijer, 1972, 1975, 1976). This subject will be examined in more detail in Chapter 10.

INDIVIDUAL DIFFERENCES AND MEMORY

The cognitive structures and processes described earlier in this chapter have largely been assumed to represent universal properties of the human cognitive system. Not all individuals are alike in their cognitive styles or abilities, however, and experimental cognitive psychology has found that memory for information may vary not only with the difficulty of the learning material but also across different categories of people.

In research on the informational effects of the mass media, mass communications researchers have long recognised that some groups of individuals know more about news and current affairs than others. In particular, it has been noted that certain demographic groups, most notably the better educated and higher social classes, seem to learn more from the media than others (Robinson, 1967, 1972; Tichenor, Donohue, & Olien, 1970). The explanation for this "knowledge-gap" phenomenon usually pointed to differences between these groups in the ways they used news media. The better educated generally read more newspapers and news magazines than other people and were exposed to greater volumes of news about current events.

With the growth of television as a news medium, however, there was an awareness that most people were regularly exposed to news messages via network and local news programmes, regardless of their educational backgrounds, and demographic indicators might provide less useful indicators of differential public affairs knowledge growth, especially if the critical dynamic factor underlying information uptake was media usage habits.

In a move away from purely demographic classification of media consumers, the uses and gratifications model attempted to isolate different motives people had for selecting one mass medium over another or for choosing predominantly to consume one area of media content (e.g., news programmes) over others (see Blumler & Katz, 1974; Katz, Blumler, & Gurevitch, 1974).

The memory literature would suggest that different motives for approaching and using the media will promote different cognitive modes of processing news information. For example, approaching media news content to obtain information might be expected to give rise to a different set of cognitive activities than when driven by entertainment-seeking motives. The evidence for the efficacy of self-reported motives as predictors of memory for news, however, is not strong. Although a comparison of memory for a television newscast among differently motivated individuals found that information seekers recalled a little more than entertainment seekers, overall, individuals' self-reported motives for watching the news were only weak predictors of news recall (Gantz, 1979).

74

Kellermann (1985) reminds us that motivation is likely to affect attention. Because, on many occasions, television viewing seems to be largely unmotivated (see Goodhardt, Ehrenberg, & Collins, 1975), attention during viewing may lack focus, thus placing a greater strain on short-term memory and increasing the rate at which new informational input is allowed to decay rather than being transferred to long-term storage.

The fact that self-reported motives or gratifications underlying media use are only weak predictors of memory for broadcast news, however, may indicate that they may also be questionable measures of individual differences in the context of cognitive information processing. This is not to say that motivational factors are unimportant as mediators of learning but, rather, that the motivational *claims* of people may be unreliable indicators of psychological processes involved in processing the news.

The audience classifications typically employed in mass communications research tend to be descriptive rather than explanatory. Demographic variables provide a convenient system for classifying populations, but finding that better-educated people know more about public affairs and learn more from the news media than less well educated people merely describes a media effects phenomenon; it does not explain why it has occurred. Understanding why one segment of the population learns more from the news than another must include some examination of the psychological processes that underlie knowledge acquisition.

Differences in patterns of media use among different population subgroups may represent only one important dynamic in relation to learning from the media. In the specific context of remembering broadcast news it may be far more important to know how individuals process information from news programmes. In the light of evidence indicating an often significant role for production variables during news retention and comprehension (see Berry, Gunter, & Clifford, 1982; Gunter, Berry, & Clifford, 1982), it is possible that some individuals are at a disadvantage because by virtue of their inherent cognitive styles or capacities to learn, they have extra difficulty in processing information presented in certain ways in news programmes.

Ability Differences in Memory

The possibility that education-related differences in memory and comprehension of television news are underlaid not just by differences in patterns of media consumption but also, and perhaps more fundamentally, by differences in cognitive information-processing abilities is something that ought to be given more serious consideration by mass communications researchers. Measures of cognitive style and mental ability are available that may begin to provide explanations as to why knowledge acquisition from news broadcasts breaks down, either among people in general or among some people more than others. And these explanations may also be linked to programme factors indicating that certain modes or styles of presentation in news programmes are especially likely to impede information acquisition among particular (possibly substantial) segments of the audience.

A high level of formal education has previously been linked by communications researchers to a high level of information uptake from the media. Likewise, a sound general knowledge about current affairs or specialised knowledge about a particular topic are thought to promote learning from the news in general and from specific news topics respectively (Berry, 1983 b; Berry & Clifford 1985; Robinson & Sahin, 1984). In addition to these factors, however, which are undoubtedly of some importance, cognitive psychologists have found that verbal intelligence tests can provide a means of identifying people who can code and manipulate verbal stimuli rapidly in situations in which knowledge per se is not a major factor.

Hunt, Lunneberg, and Lewis (1975) found that individuals who scored high on a test of verbal ability performed significantly better on a large number of memory tasks than did others of low verbal ability. In particular, individuals with high verbal intelligence exhibited better short-term retention of information even though distracted by another task after presentation, and showed greater release from proactive interference when a shift occurred from one category of verbal material to another.

Individuals with high verbal intelligence seem to be more able to extract meaning from input and at a more rapid rate than those with low verbal intelligence. Highly intelligent individuals are also better able to distinguish between items in short-term memory and may therefore suffer less from the effects of interference between similar items of information. Hunt et al. speculate that "it seems plausible to believe that high verbal subjects know more about the linguistic aspects of their culture because they are more rapid in CIP (cognitive information processing) tasks" (p. 225).

Other research has shown that individuals differ in their organizational strategies when processing information. People may vary in the extent to which they impose their own organizational frameworks on information at input. Individuals who exhibit high levels of subjective organization tend also to show superior performance on a number of memory tasks (Ozier, 1980). There is some indication that individuals who are more active in organizing information in memory are able to distinguish more clearly between different items of information. This might mean that more active processors of information may be less likely to suffer the effects of interference between news items in a television bulletin.

Sex Differences in Memory

From what is known about the cognitive abilities of males and females, one might expect certain differences in the way the sexes process television news information. Differences in the visual-spatial and linguistic abilities of males and females have been hypothesized by some writers to have a genetic component (Maccoby & Jacklin, 1974). In a review of 22 studies involving verbal content, 12 studies showed no difference in the performance of males and females, and 10 studies showed that females recalled more than males. In general, females tend to be superior to males on tests of verbal ability, while males perform better on tasks involving visual and spatial abilities.

Goleman (1978) demonstrated that females perform particularly well on verbal tasks that involve hearing, whereas males perform better on tasks that involve seeing. Elsewhere, however, researchers have found no differences in the listening abilities of males and females (Bostrom & Waldhart, 1983).

In general, males and females probably do not differ in their memory capacity or in the skills involved in storing and retrieving information. But there is some indication that they do react differently to different kinds of content. A preference among females for processing verbal content over visual content may mean that visual embellishments in the news may be less useful to women viewers than to men in the audience. There is some indication from experimental research with news materials that exciting (violent) film footage may impair memory for information in accompanying narratives more among females than among males (Furnham & Gunter, 1985; Gunter, Furnham, & Gietson, 1984).

Aging and Memory

The literature is not consistent, but there are indications that changes do occur with age in cognitive information-processing capabilities. This might lead one to predict differential news acquisition from broadcast news among young people and old people.

One hypothesis that has been put forward as a conceptualisation of age-related deterioration in high-level cognitive processing is the processing deficit hypothesis (Craik & Simon, 1980). This hypothesis suggests that as people grow older the cognitive resources available to enable effective processing of new information become diminished. Any new learning requiring effort occurs less efficiently among older people. As yet, the empirical psychological evidence for this hypothesis has not produced universally accepted results, but there are indications from some studies that differences between age groups in information uptake from news broadcasts could be expected and are a function of respective information-processing abilities.

A detailed review will not be presented here, but some findings are worthy of mention. Although on many tasks of verbal learning old people perform as well as young people, on others differences have been observed (Meudell, 1983). These discrepancies in learning related to age can be broken down into those involving encoding, storage, and retrieval of information.

On encoding-involved differences, there is evidence that the elderly may require more time to learn than do younger people under certain conditions of verbal information presentation. When subjects are learning lists of words, for example, increasing the time for which the words are presented may aid older people's memories to a much greater extent than it does younger people's (Canestrari, 1968; Arenberg, 1965). Giving the elderly more time to think about their answers during recall can also help their memory performance (Monge & Hultsch, 1971; Treat & Reese, 1976). Elsewhere, researchers failed to replicate either of these findings (Hulicka, Sterns, & Grossman, 1967). Clearly, more consistency of results would be desirable, but the indications of this research ought not to be ignored by those investigating individual differences in memory for news. Age-related differences in learning from the news carry implications as well for producers of news. The fairly rapid presentations of complex information that typify news broadcasts might impair learning among older viewers and listeners more than among younger audience members. And let us not forget that older people watch the news on television more often and in greater proportions than do younger people.

Turning next to storage of information, do old people forget more rapidly than the young? The old appear to forget at pretty much the same rate as the young, although some age differences have been observed at longer retention intervals. Some researchers have observed that if new learning is tested inside a day, the elderly forget no more than the young. With longer delays, however, older people exhibit greater forgetting (Davis & Obrist, 1966; Hulicka & Rust, 1964; Wimer, 1960). Others have failed to observe the same results, however, so the evidence for age-related storage and forgetting differences remains equivocal (Hulicka & Weiss, 1965; Desroches, Kaiman & Ballard, 1966).

Finally, looking at retrieval, do old people have more difficulty recalling what they have learned? Results indicate that the elderly tend to perform less well than the young when required to recall spontaneously what they have just learned and when given cues by the researcher to aid memory (Meudell, 1983). There is some evidence also that the elderly may be more susceptible to interference across a set of to-be-remembered items (Traxler, 1973). This, it seems, may be most likely to occur among the less intelligent and less well educated older people (Winocur, 1981).

Studies of learning from complex verbal materials more akin to news stories have produced conflicting evidence for adult age differences in memory performance. On the one hand, several studies have found that age-related differences are greater for recall of the main ideas of texts than for their details (Cohen, 1979; Dixon, Simon, Nowak, & Hultsch, 1982). For example, Dixon et al. asked younger, middle-aged, and older adults to read or listen to short news articles. In general, the younger adults recalled the articles better than either the middle-aged or older adults, and all individuals recalled the main ideas better than the details. However, age-related differences in recall were somewhat larger in the case of superordinate (main idea) propositions than in the case of subordinate (detail) propositions. Cohen (1979) asked younger and older adults to listen to a short story and found that the older adults recalled significantly less information about it than did younger adults. Furthermore, the older adults produced fewer summary statements that represented the gist of the story than their younger counterparts.

On the other hand, the results of several studies have indicated that age-related differences are greater for the details of texts than for the main ideas (Byrd, 1981; Zelinski, Gilewski, & Thompson, 1980). When Byrd asked younger and older adults to recall a structurally complete and temporally ordered story, he found that both age groups recalled the main ideas equally well. However, older adults recalled significantly fewer details.

Zelinski et al. (1980) found no age differences in recall of higher-level propositions, but younger adults recalled more of the details once again. Thus, in some instances, age-related differences are greater at the level of memory for main ideas, and in other cases at the level of memory for background details.

One possible reason for this discrepancy that has been suggested is that performance differences in text retention may be mediated by individual differences in verbal ability. Dixon, Hultsch, Simon, and von Eye (1984) investigated this issue by including verbal ability along with age as separate independent variables. They hypothesised that age-related deficits in the recall of main ideas from a text would be present for individuals with relatively low levels of verbal ability, whereas age-related deficits in the recall of background details from a text would be present for individuals with relatively high levels of verbal ability. Put simply, the reasoning behind these hypotheses is that high-ability people could be expected to show accurate retention of the central theme and main ideas of a text regardless of age, but that age-related deficits might appear for less important content. In contrast, among low-ability individuals memory for background details is likely to be poor across all age-bands, but age might make a difference to retention of the main points in the text.

This investigation involved three age groups of 20 to 39-year-olds, 40 to 57-year-olds, and 60 to 84-year-olds. They read and recalled short texts on health and nutrition. The texts were carefully designed, with the main ideas always appearing early in the passage. Texts were varied in terms of the number of arguments or items of information they contained.

Results showed that young adults were generally better than older adults at remembering information from text materials. However, age-related differences in recall were found to be mediated by verbal ability and text structure variables. For adults with low verbal ability, age-related differences in recall were greater for the main ideas than for the details of texts. For adults with high verbal ability, the reverse was true.

There was no indication that age-related differences in recall were minimized when there was less information in the text.

In the case of adults with relatively low verbal ability, age-related differences in recall were greatest for the main ideas of the text. Younger adults recalled a significantly greater percentage of main ideas than did middle-aged adults, who in turn recalled significantly more than older adults. In contrast, in the case of adults with relatively high levels of verbal ability, age differences in recall were greatest for the details of texts. There were no significant differences among the three age groups in recall of main ideas. At this level of text structure, the three age groups performed at a high level, similar to that of the young adults with low verbal ability. In recall of main ideas, the high-verbal-ability middle-aged, and older adults performed better than their low-verbal-ability counterparts. And in contrast to the pattern displayed by low-verbal-ability people, the high-verbal-ability young adults recalled a significantly greater percentage of details than the middle-aged adults, who in turn recalled more than the older adults.

Personality Differences and Memory

Individual difference variables other than the standard demographic ones have been found to mediate memory performance. Measures of introversion-extraversion have been observed to be related to memory for new information and to ability to retrieve information from existing knowledge stores. Personality variables as such do not just function as supplementary descriptors of audiences to demographic variables but also embody theoretical assumptions about the dynamics of individual differences in cognitive information-processing abilities under different conditions of learning. There are two major hypotheses relating the dimension of introversion-extraversion and memory performance. The first of these states that extraverts will show faster learning of new material than introverts in tasks that are difficult. The second derives from H.J. Eysenck's (1967) modification of Walker's (1958) action-decrement theory and states that the period of consolidation of new learning is longer for introverts than for extraverts, with the result that the short-term retention of extraverts exceeds that of introverts, but introverts show better long-term retention. Research has shown that in general extraverts do show faster learning under difficult conditions (M.W. Eysenck, 1977).

Learning differences between extraverts and introverts may reflect differences in encoding processes. One possibility is that introverts simply take longer than extraverts to discover suitable verbal and imaginal mediators. Another possibility is that high arousal (a functional characteristic of introverts) orients memory towards the physical attributes of verbal material, while adversely affecting memory for its semantic aspects (Schwartz, 1975).

Another indication comes from work showing that extraverts show more vivid imagery than introverts and may be able more effectively to use imaginal mediation to aid recall of verbal material (Morris & Gale, 1974).

Introverts have been found to be inferior to extraverts in retrieving information from semantic memory. Introverts search semantic memory more slowly than extraverts, and it is possible that information may be less well organized in the semantic memory of introverts than in that of extraverts. One suggestion also is that introverts show greater cognitive complexity than extraverts and therefore find information more difficult to retrieve from memory (M.W. Eysenck, 1977). Another interesting finding is that introverts may be more likely than extraverts to re-retrieve information from semantic memory (Roediger, 1973, 1976). Thus when presented with a list or sequence of verbal items, introverts may be likely to repeatedly recall the first few in the sequence at the expense of the later ones.

Personality variables such as these may represent potentially significant predictors of memory and comprehension of broadcast news. Television news programmes, for instance, consist of rapidly presented sequences of complex verbal items about diverse topics. They are often presented with film footage to which the arousal responses of introverts and extraverts are likely to differ. Recent research on memory for news in which these variables have been measured has found that introverts do show better delayed retention than extraverts, consistent with H. J. Eysenck's (1967) hypothesis (Gunter, Furnham & Jarrett, 1984). Another experiment by Gunter and Furnham (1986) found that introverts exhibited poorer immediate retention than extraverts of television news items accompanied by violent and potentially highly arousing film footage. In the latter study, personality variables (which included measures of neuroticism and psychoticism) were better predictors of news recall than were demographic variables, indicating the significance of these psychological factors in the search for useful explanatory measures of individual differences in cognitive information processing.

4

News Awareness and Retention Across the Audience

Most research connected with the informational effects of television content has been carried out within what might be broadly labeled a "sociology of mass communications" research framework, in which the acquisition of information from the mass media has typically been traced to a complex set of determinants existing among individuals and usually involving their so-called informational "needs." For example, does a media message have instrumental utility for the receiver? In other words, will it provide him or her with a helpful input for responding to everyday environmental stimuli or for defending personal beliefs and attitudes? A degree of selectivity of attention to and assimilation of news messages is implied. Such selection may also be based on non-instrumental factors, such as personal interest in the subject matter or even the entertainment value of the material. In the latter instance, the individual supposedly derives a certain intrinsic satisfaction during exposure. Intrinsic motivational influences are, in turn, often closely interrelated with demographic characteristics of individuals, such as their socio-economic background or level of formal education, which may act as mediators of likes and dislikes concerning media content and of use of different media.

Not surprisingly, this perspective has resulted in emphasis being laid upon the importance of audience variables in relation to the impact and retention of news media messages. Although this book is concerned principally with effects of programme factors on retention of broadcast news, there is no doubting that news acquisition does not occur at a constant level across the audience. Some individuals are more news-aware or exhibit a higher level of comprehension of current events than others. And this variability in news memory comprehension across individuals is often related significantly to personal characteristics of audience members that may act as mediators either of media use or cognitive information-processing style. In this chapter we examine evidence on levels of news knowledge and on learning from news broadcasts among different types of audience members. Among the audience variables that were most emphasised during early research concerned with media impact on public knowledge of domestic and world affairs were socio-economic and educational background. However, as we see in this chapter, researchers have also observed differential information uptake from broadcast news in relation to other audience characteristics, including the sex, age, and psychological profiles of audience members. We will see that each of these factors relates to how much individuals know about recent news events and how much they seem able to learn and retain from recent news broadcasts.

It has been widely argued that the best-educated members of society keep most informed about contemporary news issues and gain most from exposure to the news media. Furthermore, it is exposure to print media, such as newspapers and news magazines (the favoured media of the better educated), rather than exposure to the broadcast media, such as television and radio, that is most closely related to being highly knowledgeable about world affairs (Robinson, 1967). Research in the early 1970s, however, indicated that the mass media had become so pervasive in the world that even the less educated groups were becoming relatively well informed (Robinson, 1972), and socio-economic and educational differences alone no longer seemed to be sufficient to predict information gain from the news media (Neuman, 1976). Other factors such as motives underlying media use (e.g., Gantz, 1979) and levels of interest in specific news issues or topics (Booth, 1970; Genova & Greenberg, 1979) were recognised as having important effects upon news recall, too.

SOCIAL CLASS, EDUCATION, AND LEARNING FROM THE NEWS

The tendency of the already well-informed to become better informed relative to the already ill-informed has been formally discussed within the framework of the knowledge-gap hypothesis (Tichenor, Donohue, & Olien, 1970). It was postulated by these authors that as the infusion of mass media information into society increases, sections of the population with higher socio-economic status and more formal education acquire this information at a faster rate than low-status groups, so that a gap in knowledge of lower- and higher-status individuals will tend to increase.

Although not always explicitly stated, the notion of a knowledge gap has been implicit throughout much research on mass communication effects. Underlying this view is the general finding that education is a powerful correlate of knowledge acquisition about public affairs and science from the mass media (Wade & Schramm, 1969). It has often been assumed that increased formal education indicates a wider and more differentiated range of interest in and awareness of world affairs, and an accompanying desire for exposure to mass communications relevant to this knowledge.

In essence, therefore, the knowledge-gap hypothesis offers one potential explanation for the apparent failure of the news media often to inform the public at large on many current news issues—even those of major national and international significance. As an illustration of this, Budd, McLean, and Barnes (1966) studied the diffusion of two major news events over a two-day period: the resignation of Nikita Kruschev and the Walter Jenkins case of 1964. Although one might expect the effects of socio-economic and educational differences to be diminished in the case of events of such major import, the results were generally consistent with the knowledge-gap hypothesis. Among those people questioned, the better educated learned information surrounding these news stories more rapidly than those with less education, and after two days the gap in awareness of these events had actually widened.

Tichenor et al. (1970) reported another test of the knowledge-gap hypothesis in which data concerning three topics were gathered by the American Institute of Public Opinion between 1949 and 1965. The topics included correct identification of earth satellites, belief that man would soon reach the moon, and belief that cigarettes cause lung cancer. Each topic received mass media attention during the study period due to the fact that more news space generally was devoted to science, technology, and medicine, and because each specific topic received heavy media treatment as a result of specific events. The late 1950s saw the launching of Sputnik I, followed by several further satellite launchings by both the United States and Soviet Union. In 1954, a major report by the American Medical Association resulted in widespread media coverage of the possible link between smoking and cancer.

While a general growth in knowledge or acceptance of each topic occurred over time, differential growth of awareness was also witnessed when groups of varying educational attainment were compared. For example, in 1949, 18% of college-educated individuals believed that man would reach the moon, compared to 14% of non-college-educated people. By 1965, the comparable figures were 81% and 37% respectively.

In another relevant study, Robinson (1967) reanalysed the findings of two surveys conducted some years before in the United States and rearranged their data so as to form a social typology. By combining the variables of media exposure habits and social strata, he hoped to create a powerful set of demographic indicators of which individuals were most knowledgeable about world affairs and which groups seemed to be gaining most from news media. In one survey, respondents had been given four questions on beliefs about China and were scored according to the number of items they answered correctly. The other survey examined the impact of science and technology news in the mass media, focusing in particular on public knowledge of the atomic capabilities and government ideologies of various countries. Robinson took the information scores from each survey and related them to a number of demographic factors, including the education, race, income, occupation, sex, and age of the respondent, and the geographic region and size of community in which he or she resided. Six combinations of these background factors were constructed, and each survey sample was divided into six social status groups accordingly. These groups ranged from Group I, who represented that 9% of the population who were nonwhites with less than high school education and low income, to Group VI, who were representative of the upper 10% of the population who had graduated from college and were now in white-collar jobs.

From the findings it became clear that level of educational attainment and type of occupation were important variables closely associated with knowledge of world affairs. For example, in the survey on knowledge about China, college graduates who were in white-collar jobs exhibited an average information score six times as high as that of individuals who failed to finish high school and were in the lowest earning bracket. High educational and occupational attainers tended to make more use of all the media and were consequently better informed in a general sense. This included reading more books and magazines, more familiarity with news in daily papers, and a higher frequency of listening to the news on radio and watching it on television. The data clearly indicated that wide differences in knowledge levels and media usage habits occur between different social strata. An important question is whether differences in knowledge levels across different social or educational strata are a function of different media consumption patterns or are related to specific characteristics of these groups that mediate their information-processing capabilities.

Does Television Induce Knowledge Gaps?

Much of the research concerning differential acquisition of news information by different sections of the public has focused on learning from print media. Whether the knowledge-gap phenomenon occurs specifically as a function of exposure to broadcast news is another question. To begin with, audience research has indicated that differential exposure to television news is not as strongly correlated with education levels of individuals as newspaper and magazine reading. Israel and Robinson (1972) showed an average difference of only 4% between the proportion of network news viewers who were college or non-college educated. This contrasts with differences of from 15 to 20% between equivalent groups for print news media usage (Robinson, 1967). The less well educated also express a general subjective preference for television over newspapers and magazines as a source of news. This preference may be partly a function of literacy problems—that is, poorly educated individuals may find it easier to understand a television news item than to read and comprehend the same story in a newspaper. Thus, Tichenor et al. (1970) speculated that television might actually prove to be a knowledge-leveler in the long run.

Weak support for the knowledge-leveler hypothesis emerged from a subsequent British survey. Rawcliffe-King and Dyer (1983) reported differential amounts of learning from a television series about Irish history among viewers from higher and lower social classes. A two-wave panel study was conducted with representative samples in Great Britain, Northern Ireland, and the Republic of Ireland to see how much was learned from the second episode of the BBC documentary series *Ireland: A Television History*. Telephone interviews were carried out two weeks before and within one day of the test broadcast in which eight questions dealing with specific points covered in the programme were asked. Amongst the Great Britain sample, greater knowledge gains were revealed for those from the middle classes than for those from working class backgrounds. In Northern Ireland and the Republic of Ireland, knowledge of Irish history was not surprisingly higher than in Great Britain, and the pattern of information gain less clearcut. However, the fact that respondents from higher and lower social classes in the Republic of Ireland exhibited greater similarities in their knowledge levels after watching the programme than before suggested a knowledge-leveling function for the programme. The higher social classes, being already more knowledgeable than the lower, learned proportionately less from watching the programme. In Northern Ireland, though, there was no evidence of a knowledge-gap reduction effect of television. Here, other factors seemed to be affecting knowledge gain. In particular, results indicated that religious persuasion was related to knowledge levels. Misconceptions or distortions of information that were evident in replies to certain questions were consistent with preexisting prejudices among the Roman Catholics and Protestant groups in Northern Ireland. Rawcliffe-King and Dyer reported that two separate versions of Irish history were identified by these religious groups, and differences between them remained even after seeing the programme. There was evidence that the information contained in the programme had been understood and absorbed differently by the two sections of the population.

AGE AND SEX DIFFERENCES IN NEWS LEARNING

In assessing the differential accumulation of information from the mass media by different segments of the audience, most researchers have focused on knowledge differences associated with education and social class. Relatively few studies have examined differences in awareness of news and public affairs connected with sex and age. Although emphasised far less than education and class, there is evidence that new awareness also varies considerably with age and sex. These differences may be accounted for at least in part by differences in media use among these demographic groups. However, research in which factors such as level of interest and attention to the news have been statistically controlled has found that differences in news awareness among men vs women and among younger vs older members of the population still emerge. Furthermore, experimental studies with captive audiences have found that even though exposure and learning conditions are standardised across all respondents, differences in the ability to understand and retain broadcast news messages as a function of age or sex occur nevertheless.

Both sex and age are known to interact with media use, and more especially with television viewing patterns (Gunter, 1985). Patterns of media use, interest in the news, and utility of information often show marked variations between the sexes. Furthermore, there is psychological evidence of age differences and to some extent of sex differences in cognitive information-processing capabilities relating to acquisition and retention of linguistic material, although the findings relating to sex differences are not as clear.

AWARENESS OF RECENT NEWS EVENTS

A number of studies have attempted to measure audience knowledge levels for news events that have been reported prominently in the news in the previous week or so. These studies have tried to ascertain just how well informed the public is about recent news stories and whether knowledge levels vary across different segments of the population. In addition the exploring knowledge differences associated with the class and education of respondents, several of these studies have also assessed age and sex differences in news awareness.

Robinson and Sahin (1984) reported a survey with over 500 adults in England. This survey was conducted on a Saturday, and respondents were asked question about items featured in the news during the previous few days. Among other things, the authors examined demographic differences in news awareness associated with social class, educational background, age, and sex. Individuals from professional occupational classes exhibited better awareness of the week's news than did those from skilled and unskilled working classes. These differences survived multivariate statistical controls for other factors. Education also emerged initially as an indicator of news awareness, with the better educated apparently having a better grasp of that week's news that the less well educated. However, these differences were much reduced after controls for other variables were employed. Fairly large sex differences were also found, with men having higher awareness scores than women. These sex differences disappeared, however, after controls for other variables were introduced. Finally, younger adults scored lower than older adults, though this difference was not great. After controls were built in, age differences effectively disappeared (see Table 4.1).

In a survey of knowledge for the previous week's news among a sample of London residents, Gunter (1984) found that knowledge about recent news events was greater among individuals from middle-class than from

TABLE 4.1

Variations in News Knowledge by Social Class and Education

	Mean Recall	Adjusted Recall
Social Class		
Higher Professional (29	3.0	2.6
Lower Professional (125)	2.9	2.4
Skilled Working (251)	2.3	2.2
Semi/Unskilled Working (102)	1.4	1.9
Education completed		
14–16 years (171)	2.0	2.4
17–18 years (196)	2.1	2.3
19–20 years (98)	2.2	1.9
21+years (42	3.4	2.6
Age		
18–34 years (133)	2.1	2.3
35–49 years (167)	2.3	2.4
50+years (207)	2.3	2.2
Sex		
Male (242)	2.8	2.3
Female (265)	1.8	2.2

Source: Robinson and Sahin, 1984.

Note: Numbers in parentheses indicate group sizes. Reprinted by permission of author.

TABLE 4.2
Differences in News Knowledge as a Function of
Education, Class, Age, and Sex

	People in the news	Major news stories	All News
Education			
Before 15	7.4	7.6	14.5
15–16	9.8	9.4	19.1
17–18	13.2	12.9	25.9
Graduate	12.7	12.9	25.5
Class			
Middle	13.4	13.2	26.4
Working	9.6	9.8	19.1
Age			
16–24	10.7	10.7	21.1
25–34	11.6	11.7	23.2
35–54	11.1	11.0	22.0
55+	13.5	13.6	26.9
Sex			
Male	13.2	13.4	26.5
Female	9.5	9.2	18.5

Source: Gunter, 1984.

working-class backgrounds and among those who had finished full-time education at 18 years or later than among those who had finished schooling earlier. Respondents from higher social classes who had better education had more knowledge about prominent political figures in the news and of details about several major news stories from the week before. Also significant as indicators of knowledge levels were age and sex. Older respondents and males exhibited higher knowledge levels than did younger respondents and females. Table 4.2. shows the mean news knowledge scores for different demographic groups within this sample. These results show that news knowledge was best among middle-class and better-educated respondents.

Table 4.3 summarises the results of a series of multiple classification analyses designed to test the significance of these demographic differences in news knowledge. The figures under the deviation-from-mean column indicate the extent to which sex, age, class, and education were individually connected with variations in levels of news knowledge in the presence of statistical controls for the influence of the other three demographic factors. The beta value is an indicator of the magnitude of variations in news knowledge associated with each demographic factor. The results indicate that differences in knowledge for the previous week's news due to education, class, age, and sex were statistically significant, even in the presence of multiple controls for the other factors. Better news knowledge was associated with being better educated, middle class, older, and male. Most of these findings were consistent with those of Robinson and Sahin (1984).

Although education, class, age, and sex were all found to be significantly related to knowledge levels for recent news by Gunter (1984), there still remains the question as to why this should be so. It is because better-educated individuals from higher social classes who are older and male are better equipped intellectually to process broadcast news, or has it something to do with different patterns or rates of news consumption, such that the better-educated and higher social classes are more frequently exposed to news and hence have more opportunities for learning? In this research, the author observed, for example, that better-educated respondents with better and more highly qualified occupations, along

TABLE 4.3

Adjusted Variations in News Knowledge as a Function of Education, Class, Age, and Sex

	People in the News		Major News Stories		All News	
	N	Deviation from Mean	N	Deviation from Mean	N	Deviation from Mean
Education						
Before 15	221	−1.08	220	−1.42	221	−2.68
15–16	133	−1.04	131	−0.71	133	−1.78
17–18	83	1.45	84	1.97	84	3.36
Graduate	82	3.13	76	3.18	82	6.68
		Beta = 0.27[a]		Beta = 0.31[a]		Beta = 0.32[a]
Class						
Middle	258	1.23	254	0.94	259	2.12
Working	261	−1.22	257	−0.93	261	−2.11
		Beta = .21[a]		Beta = .16[a]		Beta = 0.19[a]
Age						
16–24	71	−2.13	70	−2.41	71	−4.65
25–34	108	−0.22	107	−0.16	108	−0.52
35–54	185	0.18	182	0.10	185	0.27
55+	155	0.91	152	1.10	156	2.16
		Beta = 0.16[a]		Beta = 0.19[a]		Beta = 0.19[a]
Sex						
Male	257	1.93	230	2.31	237	4.26
Female	282	−1.62	281	−1.89	283	−3.56
		Beta = 0.30[a]		Beta = 0.36[a]		Beta = 0.34[a]
Grand Mean		11.51		11.52		22.81
Multiple R^2		0.28		0.32		0.33

[a] $p < 0.001$

Note: Original analyses, not previously published, based on data from Gunter, 1984.

with older respondents and men, reported more frequent reading of serious newspapers and more frequent viewing of network television newscasts. What happens to each of these demographic differences in knowledge of recent news when controls are introduced for amount of claimed news consumption?

To answer this question, the author computed additional multiple classification analyses relating education, social class, age, and sex to knowledge about news, while statistically controlling for certain news consumption factors. Table 4.4 shows that even in the presence of single or multiple controls for reported viewing of network television news, frequency of newspaper reading, type of newspaper news, frequency of talking about the news with other people, both class and education remained significantly related to knowledge levels. In fact, multiple statistical controls for claimed use of these various news sources did not weaken the difference in news knowledge due to class or education at all.

TABLE 4.4

Differences in Levels of News Knowledge as a Function of Social Class and Education Following Controls for Use of Major News Sources

	People in the News		Major News Stories		All News	
	N	Deviation* from Mean	N	Deviation* from Mean	N	Deviation* from Mean
Class						
Middle	257	1.52	254	1.35	258	2.83
Working	269	−1.44	265	−1.30	269	−2.72
		Beta = 0.25[a]		Beta = 0.23[a]		Beta = .25[a]
Grand Mean =		11.53		11.52		22.86
Multiple R[2]		0.19		0.16		0.19
Terminal age of Education						
Before 15	216	−1.00	215	−1.22	216	−2.35
15–16	131	−1.38	130	−1.05	131	−2.53
17–18	82	1.52	83	2.06	83	3.51
Graduate	82	3.33	76	3.01	82	6.69
		Beta = 0.30[a]		Beta = 0.30[a]		Beta = 0.32[a]
Grand Mean =		11.54		11.52		22.86
Multiple R[2] =		0.21		0.20		0.23

[a] Significance level, p <0.001

*Adjusted deviations following controls for claimed frequency of newspaper reading, type of newspaper read, claimed frequency of network TV news viewing, and claimed frequency of talking about the news.

Note: Original analyses, not previously published, based on data from Gunter (1984).

FIELD STUDIES OF RECALL AND COMPREHENSION OF BROADCAST NEWS

The cognitive impact of broadcast news has been assessed more immediately in terms of how much information audiences can remember from single radio or television news programmes they have just heard or seen in their own homes. And a number of these studies have provided evidence on comparative levels of direct retention of news from news broadcasts among different demographic segments of the population. Findings from these studies not only indicate that certain sections of the public possess more general knowledge of recent news and current affairs issues but may also reflect differences in the cognitive abilities of individuals to process the news effectively from information broadcasts.

A common method is to conduct telephone interviews with respondents in which questions are asked about a news bulletin they saw or heard just a few hours earlier. Some researchers have had the funding and facilities to carry out face-to-face interviews with audience members. Sometimes interviews are not expected by participants, whereas on other occasions researchers may provide respondents with an early warning upon recruiting a few days before. In the latter instance, certain experimental manipulations may be employed, such as asking certain parts of the sample to pay careful attention to the news broadcast and requesting the rest simply to watch as they would normally. The mediating effect of attentional level can then be assessed in relation to comprehension and memory performance.

In one study, a sample of over 200 San Francisco Bay area residents were interviewed unexpectedly by telephone shortly following early evening news transmissions and were questioned directly about the particular newscast they said they had watched (Neuman, 1976). Respondents were given tests of *unaided recall* ("Can you recall any of the news stories on the network news this evening? Do any details come to mind?") and *aided recall with* and *without details*. In the latter case, the interviewer read a list of headlines from the particular newscast seen, and whenever respondents indicated they remembered the story the interviewer would then probe for further detail about it.

Neuman found only small differences in recall from single television newscasts as a function of education. College-educated respondents did have a higher overall rate of news recall than non-college-educated individuals, but the difference between them was only 5% which translated into one more story recalled on average out of a possible 19 or 20 per bulletin (see Table 4.5). Although the difference in *overall* news recall between educational strata was small, it was still possible that respondents paid differential attention to different kinds of news story as a function of their educational background. To examine this question,

93

TABLE 4.5
Average Recall of Television News as Percent of Total Stories in Newscast

	Total Recall	Unaided Recall	Aided Recall with Details	Aided Recall without Details	(N)
	%	%	%	%	
Education					
Non-college	47.1	4.0	20.8	22.3	(88)
College	52.4	7.0	23.6	21.7	(142)

Source: Neuman, 1976. Reprinted by permission of publisher.
*Significant at p <0.05 level

TABLE 4.6
Average Recall of Types of News Stories by Education

	Education	
Level of Abstraction	Non-college	College
	%	%
Low (human interest and weather stories)	60	61
Moderate (racial issues, Vietnam, and ecology stories)	48	51
High (political commentaries, economic issues, foreign affairs)	47	51
TOTAL	47	52

Source: Neuman, 1976. Reprinted by permission of publisher.

TABLE 4.7
Percent Who Could Not Recall Any Item of Broadcast News

Education	Listeners to Radio Bulletin	(N)	Viewers of TV Bulletin	(N)
	%	(N)	%	(N)
Elementary	46	(13)	31	(26)
Secondary	26	(46)	20	(56)
More than 12 years	36	(59)	9	(33)

Source: Katz et al, 1977. Reprinted by permission of publisher.
Note: Base sizes in parentheses

Neuman compared more and less well educated individuals on their recall of relatively complex and less abstract story types. Again, regardless of the complexity or level of abstraction of the news, differences in average recall as a function of education were small. Neuman in fact observed that level of motivation for watching the news was a better indicator of news recall than education. The latter relationships are examined in the next chapter when we turn to the subject of attention to the news, and news awareness and comprehension (see Table 4.6).

Katz, Adoni, and Parness (1977) reported two field studies conducted in Israel during the early 1970s. In both studies the authors compared average levels of recall from particular news broadcast on radio or television among better and less educated people.

In their first study, they conducted personal interviews with respondents within an hour or so of the evening's major radio news broadcast or major television news programme. Respondents were divided into three categories according to education, and as the data shown in Table 4.7 demonstrate, the least well educated were most likely to be unable to recall even a single item from a news broadcast they had just heard or seen. It is noticeable also that the best educated appeared to benefit most from television presentation of the news.

In the second study a panel of 200 people were approached on three consecutive evenings and asked either (a) to view the evening's major television news bulletin (at 8:00 p.m.); (b) to tune out or turn away from the television screen while the programme was on; or (c) not to watch or listen to the programme at all. Following the broadcast, respondents were telephoned and asked to recall as many items as they could from it.

Results indicated that seeing the pictures on the screen during the news had the greatest effect on the best educated in that these people showed most improvement in remembering something and also showed the largest increase in the proportion able to recall spontaneously five or more items. Inspection of the data as a whole, however, indicated relatively small differences among people as a function of education. The least-educated group was somewhat more likely to remember no items or to remember only one item but, the other two groups differed little (see Table 4.8).

Stauffer, Frost, and Rybolt (1983) conducted a telephone survey in which 597 respondents from ages 18 to 87 were questioned about the content of the same evening's network television newscast within two or three hours of transmission. Results showed that education was positively related to recall. Of those who had attended graduate school (23% of the total sample), 22% recalled more than three items, compared to 24% with at least some college, 13% who were high school graduates, and 8% with less than high school.

Large differences in recall emerged between those below age 60 and those above. A total of 46% of those aged 60 and older recalled no more

TABLE 4.8
Percent Recalling Broadcast News Items by Education and Type of Exposure

	Number of Items Recalled				
	None	– 12	3–5	5+	N
Listened only					
Elementary education	20	48	20	12	25
Secondary education	21	25	31	21	68
12 years or more	17	26	44	11	75
Listened and Viewed					
Elementary education	13	53	31	3	38
Secondary education	11	33	32	21	83
12 years or more	4	34	42	20	83

Source: Katz et al., 1977. Reprinted by permission of publisher.

TABLE 4.9
Respondents' Level of Education and Percent of News Items Recalled

	News Items Recalled		
	0–1 %	2–3 %	4+ %
Education			
Less than high school	36	56	8
High school graduates	38	49	13
Some college	34	49	17
College graduates	28	61	11
Graduate school	22	56	22
Age			
18–39	21	62	17
40–59	28	54	18
60–87	46	45	9

Source: Stauffer, Frost, and Rybolt, 1983. Reprinted by permission of publisher.

than one news story. Below age 60, the number was 25%. There were only small differences between the 18 to 39 and 40 to 59 age groups (see Table 4.9). Sex was not significantly related to recall.

A British study on recall of news items from a single broadcast was conducted by Robinson and Sahin in the late 1970s. Face-to-face interviews were carried out with 489 viewers of the BBC1 early evening newscast within a short time after transmission on four consecutive evenings. Respondents were asked for their spontaneous or unaided recall of all the items they could remember from the bulletin that evening, and this test was followed by another in which they were provided with "bullets" or brief headline cues for each story.

96

Each recall account was scored for comprehension according to a nine-point coding scheme. The mean score per evening was 27.7. Comparisons were carried out across various educational, social class, and age strata among the sample. Across different social class/ occupational classes Robinson and Sahin found that those with professional qualifications and skilled manual workers recalled more from the news than did semi- or unskilled manual workers. There was also some initial indication that level of education was positively associated with news recall. However, variations in recall with social class and education level diminished when controls for other audience factors and media use variables were statistically built in. No systematic zero-order relationships of age with recall were found, though the under-25 group remembered less than any other older groups. Following statistical controls (via multiple classification analyses) for other demographic variables and use of different news source, age differences in recall from this news bulletin were even smaller (see Table 4.10).

TABLE 4.10
Recall of News from a Single Television Broadcast as a Function of Education and Social Class

	Mean Recall Score	Adjusted Mean Recall Score
Education		
Leaving age: 14–15	27.1	28.0
16–17	26.3	27.5
18–20	28.3	24.6
21+		
Social Class		
Occupational Type:		
Unclassified	21.8	25.8
Unskilled	20.2	24.4
Semi-skilled	26.5	28.5
Moderately skilled	27.4	28.7
Skilled	27.7	27.5
Highly skilled	28.7	26.3
Lower professional	34.2	30.2
Higher professional	28.5	26.9
Age:		
Under 25	22.9	26.7
25–34	30.6	29.3
35–44	28.4	27.4
45–54	29.4	28.3
55–64	26.2	24.6
65+	28.0	28.8

Source: Robinson and Sahin, 1984. Reprinted by permission of author.

In a series of studies beginning in the early 1980s, Cairns has examined the role of television news broadcasts in providing knowledge about the "troubles" in Northern Ireland to younger viewers. This research has been interpreted to show differences in children's knowledge about current social and political problems in the province associated with television news viewing and has indicated age-related differences in learning from the news among child audiences.

In the first published study of this series, Cairns, Hunter, and Herring (1980) suggested that even young children living in relatively peaceful areas of Northern Ireland who had not been directly exposed to violence were still aware of the violence going on in other parts of Northern Ireland. Cairns and his colleagues went on to suggest that at least some of this knowledge was probably acquired by children from the news media, particularly from television news, and this they claimed to have demonstrated in a study involving children from Northern Ireland plus children from Scotland, some of whom were exposed to Northern Irish television news broadcasts and some of whom were not.

From this study it was apparent that whereas Scottish children who had seen Northern Irish television news broadcasts were more aware of the violence and problems in Northern Ireland than were a control group of Scottish children who had seen none of these broadcasts, the children who revealed the greatest level of awareness were those actually living in Northern Ireland. Two possible explanations were offered for these results. Firstly, although both Northern Irish children and some Scottish children had seen television news from Northern Ireland, the Northern Irish children were probably also exposed to other information sources (e.g., newspapers, family, and friends) and hence had greater overall knowledge of events in the province. Secondly, it could be that the Northern Irish children, because of their greater background knowledge about the "troubles," were able to absorb more information from television news programmes about this topic and thus increase their superiority. The latter explanation is akin to the knowledge-gap hypothesis, whereby the already well informed benefit more from exposure to the news than do the less well informed, so that the gap in knowledge between the two group widens.

More recently, Cairns has reported further studies of the impact of television news viewing on Irish children's knowledge about the problems in Northern Ireland. Cairns (1984: Experiment 1) described a study with nearly 500 11-year-olds living in five different parts of Ireland, some of which were closer to actual violence than others. The children were asked to estimate personal frequencies of watching television news (never, sometimes, frequently) and also responded to an 11-item knowledge test. The latter consisted of "items relating to what were felt to be relatively enduring features of the violence (for example, what the initials RUC and UDR stand for, where the Falls Road and Crossmaglen are, what a control zone and road block are and what the confidential telephone is used for)" (p. 34).

Cairns found main effects of sex, area, and reported television news viewing on knowledge levels. Boys were more knowledgeable than girls, children who lived closer to the violent areas knew more than those who lived further away, and those who claimed frequent news viewing knew more than those who claimed otherwise. The study falls down on a number of points, however, and solid evidence for a television influence here must be questioned. Although a number of main effects were examined, the statistical analyses were inappropriate to show the independent effects of these variables while controlling for effects of the others on knowledge levels. We do not know whether boys watched more news than girls or whether children living in violent areas watched more news than those living farther away from trouble spots. Other writers have suggested that at times of trouble, people do turn to the news media more often for information about the latest developments (Katz & Peled, 1973).

Cairns (1984: Experiment 2) replicated the first study with a sample of nearly 600 children from the north and south of Ireland. This time there were two age groups: 18 years and 11 years. Children in the north were from two distinct locations once again: those who had experienced relatively little violence and those who had experienced above-average levels of violence. The news viewing and knowledge measures were the same as before.

Results showed main effects on knowledge for sex and area, and also for age, but this time not for claimed television news viewing. There was, however, an interaction of television news viewing with age. Eleven-year-olds who reported greater viewing frequencies knew more. Claimed frequency of news viewing was not related to knowledge levels among the younger children.

This study suffers from similar problems to the first. In addition, neither study attempted to measure the influences of other important factors mentioned by Cairns et al. (1980). For example, to what extent were differences in knowledge in different areas affected by exposure to other media, such as newspapers and radio, or by talking with family and friends? The relationships between reported television news viewing and knowledge about the "troubles" may indeed indicate that more knowledgeable children were also more active news seekers. But were they more active seekers of news not only through television but also through radio, the press, and elsewhere? Without controls for these other important variables, the independent effects of television news viewing on knowledge cannot be properly ascertained.

EXPERIMENTAL STUDIES OF RECALL AND
COMPREHENSION OF BROADCAST NEWS

In addition to studies conducted in the field, a great deal of research on memory and comprehension of broadcast news has been carried out with captive audiences exposed to the news in theatre or laboratory settings. Under these conditions, the researcher has much more control over what is shown and the degree of attention that audience members pay to the screen while the news is being shown. Of course, experimental conditions seldom come close to resembling normal viewing and listening conditions, and this environmental difference needs to be taken into account when attempting to generalise from findings obtained in the laboratory or theatre to predictions about news impact in real life. Nevertheless, experimental work has its place in the investigation of news retention and understanding and has revealed things about the cognitive processing of the news no other paradigm could do. Although laboratory experiments have often been primarily concerned with the significance of structural features of news programming for news recall and comprehension, some of these studies have obtained background information from respondents that has been related to their immediate recall of simulated news presentations.

Several important early studies were carried out by Belson in the 1950s and early 1960s, which he reported subsequently in his book *The Impact of Television* (Belson, 1967). These studies examined audience retention of information from radio and television broadcasts concerned with public affairs topics in a series of theatre tests conducted by the author for the BBC's Audience Research Department.

Belson reported one investigation that looked at audience comprehension of a programme called "Topic for Tonight." This consisted of a series of short talks on radio that presented the background to events currently in the news. Tests of comprehensibility were made on all 26 talks in the series. Between 35 and 50 people were tested on each talk, totaling over 1,000 people. Respondents were recruited from the London area via the BBC's Daily Survey of Listening, in which interviews were carried out with people nationwide everyday concerning their use of and attitudes towards broadcast output. Participants were invited to a central listening location where they were played a recording of one of the talks. After this their comprehension of the broadcast was tested via written replies to a series of questions about major and minor points of the talk.

Although Belson studied the effects of a number of factors relating to the audience and the programmes, we will for the time being discuss his findings concerning variations in comprehension performance that were associated with education and social class. Comprehension scores varied with listeners' educational background: The higher the listener's educa-

100

tional level, the more he or she was likely to understand. What Belson found surprising, though, was that even university graduates, when listening under optimum conditions, scored only about 50% on the average talk. Most of the sample left school at 15 years or less, and the average comprehension score overall was only about 25%.

There was an appreciable correlation between educational and occupational levels, hence the relationships between occupation and comprehension were much the same as those between education and comprehension. The higher the occupational level, the higher the comprehension score. But even for the professional, semiprofessional, and executive groups, the score for the average talk was only 45%. Among semi- and unskilled participants, comprehension levels averaged out at around 17%.

Belson also examined comprehension for these radio broadcasts in relation to intelligence levels as measured by a standard test of intelligence. Comprehension was found to be much better among those listeners with high intelligence scores than among those with low intelligence scores. In fact, comprehension was correlated more powerfully with intelligence level (+.62) than with education (+.55), occupation (+.53) or any of the other personal characteristics on which information was obtained from respondents, with the exception of background knowledge (+.66). As we see later, other researchers have found background knowledge to be one of the most powerful predictors of effective comprehension of broadcast news.

In another investigation, Belson (1967) reported a study of audience comprehension of *Facts and Figures*, a monthly 10-minute television broadcast that gave, in diagrammatic form and with a spoken commentary, information about economic and related trends. The programme's target audience had been defined as the top 70 to 80% of viewers in terms of occupational background. Comparisons were made between four distinct occupational levels: (a) professional, semiprofessional, executive, and administrative; (b) highly skilled; (c) skilled; and (d) moderately skilled. Altogether, 550 viewers took part in theatre tests in groups of about 40 at a time.

Respondents saw one of two programmes, each projected before them on film. Each programme was made up of seven or eight independent units averaging a little over a minute in length. In each unit, presentation was through simple animated drawings that were designed to match closely the verbal narrative. The drawings varied from unit to unit, but across each 10-minute programme there were charts, histograms, moving arrows, and cartoon like drawings of people and things. The respondents were tested on units one at a time immediately after presentation of each one.

Comprehension was classified on a number of levels as shown in Table

TABLE 4.11
Differences in Grasp of Major Points and of Detail by Viewers According to Occupational Background

	1	2	3	4	Weighted Average for Total Target Audience
Percentage showing:	%	%	%	%	%
A sufficient grasp of a useful part of the average major point	88	84	81	71	79
A sufficient grasp of the average major point	82	75	71	62	70
A really good grasp of the average major point	40	35	33	24	31
A sufficient grasp of the average point of detail	78	76	75	68	73

Source: Belson, 1967. Reprinted by permission of author.

4.11. For the target audience as a whole, 70% showed a "sufficient grasp of the average major point" being presented, while nearly 80% had a "sufficient grasp of at least a useful part of the average major point." At the same time, only 31% had a really good grasp of the average major point.

Comparing the performance of occupational groups, the difference in grasp of major points was comparatively small, with even the moderately skilled doing quite well. Thus, 62% of the moderately skilled showed a sufficient grasp of the average major point and 71% a sufficient grasp of at least part of it. The occupational differences were larger when it came to a really good grasp of major points (see Table 4.11).

In another series of studies conducted with the BBC's Audience Research Department on the comprehension of educationally oriented television programmes during the 1960s, Trenaman (1967) also reported learning differences associated with certain demographic factors. The test programmes covered a variety of topics, such as science, history, and art, and were presented audio-visually (as on television), in audio only (as on radio), or in written form. Groups of subjects were recruited from the general public. The test pieces were presented to each group, either two sound broadcasts or a television programme and a written version. Before and after tests were used with comprehension tested via open-ended and multiple-choice questions.

Results showed that both education and social class (estimated via occupational status) were significantly correlated with comprehension from all these media. Indeed, Trenaman found that occupational status accounted for more of the variance in comprehension than did either topic or mode of presentation. Whatever the subject matter of the programme or the medium through which it was presented to the audience, occupational status was significantly related to comprehension, as was education. On the other hand, neither sex nor age was significantly related to comprehension, although men's scores were slightly higher than women's, and there was a tendency for comprehension scores to decline with increasing age. Trenaman suggested that the sex difference may partly reflect the association he also observed between level of occupation and sex—men tended to be in higher-level jobs than women.

Recent Experimental Research

Experimental research on memory for television news materials has also revealed differences in news retention associated with demographic factors. More recently, research evidence has emerged from other laboratory-type studies of broadcast news recall that indicates apparent differential capacities to absorb information effectively from news bulletins on radio and television. Stauffer, Frost, and Rybolt (1980) tested for recall from a radio news broadcast recorded some 4 months earlier among adult illiterates, tenth-graders, college students, and out-of-school adults who were literate. Participants were told to listen carefully to the recording but were not informed that they would be questioned about it later. Immediately following the newscast, were given an unaided test of memory for news in which they provided brief verbal labels of all the items they could recall. After this unaided recall test, they completed a 15-item multiple-choice test on the programme's content. Questions tested for recall of names of persons, place names, and knowledge that could be inferred from the news content.

Stauffer and his colleagues found that spontaneous recall was best among the best-educated group and worst among the illiterates. The college sample recalled an average 6 items out of 13 without help (or 46% free recall). They were followed by out-of-school adults with 34 items (26%), high school students with 3.2 items (25% and finally by illiterate adults with 2.8 (22%). Ten percent of the illiterates and high school students could recall none of the items, compared to 9% of the out-of-school adults and 3% of the college group. On the multiple-choice test, college students once again performed best, with 42% correct response on average, compared with 32% for the high school students, 28% for the out-of-school adults, and just 23% for illiterate adults.

In an earlier study, Stauffer, Frost, and Rybolt (1978) tested literates and adult nonreaders' abilities to recall and use information from a national network television news programme. The programme had been recorded 7 months prior to the experiment and viewers were tested for unaided recall and with a multiple-choice test immediately after programme presentation. The literate group recalled without help an average of 7.3 items out of 12 (61% free recall) against 4.7 items out of 12 for the adult illiterate group (39% free recall). In the multiple-choice test, literates scored 17 out of 23 correct answers compared to 10.5 for the illiterates.

Recent reported Swedish research has further indicated that certain sections of the audience may be less capable than others at remembering broadcast news information, even when tested immediately after presentation. Findahl and Hoijer (1985) tested over 600 Stockholm residents for recall and understanding of the content of a 7-minute television news bulletin that had been specially prepared for the experiment. Questions probing memory for story details were presented immediately after the programme had been shown. On average, men remembered more news information than women, and individuals with higher levels of education remembered more than those with less education. Sex and education differences were robust enough to survive statistical controls for other background variables. Differences between age groups also occurred, though these were more complicated and interacted in specific ways with sex and education. Thus, at one extreme, with very high recall of the news, were middle-aged viewers (36–45 years) with high education, and at the other extreme, with very low recall, were older women (56–65 years) with low education.

British Evidence

A series of recent laboratory-based experiments by several British researchers have indicated that recall from specially edited broadcast news sequences, tested immediately after presentation, was often related significantly to demographic characteristics of the audience (Berry & Clifford 1985; Furnham & Gunter, 1985; Gunter et al., 1984. Sometimes, interesting interactions emerged between production features and demographics, with certain viewers performing better on items presented in a particular way than did other viewers. In some studies, viewers characteristics were also found to interact with the type of news content to affect levels of news recall.

Berry and Clifford (1985) reported an experiment on the effects of text organization or reorganization on recall of televised news. Rearranging the grammatical structure of a news story in order to make clearer the setting of the events and the various plots and subplots that made up the story enhanced recall of its narrative content. The beneficial effects of the well-organized test, however, were greater among females than among males, although both sexes actually improved following the experimental treatment. Unfortunately, Berry failed to replicate these sex differences in a subsequent repetition of this study. Better text organization resulted in increased memory performance for better-educated audience members, but, at least with the stories used by Berry, produced no comparable effects among less well educated audience members. Berry suggests that text-organization enhancement effects among the less able audience members may be more likely to occur with less complex news stories than the ones he used.

Further evidence that the effects of audience characteristics may be more pronounced with certain types of news presentation styles than with news generally emerged from two more experiments by Berry and Clifford (1985), designed to examine the effects on learning of televised news of alternating presenters across items. Two versions of a news bulletin were produced, using items recorded from actual televised news transmissions. A *blocked* condition was produced where the first six items were introduced by a female news reader followed by six presented by a male colleague, and an *alternating* condition was produced in which the same items alternated with respect to presenter. Results showed that although presentation condition did not affect overall performance, it did interact significantly with sex of the viewer. Female viewers did slightly less well in the alternating condition than in the blocked condition in both experiments, while the alternating format produced significantly better recall from males.

Other recent British studies have shown that demographic characteristics of viewers interact not only with presentation styles but also with the type of news story being reported, to influence significantly how much information is recalled.

In an experiment concerned with recall of violent news from television bulletins, Berry and Clifford (1985) compared memory for two visual treatments of a horrific news item about El Salvador concluding with the execution of a student by the army. Recall of detail from this item was compared for the television versions and a sound-only version. Retention was tested immediately after presentation and 6 weeks later. The portrayal of violent action reduced the informational impact of the news text under both immediate and delayed retention. However, this overall effect was due principally to the performance of females, who did significantly less well under each visualisation condition than following the sound-only condition. Presentation style did not affect memory for news among males in the audience.

Other experiments have found that males and females differ in the reactions to and recall of violent news on television. Gunter, Furnham, and Gietson (1984) reported a study in which male and female teenagers at a sixth-form college were tested for recall of violent and nonviolent news stories presented either audio-visually, in soundtrack only, or as written transcripts. Subsequently, Furnham and Gunter (1985) replicated the experiment with a slightly older group of university students.

The results of the first experiment (See Table 4.12) indicated that recall was significantly related to the sex of the respondent, the presentation modality, and the type of news content. Males recalled significantly more than females, and print produced significantly better recall than audio-visual or audio-only presentation. Of specific importance to the present discussion, it also emerged that violent material was recalled significantly better than nonviolent material. However, the effect of content type on recall was not a simple one. Recall of violent and nonviolent news content varied as a function of presentation modality and with the sex of the respondent. An interaction between modality and content reflected the far better recall of violent content in the print condition than in either the audio-visual or audio-only conditions. Much smaller differences existed between presentation modalities for recall of nonviolent news content. An interaction between sex and content indicated the far better recall by males than females of violent news content.

The second experiment reproduced the presentation modality effect on recall observed in the first study, but the significant overall differences in recall associated with sex of respondent or type of news content did not reemerge. Within modalities of presentation, however, there were significant variations in recall of different types of news, associated also with the sex of the receiver (see Table 4.13).

The most important interaction was between sex and news type within the audio-visual condition. Here, males recalled violent news significantly better than nonviolent news, whereas females recalled nonviolent news significantly better than violent material. Within the audio-visual modality, males recalled violent news significantly better than did females, and females scored significantly better on nonviolent news. In

TABLE 4.12

Mean Recall of Violent and Non-Violent News Content as
a Function of Presentation Modality and Sex of Subject

	Violent News			Non-Violent News		
Presentation Modality	Males	Females	All	Males	Females	All
Audio-Visual (n = 46)	18.1	10.3	14.2	6.1	5.7	5.9
Audio-Only (n = 36)	14.8	10.1	12.5	6.1	4.1	5.1
Print (n = 46)	19.3	16.6	18.0	7.3	6.6	7.0
Mean recall: all modalities	17.4	12.3	14.9	6.5	5.5	6.0

Source: Gunter, Furnham, & Gietson, 1984

TABLE 4.13
Mean Recall of Violent and Non-Violent News Content as
a Function of Presentation Modality and Sex of Subject

Presentation Modality	Violent News			Non-Violent News		
	Males	Females	All	Males	Females	All
Audio-Visual (n = 24)	11.1	6.9	9.0	8.8	12.9	10.9
Audio-Only (n = 22)	13.1	12.1	12.6	13.0	11.1	12.5
Print (n = 22)	17.7	17.9	17.8	13.7	16.1	14.1
Mean recall: all modalities	13.0	12.3	13.1	11.8	13.4	12.5

Source: Furnham & Gunter, 1985

each of the other two presentation modalities, both males and females recalled violent content better than nonviolent content.

It would seem that something peculiar to the audio-visual presentation of these news stories caused males and females to process their information content differently. The important feature may have been the nature of the film footage accompanying the narrative content of the violent and nonviolent stories. It is possible that the female subjects who took part in this experiment were more distracted by footage of street fighting, shootings, and riots than were the males, and that the visuals disrupted females' learning of the narrative content.

Males apparently were not affected in the same way by the film content of these stories and were relatively better able to attend to and absorb the narrative information from these violent news stories. The results also suggest that the violent items were relatively more salient for male subjects in this experiment, insofar as they recalled the content of these items much better than that of the nonviolent items. For females in the audio-visual condition, however, the nonviolent items were recalled and possibly initially learned more effectively. It is possible that males tuned in more attentively to the violent film items in the audio-visual sequence, while females may have tuned out from violent audio-visual content that they found too distressing or distracting to learn from comfortably.

CONCLUDING REMARKS

This chapter dealt with the character of the audience. In the first part we saw that levels of news awareness and public affairs knowledge vary across different sections of the population. It has been known by mass communications researchers for many years that better-educated people and people from higher socio-economic classes tend to have better knowledge of what is going on in the world. More recent research has indicated that differences in news awareness also occur across different age groups and between men and women. These differences may be related to the way individuals use the media. Thus, some more knowledgeable types of people may be the ones who pay more attention to the news either on television or in the newspapers. Cognitive psychologists have found, however, that ability to learn from verbal materials varies as a function of intellectual ability (as reflected perhaps in educational attainment) and age. Therefore, some of the differences in news awareness across these demographic subgroups could be explained in psychological terms relating to cognitive information-processing capabilities, quite apart from patterns of usual media exposure.

In the second part of this chapter evidence was reviewed that provides some support for this last assumption. It is not simply the case that certain types of people know more about the news than others; it also appears that there are pronounced differences in the extent to which the news is remembered and understood by different sections of the audience. The picture becomes even more complicated following research that shows that certain types of individuals are better able to learn certain types of news or news presented in a certain way. The finding, for example, that women remember news stories accompanied by violent film footage less well than do men cannot be explained by patterns of media use or news interests alone. There are other, deeper psychological reasons why women react to violent news content in a way men do not.

The fact that there are sex differences (or age differences or education differences or whatever) in memory for the news does not provide explanation of why these differences occur. Demographics are merely descriptor variables and serve as a convenient taxonomy for classifying audience members. The reasons for differences among individuals in their recall of broadcast news may require a deeper examination not only of the way they use the media but of the way they process information.

Support for the need to consider psychological explanations of breakdowns in news memory and comprehension has emerged from recent unpublished research that has indicated that personality factors (which may cut across demographic characteristics of news audiences) may provide even more valuable indicators of information uptake from news messages than demographic variables. Gunter and Furnham (1986) found that individuals characterised by their Eysenck Personality Questionnaire (Eysenck & Eysenck, 1969, 1975) profiles as more extraverted, emotionally stable, and tough-minded were better able to recall the narrative content of news stories accompanied by violent film footage than were individuals who were introverted, anxious, and tender-minded. Personality did not predict retention of nonviolent news content presented in the same sequence of audio-visual news items, or memory for the same story narratives presented without violent film footage in sound track-only and written transcript conditions.

The psychological explanations invoked to account for these results include an assumption about the effects of arousal on learning and about the basal arousal levels characteristic of certain personality types. High levels of arousal are known to interfere with learning of new and highly complex verbal information. Introverted and anxious individuals are known also to have higher base levels of arousal than extraverted and calmer people. Violent film footage may be highly arousing stimulus material; this arousal level, added to the already fairly high natural levels of arousal of introverts and anxious individuals, may have passed the optimal level for effective learning.

Further details of this experiment will not be gone into here, but it is mentioned briefly to illustrate the important point that learning from the news is a psychological process, and audience differences in memory and comprehension require psychological explanations. In the next chapter we turn to the topic of attention to the news. Quite apart from the character of the audience, how important are levels of news consumption and attention to news as predictors of memory and comprehension of broadcast news content?

5 Attention to the News

The audience for television news is often described in terms that suggest the television audience at its most active. During political campaigns special attempts are made by broadcasters to provide additional coverage over and above the norm for political events, while the politicians themselves often stage events that are likely to attract the attention of the newsmakers, in the firm belief that viewers may be extraordinarily thirsty for political news information during campaign periods and may as a result of such exposure be swayed in the desired political direction, or at least encouraged to stay with the side they have already chosen.

It has been suggested that at times of crises the public turns to the news in order to meet urgent psychological and social concerns (Peled & Katz, 1973). Television, being the most vivid and immediate of all news sources available today, is the one people turn to most. In more mundane times, audiences have still been assumed by some writers to pursue news in an active way to satisfy a variety of routine needs (Levy, 1978; Rubin, 1984). The television news audience is often pictured therefore as an active and attentive one. To what extent is this true, however? And what bearing does the level of activity inherent in keeping up with the news have on how much is learned?

In this chapter we are concerned principally with the nature and characteristics of viewing behaviour in relation to television news. We examine how the volume of and attentiveness to news consumption on the part of the audience member, particularly with respect to the news on

111

television, relate to comprehension and retention of the news. To begin with, we need to establish some idea of how active television news viewing really is. This, as we see, can be done in a variety of ways. Some researchers have tried asking people to describe their own viewing behaviours and to describe in their own words how regular and attentive it is. Another approach, however, is to examine the behavioural records of news watching provided in specially prepared viewing diaries. Such records can indicate either over a fairly short period or over extended periods of time just how often individuals watch the news and can provide data from which a measure of intentionality to follow the news can be inferred. One can examine, for example, the extent to which audience members watch a number of different news programmes on the same day, or over several days, and the extent to which viewers switch between television channels in order to catch different news broadcasts.

In a study of the audience's experience with television news, Levy (1978) pursued the course of asking respondents to describe for themselves the way they watched television news. Specifically, Levy asked, "How do you manage to tune in at the right time for the news so that you don't miss the first part of the programme?" Answers that indicated a deliberate decision to watch the news were coded as "active," and others that suggested exposure to the news consequent on relatively nonselective use of television were coded as "passive." Levy found no significant difference between percentages of respondents who endorsed either "active" (52.2%) or "passive" (46.8%) watching of television news. Among specific descriptions given of news watching behaviour, about 44% said they caught the news because their television set was already switched on ("passive"), whereas just 12.5% said they "watched the clock" to make sure the set was switched on in time for the news ("active").

There were demographically associated variations in the extent of accidental versus deliberate viewing of television news among Levy's respondents. Men were more likely than women to say they viewed "by appointment." Additionally, a larger percentage of college-educated respondents than of respondents without a high school diploma said they were selective about watching the news.

One other interesting finding to emerge from Levy's investigation was a curvilinear relationship between type of news exposure and how much television news respondents reported watching. It was among individuals with "moderate" levels of news exposure that a majority were active viewers of television news (nearly 60%), while among those who reported "high" or "low" levels of exposure, about two thirds in each case were nonselective news watchers. Although it might be expected that, among individuals with low levels of exposure, viewing generally would be fairly selective, this expectation was not supported by Levy's findings. Among heavy viewers, nonselectivity of news viewing was more expected, in as much as such individuals will tend to see a great deal of all kinds of programming on television. It was among moderate viewers only that any implication of goal-directed news viewing behaviour materialised. For all this, however, Levy still noted, significantly, that at least half his sample failed to indicate deliberate or active news viewing behaviour.

METHODS OF MEASUREMENT

There are three distinct levels at which attention to the news can be measured:

1. Regularity of watching the news.
2. Deliberateness of watching the news.
3. Degree of attentiveness to the screen when the news is on.

The first level—regularity of watching the news—refers to how often a person watches television news. This can be measured in more ways than one and is a source of some methodological argument. Operational definitions of news viewing include subjective claims or estimates by viewers themselves of how many times a week they watch the news; report of particular news programmes seen; self-completion viewing diaries; and diary measures supplemented by television meters that record electronically when the television set is switched on and the channel to which it is tuned. The second level refers to viewers' motivations to watch the news, the reasons why they do so, and specific topic-related interests they have concerning news. Do viewers feel a need to follow the news deliberately on a regular basis to find out what is happening in the world? Or is most news viewing fairly casual in nature? The third level refers to the act of television watching itself when the news is on. When sitting in front of their television sets at home are viewers glued to the box or is television watching only one of a number of activities among which they divide their conscious attention?

This chapter examines evidence on all of these aspects of television watching. In the course of this examination evidence is also discussed on the relationships between amount of and attentiveness to television news viewing and news comprehension and retention. Do regular viewers know more about the news than less regular viewers or nonviewers? Is strength of motivation or type of reason for watching the news related to how much viewers learn from television broadcasts? Does greater attention to the screen promote better learning from broadcast news? Over and above all these considerations, however, something is also said about the level of uncertainty connected with most measures of how much broadcast news audiences actually attended or tune into. And to what extent does uncertainty in this context limit what we actually know about the influence of broadcast news on public awareness of current news events?

PROBLEMS WITH MEASURING NEWS WATCHING

How often do people really watch the news—more than once an evening, several times a week, several times a month, or less often on average? When watching the news, how much attention do viewers pay to the screen itself? Do viewers usually and mostly watch news programmes in their entirety or only in part? Is attention to the television screen undivided or shared with other distractions? Do those segments of the audience who watch news most often and pay most careful attention to news programmes also learn most about current news events and issues? These are all important questions concerning audience behaviour towards the television screen and specifically towards television news, the answers to which may provide some insights into further questions concerning public levels of news awareness and why knowledge about prominent news stories on television is often so poor.

As we will see, watching the news is something that is difficult to define and measure accurately. It varies not only across different segments of the audience but also according to the techniques used to measure it in the first place. Large proportions of the audience may watch the news on television only relatively infrequently or not at all over long spells, even though they might claim via self-reports that they are avid news viewers. The longer the term over which individuals are required to estimate their own television news viewing, the less accurate such estimates tend to become (Bechtel, Akelpohl, & Akers, 1972). And even if we ask a group of respondents if they watched the news last night, and they say yes, what does this mean? Does it mean that they watched the programme carefully and attentively from beginning to end? Does it mean that they caught a few minutes here and there in between playing with the children, eating dinner, or reading the newspaper? Or does it mean that they saw the first couple of minutes before having to go out? Or could it be that they did not see the news at all last night, but the night before, and confused the two occasions?

Clearly, whether or not people actually watch the news and how often or how much they watch are important antecedent conditions for learning from television news. In a great deal of survey research that has investigated the significance of relationships between amount of television news consumption and news awareness or news comprehension, or that has tested recall from the same or previous evening's main television newscast, measures of viewing have invariably consisted of personal reports.

For example, measures may consist of personal estimates of how much television news respondents normally watch in terms of days per week, or numbers of broadcasts seen the week before, or whether they viewed last night or a few hours ago. However, the question of the accuracy of these self-report measures is rarely questioned. It is often taken for granted that they are sufficiently accurate to serve as useful indicators. And maybe they are. If they are far off the mark, however, then much of this research is in trouble. The less accurate subjective estimates of viewing turn out to be, the more the findings of studies that employ these kinds of measures may be invalidated.

Although self-report measures of television news viewing often do relate in a statistically significant sense to how much individuals know about recent or current news events, we will also see that such reports may paint one picture of television news watching behaviour, and that other, less purely subjective measures may provide a different impression of the extent to which news is viewed.

TV NEWS VIEWING AND KNOWLEDGE ABOUT RECENT NEWS EVENTS

Two studies published in Britain have indicated relationships between reported viewing of television news and knowledge about news events reported in the news during the previous week or so. The author conducted a study with over 500 residents of London who were telephoned on two evenings and questioned about events in the news during the week before (Gunter, 1984). News knowledge questions focused on a number of prominent political figures in the news and on three major news stories. Respondents were also asked to estimate how many radio news programmes and radio political and current affairs discussions they had heard, and how many network and local news programmes they had seen on television during the last week.

Table 5.1 shows the mean news knowledge scores as a function of respondents' claimed frequency of radio news listening and television news watching over the previous week. Casual examination of these scores indicates that higher knowledge scores were associated with more frequent claimed use of radio news and radio discussion programmes and of network television news programmes. Personal estimates of viewing local news programmes on television, however, were less clearly linked with knowledge of recent news items.

In order to find out if these apparent associations are significant in a statistical sense, correlational analyses were computed between listening and viewing claims and news knowledge scores. The results of these analyses are summarised in Table 5.2 This table shows the results of

TABLE 5.1
Mean News Awareness Scores for Different Types of News as a Function of Frequency of Broadcast News Consumption

	Frequency of Radio Listening								Frequency of Television Viewing						
News Category	News Broadcasts				Political Discussion				Network News			Local News			
	None	1–5	6–9	10+	None	1–5	6+	3	3–5	6–9	10+	None	1–2	3–5	6+
People in News															
Who	7.2	7.5	7.6	9.8	6.9	6.7	8.2	7.1	7.9	7.2	8.9	7.5	7.5	8.1	7.7
Why	3.9	4.1	4.1	5.2	3.7	3.6	4.4	3.8	4.2	4.0	4.8	4.2	4.0	4.3	4.2
Total	10.6	11.3	11.2	14.7	9.8	9.9	12.3	10.6	11.7	10.9	13.4	11.3	11.1	12.0	11.6
Major News Stories	10.8	11.4	11.2	14.3	9.3	10.3	12.2	10.8	11.5	10.6	13.7	11.3	10.5	12.3	11.8
Total News Awareness	21.2	22.3	22.2	28.8	18.5	20.0	24.4	21.2	23.0	21.4	26.9	22.3	21.5	24.2	23.3

Source: Source: Gunter, 1984.

Note: All Frequencies represent number of programmes seen or heard over last seven days

TABLE 5.2
Partial Correlations Between News Awareness and Use
of Different Sources of Broadcast News

News Category	Radio News Listening	Radio Discussions Listening	Network TV News Viewing	Local TV News Viewing
People in News				
Who	.12*	.07	.13*	.06
Why	.07	.09	.11**	.02
Total	.11*	.09	.13*	.05
Major News Stories	.07	.10*	.12*	.02
Total News Awareness	.10**	.10*	.14**	.04

Source: Gunter, 1984.
Note: Fourth-order partial correlations with sex, age, class, and education controlled.
** p <0.001
* p <0.01

fourth-order partial correlations in which simultaneous controls were employed for the influence upon either media use claims or news knowledge of respondents' sex, age, and social class.

The results indicate that claimed frequency of listening to radio news programmes and radio discussion programmes were both related significantly to total news knowledge. Claimed frequency of watching network television news bulletins was also significantly related to overall knowledge level for recent news items. From both tables it can be seen that news listening and viewing claims of respondents were related to their knowledge of specific subcategories of news as well as to news in general. These subcategories included knowledge about prominent figures in the news— who they were and why they had been the objects of reports—and knowledge about particular major news stories. Table 5.2 indicates that claimed radio news listening was linked particularly with knowledge about prominent figures in the news, whereas claimed listening to radio discussions was more closely related to knowledge about major news stories. Personal estimates of network television news viewing, however, were significantly related to all aspects of news on which knowledge was tested in this study. Claims of viewing local television news, on the other hand, was not related very powerfully to any aspect of news knowledge.

The extent to which respondents who claimed frequent viewing of television news correctly answered questions about specific political figures and about different elements of specific major news stories was consistently better than among relatively infrequent viewers of these programmes. Respondents who said they had watched more than ten national television newscasts in the previous week were most likely to

identify correctly various prominent political figures—domestic and foreign—and to know why these politicians were in the news.

Looking back to Table 5.1, it is interesting to note, however, that the
actual numbers of news broadcasts respondents claimed to have seen over
a certain number made little differences to level of news knowledge. In
general, respondents who claimed to have seen between three and five
national news broadcasts exhibited practically the same knowledge levels
for recent news as did those who claimed to have seen more than ten news
programmes. This could mean that, provided respondents have seen a
certain minimum number of news broadcasts, seeing a few more does not
make any difference to their news knowledge. Or it might mean that, over
a certain number, respondents are unable to estimate with any real
accuracy how many news broadcasts they may have seen during a certain
period of time and at best can offer only rough guesses. Consequently,
those who said they had seen five may in fact have seen any number
between three and seven, whereas among those who said they had seen
more than ten, many may in fact have seen only six or seven or eight. The
net results would be that these two categories would overlap and would
probably provide only a very approximate differentiation of respondents
in terms of their television news viewing levels.

One promising finding to emerge from this study, however, was that
knowledge about some news was differentially related to national and
local television news viewing claims. Knowledge of events in one foreign
news story that had broken only the previous week, for example, was
positively related to estimates of the number of network television newscasts seen, while being inversely related to claimed viewing of local
television news. This indicated that, with regard to recent foreign or
international news, those people who claim to be particularly loyal to
local news on television are less likely to be aware of the details of such
stories.

In addition to getting information about public and world affairs
directly from different mass media, people may sometimes learn about
recent news events through talking to others. Furthermore, the extent to
which people talk to others about the news may indicate how interested
they are in news and current affairs. The news obtained in the first
instance through mass media sources may be further elaborated and
reinforced by discussing it with family, friends, or workmates, thus
increasing the strength of learning. In view of these possibilities, the
author also asked his respondents to say how often they talked about the
news, and related this variable to news awareness. It was found that
respondents who claimed to talk about the news had greater news awareness for recent news events than those who said they hardly ever or never
talked about news with others. Indeed, this variable was as powerful as
any mass media indicator of news awareness.

Respondents who said they had not once talked about news with others during the previous week as far as they could remember were far less likely than those who said that they had talked about news with others to identify correctly prominent politicians in the news and to know why those political figures had been in the news, and had a poorer grasp of the facts from several major news stories from the last week's news. Knowledge about recent events in the Middle East, Cyprus, and Britain was considerably more extensive among those respondents who said they had talked about the news during the last week. The margin of difference between news discussants and nondiscussants was often considerable, with the former being half again as likely or even twice as likely as the former to answer certain questions correctly (see Gunter, 1984).

On the surface such results indicate that levels of news consumption via the mass media or through conversations with other people were positively related with knowledge levels for recent news stories and events. But just how real are these relationships?

During his research with the BBC in Britain, Robinson discovered that one of the questions news editors wanted to know the answer to was to what extent "tonight's" audience could be assumed to have seen "last night's" stories, or those on the previous evening(s). Plenty of information is regularly supplied on audience sizes by the ratings' services in Britain and the United States. But what is needed in order to answer this kind of question is an analysis of the cumulative nature of the audience for television news over a period of days or weeks.

Robinson and Sahin (1984) refer to Goodhardt, Ehrenberg, and Collins (1975) who examined JICTAR data for Britain and Nielsen data for the United States to see the extent to which the audience for a programme (or type of programme) at one time period would be the audience for the same programme (or type of programme) the next time it was shown. Briefly, Goodhart et al. concluded that news was little different from other programmes in terms of audience loyalty. In other words, one could predict the size of the news audience by knowing the overall proportion of people in the news audience on one day and the proportion on a second day and multiplying the product of the two numbers by a channel-loyalty factor.

Robinson and Sahin examined data on viewing patterns for TV viewers using the 1975 BBC Survey "The People's Activities and the Use of Time." In this survey, respondents reported all their daily activities, making it possible "to examine programme viewing in the full context of daily life away from the set" (p.16). The authors were able to carry out only exploratory research using a small random sample of 153 respondents selected from the original survey. Nevertheless, they were able with this group to discover a number of interesting features of television news viewing behaviour.

Individuals viewing each half-hour across the evening period between 7:00 p.m. and 11:00 p.m. were recoded into one of four categories: watching BBC, watching ITV, watching another channel, or engaging in some other activity. From this subset of activity diaries, Robinson and Sahin identified, for each day of the week, which people at 9:00 p.m. were watching BBC news or at 10:00 p.m. were watching ITV news. They found that the proportion of this small sample on one evening during the week that did not watch the 9:00 p.m. BBC newscast was 55%. Some 16% watched the newscast on one evening only across the week, 16% more watched two, 7% saw four, with only 2% watching all five.

These figures, however, did not take into account viewing of news on the opposite channel. By including opposite-channel news viewing, the researchers found the news audience for any given night to be even less random in terms of its prior exposure to news on another weekday evening. Well over half the BBC nightly news audiences or ITV news audiences for the period and among the sample covered has seen a newscast on three or four of the previous weekday evenings. Averaged out, the viewer of BBC's *Nine O'Clock News* bulletin one night had seen 2.7 late evening newscasts on one or other of the two main channels over the last four weeknights (of which 1.8 were on BBC and 0.9 were on ITV), and the average viewer of ITV's *News at Ten* had seen 2.4 newscasts (1.8 on ITV and 0.6 on BBC). In contrast, a person who had seen neither of these newscasts on a given evening was likely on average to have seen only 1.3 newscasts over the previous four evenings. Robinson and Sahin concluded that their data portray the news viewer as somewhat more selective than does the Goodhart et al. analysis, and this is without consideration of viewers of news programmes shown by BBC and ITV earlier in the evening, at 5:45 p.m. A substantial part of the BBC nightly news audience is, according to their analysis, made up of people who have seen the ITV version of the news on a previous evening.

This is not to say that channel loyalty is unimportant; however, the news viewing data reported by Robinson and Sahin from the BBC's "People's Activities" survey still indicated a somewhat more loyal and selective audience for newscasts on the same channel than did Goodhardt et al.'s. Some 13% of the small sample had watched 3 to 5 BBC newscasts during the week, compared to the 6% expected on the basis of chance alone, and 18% had seen 3 to 5 ITV newscasts, compared to a 9% random expectation. Taking into account the channel-loyalty factor identified by Goodhardt et al, Robinson found that these figures reduced to a 13% (actual) versus 8% (random) contrast for BBC, *Nine O'Clock News* and to 18% versus 17% figures for ITV. Moreover, in a separate comparison with other programmes on BBC between 8:00 p.m. and 10:00 p.m., in which there was 48% viewer overlap from one evening to the next, duplication for the news was 59%. For ITV, the news duplication figures of 68% was less distinguishable from viewing that channel at other periods (64%), indicating a somewhat greater loyalty among BBC news viewers.

REMEMBERING THE NEWS FROM INDIVIDUAL BROADCASTS

We turn now to consider recall of news from specific broadcasts. Although there is evidence that knowledge of recent events in the news generally may be related to self-reports concerning regularity of listening to or watching the news on radio and television, to what extent does reported use of broadcast news relate to or indicate something about the recall of news from individual editions of the news? Do individuals who claim to be regular watchers of television news, for example, recall information from particular news broadcasts better than those individuals who say they watch television news relatively infrequently? Those segments of the audience for whom television is a customary and regular source of news information may also be better equipped, perhaps through reasons associated with their extensive experience with the medium, to absorb news from television news programmes.

A study conducted in Britain by Robinson and Sahin (1984) sheds some light on this question. These researchers examined comprehension of a single evening's television newscast among 489 viewers of BBC1's early evening newscast at 5:45 p.m. Interviews were carried out in respondents' homes over four evenings shortly after the programme had been broadcast. Respondents were given unaided and aided tests of recall for the content of that evening's bulletin.

Robinson and Sahin found that those respondents who were relatively frequent newspaper readers and who read serious newspapers had better comprehension. Those who said they listened most often to Radio 4, the BBC's serious radio station featuring a good deal of news and topical discussion programmes, also had better comprehension than listeners to other radio channels. Viewing of BBC TV news was monotonically related to news comprehension, while heavy viewing of ITN news on the independent television channel was negatively related to news comprehension from single BBC newscasts. Robinson and Sahin were quick to point out several notes of caution when interpreting the latter potentially provocative findings, however. First, their sample sizes were fairly small; second, scores were based on comprehension of one week's news only; and third, controls had not been built in for demographic variables.

On subsequently building in demographic controls, the authors found that not only was BBC TV news viewing positively related to retention and comprehension of news from single news broadcasts, but, so too, now was ITN news viewing. After statistical controls were added, comprehen-

TABLE 5.3
Variations in Comprehension of News From a Single Broadcast as a Function of News Media Use

	Initial Information Score	Following Statistical Controls
Total sample	507	2.3	2.3
Newspaper Reading			
0–1 days	120	1.7	2.1
2–7 days	387	2.4	2.3
Newspaper Type Read			
None	53	1.7	2.2
Popular tabloid	362	2.2	2.3
Serious broadsheet	92	3.0	2.4
Radio News Heard			
0–1 days	215	2.1	2.2
2–7 days	292	2.4	2.3
Radio Station			
None	139	2.0	2.2
Radio 1	133	1.9	2.1
Radio 2	58	2.6	2.4
Radio 4	87	3.1	2.8
Local	90	2.3	2.0
BBC TV News			
0–1 days	150	2.0	2.1
2–3 days	212	2.2	2.2
4–7 days	145	2.7	2.6
ITN TV News			
0–1 days	158	2.3	2.1
2–3 days	172	2.5	2.4
4–7 days	177	2.0	2.3

Source: Robinson and Sahin, 1984. Reprinted by permission of author.

sion differences related to BBC TV news viewing were virtually unchanged, while for ITN news increased viewing was now related to better comprehension. The latter control, however, reduced the effects of newspaper reading and radio listening to nonsignificance, with the sole exception of listening to Radio 4 (see Table 5.3).

MOTIVATION, ATTENTION TO THE NEWS, AND NEWS KNOWLEDGE

The extent to which audiences learn from broadcast news may depend not simply on how often they habitually watch or say they watch the news on television or listen to it on radio but, more importantly, also on the particular reason they have for watching in the first place. Audience

122

members' level of motivation to listen to or to watch the news generally or on specific occasions, and their level of interest in the content of particular news broadcasts, has been found by some researchers to influence how much they assimilate and remember from the news. Some researchers have asked respondents to state their most important news sources and their perceived dependence on one mass medium or another for news of different kinds, and have found that levels of media dependency may have some effect on retention of news from particular media. Selective attention to or retention of news messages has also been considered, however, in relation to clusters of motives underlying news consumption in general, and more specifically to personal interests in the subject matter of individual stories.

Research has indicated that the choice of media information to consume and the learning of such material may depend fundamentally on specific news interests that may vary widely from one individual to another, often quite independently of education or other demographic indicators of news consumption (Ettema & Kline, 1977). In this section we examine evidence concerning relationships between news knowledge or news recall and media dependencies, motivation to consume news, and interests in particular topics or subject matter.

Media Dependencies and Information Gain

A number of researchers have investigated relationships between how dependent people say they are on particular media for their political and current affairs information, and the nature and extent of the messages assimilated from the media. Some studies have examined media impact during short-term information campaigns, while other writers have focused on broader and more long-term effects associated with certain patterns of media dependencies. Michael Robinson has reported, for example, that dependence on television for political information is associated with political cynicism, political inefficacy, partisan disloyalty and acceptance of third-party candidates, and misperceptions of candidate strength. People relying on television are more likely to think they cannot understand politics than those dependent on other media such as print. The television dependent are also more likely to believe that governmental leaders are crooked and that members of Congress tend to lose touch with their constituents once they are elected. These relationships were found to hold even after controls for education were introduced (Robinson, 1975, 1976; Robinson & Zukin, 1976; Robinson, 1977). In a 1974 paper, Robinson reported that persons watching the televised Watergate hearings showed an increased hostility to government and a sense of personal perplexity. The television-dependent were less knowledgeable about the scandal than newspaper-dependent respondents. Thus heavy reliance on television on this evidence would appear to inculcate a sense of political distrust. This tells us something about a possible influence of television news and current affairs programming on impression formation, but we still need to know more about television dependency as a mediator of learning from television news.

More recently, Becker and his colleagues have demonstrated that reliance on television for current affairs information may be associated with lower levels of knowledge than dependency on print media. Becker, Sobwale, and Casey (1979) reported that television dependency was associated with lower levels of knowledge about local affairs, while newspaper dependency showed the reverse relationships. There was some slight evidence that people dependent on newspapers were more favourably inclined towards local governmental officials than people not newspaper dependent. Television-dependent people tended to be less favourable towards and trusting of local political leaders.

In a subsequent study, Becker and Whitney (1980) examined relationships between dependency on newspapers or television for news and knowledge of local and national issues, perceived comprehension of these issues, and trust in local and national government and politicians. Dependency on a particular medium was a composite index based on self-reported reliance on newspapers or television for local or national news, and degree of attention to local and national news issues. Knowledge of local affairs was assessed by asking for the name of the mayor of Columbus, where the study took place, and his party affiliation, and on the provision of information by respondents on two local issues being discussed in the media at the time, namely school busing and solid waste disposal. Knowledge of national affairs was assessed via questions concerning the name of the local Congressman, his party, the effective date for the Panama Canal transfer under a proposed treaty, and solutions for U.S. dependency on foreign oil.

Newspaper-dependent people were higher in knowledge of local affairs than people not dependent on newspapers, while television-dependent people were more likely to be low in knowledge of local affairs than people not reliant on television. Newspaper-dependent people were also more likely to think they comprehended local affairs than those not so dependent. Television-dependent people, on the other hand, were less self-confident in their local news knowledge. With regard to national news issues, newspaper dependence was associated with higher knowledge levels, while television dependency was correlated with lower knowledge levels on these matters. Media dependencies were not related to perceived comprehension of national level issues, however.

Finally, Becker and Whitney found that in actuality the differences in knowledge between those who are newspaper dependent and those who are television dependent were small. Using multiple classification analysis and controlling for age and education, they found that the mean score for local knowledge was only .29 point higher on a five-point scale for newspaper-dependent than for television-dependent people. On national knowledge, the difference was just .48 point. Thus, although media dependencies can make some difference, it was not in this instance a very great one.

Although reported dependencies on different media for news or political information may not appear to be very good predictors of knowledge acquisition during information campaigns, several studies have indicated that motivations related to watching the news on television may mediate memory for broadcast news content quite independently of educational background, social class, or other demographic characteristics of the audience.

Media dependency research is not without its problems, however. Results have not always been consistent, but differences in design and procedures make comparisons between studies difficult. Media dependency studies have varied in the kinds of dependent variables they have studied and in the extent to which they control for demographic variables. Some studies have examined cognitive dependent variables such as knowledge gain, issue awareness, and so on, whereas others have investigated affective variables such as attitudes towards issues or objects, or behavioural variables, such as intention to vote and participate in the political process. Perhaps the most serious problem of all in media dependency studies has been the lack of consistency in the conceptualisation and measurement of the independent variables of television and newspaper dependency.

Some studies have used only simple claimed exposure measures (e.g., hours of watching television per day); others have measured exposure to specific content (e.g., frequency of watching news programmes); and others have asked questions about subjectively perceived reliance for news on a particular medium. Another point of confusion is that television dependence is at times used as an *absolute* measure in contrast to television use (i.e., high versus low television dependence), whereas in other research it is viewed as a *relative* measure in contrast with newspaper use (i.e., television dependence versus newspaper dependence). In the latter case, television dependence may be confounded with newspaper dependence, and any effect found could be a function of either, both, or neither of these types of dependency.

In an attempt to over come these shortcomings, McLeod and McDonald (1985) examined three different dependent variables representing cognition, attitude, and behaviour in relation to multiple measures of media dependence that consisted of time spent with a medium, reliance on a medium for news, exposure to news and current affairs content in a medium, level of attention to news, and gratifications sought from watching television news and current affairs programming or from reading newspapers. The authors assessed both their individual main effects and their interactive effects on various dependent variables.

McLeod and McDonald found that there is more to media impact than simple exposure. The two exposure measures—number of days per week a newspaper is read, and time spent with television—accounted for less than 2% of the variance averaged across the three dependent variables after the application of demographic controls (for age and education); of which only a minor proportion was actually accounted for by television viewing. More than three times as much variance was accounted for by the other media variables, reliance on a medium, exposure to news content, attention to news, and gratifications sought from a particular news medium.

Overall amount of television watching and television reliance were both negatively related to economic knowledge and political participation after the application of demographic controls, but level of attention to news showed a reverse pattern and was positively related to these variables. This finding indicates the importance of considering multiple measures of television use. McLeod and McDonald argued that simple exposure to television is made up largely of viewing of entertainment programmes and only incidentally involves watching news and documentaries. Attention may be the ingredient necessary for the television medium to have an integrative and politically motivating function.

Motivation to Watch and Information Gain

Neuman (1976) found more substantial differences in mean news recall from television bulletins by motivational level than by educational level among respondents interviewed by telephone shortly after the evening's network newscast. Individuals who admitted that they watched the news primarily for relaxation had significantly lower rates of recall than those who claimed to want to keep informed. Overall though, the evidence for positive mediating effects of interest or motivational levels on information uptake from television news is not conclusive. There is some evidence that how well the news is remembered may depend on the nature of the motivational patterns influencing the way individuals use the media. Some motivational sets are conductive to learning, while others are not. At the same time, however, recent experimental work has emerged, which we look at later in this chapter, that indicates that motivation or interest per se may be rather less important than background knowledge as mediators of comprehension and retention of television news. In the presence of statistical controls for the effects of knowledge, the effects of motivation and interest may be considerably weakened.

In the context of motivational effects on news recall, however, a lot seems to depend on the way individuals approach and use television.

Most people tend to think of or use television principally as a source of entertainment, whereas they read newspapers mainly because they want to be informed. Research has indicated that less well educated sections of the public generally have weaker information-seeking motives than better-educated groups, but it has not yet been clearly established to what extent people (irrespective of their educational attainment levels) differentiate news and current affairs programmes as a special and distinct category of television content—to be watched specifically for purposes of information rather than for entertainment. It is possible that large numbers of people do not make this distinction and watch news programmes as one form of entertainment. Does this mean, however, that they will also be less likely to remember information from newscasts?

According to the proponents of the uses-and-gratifications perspective, motivational factors can have a profound influence on information recall from television programmes. Those individuals who actively seek information from the media will tend to learn more than those who approach the media for some other purpose, such as entertainment. In a field survey of news recall within this empirical framework, Gantz (1979) questioned a sample of over 500 people by telephone about their reasons for watching television news and on their memory for the content of a major newscast that had been aired shortly before the interview. On the basis of their expressed attitudes towards the news, Gantz divided his sample into four types of news viewers: information seekers, recreation-diversion seekers, information and recreation seekers, and casual viewers. Results showed that recall of news items from the test bulletin correlated significantly with both information-seeking and recreation-diversion-seeking motives, but with information seekers tending to remember slightly more than recreation-diversion seekers. Interestingly, individuals who viewed television news for information and entertainment purposes generally produced the lowest recall scores of the four types, performing even worse than casual viewers. It seems that individuals who have a single, fairly precise reason for watching the news, even though not necessarily representing a need for information, remember more from news bulletins than individuals who have a number of possibly competing reasons for doing so. Indeed, the fact that the latter type remembered fewer items than people who had no particular reason for watching the news suggests that competing motives may interfere with the processes of learning and/or remembering news content.

How important then is motivation to news recall? Unfortunately, it is difficult to form any kind of positive conclusion on the evidence available so far. Closer examination of the Neuman and Gantz studies indicates that motivational differences among television audiences provide only weak indicators of news diffusion. For example, although Neuman (1976) found that individuals who wanted to keep informed remembered more news items than those who watched news for entertainment purposes, these two groups comprised only one third of the sample. The great majority of viewers consisted of individuals who "just happened to watch the news" and who had no regular news viewing habits or special reasons for watching. Indeed, the combined effects of motivation and education accounted for only 2% of the variance in recall. Likewise with Gantz's study, motivational data offer no clear picture of how memory for news is affected by specific reasons for tuning in to the broadcast in the first place. To begin with, both information needs and recreation-diversion needs were positively correlated with memory performance, and the difference between their respective associations with news recall was only small. Further, even when considered together, these motivational factors accounted for only 5.4% of the variance in recall scores.

In one of several studies they reported on comprehension of television news, Robinson and Sahin (1984) tested respondents for their understanding and retention of content from an early evening television newscast they had just watched. In addition, the authors asked respondents to give their reasons for watching the news and to say how much attention they had paid to the newscast. Results indicated that those who said they

TABLE 5.4
Motives for Watching the News and News
Comprehension

	Percent of Sample	Comprehension Score
Watch news for reassurance		
Low	38	29.5
Medium	40	27.0
High	22	25.6
Watch news for curiosity		
Low	38	27.8
Medium	39	28.0
High	23	26.9
Watch news to feel informed		
No	21	25.6
Yes	79	28.1
Attention paid to newscast		
Partial	65	25.6
Complete	35	32.2
Feel able to understand news		
Almost all	67	31.8
More than half	14	23.6
About half or less	19	16.8

Source: Robinson and Sahin, 1984. Reprinted by permission of author

watched the news for reassurance about the state of the world scored lower on comprehension than those who did not watch principally for that reason. Furthermore, those audience members who said they watched mainly out of curiosity tended to exhibit lower comprehension scores for the broadcast they had just seen. Instead, viewing to keep informed was the best predictor of comprehension out of the motivational variables looked at. Also, those who said they paid complete rather than just partial attention to the newscast, and those who said they felt able to understand its content, were the ones who produced the best comprehension scores (see Table 5.4).

News Interests and Information Gain

Although it may not be the sole source, television for most people these days is the main source of information about events and happenings in the world. Many people find television news useful and gratifying (Levy, 1978). At the same time, however, viewers' attention and interest vary depending on the content of news programmes. Sometimes the news is found interesting and relevant and at other times irrelevant and difficult to understand.

Levy's study of the audience experience with television news found that viewers may have a variety of reasons for watching the news. For some people, news watching may provide an opportunity "to exercise their critical capacities, testing their perceptions and attitudes on 'fresh' events and personalities" (p. 24). The news also provides the raw material for opinion formation, which in turn may serve a variety of social functions.

Television news, through its highly stereotyped and routinised format of presentation, can reassure as well as inform audiences. History is seen in the making, but the distressing elements associated with certain real-life occurrences are filtered or shaded out, and the familiar presence of the resident anchorperson lends an ingredient of security and sanity to an ever-changing and often conflict-filled world.

Television news is also entertainment for some segments of the audience, and in common with fictional genres of television programming can provide an escape from everyday cares. Not entirely unaware of this function, the broadcasters and newsmakers themselves play on the entertainment angle and in some instances adopt a deliberately contrived light-hearted approach or "happy talk" format. Although this excessively stylized format is not suited to everyone, in general most of the television news audience feel positively towards newsmen and newscasts most of the time.

Levy notes, for example, that while viewers do say they enjoy television news that is funny, relaxing, and otherwise entertaining, most also watch with the serious intention of finding out about what is happening in the world. Moreover, well over half the people surveyed by Levy complained that television news did not provide them with enough background on complicated and important issues. We have seen already that the general reasons people have for watching the news may affect what they take from news broadcasts. But how important are the effects of more specific content-related interests on the apprehension of information from news programmes?

The knowledge-gap hypothesis proposes that socio-economic and educational factors are the crucial determinants in identifying individuals who are more likely to be knowledgeable about public affairs. Certainly, background characteristics such as educational attainment can affect the capacities of audience members to assimilate some mass media information (Budd, MacLean, & Barnes, 1966; Wade & Schramm, 1969). However, although education is related to reception of information campaign knowledge, other writers have indicated that the choice of media information to consume and the consequent learning of such material often stem more immediately and directly from specific motivational interests of the public (Ettema & Kline, 1977), which in turn may mediate how much is learned independently of or in addition to demographic factors.

A study by Atkin, Bowen, Nayman, and Sheinkopf (1973) of audience attention to television commercials for two gubernatorial campaigns showed strong ties with campaign interest and little support for demographic predicators such as education or occupational status. Greenberg, Brinton, and Farr (1965) found interest strongly related to knowledge about an ongoing sports event. Two further studies sought to isolate factors playing a role in political knowledge acquisition and concluded that interest predetermined media use, which, in turn, was related to political knowledge levels (Johnson, 1973; Bishop & McMartin, 1973). These studies suggest that specific news interests of the media consumer may be crucial when considering what public affairs knowledge is gained. Many studies have implied that news interests may be associated with education or socio-economic status differences within the knowledge-gap model, but few have actually directly assessed their effects. Although it may be reasonable to postulate that education can broaden an individual's interests, it is not reasonable to assume that similarly educated people necessarily have the same interests.

In another test of the effects of interest on news acquisition, Funkhouser and McCombs (1971) traced the actual diffusion of several news messages by surveying the audience while diffusion was in progress. In order to preclude people falsely claiming knowledge of an event (a shortcoming that results in distortions or inaccuracies in the data of many surveys) these researchers asked each respondent a question that, if answered correctly, indicated knowledge of the event. In addition, whether or not respondents had heard of an event, they were each asked how interested they were in that type of news. It was found that the higher the audience interest in a news event, the larger the proportion of audience members that would be aware of it at any given time during its diffusion and the less susceptible its diffusion would be to forgetting or to competition from other news events.

Focusing specifically on interest in assessing public affairs and news information learning within a knowledge-gap framework, Genova and Greenberg (1979) predicted that different news items would hold varying levels of interest for audience members and that information gain could be presented as a function of those interests. They speculated that specialised interest in ongoing news events might yield more sensitive expectations about public knowledge acquisition from the news than demographic indicators such as education or socio-economic class. Tracing the diffusion of two well-publicised news events over a ten-day period, Genova and Greenberg indeed found that interest alone generated a knowledge gap. For each news event at each of two interviews conducted respectively at the beginning and at the end of the survey period, respondents who showed the greatest interest in a story knew more about it than those who showed less interest. Furthermore, when four new questions were introduced about each news event on the second interview, convening new developments that had taken place in each case, those respondents who had maintained a high level of interest had learned significantly more about the new information than those who had remained uninterested.

Research has quite clearly established that specialisations of interest do exist within heterogeneous television audiences and that levels of claimed knowledge about news tend to vary with these news interests. In an investigation into audience attitudes towards television news, Wober (1978) questioned two samples of viewers in two regions (Lancashire and the Midlands) about their news preferences. Respondents were given nine news topics: industrial news in Britain, what goes on in Parliament, the Royal Family, immigrant affairs in Britain, human rights in communist countries, problems of Northern Ireland, Rhodesia, the Middle East conflict, and the National Front. Respondents indicated whether they thought each topic should be given continuous coverage, whether they personally wanted to see more or less of each topic, whether they claimed any knowledge of such topics, and whether they felt that coverage was biased in any way. Results indicated clearly defined attitudes about news topics among both samples. Industrial news, Parliamentary news, and the Royal Family were widely cited as things that should be treated more extensively by news and documentary programmes. However, respondents sampled wanted to see less about Northern Ireland, Rhodesia, the Middle East, and the National Front.

Most knowledge was *claimed* about industry, Parliament, and the Royal Family (all of which respondents wanted to see more) and the problems of Northern Ireland (of which they wanted to see less). Lowest knowledge was admitted about the National Front and the Middle East. Claimed knowledge across the nine news topics did not relate in a simple way to the amount of news seen, or to the proportion of news within a week's viewing diet. It did, however, relate to the attitude that more news across the nine news topics should be shown to the public, that one would personally want to see such material, and to the perception that news treatment sometimes contains bias. The usefulness and relevance of this investigation to the current discussion lie in its demonstration of well-formed news interests and preferences among heterogeneous publics, but how do these interests relate to knowledge acquisition? Although Wober (1978) found an association between attitudes towards television news topics and *claimed* knowledge, he did not obtain any direct measures of knowledge levels. To what extent is televised informational material that is found most interesting and/or enjoyable to watch also the best remembered?

Although audience-based factors such as educational background and levels of general interest in news and current affairs are undoubtedly influential mediators of news retention, precisely how important their influence is during the learning process remains to be further clarified. One important point to emerge from survey research is the need to investigate more thoroughly the ingredients of news programmes and news stories, whose effects on learning and memory performance may interact with or even override those of the personal significance of news generally or of certain story-types in particular for the audience. Research developments in this respect are imperative if sound recommendations on how to improve the informational quality of news programmes on television are to be forthcoming in the future.

Important implications of the last point emerged from the field survey of news recall from TV bulletins by Neuman (1976). He examined viewers' memories for various types of news stories to find out whether individuals who differed in terms of educational attainment or motives for watching TV bulletins paid more attention to some aspects of news than others. Neuman combined types of news stories according to an intuitive scheme of complexity in which political, economic, and foreign affairs stories were classified as the most abstract and impersonal, and human interest and weather items as the least abstract. Comparisons of recall rates between groups differing in education and interest levels showed consistent small differences in memory performance on items at all levels of abstraction (see Table 5.5).

Although overall real scores for groups who differed in their motives for watching the news showed statistically significant differences, these

TABLE 5.5
Average Recall of Types of News Stories, by Education
and Motivation for Watching News

| | Education | | Motivation for Watching News | | | |
Level of Abstraction	Non-College	College	Watch To Relax	Casual Viewer	Keep Informed	Total
	%	%	%	%	%	%
Low (human interest and weather stories)	60	16	53	61	73	10
Moderate (racial issues, Vietnam stories and ecology	48	51	40	50	68	50
High (political commentaries, economic issues, foreign affair, and general U.S. politics)	47	51	43	50	51	50
TOTAL	47	52	42	51	57	52

Source: Neuman, 1976. Reprinted by permission of publisher
* Significantly different from each other at the .05 level.

differences were less substantial within each level of abstraction. Also contrary to expectations, the greatest differences in recall due to interest levels occurred for the least abstract stories.

ATTENTION TO THE SCREEN WHILE THE NEWS IS ON

So far in this chapter we have seen that the amount of time people claim to watch television has often been found to be significantly related to how much they know about the news and to some extent also to how much they remember from particular news broadcasts or short-term news campaigns. We have also seen, however, that how much people say they watch the news and how often they actually watch may be two completely different things. The old problem of correlation and causation is still with us, and simply because two variables such as news knowledge and claimed consumption of the news are associated or vary concurrently in certain fairly systematic ways cannot be offered as proof of the informational effectiveness of a particular news medium. It is even more troublesome, however, when one of those variables lacks any real accuracy or validity. That being the case, the whole relationship in which we are interested is threatened with invalidation, too. But even supposing that individuals are capable of providing reasonably accurate indications of how much broadcast news they consume over a given period, and that the overlap between how much is actually watched by heavy and light news consumption categories classified via subjective reports of consumption is fairly small, we are still left with the fact that levels of retention are often fairly low across the audience. Even those who say they watch or listen to a lot of news not unusually exhibit extensive failure to recall all but superficial details of one or two stories, especially when the test of memory and comprehension is unexpected.

Poor retention has reliably been found to occur also within a short time of exposure to a news broadcast. One reason for this, which we have not discussed yet, may be connected with the amount of attention viewers or listeners pay to broadcast news bulletins when they are being aired. How much attention does the viewer pay to the television screen when watching television? It might be intuitively assumed that someone watching television is looking at the screen and listening to what is being said for much of the time. Experimental research on this question, however, has indicated that this is often far from what actually happens.

Two major sources of evidence are available on the attentiveness of the audience to the television screen while the news is on. Survey studies have questioned people about the various other activities they engage in while watching television. On the evidence of self-reports it has become clear that the television screen may not be the only focus of attention even when the set is switched on. In the context of watching the news, it is evident that whether or not a viewer has made the deliberate decision to tune into a particular bulletin, he or she may not pay constant, uninterrupted attention to the television screen while the programme is on.

In his study of the audience's experience with news, Levy (1978) asked his respondents: Do you sometimes do something else, like eat dinner, work, read, or things like that? Respondents were permitted more than one answer, and their multiple responses were coded to provide a list of viewer activities while watching television news. The results of this investigation are summarised in Table 5.6. Just one quarter reported no other activity while they were watching the news, and just one other behaviour, "eating dinner" was mentioned by more than a quarter of the sample. Of course, not all of these alternative or concurrent behaviours are likely to be equally distracting. One could still give fairly complete attention to the news while eating, whereas reading, caring for children, or talking to other people in the room might cause auditory and visual distraction from the screen.

It is also worth adding that Levy found that over 70% of his respondents said they generally watched the entire newscast. This, however, might mean that they leave the set switched on for the duration of the newscast, rarely switching off before it is finished, rather than that they attentively watch the programme all the way through. There is no reason to suppose that viewers should watch a newscast with undivided attention

TABLE 5.6
Viewer Activities While Watching TV News

Activity	Percent mentioning
Eating dinner	41.2
Reading newspaper, books, etc.	25.8
Talking to people in room	23.3
Smoking, drinking	22.5
Working in kitchen	19.6
Sewing	17.1
Caring for children	15.0
Doing housework	14.2
Preparing for bed	9.6
Miscellaneous	5.0
No other activity	24.2

Source: Levy, 1978. Reprinted by permission of publisher
Note: Multiple responses allowed. N = 240

from beginning to end. Most people may be content to monitor bulletins selectively, listening for items that are important or relevant to them.

In asking people what other activities they engage in while watching television we are relying on the accuracy of their memories, just as when we ask them to provide personal estimates of how much television they watch. These personal-activities estimates may suffer from the same unawareness and distortions as personal viewing estimates. Another approach that offers a way round the fallibility of human memory is to obtain independent observational evidence of viewers' behaviours in front of the television screen. We go on now to examine such evidence.

Studies of the way people watch television have revealed that viewers pay far less constant attention to the television screen than might be commonly believed. Bechtel, Achelpohl, and Akers (1972) conducted an investigation that was designed to test the validity of various self-report measures of television viewing against actual behavioural evidence on film of people watching television in their own homes. The technique they used was to install video cameras in the television viewing room at the homes of 20 families who volunteered to take part in the study. One camera was mounted over the television set and filmed the family watching television; the other camera was aimed directly at the set so as to film the programmes actually being watched. These pictures were then relayed to a video-recorder in an equipment truck outside the home.

Participants also filled out a variety of questionnaires designed to estimate viewing behaviour. These consisted of a diary consisting of 15-minute time intervals for each day of the 5-day observation period. Respondents had to mark off the intervals during which they had watched

television; another questionnaire asked respondents to specify programmes watched the previous day and to fill out one sheet for each
programme, estimating the amount of time each programme was actually
watched; and finally another questionnaire, administered following the
sixth day, asked for an estimate of family viewing during the 5 days for
which viewing was filmed.

A number of important findings emerged from the comparisons between self-reports of television viewing and behavioural measures. With
respect to diary estimates, for example, cases of underreporting amount
of viewing were infrequent (5.5% of the total time), whereas overreporting
was more generally the case (24.8%). This means that for roughly every 4
hours watching reported, only 3 hours were actually spent watching.
Comparisons of previous day reporting and behavioural observations
produced even less agreement. The average percent agreement between
these two measures was in fact only 45.5%. This meant that for over half
the time respondents reported watching television, they were not actually
doing so. Finally, the comparison between 5-day questionnaire estimates
of amount of television viewing and observational behaviour measures
produced even less agreement. With this particular self-report measure,
respondents were required to estimate the number of hours viewed per
day during the 5-day period, both for themselves and for each member of
their family. Respondents actually reported their 5-day viewing
behaviours in three ways: first, in terms of how much time they generally
watched television per day during the 5-day period, and third, in terms of
how much each member of the family watched television each day of the
five. The first two estimates correlated very highly, whereas the first and
third and second and third did not. Comparisons with behavioural measures indicated that nearly all respondents overreported the amount of
television watching both for themselves and for others. Average percent
agreement was about 44%.

Comparing the diary with previous-day estimates and each of these
with the 5-day estimate showed a decreasing continuum of accuracy. The
further removed in time the respondent was from the immediate situation, the less accurate were the estimates he or she gave for amount of
viewing. The respondent began this continuum, however, with a fairly
high degree of accuracy (about 25% error).

In the context of the present chapter, however, the really interesting
findings emerged with regard to the amount of attention viewers invested
in watching the screen for different kinds of programmes. Bechtel et al.
used three kinds of measures here: firstly, percent of total watching time
devoted to different types of programmes; secondly, percent of time not
watching while in the television viewing room with the set on, by programme type; and, thirdly, percent of time watching the television set
while a particular type of programme is on.

Results indicated that less than 6% of total viewing time observed on camera was devoted to news programmes. The most popularly viewed shows were family shows and movies, which were each watched at least three times as often as the news. When the news was being shown on television, about 10% of the total programme duration on average was spent not actually paying attention to the television screen. Individuals were actually least likely to be paying attention to the television screen when commercials were on. After commercials, however, least attention was paid to the set during news programmes. On average, just over half the duration of television news was visually attended to.

More recently, similar in-home, video-recorded observational studies of viewers' attention to the television screen have been reported by Anderson and his colleagues (Anderson, Lorch, Field, Collins, & Nathan, in press). They installed time-lapse video cameras in the homes of 99 families and recorded family viewing behaviour and what they were watching for 10 full days in each case. The equipment automatically began recording when the set was switched on. Altogether 4,672 hours of recordings were made.

Results showed that the main family viewing room contained no people 14.7% of the time that the TV set was on. Even when someone was in the room with the set on, visual attention to the screen was far from 100%. Attention increased dramatically among children of preschool age, leveling off during school years and declining in adulthood. Adult men looked at the television 63% of the time they were with the television, which was more than adult women (54% of the time) and less than children (70% of the time).

At the time of this writing, Anderson and his colleagues had not yet produced an analysis of levels of attention to different categories of programming. They did, however, compute comparisons between self-reported viewing and observed viewing. According to Anderson et al., the analysis done on this by Bechtel et al. was insufficient. The latter found only that families overestimated viewing when the criterion was eyes actually directed towards the TV screen. They did not determine whether families may have accurately reported the presence of family members in the viewing room. This is an important distinction. Anderson et al. found that when they compared diary records with observational data with the criterion of viewing set as eyes looking at the screen, self-reports did indeed underestimate amount of viewing. But when diaries were compared with presence in the viewing room, self-reports proved to be much more accurate. The diaries may therefore have been accurate records of what most people consider to be "watching TV," namely being present in a room with a set in use.

Visual attention to the screen may not be too strict a definition of viewing, not only because this is not what viewers themselves mean by watching television but also because attention to the television does not depend on actually looking towards the screen. Indeed, Anderson believes that attention may be comprehension-driven rather than the other way around (Anderson & Lorch, 1983). Thus, the increase in visual attention during childhood reflects the increasing comprehensibility of TV programming as the child's cognitive information-processing skills develop. Once the child has mastered cinematic and linguistic codes, television provides a continuous, easily understood source of entertainment and social information. Anderson and Smith (1984) suggested that, for adults, television viewing is highly overlearned and easily time-shared with other ongoing activities. As such, less visual attention is necessary for full comprehension, especially because the correlation between looking at television and listening to it decreases with age (Field & Anderson, 1985).

Anderson and his colleagues at no stage tested whether retention of programme content among observed families was related to level of visual attention to the television. In subsequent chapters we see that a variety of production factors determine the way broadcast news is reported and can affect how well audiences understood and remember what was said. Despite the fact that attention may be comprehension-driven, such that viewers look back at the screen in response to meaningful auditory cues in the story narrative, it may be that on doing so the pictures prove to be distracting nevertheless, causing attention to focus on visualised events that do not in themselves provide an explanation of what the story is about.

Other researchers have examined in greater detail the attention the audience pays to television news while watching bulletins. Robinson and Sahin (1984) conducted seven focus group interviews in the London area and Leeds area of Great Britain to examine how people actually process television news. Groups of between six and ten respondents took part in 3-hour sessions in which they were shown a news programme and were invited to discuss the features of BBC and ITN news coverage in Britain they liked and disliked. At 9 o'clock each group watched that evening's BBC main evening news. While the newscast was on air the researchers developed questions about the news items in the programme to measure the group's understanding of them. The researchers had already gathered some idea of appropriate questions following discussions with news editors about the content of the newscast that afternoon.

In order to gain some notion of how much attention viewers were paying to the newscast, Robinson and Sahin switched off the television set three or four times during the programme and asked participants what they were thinking about at that exact moment the set was turned off. Even though this was a group watching-situation dealing with the news they were about to discuss, fewer than half the respondents reported attention to the news item that was on the screen at the time. This happened more often with impersonal news items concerning politics, economics, or foreign affairs than with some human interest items.

This small study, though limited in terms of sampling, was nevertheless informative about the irregular attention viewers give to the news while it is on air. As Robinson and Sahin correctly point out: "If the viewer's attention wandered this much in a focused group setting, it must be much greater in the unfocused confusion of the home viewing environment" (p. 12). They recommended that broadcasters need to think perhaps about building some degree of repetition of the central points of news stories into the newscast to increase the likelihood that viewers will catch them.

Stauffer, Frost, and Rybolt (1983) sampled 593 people from the western suburbs of Boston to take part in a study of memory for a single news broadcast. Among those contacted, 170 were warned in advance to watch their favourite national news programme on the following evening. They were asked to pay very close attention to the news stories as they would be called again and asked questions about the content of the bulletin. The rest of the sample were telephoned after the bulletin without prior warning.

Stauffer et al. found that there were substantial differences in news recall between those respondents who had been forewarned and those who had not. Those who had been warned in advance to watch that evening's network news recalled 3 news items on average, against an average of 1.9 items for those tested without prior warning. Thirty-one percent of the warned sample recalled five or more of the news stories per bulletin, compared to only 3% of the nonwarned sample. These averages were for newscasts that over four evenings of tests contained between 10 and 18 news items (mean = 13.3). Eight percent of those who were not forewarned failed to recall any news stories at all from a broadcast, versus just 2% of respondents who received prior notice. The warned sample also recalled more details about new stories. Eighty-seven percent remembered an additional two or more details of at least one story, compared to 64% of the respondents tested unexpectedly. The attention manipulation by the researchers seemed to work in that respondents who were contacted in advance reported paying significantly greater attention to the newscast (7.4 on a 10-point scale) than those who were not forewarned (6.9 out of 10).

Stauffer and his colleagues also asked their respondents about their reasons for watching the news and about the level of attention they paid to the news when it was on. Statements of motivation for viewing the news relating to the need for information were reported as a more important influence on the decision to watch the news than those concerning recreation/diversion needs. The statement with the highest average rating (8.4 out of 10) was "to keep up with political events in our country." The lowest average rating was given to "Because you like to watch TV and there's nothing else on" (1.5 out of 10). Differences in motivation to watch the news were not found to be significantly related to recall, however.

How well the news is attended to and as a consequence remembered may depend on the viewing circumstances. In particular, whether viewing takes place alone or with someone else may make a difference. When viewing with someone, the individual may have his/or her attention distracted from the screen during conversation with the other person. On the other hand, two or more people watching the news together may talk about the stories reported in the bulletin, and hence learning may be reinforced. Seventy-three percent of Stauffer et al's sample watched the news with one or more other persons in the same room. Fifty-nine percent said they discussed the news with others while the broadcast was in progress. However, neither the presence of someone else nor whether or not the news was discussed with that other person made any difference to recall from a single television news broadcast seen a short time before.

Deliberation in watching the news might be expected to have some bearing on how much attention is paid to a broadcast and in turn to how much is learned from it. Sixty-four percent of Stauffer et al's. sample said that they normally plan ahead to watch the news, compared to 36% who said they usually tune in spontaneously. The effect of this factor upon news recall depended on whether respondents had been forewarned or not about watching the news. Whether or not respondents normally planned ahead to watch the news made no difference to recall rates among those individuals in Stauffer et al.'s sample who had been asked in advance to pay careful attention to the following evening's network news. Presumably the warning canceled out any effect of respondents' normal degree of deliberation about watching television news. However, among those respondents who were called unexpectedly, those who said they normally planned ahead when viewing the news exhibited better news recall than those who said they did not usually plan to watch the news. Sixty-nine percent who planned ahead recalled two or more stories from that evening's network news, compared with 59% of those who did not normally plan ahead.

In a comparison of news recall from radio and television news broadcasts in Israel, Katz, Adoni, and Parness (1977) found that memory for television news was better than memory for radio news. Among several reasons offered by the authors to account for this difference was the fact that respondents often reported that they were engaged in other activities while the radio news was on, whereas this was less often the case when watching television news. Stauffer et al. reported that 72% of their sample said they spend a sizeable proportion of their news viewing time engaged on other things, however. The most common of these was eating and drinking (mentioned by 45%), followed by reading and writing (30%), household chores (26%), talking (4%), and so on. The amount of time respondents reported spending on other activities while the television news was on, however, was not significantly related to news recall.

CONCLUDING REMARKS

This chapter has been concerned with the nature of audience attention to the news and the significance of viewing patterns for memory and comprehension of television news. Three principal features of the viewing experience and their significance for knowledge gain were examined: frequency of watching the news, motivation for tuning in to the news, and degree of attention to news broadcasts when watching them on television.

There is fairly consistent evidence to show that individuals who claim to watch television news more often also know more about recent news stories. However, television news viewing appears to be more effective at imparting certain kinds of information than others. Thus, frequent television news watching is related to knowing more about personalities in the news but not necessarily to knowing more about the details of major news stories. The latter seems to be enhanced more by reading of quality newspapers.

Motives for watching or reading about the news can influence information uptake, but the extent to which uses and gratifications factors are important seems to depend on how specifically they are related to certain areas of news content rather than to a medium as a whole. In other words, saying that one watches television because it offers good news coverage may be a poor predictor of memory and comprehension of news from television, but saying that one has a particular interest in politics may be a powerful predictor of learning about political news stories seen in a recent news broadcast.

It is often assumed that whenever the television set is switched on in a household, members of the household must therefore be paying attention to it. This is not necessarily true, however, as studies of people watching television at home have shown. Clearly, if attention is not given to the set when the news is on, learning from the programme is likely to be limited. Several surveys reported in this chapter indicated that people reported being engaged in a variety of other activities while watching television. Although no relation has so far emerged between the extent to which other activities are reportedly engaged in while watching the news on television and failure to recall news from broadcasts shortly after viewing them, it has been found that people who are warned that they will be tested on a news programme's content remember more than those called up unexpectedly. This finding suggests that more deliberate viewing by those who were forewarned led to better absorption and retention of the news just seen.

6 Story Attributes and Memory for News

This chapter examines variations in audience retention of different categories of news from news broadcasts. We also take a look at the extent to which learning from the news is related to attributes of "newsworthiness" employed by news editors and producers to guide their selection of events to be reported. Most often, news programmes feature a great deal of news about politics, economics, industrial matters, and foreign affairs, otherwise known as "hard" news. On other occasions, the news may be dominated by emotionally arousing items, such as crime, violent civil disturbances, terrorism, or some natural or man-made disaster. On rarer occasions, the main news of the day may be a report of a major sports event, or stories of "human interest" that feature some dramatic, humourous, bizzarre, or curious event.

It is not unusual, even in a programme dominated by "hard" news, for the final item in the show to be a human interest story, often with an element of humour. Research has indicated that audiences may voice distinct preferences for different types of news. In the United Kingdom, for example, one survey found that people wanted more of certain kinds of news and less of other kinds on their nightly television news programmes (Wober, 1978). Preferences tended in the latter case to lie in the direction of more human interest news and less political news, less news about industrial disputes and less news about terrorist violence (specifically, in this study, news about the troubles in Northern Ireland). But is the content profile of a news broadcast related to how much its audience remembers from it? Are certain categories of news recalled better than others? And if so, are there any implications for the production of news to be gained from the demonstration of such differences in recall by news category and of the effect of this phenomenon on information uptake from the programme as a whole?

Network news programmes have become a popular form of journalism. Given their position at the front of peak-time programming each evening, they have to be. The networks expect the news to capture an early audience that will stay tuned for the rest of the evening's scheduled programmes. The networks pour resources into these flagship news shows with the aim not just of fulfilling their responsibilities for news coverage but, just as significantly, of building a large audience.

In the early 1970s, the "eyewitness news" concept introduced the phenomenon of friendly newspeople who not only have engaging personalities but cover events on the scene and report back their findings "as they happen" during the course of the programme.

The highly competitive battle for bigger audiences has led some local TV stations in the United States to seek specialist advice from so-called "programme doctors." These consultants provide advice on programme formats that are designed to help the station boost the ratings for its news shows. The recommendations that often follow qualitative audience research to find out about attitudes favourable or otherwise to the existing format and responses to new pilot formats may focus on cosmetic changes to style of presentation or on more fundamental shifts in the types of stories on which most coverage is provided. Cosmetically, many news programmes have chosen to adopt a show-business approach to news presentation in which cheerful smiles and "happy talk" are exchanged between presenters who themselves are selected on the basis of their sex appeal or sexual chemistry.

Changes in content may mean more "good news" or more dramatic news. The inextricable links between format and content, mentioned earlier, are often most evident in the case of events that are not themselves inherently exciting but are made that way through appropriate treatment in the story-telling and style of visual presentation. As Bogart (1980) observed, some senior television executives have been known to order their news staff to produce more news about famous or currently popular or fashinable people in a style that is both humourous and, on occasion, controversial. The assumption is that this is the kind of item people are really most interested in, and not the routine reporting of political affairs or the state of the economy. However, styles of presentation such as the "action news" format endorsed by one leading news programme consultant, Frank Magid, are designed specifically to attract and maintain a large and loyal following. But what do people learn from these programmes?

Through a chain of assumptions (for instance, that happy news is what most people really want, and what people want they are usually most likely to remember) one might expect this sort of programme to be extensively absorbed by its viewers. But are the motives for news watching that may eventually be cultivated by news shows, which often perhaps unnecessarily dramatise events or adopt an entertaining "happy talk" style of presentation, the ones that are most conducive to effective learning from information broadcasts? Some critics of the "happy talk" format argued that too much emphasis on entertainment reduced the professionalism and quality of the journalism in television news. Although not given as much consideration at the time, it is not unlikely that the attention to slickness by television newsmakers also had (and still has) consequences for audience apprehension and comprehension of news from their programmes.

Wamsley and Pride (1972) argued that news or public affairs programmes that attract some people primarily because of their entertainment value should influence these people in several ways. These authors contend that broadcasts that highlight dramatic events have an emotional impact that makes the information they contain more significant. During a political campaign, for example, coverage of specific dramatic events may stand out and serve as potent symbols that focus people's attention. Wamsley and Pride further argued that this focusing may result in gradual, long-term shifts in public attitudes, especially among those who use the media for entertainment-related gratifications. They are less clear, however, about the impact of a dramatic format in such political communications on audience comprehension of issues.

It was not only the changes to format brought about by the *Eyewitness News* concept that carried implications for audience comprehension but also the suggestion that the new-style programme placed more emphasis on the coverage of certain kinds of news, hence restricting the areas about which the public were being informed. There was an indication in the mid-1970s that many news stations in the United States were reporting more violent news and more humorous and emotionally arousing (human interest) content.

Dominick, Wurtzel, and Lometti (1975) compared the story content of WABC's *Eyewitness News* with the WNBC and WCBS news programmes. Their results showed that the *Eyewitness* format did spend significantly more time on human interest stories, violent stories, and humorous stories. There was no strong indication, however, that coverage of "hard" news suffered significantly in consequence.

Emphasis on violent, human interest, or comic material is directed at gaining larger audiences but raises questions about the quality of their journalism and the ability of news programmes to inform the public about what is happening in the world.

NEWS VALUES AND THE SELECTION OF EVENTS

News editors are well aware that the appeal of their news broadcasts depends significantly on the quality of the stories they report. Researchers concerned with the selection practices and profiles of news in the media have identified a number of basic news values—attributes of events— that seem to be the ones news editors use to decide what events in the real world are reported in the news.

According to Galtung and Ruge (1965), events are more likely to be reported if they concern short, dramatic happenings, have a clear inter- pretation, have meaning and familiarity for the audience, are relevant to the audience, are about things one expects to happen, or are highly unexpected. Another important factor is the composition of the news. The news must have balance across types of stories. The more items of a given variety that have already become available, the greater will the news value have to be for any new item of the same type to be included. Finally, the probability of an event becoming a news item is increased if it concerns elite nations or elite people, the more personalised it is, and the more negative its consequences. These latter criteria are not surprising inasmuch as the actions of the elite (nations or people) usually have the most important and substantial consequences. Personification of the news is also important, however, because persons can serve easily as objects of positive and negative identification. Negative news, especially that which involves violence, satisfies a whole range of other important news values, often being dramatic, unambiguous, and unexpected.

Although a subsequent analysis of media news profiles by Galtung and Ruge seemed to support their claims that these news values do character- ise reported events, to what extent do they relate to the uptake of news by the audience. In a study of television news coverage and voter behaviour, McClure and Patterson (1973) listed five criteria necessary to produce television news that they claimed would leave the viewer with "a unique and powerful impact." There were clearcut parallels between the qualities listed by these researchers and those identified by Galtung and Ruge as important for news selection in the first place. According to McClure and Patterson, the news coverage should be of real live events; it should have an exciting visual context; it should have an uncomplicated storyline; there should be repeated and/or saturation coverage; and it should be outside the context of a political campaign. As an example of television news that fulfilled these requirements, the authors offered the "violence and brutality of the 1968 Democratic National Convention" (p. 25).

NEWS VALUES AND AUDIENCE INTEREST

Sparkes and Winter (1980) systematically tested whether supposed journalistic news values such as those outlined by Galtung and Ruge are the same values the audience places on the news. Galtung and Ruge (1965) suggested that two principles operate in the reporting of news. First, the more characteristics or news values an event possesses, the more likely it is to be selected as news (the *additive hypothesis*). Second, the value of stories is enhanced by stressing (or indeed overemphasising) aspects of an event that are judged as particularly newsworthy (the *complementary hypothesis*).

Sparkes and Winter began by drawing up a list of eight basic news values that they condensed from a review of literature on news selection criteria. These values are listed in Table 6.1. The list is not exhaustive, but it does represent those news values previous research had indicated to be most important in the news selection process. In particular, the values of impact and conflict had previously been singled out as the qualities of an event that will most certainly ensure attention by the news media. Furthermore, these two news values were found to be related also to newspaper readers' story preferences (Atwood, 1970).

Interviews were conducted with 201 households in Syracuse, New York. Respondents gave an interest rating on a selection of news stories.

TABLE 6.1
News Values

1. Duration: short time span events are more likely to receive coverage than continuing developments. They can be quickly investigated and reported. (Galtung and Ruge, 1965; Sande, 1971)
2. Simplicity: simple events will be reported before complex events which might be difficult to understand or explain. (*ibid.*)
3. Impact: items which are thought to have relevance for the audience will be selected more often than matters which have no immediate bearing. (*ibid*, Hester, 1976)
4. Prominence: large-scale events will be covered more often than similar developments on a smaller scale. Prominence could also involve the importance of the persons or countries involved (elite persons and nations). (*ibid*, Rosengren, 1977)
5. Conflict: included here are the areas of violence, crime, confrontation, catastrophe, etc. Such matters will be more often reported than peaceful developments. (Galtung and Ruge, 1965)
6. Novelty: unusual occurrences or oddities will receive press attention far beyond their actual importance. So-called human interest stories would fall in this category. (*ibid.*)
7. Affinity: events socially or culturally familiar will receive more attention in the news than the unfamiliar. (*ibid*, Hester, 1976; Lent, 1977)
8. Personification: events with strong personal dimensions will receive more attention than broader social or natural events. (Galtung and Ruge, 1965; Sande, 1971)

Source: Sparkes and Winter, 1980. Reprinted by permission of publisher

147

The stories themselves were fictitious accounts written and prepared to look like actual stories that had been clipped from a newspaper. These stories covered six event topics supposedly occurring in four countries and were presented under four treatment conditions. One condition, called the "straight" treatment, was designed as a control condition against which three special treatments could be compared. The latter were "conflict emphasis," "impact emphasis," and "personification," in each of which the appropriate news value(s) had been stressed.

A majority of Sparkes and Winter's respondents reported that they were at least moderately interested in foreign news, with 26% indicating they were very interested and 18% indicating slight or no interest. Attitudes towards various types of news varied. Respondents generally believed they were too many stories on violence and too few on cultural and social customs. Many respondents also expressed an interest for more news of "ordinary people" and of social problems in other countries.

Sparkes and Winter also asked their respondents an open-ended recall question about news stories in general that had caught their attention over the preceding week. This question produced a higher level of recall of foreign or international stories than for local or national news, suggesting that foreign news was a salient category, at least for this sample of individuals (see Table 6.2). Next, a test of aided recall was given in which respondents were asked more specifically about countries that were known to have been covered in the locally available news media over the preceding weeks. Around one-half of the sample were able to recall four stories (see Table 6.3). Significantly, very high numbers confessed they had seen or heard nothing about important political developments in Bolivia and Afghanistan.

In controlling for both media use and demographics, foreign news story recall was found to be associated with both network news viewing and education. The fact that foreign news recall was found to be more highly associated with network television viewing than with newspaper

TABLE 6.2
Free Recall of Foreign News Stories

Catogory	Recalled none	Recalled 1	Recalled 2	Recalled 3	Recalled 4
Local Stories	111	59	24	6	1
	(55.2)	(29.9)	(11.9)	(3.0)	(0.05)
National Stories	84	60	34	20	3
	(41.8)	(29.9)	(16.9)	(10.0)	(1.5)
International Stories	59	69	54	14	5
	(29.4)	(34.3)	(26.9)	(7.0)	(2.5)

TABLE 6.3
Aided Recall of Foreign News Stories

Story Location	Didn't Remember	Vaguely Remembered	Definitely Remembered
Russia	60	11	130
	(29.9)	(5.5)	(64.7)
Canada	111	22	68
	(55.2)	(10.9)	(33.8)
West Germany	108	7	86
	(53.7)	(3.5)	(42.8)
Bolivia	183	12	6
	(96.0)	(6.0)	(3.0)
Afghanistan	180	9	12
	(89.6)	(4.5)	(6.0)
Vietnam	122	31	48
	(60.7)	(15.4)	(23.9)

Source: Sparkes and Winter, 1980. Reprinted by permission of publisher
Note: Sample size = 201. Figures in parentheses are percentages of that sample.

readership suggested that the self-reported preference for television for foreign news might indeed be valid.

The main aim of this study, however, was to investigate the significance of journalistic news value for levels or audience interest in news stories. Which news values, among those identified as the major criteria of news selection, were related to interest in the news? To answer this question, an average interest score was computed across all stories contained within a particular news value category.

The violence factor emerged as a news value important to story interest, despite previous expressions against too much violence in the news. This reversal of opinions on different measures was not universal, however. The conflict treatment was a poor second to the impact and affinity treatments. In summary, relating interest ratings for stories with self-reports of wanting more or less coverage of certain types of events, Sparkes and Winter found that people seem to underrepresent their interest in violence and overestimate their interest in cultural affairs and human interest. What did appear to hold was interest in economics and disinterest in politics in foreign news. Respondents were most interested in foreign news stories with political or economic themes when they were made more relevant by being written from the standpoint of the benefits to or effects of their own country.

The story interest scores also provided some test of the elite-nation hypothesis. Among their original fictitious stories on which respondents provided interest ratings, Sparkes and Winter reported events from four countries, two of which were classified as elite (England and Japan) and two nonelite (Canada and Nigeria). Interest ratings for stories from the elite nations were higher than those for stories from one nonelite nation (Nigeria) but lower than stories from the other nonelite nation (Canada). These findings suggest that eliteness might not be as important as affinity in determining reader or listener interest.

Manipulation of topic and treatment produced marked differences in levels of respondent interest in news stories. In general, these differences were in the direction that news value research would indicate. Sparkes and Winter add an important caveat to this conclusion, however. The conflict treatment manipulation did not result in interest scores comparable to those for the violent story theme. This suggests that the observed journalistic tendency to emphasise the negative aspects of events from abroad does not bear consistency with qualities associated with enhanced public interest in foreign news items. Journalists keen to boost interest in a foreign item whose inherent appeal may be suspect might instead play on the "home country" angle.

RECALL OF DIFFERENT TYPES OF NEWS

Journalistic news values have been found to be good predictors of audience interest in news stories, but to what extent do they have a direct influence on recall of news stories? Sparkes and Winter observed that foreign news stories were better recalled than were either national or local news stories from the preceding week's news, and that television was identified as the major source of this news information. Unfortunately, they did not attempt to relate their news value treatments of news stories to news recall. Research elsewhere that has focused on news awareness or news recall has found variations in the extent to which different categories of news are remembered from broadcast news programmes. In some cases, memory performance has also been related to journalistic criteria of newsworthiness. It is to these studies that we now turn our attention.

Following a telephone interview survey of recall of news from that evening's network television broadcast, Neuman (1976) examined viewers' memories for various types of news stories to find out if one category of news was better remembered than another. Table 6.4 lists the different story-types analysed by Neuman and shows some variation in levels of recall by type of news content. Results indicated substantial variations in the salience and memorability of different story-types. Overall, best recall was recorded for weather items and human interest stories, but the most salient items, as indicated by unaided or spontaneous recall scores, were those about Vietnam—a particularly important news topic in the United States in the early 1970s when this study was carried out. However, when

TABLE 6.4
Recall of Various Types of News Stories

	Total Recall	Unaided Recall	Average Aided Recall With Details	Aided Recall Without Details	No. of Stories Per Newscast
	%	%	%	%	%
Weather	63.7	6.9	38.4	18.3	0.5
Human Interest	58.7	7.5	32.2	18.9	0.9
U.S. Politics	53.9	6.7	24.2	23.0	1.7
Race Relations	53.0	5.9	22.9	24.1	0.4
Foreign Affairs	53.0	5.5	21.4	26.1	3.9
Vietnam	52.3	9.9	19.2	23.2	4.1
Economy	50.5	0.8	22.9	26.9	2.3
Ecology	45.2	6.9	20.4	17.9	1.0
Miscellaneous	44.4	4.2	23.8	16.4	4.5
Commentaries	34.1	8.2	5.9	20.0	0.4
TOTAL	50.3	5.9	22.5	20.0	19.8

Source: Neuman, 1976, p. 120. Reprinted by permission of publisher

further cues were provided to aid recall, memory performance improved more for nearly every other category of news than Vietnam stories relative to unaided recall. This is an important point that requires further consideration.

It is interesting to note that for several story categories on which spontaneous recall was high, detailed memory for their content was relatively poor. One possible explanation for this relates to the actual number of items from a particular category in a television bulletin. From the table it can be seen that the mean number of items for each story type per newscast was nearly 2.0. Leaving aside the miscellaneous category, it is noticeable for the remaining categories with well above the average number of representatives per programme (e.g., Vietnam, foreign affairs) that smaller improvements in memory performance occurred from unaided recall to aided recall than for those categories with fewer representatives on average per bulletin (e.g., weather, human interest). Clearly, those categories exemplified by many items per bulletin may be quite salient and at a superficial level are the ones most readily and spontaneously recalled by viewers in the absence of specific reminders. It is possible, as experimental research on learning of simple verbal materials has shown, that items from a common category are clustered together in memory so that the learner can retrieve all of them only via a superordinate category heading (e.g., Tulving & Pearlstone, 1966). At the same time, however, as we see later, when it comes to detailed retention of

content from news items, such clustering may impair memory performance as topically similar items become confused or interfere with each
other during learning and retrieval from memory.

Katz, Adoni, and Parness (1977) reported two studies of recall of
broadcast news in Israel in which they examined retention of different
categories of news. In their first study, which was conducted in 1971, they
carried out 387 interviews with adults in Jerusalem within an hour of the
broadcast of the evening's major radio news programme and the major
television news programme over five consecutive evenings. In the second
study, in 1972, 200 people were recruited on three consecutive evenings
either to watch, just listen to, or ignore each evening's main television
news bulletin in their own homes. Shortly afterwards they were contacted
and tested for their recall of the programme's content.

Katz et al. looked at several schemes of classification of news programme content in relation to rates of news recall. Firstly, they divided up
items according to whether they dealt with internal (Israeli) or foreign
affairs, and the foreign items were further subdivided according to
whether they had an explicit bearing on Israeli or Jewish interests. Relevance was found to have important effects on recall. Results showed that
domestic items were recalled much better than foreign items. Among
foreign items, however, those with implications for internal affairs were
recalled better than those with no such relevance. There was also an
interaction between subject matter and presentation style that affected
likelihood of news recall. Recall of domestic items was not affected
significantly by presentation style. On the other hand, foreign affairs
items did benefit from certain styles of presentation. On average, foreign
affairs items were recalled twice as well by those who viewed and listened
to the news as by those who listened only.

Secondly, news items were also classified according to institutional
content, such as economic, cultural, political, etc. Items dealing with
defence policy emerged as best recalled under this taxonomy. Seeing the
picture when tuning in to television news led to better recall than simply
listening to the telecast, though not appreciably more in one area of
content than another.

A third scheme of classification was used based on Galtung and Ruge's
(1965) analysis of newsmen's implicit criteria of newsworthiness. The
latter writers outlined 12 criteria, of which three—suspense, negativeness, and meaningfulness—were found by Katz and his colleagues to be
the best predictors of recall.

In their first study, Katz et al. attempted to score each news item in
terms of the number of Galtung and Ruge's criteria that it met, giving
each criterion equal weight. They found a direct relationship between the
score and the rate of recall for television viewing, but a confused relationship for radio listening, which they suggest might have arisen because of

TABLE 6.5
Recall of Broadcast News by Type of Content

| | Domestic | Foreign | Foreign with Domestic Implications | Major Criteria | | |
				Suspense	Negative	Violent
Total number of items of this type in nine programmes	60	44	44	21	18	20
Average number of recalls of items of this type by those who listened only	4.0	1.5	2.7	5.0	5.0	3.9
Average number of recalls of items of this type by those who viewed and listened	4.4	3.0	4.5	4.0	7.4	3.3

Source: Katz, Adoni, and Parness, 1977. Reprinted by permission of the publisher

153

the smaller number of items in the typical radio bulletin. In this study, Katz et al. report that 5 of Galtung and Ruge's 12 criteria emerged as better predictors of news recall than the others, of which we are told about 3. Surprise, negativeness, and meaningfulness recurred as important predictors in the analysis of recall by both radio listeners and television viewers.

In the second study, recall of television news among viewers and listeners only was compared for items according to their loadings on three criteria: surprise, negativeness, and violence. From Table 6.5 it can be seen that recall varied across items of each type and also that different categories of news content benefited differentially from different presentation styles. Seeing the picture added substantially to the rate of recall of negative events but had no real bearing on recall of items of the other two types.

NEWSWORTHINESS FACTORS AND NEWS AWARENESS

Schulz (1982) conducted a study in West Germany of news event awareness in relation to claimed use of four media news sources that had previously been content-analysed. The study began with a 3-month period of monitoring of news stories concerned with political events reported in both German national television channels, a national newspaper, and a local newspaper in the region where the news awareness survey was eventually to be carried out. During the content analysis each story was characterised by an identity of time, location, actors, topic, and form of presentation. The analysis was designed to identify events. Schulz's definition of an event as "what journalists make it" is a little unclear, however. Whatever the precise nature of the criterion used by coders, the monitoring exercise produced a total of 555 different political "events."

Despite the haziness of its definition of what exactly constitutes an event, however, the Schulz study is particularly interesting because it combines an extensive analysis and classification of media news content with an assessment of news awareness. Earlier research had indicated that those events that stand out in the news as highly prominent (but in terms primarily of content analysis rather than audience criteria) tend to have a characteristic content structure (Sande, 1971; Schulz, 1976). This has been explained by the concept of *news factors*, which was introduced by Ostgard (1965) and Galtung and Ruge (1965). Briefly stated, news factors are defined as those features of an event that determine its newsworthiness. For instance, factors like proximity, personification, negativism, or unexpectedness are hypothesised to affect the chances of an event being reported by the media and particularly the prominence of its coverage. But are "newsworthy" items, identified in these terms by researchers, also the ones of which audiences become most aware following exposure to media coverage of them?

Schulz (1982) examined relationships between content structure features of news and news awareness among 260 young adults in the Rhein-Main area of West Germany. Events with highly prominent coverage were found to satisfy to a high degree certain news factor criteria. In other words, prominent political news events usually had a particular content structure. To identify these stories, Schulz adopted a system of content structure categories similar to those developed by Galtung and Ruge (1965). Schulz also found relationships between a number of content dimensions and the degree of prominence events were given in the news, such as their frequency of occurrence, position, length, and pictorial presentation style.

Schulz's taxonomy of content structures and the way they were found to relate to various aspects of presentation are shown in Table 6.6. Elite people and emotional as well as predictable events were particularly emphasised by extensive coverage. Extensive coverage was given to stereotyped political happenings and to events that satisfied various criteria of the valence dimensions. Besides predictability, the factors of proximity and timeliness were characteristic for events that stood out through pictorial presentation.

A prominent position in a broadcast news bulletin was given primarily to events that were high in consequence, that related to one of the predominating political themes and rituals, and that involved elite institutions and elite people. Events in the top positions in television news were also highly personalized. In addition, most of the factors of the valence dimension, as well as uncertainty, unexpectedness, emotional content, and relation to a dominant theme, characterised events that were frequently covered by television news programmes.

Schulz employed three measures of event awareness: (a) recognition of events, based on a question whereby people were asked to identify from a sample of events those which they had seen or heard something about on television, radio, or in the newspaper; (b) all events from the last 3 or 4 weeks they could mention, either from Germany or abroad; and (c) all such events they could mention that had been on reports that had been identified in the four news media monitored.

Schulz found that the structure of events was related not only to their prominence in the news media but also to levels of awareness of them. This finding indicated that people's awareness of political reality is shaped by the news value criteria of the mass media.

More recent experimental studies have also indicated that memory for television news may be affected by news structures. After watching a live

TABLE 6.6
Correlation Between Content Structure and Prominence of Coverage of Events

Dimension	News Factor	Prominence (news value indicator)			
		Frequence	Position	Length	Presentation
Status	Elite nation	.03	.06	−.04	−.05
	Elite institution	.05	.15*	.02	−.13
	Elite person	.06	.11*	.25*	.24*
Valence	Aggression	.08*	.01	−.09*	−.02
	Controversy	.10*	.10*	.12*	.01
	Values	.08*	.09*	.09*	.09*
	Success				
Relevance	Consequence	.15*	.27*	.25*	.15*
	Concern	.01	.06	.11*	−.03
Identification	Proximity	.06	.05	.06	.14*
	Ethnocentrism	.01	.00	−.07	−.06
	Personalization	−.03	.21*	−.15*	−.09*
	Emotions	.09*	.02	.18*	.23*
Consonance	Theme	.08*	.21*	.00	.10*
	Stereotype	.07	.11*	.16*	.22*
	Predictability	.01	−.01	.29*	.40*
Dynamics	Timeliness	.05	.00	.06	.14*
	Uncertainty	.09*	.09*	.08*	.05
	Unexpectedness	.09*	.09*	.08*	.05
Multiple correlation of all news factors		.36	.49	.57	.58

Source: Schulz, 1982. Reprinted by permission of the publisher
* Significance level p <.05

television newscast broadcast by BBC television in the United Kingdom, Robinson and Sahin (1984) questioned focus groups about the content of the programme. Under these viewing conditions, the researchers found that, contrary to earlier findings, participants exhibited a reasonable level of understanding of the news. They were able to grasp the central point of many of the stories in the bulletin they had just seen.

There were variations, however, in the types of story they were best able to comprehend properly. Highly technical stories about abstract political or economic issues were understood poorly. However, items containing human interest elements, such as how a Scottish driver was able to survive being covered in a snowdrift for several days, a story about Soviet cosmonauts in space, another about why a woman doctor became involved in an LSD ring, and another about a soccer official's reaction to a report on soccer hooliganism, were all comprehended quite fully. According to the researchers, high audience comprehension can be accomplished particularly if the viewers find the story or its presentation done in an interesting or visually appealing way.

Robinson and Sahin reported that viewers preferred accounts that "brought the story to them" in human "eyewitness" terms. They have as examples a *doctor's* account of how the Scottish driver was able to survive being buried alone in the snow; the dangers of an oil rig going aground as retold by *sailors* in the pub rather than by the ship's officers or company officials; and interviews with train riders affected by a rail strike (Robinson & Sahin, 1984, p. 13).

Viewers sometimes enjoyed having specific story details described to them rather than a single summary statement. The use of diagrams and mock-ups to embellish a story were generally liked. What was not so welcome was statistical and quantitative information. Indeed, Robinson says that statistics were often greeted with scepticism because the same figures were often seen to be used by different politicians to support opposite sides of an argument.

The focus groups indicated that viewers do want to have things ex-

TABLE 6.7
Correlation Between Content Structure and Frequency of
Coverage and Awareness of Events

Dimension	News Factor	Frequency	Awareness
Status	Elite nation	.03	.02
	Elite institution	.05	−.01
	Elite person	.06	.09*
Valence	Aggression	.08*	.09*
	Controversy	.10*	.03
	Values	.08*	.09*
	Success	.02	.02
Relevance	Consequence	.15*	.11*
	Concern	.01	−.01
Identification	Proximity	.06	.11*
	Ethnocentrism	.01	.00
	Personalization	−.03	.03
	Emotions	.09*	.12*
Consonance	Theme	.08*	.07
	Stereotype	.07	−.05
	Predictability	.07	.01
Dynamics	Timeliness	.05	.01
	Uncertainty	.09*	.11*
	Unexpectedness	.09*	.11*
Multiple correlation of all news factors		.36	.27

Source: Schulz, 1982. Reprinted by permission of the publisher
* Significance level p <.05

plained to them but in simple terms that they can readily understand. Emphasising the human elements of a story can boost interest and appreciation, while excessive statistical information turns people off.

In a separate study of viewers' recall of information from a single evening's newscast on each of four evenings, Robinson and Sahin examined relationships between memory performance, and story structure and presentation characteristics.

Some of these stories were recalled by over 75% of the audience, others by less than 10%. How did the various characteristics of the stories themselves relate to their comprehension and retention by the audience?

Robinson and Sahin identified and measured some 25 story characteristics in terms of their relation to comprehension. Included among these were: length of the item, position of the item in the bulletin, percentage of story time for which the presenter was on screen, and use of film or graphic material.

Other characteristics in terms of which news stories were analysed were inspired by the work of Schulz (1976). He developed a specific coding instruction for such news item characteristics as "ethnocentrism," "personalization," "degree of conflict," "surprise," "complexity of portrayal," "proximity," "pre-eminence," and "centrality." Robinson and Sahin added four more factors to the list: "extent of human interest," "overall excitement," "connection to the preceding item," and "extent of editorial interpretation in the verbal content accompanying the story." The length of the item, its position in the newscast, and the percentage of time the newsreader was on the screen could be measured objectively. The other 22 factors required the subjective judgment of three judges.

Both presentation and content factors were found to be related to news comprehension. The position of the item in the bulletin was found to affect how well it was comprehended. However, the findings did not corroborate previous research evidence on serial position effects during learning; the first item in the newscast was not the item that was most highly comprehended. Instead, Robinson found that peak comprehension often did not occur until well into the middle of the newscast.

The last story, in line with the evidence of previous research, however, generally scored above average in comprehension, and always higher than the story that preceded it. Robinson suggests that we should not be too surprised by this, inasmuch as the last story is usually deliberately chosen to be interesting, attention-grabbing, and upbeat.

Length effects were evident. Longer stories were comprehended at a higher rate. In the four evening newscasts from which memory and comprehension were tested, of the 14 stories that had high comprehension, only one was shorter than 30 seconds. On the other hand, of the 12 stories that had low comprehension, seven were shorter than 30 seconds.

Robinson and Sahin examined all their story factors in relation to comprehension and found that just 9 out of 25 correlated significantly with comprehension. Of these nine, four predominated: length of item; lower proportion of time with the newsreader on camera (usually true for longer stories); human interest; and overall excitement. All of these factors correlated over .50 with comprehension. The fifth most important story factor was degree of personalization in the story, which correlated .45 with comprehension. Factors such as conflict, proximity, relevance, ethnocentrism, and amount of interpretation showed virtually no significant relation to comprehension.

Robinson and Sahin conducted a series of multiple classification analyses in order to find out the independent contribution of each news factor to news comprehension with the effects of all the other factors statistically controlled. From these analyses, degree of human interest emerged as the major predictor of comprehension. Greater quantities of that factor were associated with 2.2 more points on the comprehension scale than were low amounts. Independently of the human interest in the story, the overall "excitement" of the story was also associated with higher comprehension. The length of the story was important too, at about the same level as excitement but well below that of human interest.

TABLE 6.8
Differences in Story Comprehension as a Function of Five
Major Story Characteristics

Factor		Stories	Unadjusted Mean	Adjusted Mean	
Length of story	Low	16	2.4	2.4	
	Medium	15	2.8	2.9	
	High	9	3.8	3.5	High-Low = +1.1
% Newsreader on camera	Low	13	2.1	3.0	
	Medium	11	3.7	3.6	
	High	16	3.5	2.3	High-Low = −0.7
Human Interest	Low	13	1.9	2.4	
	Medium	10	2.7	2.6	
	High	17	3.8	4.6	High-Low = +2.2
Excitement	Low	14	1.7	2.0	
	Medium	16	3.4	3.3	
	High	10	3.6	3.5	High-Low = +1.5
Personalization	Low	15	2.3	3.3	
	Medium	13	2.5	2.0	
	High	12	4.1	3.2	High-Low = −0.1

Source: Robinson and Sahin, 1984. Reprinted by permission of the author
Note: Overall average for all stories = 2.9 Entries are average comprehension scores for each story on 1–8 scale.

CONFLICT IN THE NEWS

At the beginning of this chapter we discussed evidence that indicated that modern news broadcasts on television, at least in the United States, have tended to emphasize conflict and violence in the news. Some writers have argued that television news tends to simplify social conflicts by focusing on their manifest characteristics and minimising coverage and discussion of their underlying causes. Murdock (1973) for instance, has referred to this as "event orientation." Television news focuses on overt actions and events, which of course can be filmed, but seldom goes into detail about why events occurred. Cognitive researchers have found that careful explication of the causes of events can significantly enhance comprehension of news stories (Findahl & Hoijer, 1976).

It has been contended elsewhere that television news tends to emphasise the more intense moments of social conflicts, again often because these events make for good film. Hall (1973) observed that in coverage of social conflicts the news media concentrate on "vivid sound and image" (p. 9). This point has been illustrated by several studies of television news coverage of riots. Tuchman (1978) noted that whereas riots in actuality seldom feature continuous intense, violent activity, being characterised rather by sporadic outbursts and periods of calm, "news reports usually ignore this, collapsing the course of riots into continuous intense activity" (pp. 190–191).

Some researchers have accused television news of bias in the presentation of conflicts. Intensive, often violent or disruptive activity tends to be associated with particular groups who are not representatives of the political and economic power centres of society. The Glasgow University Media Group (1976) found in their extensive content analysis of British network television news that coverage of industrial disputes tends to depict management in calm office settings and as sources of authority, reason, and responsibility, whereas strikers are shown in noisier location settings at mass meetings or picket lines.

Sociological theorists tell us that most social conflicts can be and are eventually solved, usually when opposing parties reach a mutually agreeable compromise. It is not unusual, however, for fresh conflict to recur, and this can be seen commonly in industrial disputes. The degree of difficulty of solving a social conflict depends on the nature of the incompatible goals of the parties and the cost of the possible outcomes (Oberschall, 1973).

Television news, however, tends to simplify matters. Conflicts are presented as matters to be resolved and as resolvable in the short term. Some sociologists have interpreted this as indicating that television news attempts to impart an impression of a society characterised by consensus, a place where agreements can easily be reached by conflicting parties, thus reinforcing the status quo.

160

In an international study of television news, Cohen and Bantz (1984) reported on the frequency with which television news in five countries—the United States, West Germany, Britain, South Africa, and Israel—reported social conflicts on domestic and foreign fronts during December 1980. In general, three quarters of all items were devoted to politics, economics, and law enforcement matters. Social issues were virtually ignored, yielding only 5% of the total items. More coverage was given to the reporting of disasters than to all the problems under such headings as environment, health, education, housing, and immigration. On the lighter side, human interest stories, cultural, and ceremonial stories and sports comprised just 10% of items. This analysis therefore revealed that much of the television news in these countries had a serious tone.

The distribution of conflict items in the news revealed differences between the five countries. South African news appeared least conflictual (34%), followed by the United States (35%), West Germany (38%), while Israel and Britain carried the highest proportion of items on social conflicts (60% each).

On the international political scene, all of the countries produced more conflictual than nonconflictual stories. Stories about domestic politics without social conflict were predominant in the United States and West Germany. This pattern was reversed in Britain. The United States, in common with Israel and South Africa, portrayed the world outside their borders as being full of tensions and disputes, but the world inside their own borders as relatively peaceful. For Britain, the political scene was presented as being synonymous with tension and social conflict both at home and abroad.

In addition to providing a count of the occurrences of social conflict on television in different countries, Cohen and Bantz also examined the characteristics of the way this kind of news was reported. Looking further at the number of items on American and British television news that contained aggression, for example, they found that 37% of U.S. conflict items (where 35% of all items were found to be conflict items) featured verbally reported physical aggression, 17% had visually shown physical aggression, 9% had verbally reported verbal aggression, 4% had shown verbal aggression, 2% had verbally reported emotional display, and 9% had visually shown emotional display. Of British conflict items (where 36% of all items were conflict items), 52% had verbally reported physical aggression, 22% had visually shown physical aggression, 33% had verbally reported verbal aggression, 14% had visually shown verbal aggression, 5% had verbally reported emotional display, and 22% had visually shown emotional display.

One point particularly worth noting is that physical aggression is more likely to be verbally reported and visually shown with foreign items than with domestic ones. Thus, the items with which viewers are likely to have less familiarity and may exhibit less interest and concern about are also the ones presented with content likely to distract attention away from the essential meaning of the narrative. But how do audiences cope with violent news? What effect does the showing of violence on film have on retention and comprehension of accompanying story narrative?

MEMORY FOR VIOLENT NEWS

There have been a small number of experimental studies that have investigated memory for violent and nonviolent broadcast news material. Cohen, Wigand, and Harrison (1976) compared young viewers' retention of emotion-arousing versus neutral events from a simulated television newscast. Six of these newscasts were prepared, each containing 12 news items, of which 6 were judged to be emotionally loaded and six were judged to be neutral. These broadcasts were prepared by professional staff at a local television station and read by the station's usual newscaster. Among the emotionally loaded items, two were designated as "sad" items, two as "happy" items, and two as "violent" items. All these items were accompanied by film footage, whereas the neutral items were read by the newscaster with a still photograph or illustration projected in the background.

The children saw the newscast and then were asked to recall spontaneously all the items they could remember from it. Following this test of unaided recall, they were given four multiple-choice questions per story, which probed for in-depth knowledge. Results showed significantly greater free recall for emotionally loaded items than for neutral items. Unfortunately, it is not really possible to ascertain from this study what precisely the effects of "tone" were on memory for the news, because emotionality was confounded with format. Emotionally arousing items were also items with film or other visual inputs, whereas neutral items were delivered by "talking heads." It has been reliably demonstrated elsewhere that such format variations alone can produce significant differences in news recall. Furthermore, the emotionality of the items was judged by independent adult judges and not by the children themselves or even by a matched sample of other children. Consequently, there could be doubts about the meaningfulness or validity of this news classification employed here from the point of view of the members of the audience.

Several experimental studies in Britain have measured retention of content from violent news stories. All of these studies were laboratory based and used small unrepresentative samples. Nevertheless, they have yielded an interesting set of findings about the effects of arousing subject matter on memory for the news.

Two experiments conducted by the author and his colleagues have already been discussed in part in Chapter 3 (Furnham & Gunter, 1985; Gunter, Furnham, & Gietson, 1984). There are aspects to them that are of relevance to the current discussion, however, so some of their findings will be mentioned again here briefly. In these studies, small samples of teenagers and young adults were presented with two violent and two nonviolent news stories audio-visually, in audio only, or as written transcripts. Recall of narrative content was then tested immediately after presentation.

The four news items had been recorded from television news broadcasts. Each item consisted of a film report with voice-overs by an unseen male newsreader. Two items depicted violent events—scenes of street clashes between rioters and police in El Salvador and in South Korea—and two depicted nonviolent events about the lifting of trade restrictions by Japan and about a visit to Yugoslavia by the Greek Prime Minister. Film footage from El Salvador depicted individuals crouching behind makeshift barricades with handguns, shooting at others across the street. Over this, the narrator described the reasons for the rioting. Footage from South Korea depicted rioters throwing rocks and stones at the police, and police officers in return were seen clubbing upturned demonstrators. The story about Japan lifting its trade restrictions told of how tariffs were being reduced on a variety of goods in respose to growing criticism from the United States and EEC. Film footage depicted delegates arriving in Versailles and settling down into a summit meeting concerning this and other trade matters. Finally, the item from Yugoslavia depicted scenes from the visit there by the Greek Prime Minister and told of the reasons for the visit.

The first experiment (Gunter, Furnham, & Gietson, 1984) found that recall was significantly better from violent stories than from the nonviolent stories across all presentation conditions. An interaction between sex of receiver and story-type indicated better recall by males than by females of content from the violent news items, whereas little difference occurred between the sexes in their recall from the nonviolent items. A marginally significant interaction between presentation modality and story-type meanwhile reflected better recall from violent news stories when presented simply as written transcripts than in either the audio-visual or audio-only conditions. Much smaller differences existed between presentation modalities for recall from nonviolent stories.

Furnham and Gunter (1985) failed to find an overall difference in recall from the same violent and nonviolent news stories across three presentation modalities with a different sample. What emerged instead were a series of significant interactions between the sex of the receiver, type of story, and presentation modality. In the audio-visual (or television) condition only, when the narratives of the violent news items were presented with violent film footage, recall from these stories was significantly better among males than females. For recall from the nonviolent stories in this modality, however, females exhibited significantly better recall than males. These experiments indicate therefore that presenting violent film footage can affect memory for accompanying story narrative, but that this effect may not be the same for all viewers.

Berry and Clifford (1985) examined the effects on news learning of two visual treatments of a horrific news item about El Salvador concluding with the execution of a student by the army. Berry and Clifford predicted that "the showing of violent action would impair the uptake of news detail, particularly in the condition in which the execution was witnessed on the screen, compared with a sound-only condition."

Sixteen male and 16 female subjects were shown a television newsfilm report from El Salvador, containing the shooting of a student prisoner by the army. There were three versions, all with the same soundtrack featuring the original sound and newsreader's voice-over: (a) the news item as actually presented on television; (b) the same as (a), except that the film was frozen at the sight of the first casualty in the street fighting preceding the execution; and (c) sound-only with no pictures.

Memory for the spoken narrative was tested via free recall immediately after presentation, followed by a cued recall test of 16 questions on the narrative's content. Both tests were repeated 6 weeks later to examine delayed memory for the news.

Berry and Clifford found that the portrayal of violent action reduced the informational impact of the news text in both immediate and delayed tests. However, this effect was due entirely to the performance of the female subjects, who did significantly less well under each of the visualisation conditions than under the sound-only conditions, though they did not differ between the visual conditions. Males showed no statistically significant differences between any of the presentation conditions. Both free and cued recall deteriorated substantially after 6 weeks delay delay—especially for males in the visual presentation conditions.

Although it was observed in earlier chapters that the provision of pictures to illustrate news stories can aid memory for story content, we see here that the enhancement effect of visuals may depend on the types of events they depict. Scenes of horrific violence can have negative rather than beneficial effects on reception of a news story's verbal narrative. Berry and Clifford recommend that words and pictures should be separated when the words carry important detailed information and the pictures depict potentially highly arousing violent events.

HUMOR IN THE NEWS

At the beginning of this chapter we saw that with the introduction of formats designed to popularise the news on television, news programmes exhibited shifts towards various affectively toned categories of story and gave greater emphasis to human interest stories, violence, and humor. We have just seen that early research indications are that care is needed with violent news, especially when violence is visually depicted, if the meaning of the story is to reach the audience. But what of the story with more positively toned content? Is humor in the news likely to influence learning and comprehension? And if so, will this influence be positive or negative?

Humorous content has been used in educational programmes for much the same reason as it has been used in news programmes—to boost popularity. Programmes that can provide gratification to audiences in terms of entertainment are likely to prove more competitive for viewers. Wakshlag, Day, and Zillmann (1980) conducted an experiment to explore the effects of humor in an educational television programme on the extent to which children chose to view it rather than other versions without humor. In addition to manipulating the humorous content of the programme they also varied the pace of the humor. Five- and 6-year old children were given the freedom to select for themselves the programme they preferred, and their selections were recorded. The presence of humor in a programme greatly facilitated popularity. Both boys and girls spent more time watching the programme with humorous episodes. The pace of the humor was important too. Fast-paced humorous episodes attracted young viewers more than slower-paced versions of the programme. The same effects were found in a subsequent study with adolescents (Schleicher, Bryant, & Zillmann, 1980).

Where programmes are designed primarily to convey information, however, it becomes important to inquire whether they can still perform this function even when they adopt entertainment-oriented formats to attract viewers? What effect does humor and the pacing of humorous episodes in a programme have on learning from it? The Singers have challenged the efficacy of fast-paced educational programmes to get information across to their audiences (Singer & Singer, 1979; Singer, 1980). They believed that rapid-fire educational or informational television formats rarely allow sufficient time for effective rehearsal or storage of new input and ultimately work to stunt the development of cognitive skills essential to effective information processing.

There are concerns also that entertaining stimuli within educational programmes serve mainly to distract attention from the instructional elements of the programme and thus impair learning. One theory is that enjoyment of a humorous segment spreads to a subsequent, educational segment and interferes with reception of the latter's information (Schramm, 1973).

Early research on the effects of humor in instructional films, mainly conducted with captive and attentive military audiences, tended to support the conclusion that the involvement of humor is more a hindrance than a help in accomplishing educational objectives (Lumsdaine & Gladstone, 1958; McIntyre, 1954).

McGhee (1980) added the suggestion that humor in educational television might create a playful frame of mind that would interfere with the acquisition of novel information mainly because it would make any rehearsal, which could be construed as effortful, seem undesirable or unnecessary.

Although humor has been considered by most writers as having negative effects on learning, and was shown to have such effects in early studies with instructional films, more recently evidence has emerged that suggests that where the humor is semantically integrated with the educational or informational content, learning may be enhanced (Chapman & Compton, 1978; Davies & Apter, 1980).

In research with specially prepared educational television materials, Zillmann and his colleagues found that humorous segments could enhance information acquisition even though not semantically related to the educational content of the programme (Bryant, Zillmann, Wolf, & Reardon, 1980; Zillmann, Williams, Bryant, Boynton, & Wolf, 1980). They suggested that humor could have an alerting function among audiences whose attention to an informational programme begins to wane after a short time. Furthermore, Zillmann suggested, in line with previous work, that enhanced vigilance produced by an orienting response to the humor could carry over to subsequent nonhumorous segments of the programme (cf. Berlyne, 1960, 1970; Tannenbaum & Zillmann, 1975) and thus facilitate learning more generally from the programme. This hypothesis was supported by their results. Humor improved learning not only for the programme segments it accompanied but also for those nonhumorous segments that followed, compared to a totally nonhumorous version of the programme. One word of caution should be noted here. These findings were all made with children under the age of 10 years, and even among these, there was some indication that the learning-facilitating effect of humor becomes weaker with increasing age. The important question is: Does this effect weaken still further with older viewers, and to what extent?

An earlier investigation indicated that with adult audiences the impact of humor on learning from educational presentations may depend more importantly than among children on the way humor is used. Kaplan and Pascoe (1977) studied the effect of humor and humorous examples upon the comprehension and retention of audio-visual lecture material. University students viewed either a serious lecture or one of three versions of a humorous lecture. The latter three included humorous examples related to the concepts in the lecture (concept humor), unrelated to these concepts (nonconcept humor), or related to only some of the concepts (mixed humor). Comprehension and retention were tested immediately after presentation and again 6 weeks later.

Results indicated that immediate test performance was not enhanced by the use of humorous examples in any way. Six weeks later, however, retention of concept-humor material was significantly improved by having viewed a lecture with humorous examples illustrating concepts. Interestingly, overall levels of comprehension did not vary significantly across different versions of the lecture. In the concept-humor presentation, audience attention was apparently focused on the humorous examples, while processing of information not humorously embellished was distracted. Perhaps the lesson to be learned from this research for news programming is that humorous content (i.e., humorous news stories) may impede learning of adjacent nonhumorous content (nonhumorous stories), unless used with great care.

CONCLUDING REMARKS

This chapter considered the importance for news retention of the types of news and characteristics (often reflecting professional judgments of newsworthiness) of news stories. It began with the observation that television news formats have undergone changes over the years that have in some cases resulted in shifts in the types of stories presented in news programmes and in the ingredients regarded by news producers as important to story selection. Stories selected for news broadcasts as currently the most "newsworthy" are assumed to be those that are likely to hold the greatest interest for audiences. Along with this judgement goes the assumption that the newsworthy stories will also have considerable impact on viewers and listeners. The extent to which stories that best satisfy the criteria of newsworthiness adopted by news professionals are the stories best learned and remembered by audience members, however, is an empirical question that in tuitive editorial judgement alone cannot answer.

Tests of broadcast news recall have indicated that certain categories of news do seem to be better remembered than others. Nationwide television news bulletins typically cover a mixture of foreign as well as domestic stories. It is usually the domestic stories that are best remembered afterwards, however. There are exceptions to this pattern when, for example, a particular foreign story has special implications or relevance on the domestic front.

Prominent among the ingredients prized by many news editors are violence, human interest, and humour. Violent events may often provide exciting film footage that lends an especially highly valued ingredient of dramatic actuality to the news, believed to enhance the programme's impact. There is mounting evidence from experimental research, however, that this sort of film footage can distract attention from the story narrative, where the essential meaning of the story is usually carried, with the result that memory and comprehension of the story are impaired.

Furthermore, certain sections of the audience may be particularly sensitive to such distracting film material and be especially likely to have their understanding of the story detrimentally affected by it.

Humor in the news is something that has been present from the early days of news broadcasting, but with the adoption of clearly more entertainment-oriented formats in television news (more especially in the United States than anywhere else), there has, according to some researchers, been an increase in the amount of humorous content in the news. Experimental research with educational television programming has pointed to the need for caution in the way humor is used with informational audio-visual material, however, because, as with violence, there is a danger that humor may distract attention away from the narrative content, thereby producing impaired comprehension. Humor can be useful when it provides direct support in a meaningful informational sense for the essential informational content carried in the narrative; otherwise it · may do more harm than good. This is not to recommend totally against the inclusion of humorous items in the news. The heaviness of hard news stories needs to be balanced by light-hearted, humorous, or human interest items to retain the interest and attention of viewers tired of highly complex issues or news of a depressing or emotionally upsetting quality. From the perspective of achieving effective cognitive information processing of programme content, however, it is important for producers to realise that extensive use of potentially distracting light material may produce an attentional imbalance towards the programme that could have a serious deleterious effect on comprehension of the informational material at the harder end of the news spectrum.

7 Telling the Story Effectively

According to many practical guides to news writing, one of the most important considerations of broadcast news style is clarity (Fang, 1968; Green, 1969). The reason for this is quite simple. Unlike the newspaper reader, the radio listener or television viewer cannot go back over a story again at his or her own pace to get the story clear in his or her own mind. Either an item is understood when it is presented or it is lost for good, or at least until the next bulletin comes around, when it may or may not be repeated. Any listener or viewer who pauses to think about what the newsreader has just said may lose not only that bit of news but also news that is being given subsequently.

Clear writing is a skill that can be developed. Furthermore, it need not rely for its development on trial and error or on good and bad experiences of the practicing journalist. Clarity of writing style and the comprehensibility of narrative structures have been empirically investigated by educational researchers and recently also by cognitive psychologists. This work has led to certain principles of discourse processing that may in turn provide practical implications for better news-writing style, thus enhancing the ease with which broadcast news can be assimilated by the audience. Studies of readability have tried to develop formulae to measure the ease with which children can learn and comprehend subject matter delivered via various writing styles in school books. The best-known worker in this field is Rudolf Flesch. Later, Robert Cunning and others applied the same principles to the analysis of business writing, periodical publications, and news wire copy. Fang (1968) reported further research on clear writing in television news. From an analysis of 36 network and local news scripts and stories from six major U.S. newspapers, Fang developed a formula which he called ELF, for Easy Listening Formula. ELF is simply this: "*In any sentence, count each syllable above one per word.* Take a second look at any sentence scoring above 20. It may be perfectly clear, but chances are it can be improved by trimming adjectives or adverbs, extracting clauses or dividing into two sentences" (p.107). Thus, one-syllable words score zero, two-syllable words score one, three-syllable words score two, and so on. The formula operates on the simple premise that short words are easy to assimilate and understand; longer words are usually more difficult.

It is not necessary always to use short sentences to produce a low ELF score, and Fang gives as an example a fairly long sentence with a zero sore: "This is the cow that kicked the dog that chased the cat that killed the rat that ate the malt that lay in the house that Jack built" (p.108). The main essential is that multisyllabic words should be kept to a minimum. Long words usually represent complex, abstract ideas. Although it is inevitable that such ideas will have to be reported in the news at some time, abstract information can best be sent in small packages or, in other words, short sentences. It is not just sentence length and word difficulty that are important to comprehension of broadcast news narratives, however, but also the way news stories themselves are structured and told to the audience. In American newspaper journalism, which was of course well founded long before broadcast news came on the scene, a style of reporting developed known as the "inverted pyramid," and although not universally acclaimed was nevertheless widely used. In this style of writing the most important facts are told first, followed by lesser facts in descending order of importance. The first sentence usually has the "five Ws"— who, what, when, where and why. The headline first tells the story in microcosm, then the five-W lead retells it more clearly and with little detail. The next three paragraphs or so may provide further retelling garnished with still more detail. The remainder of the story may repeat it over again. Hence, there is a great deal of repetition. One advantage of the inverted pyramid style of writing was that it enabled busy newspaper copy editors to trim a story from the bottom to the top as it was assembled, without losing essential elements of the story.

With the emergence of broadcast news, first on radio and then on television, a new style of writing developed that was more suited to these new media. For example, stories on radio and television have to be told in a more conversational style, which resembles that of ordinary spoken dialogue. The difference between news-speak and ordinary speech, however, is that the former attempts to communicate with grammatical sentence structures more so than is generally true of the latter. Writing styles for radio and later for television news developed over the years largely through trial and experience. In general, changes were ad hoc rather than systematic and planned. If a particular style sounded good, it was retained and used again.

Television news grew out of radio news, and although there are certain similarities between them, the style of radio news writing is not exactly the same as that required for television newscasting. The principal difference between the two media, of course, is the visual channel of television. When visual illustrations such as moving film or stills and graphics are used, the narrative must relate in some way to the pictures. It is important that the visual and narrative elements relate to and support one another. When they do not, gross miscomprehension and failure to learn the essential facts and meaning of a news story can result. Unfortunately, it is often the case that pictures on television news have priority, while the words are built around them. This can give rise to awkward or disjointed narrative structures, which may function to impair significantly the uptake and comprehension of televised news stories. In this chapter we examine the narrative structures of broadcast news and look at work that has been done on the psychology of discourse processing. This research is concerned with learning from connected/spoken or written/discourse and may have implications of fundamental importance to mass communication research and producers of broadcast news.

An area of human learning research that may be labeled "the psychology of discourse processing" has developed over the years and is concerned with elaborating the cognitive principles of comprehension and remembering texts or narratives. Cognitive pscyhologists have developed models designed to show how extended discourses are processed and entered into memory This may provide an interesting new perspective in research on comprehension and memory of broadcast news and provide fresh insights into why this particular communication process often seems to break down. Such research may also carry important practical implications for news writers regarding how to tell their stories more effectively from the point of view of achieving higher levels of audience news comprehension. Psychological research into the way we process extended prose materials has indicated that narratives may have different structures, and some structures can be more easily and effectively processed than others, even though the contents of the narratives are essentially the same. Another important finding to emerge from this work, however, is that understanding discourse efficiently often depends on having a certain amount of relevant background knowledge of the world.

BASIC PRINCIPLES FOR THE ANALYSIS OF DISCOURSE

Verbal narratives such as those occurring in broadcast news can be analysed on a number of different levels and with respect to a variety of different elements, both structural and semantic. There are *surface structures,* which include *phonological features* such as the sounds and intonations of words; *morphological features* concerning the formation of words (number of syllables per word) and *syntactical features* that provide a set of rules according to which words can be strung together to form sentences. Then there are *semantic structures* which concern the meanings carried by words, phrases, sentences, or passages of discourse. These meaning structures are assumed to exist at a deeper level than the more physical surface structures. In addition to these levels of analysis, there are different units or elements that make up narratives. These include individual words (or lexical items), clauses embedded within sentences, complete sentences, sequences of sentences or paragraphs, and finally whole discourses. A distinction can be made here between *local* and *global structures;* the former refer to sentences or particular connections between sentences, while the latter refer to paragraph structrures or even the entire discourse.

It is possible to carry out analysis of discourse at these various levels, focusing on the local dimensions, such as the meanings or physical structures of words and sentences, or more globally looking at the themes conveyed by the discourse as a whole. Any mode of analysis that directly concerns the contents of the discourse is called *textual.* Some researchers have pointed out in addition, however, that discourses are not simply isolated linguistic entities but exist in a socio-cultural framework that is also important to the way the discourse is interpreted and understood. A narrative may therefore be analysed also in terms of the latter *contextual* properties.

DISCOURSE ANALYSIS AND MASS COMMUNICATION RESEARCH

Sociological studies of newsrooms have indicated that news is not simply a description of events but is a specific kind of reconstruction of reality. This reconstruction is determined by professional practices concerned with ways of how best to present news and in line with the norms and values of the society in which the news is made. News production has been revealed as a complex set of processes and professional routines that govern the selection and appropriate formulation of news stories for presentation to mass audiences. News production is not a direct representation of events, however, no matter what many journalists might claim

172

and irrespective of the supposed intentions of "eyewitness" news formats. Often reporters are not direct witnesses to events; instead their accounts are derived from discourses from other sources, such as eyewitness reports, press conferences, official statements, interviews, or news input from other media or press agencies. Hence, the construction of the news as we see or hear it is frequently a reconstruction of available discourses. The way news editors and reporters place their own interpretations on these discourses has an important bearing on the way the news is structured and presented, which in turn may have significant consequences for the comprehensibility of the final news product received by the audience.

Work in the psychology of discourse processing has made progress towards a better understanding of how readers and listeners assimilate and comprehend narratives. This work has provided important insights into how narratives are operated upon in short-term memory during the initial stages of comprehension and then how discourses are finally represented in and retrieved from long-term memory, and in particular have indicated the crucial role of world knowledge in these processes of understanding and representation. Discourse-processing research has shown that memory for extended narratives tends principally to be semantic. However, effective comprehension and retrieval of the theme or topic of a narrative depends to a considerable extent also on the schematic or structural organization of the text itself and upon the perspective or goals of the receiver. We have seen already in earlier chapters that background knowledge and degree of attention to the news are important mediators of comprehension and retention of broadcast news messages. Over and above these factors, however, is the question of how the narratives of news are themselves formulated. And as we see in the remainder of this chapter, narrative structures can be manipulated in specific ways to improve levels of news comprehension even among those audience members who may lack appropriate background knowledge concerning the events in question or current affairs more generally.

LEXICAL AND SENTENCE FEATURES

Comprehension of discourses may be affected by the style of the surface structures they employ. This means that the kinds of words they use to describe events and also the length and complexity of sentences can either be such that a narrative is easy to follow and process or such that it is difficult to assimilate information from. Avoidance of too many abstract concepts or unusual words and use of short sentences with standard noun-phrase/verb-phrase (or subject-predicate-object) structures may enhance comprehensibility of discourses.

Again at the level of the lexicon, research on the cognitive processing of connected discourse has shown that concrete analogies can make abstract, complex information more imaginable, vivid, and hence easy to understand and learn (Davidson, 1976; Ortony, 1975). Other research suggest that the benefits of analogies lie in the fact that they allow learners to use existing and relevant background knowledge while assimilating new information, and this aids the overall learning process (e.g., see Norman, 1978; Rumelhart and Ortony, 1977). Another important function that has been identified for deeply and actively (Mayer, 1979a, 1979b).

Some writers have argued, however, that more interesting than these fairly straightforward relationships between the structural features of narratives and understanding are the possible social implications of stylistic variation (van Dijk, 1983). The kinds of words or sentence structures that are used to describe certain news events may indicate specific ideological perspectives placed on analysis of these events by news producers. Halloran (1970) has shown, for instance, that the descriptions used in the press to characterise participants in demonstrations against intervention in Vietnam—"hooligans," "thugs," "horde," etc.—often carry negative connotations or implications, and the same holds for the actions and properties described by verbs and adjectives. Van Dijk (1983) noted similar systematic differences between the lexical description of demonstrators by the national press agency and the popular newspapers in the Netherlands, following police action against squatters. The Glasgow University Media Group (1976) has shown that, in the coverage of industrial affairs, the news will typically choose lexical items to denote workers and their actions ("strike," "disruptive actions," etc.) that are more negative than the items chosen to denote the actions of the employers or management.

Other researchers have focused on the syntactic structures of sentences and have found differences in the way various groups are reported in terms of the tense of the sentence. Fowler, Hodge, Kress, and Trew (1979) discovered, for instance, that if the police are reported to be the agents of violent actions, such agency is not expressed in the more active first-position-subject proposition, as is usual, but rather "suppressed" in passive sentences, such as "Many demonstrators were hurt."

Although lexical choice is a typical phenomenon at the local level of sentence structure, it is also relevant for discourse analysis because a whole discourse will typically exhibit some kind of stylistic coherence. The choice of certain descriptors can affect the whole tone of a narrative and hence determine to a great extent the impression of events transmitted to the audience. Cognitive psychologists have found that it is this overall concept that often is most readily retrieved in memory (Kintsch & van Dijk, 1978). Thus, although lexicalisation is usually treated as a surface structure phenomenon of language use, it is in fact halfway between the surface structure and underlying semantic structures of meaning.

Belson (1967) reported a study of comprehension of a series of radio broadcasts called "Topic for Tonight," which consisted of short talks presenting the background to current news events. Among other things, comprehension of these programmes was related to the structure and composition of the talks themselves. Altogether, over 1,000 people were recruited from the London area to listen to single talks in groups of 35 to 50 people. A recording of a talk was played to the group in a theatre setting, and comprehension of its content was tested via written replies immediately afterwards.

A number of programme factors were found to be related significantly to comprehension levels. The most important factors were the degree to which the talk was systematically presented, with its main points emphasised, and the frequency with which difficult or unfamiliar words were used. Talks that were presented in a well organized, economic way and that placed emphasis on the main points of the topic under discussion tended to be better understood. Talks in which the argument or theme was not systematically developed, where summaries and other ways of emphasising points were not used, and where the task of organizing the material was left to the listener were relatively poorly understood and remembered.

TABLE 7.1
Narrative Structure Correlates of Programme Comprehension

Variables	Correlation with comprehension
Goodness of logical structure and emphasis on main points	0.65
Frequency of difficult or unfamiliar words	−0.56
Estimated ease of the talk as estimated by independent judges	0.52
Frequency of numerical references	0.47
Flesch Readability Index	0.27
Estimate of simplicity of sentences by independent judges	0.24
Sentence length	−0.12
Speed of reading	0.05
Frequency of use of various parts of speech (per 100 words)	
adverbs	0.23
number of active verbs	0.21
personal pronouns	0.24
prepositions	0.02
abstract nouns	−0.27
adjectives	−0.34

Source: Belson, 1967, p. 143. Reprinted by permission of the author.

Belson observed that in fact structural weaknesses such as those just outlined tended to characterise many of the talks, and it was therefore not surprising that listeners often picked up only random snippets of information from them, with the main points being retained little better than minor or incidental details. He argued that had listeners perhaps been given more time to ponder over the narrative, understanding might have been better. However, in broadcasting, whether on radio or television, the audience must move at a pace determined by the programme-maker.

Looking at the other programme factors analysed in this study, Belson found that the Flesch Index of Readability, based upon counts of sentence length, number of affixes per 100 words, and number of personal references per 100 words was predictive of comprehension to only a small degree. On the other hand, direct rating of comprehensibility of specific talks by independent judges provided a much better predictor of comprehension by the audience.

TEXT ORGANIZATION AND MEMORY FOR DISCOURSE

Educational and cognitive psychologists have extensively investigated the influence of global organizational features of texts on learning from passages of discourse. Research has indicated that a text whose information has been organized in a certain way can be learned and understood better than one lacking a structural coherence.

Structural frameworks that embody specifications concerning how information in narratives can best be organized to produce meaningful stories may be represented in the knowledge systems of individuals as text schemata. A text schema consists of a set of rules on how events and their consequences can be combined to produce meaningful episodes and how a set of episodes, in turn, can be linked together so that they produce a complete story with a beginning, middle, and conclusion.

It was Bartlett (1932) who first proposed that narrative discourse is remembered with the aid of an abstract structural schema. Since then, a number of cognitive researchers have tried to develop models that reflect the way texts are organised in memory. Different writers have provided empirical testimony for the efficacy of various text structures in enhancing acquisition and retention of information from narrative passages (Frederiksen, 1977; Kintsch, 1974; Mandler & Johnson, 1977; Meyer, 1975; Rumelhart, 1975; Thorndyke, 1977).

From this research has emerged a general theory of schemata (Anderson, 1977; Rumelhart & Ortony, 1977; Thorndyke, 1978). This theory assumes that a person has in memory a set of prototypical structures for use in comprehending and encoding prose information. When a person reads (or listens to) a story, it is presumed that he or she uses an appropriate stored schema to guide comprehension of the story by imposing the constraints of the schema on the interpretation of the incoming information. When a story fits the stored schema, comprehension and retention of its information are facilitated by the organizational and integrative benefits provided by the schema. In other words, a schema provides a ready-made mental framework in which a story can be absorbed and made sense of.

It is a general feature of much discourse-processing research, unfortunately, that the kinds of texts studied have been lacking in variety and have not represented the range of narratives that people normally experience and obtain information from in everyday life. The generality of the schemata defined by cognitive researchers needs therefore to be tested more widely to find out if they specify organizational mental sets optimal for effective learning from everyday information sources. News reports are one such information source whose contents seem to be appropriate for meaningful text structure analysis.

NARRATIVE STRUCTURES OF NEWS

News stories are often expressed in a highly regular manner. This should not come as too much of a surprise because the requirements of the production process place fairly rigid and routinised constraints on the selection, telling, and presentation of news. Thus, it would not be unreasonable to assume that people who regularly read, listen to, or watch the news become familiar with at least some features of the normal structure of news reports—and that they have internalized a news schema applicable to the processing of news in general or a number of different schemata through which the learning of different kinds of news stories may be facilitated.

Van Dijk (1980), for instance, has proposed a preliminary description of a schema for newspaper articles, consisting of three main parts: Introduction (which also functions as a summary), Specification, and possibly various Details that may be cut by the editor if there is lack of space. Thorndyke (1979) assumed a similar schema to be usual in news. He went on to compare learning from newspaper reports that already conformed to a standard format of text organization with learning from alternative, experimentally imposed formats.

In addition to the concept of a generalised schema conditioned by standard narrative structures common to story-telling practice across topics, there is growing evidence of the need to consider topic-specific schemas. Some mass communications researchers have observed rou-

tinised or stereotyped story-telling practices specific to particular categories of news event. Recently, Vincent, Crow, and Davis (1985) analysed
news stories about U.S. air crashes and found similarities across all stories
and all television networks examined in their use of visual devices and
narrative structure.

Vincent et al. identified three standard themes that typified the way air
crash disaster stories were told. These themes emphasised the tragic
intervention of fate into everyday life, the mystery of what caused the
crash, and the work of legitimate authority to restore normality. These
authors argue that the news appears to serve the function of dispelling
rumour by providing people with plausible, credible, and immediate
accounts of events.

Each of these themes is developed over a period of several days. Initial
coverage develops the first theme, which is the most dramatic of the three
and the one that can readily be supported by the often diverse story
elements found in proximity to the crash. This theme derives from the
oral story-telling tradition and enables apparently random, discrete bits
of evidence to be quickly woven into a narrative suitable to the gravity of
the event. Initially, the journalist as story-teller is caught off guard by the
event. He or she rushes to the scene to graphically convey to the audience
the experience of being present as a modern tragedy unfolds. By the
second day, the pieces of the event have begun to be sorted into thematic
categories, and its overall sequence has been identified. The disaster had
been foretold but predictions were ignored. On the day of the crash,
everything was proceeding routinely until suddenly fate intervened, causing a sudden break in normality. A heroic struggle ensued in which some
were saved, but most died. Family, friends, and neighbours gather to
express their shock and grief. Religious rituals serve to structure expressions of grief and bring closure to this theme.

The second theme requires more time to develop and is much more
limited in the elements that can be used to develop it. The mystery of the
crash is probed by examining alternate plausible causes. Only those
deemed by the reporter to be highly probable are mentioned. Typically,
these are causes that government investigators or aircraft technology
experts have suggested. Mechanical failure and weather conditions are
favoured causes. Both can readily be supported by the types of evidence
found at crash sites. After weighing available evidence, a probable cause
can be declared with appropriate reservations.

The third theme is one of restoration of normality. Of the three themes,
it is the least dramatic, but its very banality provides reassurances. Within
hours, government bureaucrats from appropriate federal agencies are at
the crash site to take control. They are shown supervising the cleanup and
holding press conferences to calm fears. Airport scenes show the restora-

tion of normalcy as airline employees deal with troubled passengers while planes routinely land and take off. Passengers are shown boarding the flight that crashed on the previous day. This theme is developed through repeated coverage of routine activity. This type of coverage is notable because television news typically avoids showing ordinary occurrences. Its inclusion serves as a balance to the highly emotion-arousing scenes of disaster and grief. The camera dwells upon FCC officials as they calmly discuss the crash and offer explanations or accept blame.

In conclusion, Vincent et al. interpret this coverage as serving to perpetuate naive beliefs about the safety of air travel. Evidence that contradicts such beliefs is either ignored or subordinated to themes that emphasise that crashes are highly deviant events. Journalists were actually shown through this analysis that they handle such stories in a responsible way and attempt to restore public confidence in air travel rather than generate needless alarm by reporting inconsistent details about an accident.

NARRATIVE STRUCTURES AND NEWS COMPREHENSION

To what extent then can the way the story is told affect the level to which it is remembered and comprehended? In a study of news story structures in U.S. newspapers, Thorndyke (1979) found that the standard structure in the papers he chose to examine (*New York Times* and *Los Angeles Times*) is to present the most significant or important information in the first paragraph and further elaborations and background details in following paragraphs. Important information is therefore presented first to catch the reader's attention. Information of decreasing importance follows so that if the story needs to be cut to fit a particular space on the page, only that content regarded as less important will be left out. Thus, the organization of news texts as such is determined by professional requirements. Furthermore, it may be assumed that this is the structure that readers come to know as the way news stories are typically organized. However, this structure may not be optimal for the learner attempting to acquire all the facts in the story.

To find out if this is true, Thorndyke (1979) conducted an experiment in which he took four newspaper articles and presented them either in their original published form or in a condensed form minus repetitions or elaborations of information already presented. Thus, important information was retained while less important, incidental, or background embellishments were eliminated. Indeed, more than one alternative version of each story was created. A "narrative" version was created by rearranging the sentences in the condensed format into a chronological sequence, and a "topical" version was produced by organizing sentences from the condensed story under topical subheadings.

The stories were presented to 60 university undergraduates, who read each passage once and then produced written free-recall accounts of each passage. The results showed that all rearranged story formats produced better recall of story facts common to all versions than did the original story format (as used in the newspapers). There were no reliable differences in recall from different revised formats.

A comparison of recall of preserved news information with recall of information excluded from condensed versions and from original newspaper accounts indicated that the condensed versions were recalled better than the original versions (22% versus 12% average correct recalls), suggesting that readers evaluated the importance or centrality of each proposition or item of information with respect to the main theme of the story and that extraneous or background information was not processed as deeply or as carefully as the more important or central information.

Thorndyke hypothesized that people possess sets of mental schemata or ready-made frameworks within which comprehension of informational texts can effectively take place. The schemata that are optimal for most effective processing of new information, however, may vary from text to text. But it seems that learning from narrative passages will be at its best when they are organized so as to convey clearly the essential or central ingredients of the story being told. This may not always be true of the news as it is told by the mass media.

NARRATIVE STRUCTURES AND BROADCAST NEWS COMPREHENSION

Larsen (1981) applied the discourse-processing paradigm to the study of memory and comprehension of news reports on radio. Larsen maintains that updating of listeners' prior knowledge is a mode of learning that should be central to the social and ecological functions of news. Larsen studied memory for a Danish radio newscast shortly after its transmission, with 20 college students as subjects.

Because experimenters cannot usually control the structure and contents of broadcast news materials prior to transmission, studies of memory for real news have been limited to dealing with global questions like the public's recall of a list of topics covered in the programme. Using this technique, studies in several countries, as we saw in Chapter 2, have found very substantial forgetting rates that often amount to more than 80% information loss from a single news broadcast. This fits in with the finding of Herrmann and Neisser (1978) that people rated their memory for news items lowest among memory for eight types of experiences frequently discussed with other people.

Such questions may be interpreted as support for the so-called agenda-setting theory of mass media effects (McCombs & Shaw, 1972), which claims that the media primarily serve to put topics on the "mental agenda" of the public, rather than providing detailed information. However, such research does not reveal anything about the actual processing of news information or explain what is remembered. This requires a more fine-grained analysis specifying the variables that may be operating, and thus it brings in again the problem of experimental control. In his experiment Larsen played subjects a 5-minute radio news bulletin consisting of four items, within a few hours of its original live transmission. None of the subjects had heard this or any other bulletins in the meantime. The four stories concerned Middle East negotiations, the crisis in Iran, Italy and Ireland's approval of the proposed European Monetary system, and a domestic item about decentralisation efforts in the Danish administration.

The subjects were asked to rate the importance of items from a 3-year-old news bulletin and were then given the bulletin from the same day of the experiment. They were not told that there would be a test of memory. The procedure was designed to encourage an orientation towards the important and interesting points in the news rather than towards textual peculiarities, and to discourage attempts to memorise by rote rather than comprehend the items. Recall was therefore unexpected and was done by writing as completely as possible the story contents of each item. Afterwards, the full transcripts of the bulletin were distributed, and half of the subjects underlined all parts of the text that contained information that had been familiar to them in advance when they heard the bulletin. The remaining half underlined new information. The text of the four items was analysed into micropropositions according to the method developed by Kintsch (1977). The macrostructure of the texts was analysed on the assumption that they could be described as sets of connected episodes, each with three components: setting, complication, and resolution. Embedding of episodes was also taken into account; eg, the complication of one episode might consist of another whole episode. The structure of these episodes makes up the scheme of the text. Recall accounts were compared with the micropropositions of the original texts. Looking first at the amount recalled, Larsen found that recall accounts were usually brief and stated in quite specific terms, with heavy loss of specific details. Errors were infrequent, amounting to only 8 (1%) of the 682 propositions recalled. Over all subjects, the proportion of story content recalled descreased steadily across the four items, and more subjects totally failed to recall the later than the earlier items in the programme. However, when only subjects who recalled at least one proposition per item were included, the proportion recalled turned out to be nearly constant over items at around 20%. The constant recall within items was similar to the phenomenon of some-or-none recall from word list categories observed by experimental psychologists (e.g., Cohen, 1966) and indicated that the news items functioned as integrated, higher-order units in the subjects' memory.

TEXT STRUCTURE AND TEXT PROCESSING

The most simple hypothesis relating text structure and recall states that recall increases with the height of propositions in the text structure hierarchy (Mayer, 1977)—the so-called *levels effect*. Larsen found that for two items out of four, significant correlations emerged between recall and level of propositions. From the text processing theory of Kintsch and van Dijk (1978) three predictions were tested concerning

1. recall of propositions assumed to be selected for a short-term memory buffer
2. recall of macropropositions
3. the effect of familiarity

Buffer Selection.   The assumption under this heading is that some propositions are held in a short-term memory buffer store from one cycle of processing to the next in order to establish coherence between successive sentences during listening, viewing, or reading. Propositions that are selected for this buffer will participate in both the preceding and the following processing cycle, and this double processing is assumed to increase their probability of later recall.

Using the "leading-edge" strategy described by Kintsch and van Dijk (1978), buffer propositions were defined in terms of height in text hierarchy and recency. Thus, "buffer" and "nonbuffer" propositions were identified. Comparing recall of these indicated that buffer propositions were recalled about twice as often as nonbuffer propositions. Thus, concluded Larsen, the processing of the microstructure of the news stories clearly contributed to the pattern of recall (see Table 7.2).

Macrostructure.   The four news stories were segmented into episodes and further into settings, complications, and resolutions (after Kintsch, 1977). Episodes were highly embedded; this embedding reflected a story structure similar to the scheme for newspaper articles proposed by van Dijk (1980). Structure was expressed thus:

$$\text{INTRODUCTION} + \text{SPECIFICATION} + \begin{array}{l}\text{DETAILS}\\\text{HISTORY}\end{array}$$

Macrostructure derivation was carried out according to so-called macrorules that delete redundant propositions, generalise specific details, and summarise sequences of events. A large number of macropropositions may be derived from any given text base (van Dijk, 1980; Kintsch, 1977).

Larsen in his analysis allowed only macropropositions that could be based directly on micropropositions present in the text. Having identified these former, any remaining propositions in the text base were defined as micropropositions. Recall of macropropositions and micropropositions were then compared.

Findings indicated that recall of macropropositions was much more likely than recall of micropropositions. This was consistent with the theory of Kintsch and van Dijk (1978), which predicts that macroproposi-

TABLE 7.2
Recall Proportions for Propositions Selected and Not
Selected for Short-Term Memory Retention

News Item	N	Buffer Number	Propositions Recall	Non-buffer Number	Propositions Recall
Middle East	19	11	.40	37	.15
Iran	17	10	.36	46	.16
EMS	15	19	.33	43	.17
Denmark	13	11	.27	23	.16

Source: Larsen, 1981. Reprinted by permission of the author.

TABLE 7.3
Recall Proportions for Macro- and Micropropositions

News Item	N	Macro-propositions		Micropropositions	
		Number	Recall	Number	Recall
Middle East	19	18	.36	30	.11
Iran	17	22	.33	34	.11
EMS	15	26	.35	36	.11
Denmark	13	19	.36	20	.03

Source: Larsen, 1981. Reprinted by permission of the author.

tions will have higher reproduction probabilities than micropropositions by virtue of the extra processing they receive during extraction of the macrostructure.

Interaction Between Buffer Memory and Macrostructure. The macroeffect may be interpreted as an illustration of "top-down" processing, where a previously known general scheme of news structure is selecting certain propositions for particular attention. This is in contrast to the "bottom-up" process that selects propositions for buffer memory primarily governed by the structure of the text itself. The effects of buffer selection and macrostructure derivation are assumed to be independent by Kintsch and van Dijk (1978). This assumption implies that all propositions are equally available for macrostructure derivation whether they are selected for the short-term memory buffer or not. Also, it implies that propositions are equally likely to be selected for the short-term memory buffer whether they are included in the macrostructure or not.

Larsen found, however, that there was an interaction between buffer and macrostructure effects during recall of radio news items. Buffer selection increased recall of macropropositions, whereas micropropositions were not affected. His explanation of this interaction is that macrostructure derivation was carried out (at least provisionally) during listening to each sentence and that only propositions selected for inclusion in the macrostructure were considered for eventual transfer to subsequent processing cycles via the short-term memory buffer.

Such a procedure is different from the strategy proposed by Kintsch and van Dijk (1978), but it appears as an effective solution to the constraints of this particular situation. First, the orienting task called for identifying information that contributed to the perceived importance of the items, and second, listening made it impossible to go back and review earlier sentences. Thus, the limited capacity of the buffer should be used only for material likely to be important in the final analysis, that is, macropropositions.

Familiarity and Updating. The model of Kintsch and van Dijk (1978) assumed that the more familiar a text, the fewer resources are required to comprehend it and, consequently, the more resources are left for storing propositions in memory. The model did not deal with the question of differential familiarity of propostions within a text, however. Larsen suggests a straightforward hypothesis might be that once a topic is activated in long-term memory, propositions referring to facts that are already known will have some probability of reproduction in advance. Thus, superior recall of familiar propositions is predicted. If, on the other hand, the purpose of listening to the news is to update and increase knowledge, then unfamiliar propositions should receive extra processing

TABLE 7.4
Proportion Recall of Familiar and Unfamiliar Propositions

News		Familiar		Unfamiliar	
Item	N	Number	Recall	Number	Recall
Middle East	19	16	.30	32	.16
Iran	17	17	.33	39	.15
EMS	15	13	.38	49	.17

Source: Larsen, 1981. Reprinted by permission of the author

in order to be retained. Of course, the previously known background cannot be ignored because it provides the basis for comprehending the unfamiliar information in the first place.

Larsen identified familiar propositions as those underlined by most subjects as ones they already knew about. He then compared recall of propositions that had been underlined with those that had not been. It should perhaps be noted, however, that only ten subjects were used for this analysis.

Familiar propositions were significantly better recalled than unfamiliar propositions for all three items on which this comparison was made. This supported the hypothesis that prior knowledge of the information in a proposition will increase its probability of recall. Even so, most of the familiar propositions were not recalled. The only three pieces of familiar information that were consistently recalled were the place, the main actor, and the topic of the news event. These three elements correspond closely to the index variables in the sketchy scripts of Schank and Abelson (1977) and Lebowitz (1979) and represent variables that are necessary to identify and instantiate the specific script and the knowledge it includes.

Although the latter result suggested that extra processing resources were not devoted to the task of acquiring new information from the news, it may be argued that, in a strict sense, the updating hypothesis is concerned only with chronologically new information, that is, information that has originated since the time of the last news bulletin consumed by the listener. Other pieces of unfamiliar information may perhaps be useful for understanding the new events, but only in the role of background. To distinguish new and background information, events described in the news stories were ordered chronologically, similar to the "narrative Organization" employed by Thorndyke (1979). Propositions corresponding to chronologically new information were in no case reported to be familiar by more than two subjects.

New information (chronologically) was consistently better recalled than background information and significantly so for three items out of four. Thus, to some extent subjects did focus on "real news" in the text

TABLE 7.5
Proportion Recall of Unfamiliar Propositions Carrying
Chronologically New Information and Background
Information Respectively

News		New Information		Background Information	
Items	N	Number	Recall	Number	Recall
Middle East	19	13	.29	19	.08
Iran	17	17	.19	22	.12
EMS	15	25	.23	24	.11
Denmark	13	20	.28	15	.04

Source: Larsen, 1981. Reprinted by permission of the author.

that could serve to update their previous knowledge. High priority is usually given to moving film in television news production, in service of the need for "actuality" footage that puts the viewer in the position of eyewitness to the news as it happens. Thus, in order to achieve any degree of narrative-picture correspondence, the narrative must often be written to fit the pictures. Some cognitive psychologists have argued, however, that because of this practice and because pictorial "syntax" and narrative syntax are by nature quite different, many television news texts tend to be disorganized, often setting out their information in a disjointed fashion that may impair uptake and comprehension of information from news broadcasts.

SWEDISH RESEARCH ON NEWS STRUCTURES AND COMPREHENSION

A more recent statement about the role of narrative structure in the comprehension of news messages has been made by Findahl and Hoijer (1984, 1985) in work done for the Swedish Broadcasting Corporation in Stockholm. This work had been developing for a period spanning more than 15 years and involved analysis of news narratives and empirical testing of audience memory and comprehension of radio and television news programmes.

Findahl and Hoijer offer a holistic approach to the assessment of broadcast news comprehension, which they contrast with an atomistic approach. Holistic approaches as such can be traced back to early classic work on memory for connected discourse, such as that of Bartlett (1932). Bartlett's conception of memory is consonant in several respects with the conceptions of text comprehension formulated in recent years in studies of narrative grammar and work on cognitive processes associated with reading. Some of these areas of investigation have already been referred to in this chapter.

In their analysis of problems of text comprehension, Findahl and Hoijer integrate classical psychology of memory with modern text comprehension studies. Their belief is that news discourse and comprehension cannot be understood solely in terms of isolated elements of discourse such as the frequency or complexity of individual words and sentences. Rather, understanding is to be gained via an analysis of the structure of the text of the news broadcast.

According to Findahl and Hoijer, news is about events. Furthermore, news stories can for the most part be synthesized, within the frame of a traditional journalistic style of reporting, into a fairly standard structure or schema. Basically, events occur in places, involve persons or things (principals), have causes or reasons for their occurrence, and may have consequences or outcomes for whomever or whatever they involve. The basic model of a news text is pictured thus:

Although variations around this standard structure may occur, most news is elaborated in this way. Sometimes, cause or consequences information may be missing. Or, another element, such as time, may be included. Also, there may be several events or places featured within a single story, linked via a causal chain.

In a detailed programme of research, Findahl and Hoijer analysed some 60 news items from one week in February 1978. The news items were selected from four major topics of high interest in both press and broadcast news at that time. These were the ongoing crisis in Swedish industry, worker–employer contract negotiations, employee-controlled investment funds, and nuclear energy.

All news materials were analysed with respect to their content structure. This meant that each item was examined to the extent to which the background to each event (i.e., the reasons why it occurred and what implications or consequences it had for those involved and any others) was made explicit and the extent to which each story had a clear narrative structure as regards the locus and actors involved.

In addition to this, 20 items were subjected to what the authors call a "theme-rheme" analysis of their internal linkages, or coherence. To do this, each item was examined sentence by sentence to check the extent to which each new sentence related to the preceding sentence and added new information (rheme) to the theme in question. Findahl and Hoijer studied *coherence* or the internal linkages in a text, without actually offering a systematic definition of the term. Their operationalisation of coherence is in terms of the interrelationship of sentences. This is a local rather than a global analysis. They were concerned specifically with the degree to which the information contained in one sentence related directly to that contained in the immediately succeeding sentence.

Local Coherence

An example of a "theme-rheme" analysis of the text of a news item, taken from Findahl and Hoijer is presented in Fig. 7.1. The analysis of the internal coherence or sentence connections of this particular news text may take two slightly different forms, depending on whether or not the so-called cluster-type technique is applied.

The main point of interest here is the extent to which a new sentence or new rheme relates to an already established or recurrent theme, or whether there occurs a break in the continuity. A break occurs in the text in Fig. 7.1 when Kockums is mentioned in the last two sentences in a context entirely unrelated to the rest of the story. The Kockums representative is the actor in these last two sentences but cannot be linked back directly to the statements in the rest of the item. On the level of text coherence, this masks a break in the structure. The last two sentences cannot be incorporated in either diagram, which means that the analysis must start anew.

Findahl and Hoijer claim that most broadcast news items, at least on the evidence of the ones they analysed in Swedish news, tend to be

---

Sample item Thursday, 2 March 1978, Item no 1, T – 0:51 seconds

SR: Today it was announced that the forestry industry and shipbuilding concern Kockums in Malmo are to receive government credit guarantees. Minister of Industrial Affairs Nils G Asling said that the Government intend to put a bill before Parliament next week, calling for 900 million in credit guarantees to forestry and liquidity assistance to Kockums. The amount of the assistance is to be specified in April. The terms attached to the credit guarantees to forestry are harsh, calling for stockholder participation corresponding to 25% of the amount of the loans. Further, there shall be a one year moratorium on dividends. These items lead some in the branch to fear that they will not be able to get any loans. Kockums announced today that they are withdrawing their application for state support toward the construction of a third liquified gas tanker. Nils Hugo Hallenborg, General Manager of Kockums, said the company wish to avoid a definitive No today and instead put their hopes in the pending Shipbuilding Bill to come in April.

FIG.   7.1   Analysis of the internal linkages of a news text (Findahl & Hoijer, 1984. Reprinted by permission of the author).

characterised by a fragmentary structure of often loose sentence connections. This conclusion is exemplified by the results shown in Table 7.6. Another feature of broadcast news texts that may cause problems in comprehension is inconsistencies on the time dimension. By this is meant a lack of synchronisation between the chronology of events and the order in which they occur in the narrative. Findahl and Hoijer illustrated this phenomenon with a fairly short item of less than 40 seconds duration, but within which several shifts of temporal perspective occurred (see Fig. 7.2).

Global Coherence

Findahl and Hoijer (1984) provided analyses of the content structure of news items and of the logical structure and presentation of news messages. With regard to the content structure, or the ways in which the event reported is explained, the authors found that news texts generally provide a lack of information on the background and causes of events, and that this impairs the average listener's or viewer's comprehension. More than half the items they assessed provided no such information whatsoever. And when it was presented, background information tended to be generally sketchy. Findahl and Hoijer reported that extensive background details occurred in less than one in four items they studied.

Although, on the evidence of this framework of news text analysis, it appears that news generally is poorly structured and elaborated, it should perhaps be borne in mind that the model applied by Findahl and Hoijer, focusing as it does on a cause-event-consequences structure, may not be appropriate to provide an effective analysis of all news. Sometimes political, economic, or industrial news, which occupy a large proportion of airtime on broadcast news, may be about conflicts of interest, policy disagreements, and negotiations rather than overt or clearly definable events. Such stories may, by the intrinsic nature of their subject matter, lack an event structure of the kind conceptualised by Findahl and Hoijer's model.

Besides scanty background information, implicit references and allusions in broadcast news stories may make the news material difficult for uninitiated viewers and listeners to grasp. Findahl and Hoijer's analysis led them to criticise interviewers for posing highly sophisticated questions, so much so that the interview often became almost like a private conversation between two experts. Overly knowledgeable interviewers may lack empathy with more ignorant audience members and have a tendency not to follow up on answers to their questions, even when the answers given are likely to be too technical, complex, and difficult for the

TABLE 7.6
Subject Matter and Text Coherence in Broadcast News

Item length (Long/short)	Crisis in industry		Contract negotiations		Investment funds		Nuclear energy		Total
	L	S	L	S	L	S	L	S	
Coherent structure	2	–	1	–	–	–	3	–	6
Structure with digressions	5	3	5	3	5	2	6	2	31
Fragmentary structure	8	3	2	5	3	1	–	–	22
									59

Source: Findahl and Hoijer, 1984. Reprinted by permission of the author

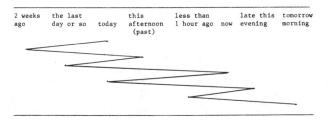

FIG. 7.2 Temporal Inconsistencies in news texts (Findahl and Höijer, 1984). Reprinted by permission of the author.

average viewer or listener to understand. Interviewers often adopted expert roles rather than acting in the role of spokesperson for and representative of the general uninitiated public. This finding is consistent with another reported by Robinson, Sahin, and Davis (1982), who found that television news editors in Britain, who had very high levels of knowledge about news stories from the previous week, by and large held the implicit assumption that the audience was as knowledgeable as they were, and therefore probably would neither need nor want extensive background to stories with which they undoubtedly would already be familiar.

News Structure, Background Knowledge, and Comprehension

Findahl and Hoijer (1985) reported two experiments in which they measured audience retention and comprehension of different structural elements of broadcast news stories and looked also at the influence of listeners' and viewers' relevant background knowledge on news comprehension. In the first experiment, over 100 Stockholm residents were recruited to attend a presentation of a 7-minute fictional radio bulletin that had been specially prepared by the news staff at Sveriges Radio. In the second experiment, over 600 residents from the same city were invited to take part in sessions in which they saw a fictional television news programme of similar length.

Participants were run in groups of about 20 persons and were not told explicitly beforehand that they would be tested on comprehension of the news. Immediately after presentation of the programme they were tested on their retention of story details via a series of probing questions.

From individual news items, Findahl and Hoijer found that some elements were remembered more easily than others. Most easily remembered was information about where an event occurred and about who or what was involved in it. Information about the causes and consequences of events was much less well recalled. Table 7.7 shows the mean percent correct recall for different ingredients of news content from each programme.

191

TABLE 7.7
Mean Recall of Different Ingredients of News Stories

	Experiment 1 Radio News	Experiment 2 Television News
	%	%
Place	35	51
Principal	30	39
Cause	6	25
Consequence	13	19

Source: Findahl and Höijer, 1975, 1985. Reprinted by permission of the author.

Previous Knowledge and Miscomprehension of News

Findahl and Hoijer identified a number of different types of miscomprehension of news information among listeners and viewers of radio and television news programmes. On some occasions, audience members would confuse facts from different stories. Confusion effects occurred particularly among stories about similar topic but was also observed to occur between relatively dissimilar stories. An example of failure to grasp the facts properly was overgeneralisation. Instead of remembering the precise location of an event, for instance, viewers would mention a wider district or region.

One type of misunderstanding, however, had its source at least in part in the level of background knowledge listeners or viewers brought with them to the news. On occasions, when subjects were attempting to remember the details from a particular news story, gaps would occur in memory. Some people would fill these gaps with alternative, although usually plausible, details derived from their prior knowledge of the events or issues in question.

Importation errors were less likely to occur with unfamiliar types of news, and the authors reasoned that when a news topic is remote and unfamiliar, many audience members lack the knowledge needed to fill in the memory gaps.

In order to clarify further the influence of prior knowledge on viewers' understanding of television news, in their second experiment Findahl and Hoijer gave participants a general knowledge test on current affairs topics in order to classify them into high-and low-knowledge types between whom news comprehension levels could be compared. Although a high level of knowledge according to the questionnaire was no guarantee that a person would remember more news, it was quite apparent from the results that a viewers with a low level on knowledge was much less likely than one with a high level of knowledge to attain a high retention score.

Comparing memory for news scores between high and low knowledge groups, Findahl and Hoijer found that only 1 out of 120 low-knowledge viewers achieved a high level of retention, whereas among 125 viewers classified as highly knowledgeable only 4 exhibited really poor retention. There was some indication also of a relationship between retention of a specific news item and knowledge relevant specifically to the topic it covered. In this context, previous knowledge was found to be very important to the way in which a news story was remembered. Although a sound background knowledge, especially one that is specifically relevant to the news topic being reported in the news, usually proves to be advantageous, there are occasions when it may lead to greater miscomprehension than would otherwise have occurred. Importation errors, for example, were found to be more frequent among individuals with high general knowledge about news and current affairs than among those people with low general knowledge. The news items that typically take precedence in memory are those that are psychologically closest to the personal experience or knowledge of audience members. One criterion of personal relevance is geographical distance. The more distant the site of an event, the less interest it has. This criterion is also important often to the selection and organization of news stories in news broadcasts. But domestic items are not necessarily better understood than foreign news (Larsen, 1981; Sahin, Davis, & Robinson, 1981), even though it has been found that people usually have more background knowledge about and feel more involved in events that are closer to home (Bjorkman, 1984).

Information that gains precedence in memory for the news may be determined by other factors than psychological involvement, however. Findahl and Hoijer observed that previous knowledge of a certain kind could operate to produce truncated memory for news, whereby retention is much better for information about places and principals than for that about causes and consequences. It is not simply that background knowledge may be called upon to fill in missing or unretrievable story details with appropriate alternatives, but more significantly that the parts of the storyline that may be distorted in this way may often be those central to the meaning of the story. In this case, the important consideration is how knowledge is organized in memory.

Schema theory has been developed by cognitive psychologists to elaborate and explain how knowledge about social experiences, events, or situations is stored in memory. Two different kinds of schemata have been proposed, one dealing with knowledge about recurrent events and situations see Schank & Abelson, 1977; Bower, Black, & Turner, 1979 and the other dealing with knowledge about the typical structure of stories e.g., Johnson & Mandler, 1980; Rumelhart, 1975 Findahl and Hoijer believe that during news comprehension both kinds of schemata—about recurrent events and about the structure of news items—are probably activated.

As news broadcasts follow set standard models and confront people almost every day, regular listening or viewing may result in the formation of a corresponding mental news schema, in which information about places and principals is foregrounded. This makes it easier to store, and later to recall, information about these aspects than information about causes and consequences. That news is structured in such a way is supported by linguistic analysis of broadcast news. In a Swedish study, Svensson (1981) noted that 76.8% of the information in newscasts dealt with persons and objects (i.e., principals), 19.2% was about places, but only 4.4% and 4.2, respectively, dealt with causes and consequences. The observation that causal information in news reporting is rare has also been made by other researchers (Glasgow University Media Group, 1980, Strassner, 1975).

We have seen already in this chapter that research into discourse processing has revealed a number of factors associated with "story grammar" that can significantly affect comprehension and memory for simple narratives. Thorndyke (1977) reported that the orderly and coherent exposition of simple stories in terms of theme, setting, and plot enhanced comprehension as reflected in the ability of readers to answer correctly questions on text content. The text structure principles developed by Thorndyke for improving the comprehensibility of written texts have recently been applied by Berry and Clifford (1985) to broadcast news narratives. Berry and Clifford reported two experiments designed to investigate the effects of narrative structures on memory for television news items. The key news story used in these experiments concerned the assassination of President Park of South Korea and the consequences of this tragic event. It was taken from a television news broadcast on a West German network and thus had not been seen by the British participants in Berry and Clifford's experiments. This particular item was selected also because it attempted to provide background details surrounding the event to an audience assumed to be unfamiliar with this history. Furthermore, it was an important story with a clear casual chain of events. Berry and Clifford reasoned also that it was apparent that extraneous factors, such as the availability of particular film and the wish to include an expert commentary in the item, had shaped its formulation and presentation in the broadcast.

An English translation of the text was recorded along with transcriptions of two news items from British television news bulletins, all were read by a professional local radio newsreader. The key Korean item was the second in the resulting three-item bulletin, which was played to subjects over a small tape recorder. Two versions of this minibulletin were in fact recorded. The first was as in the original broadcasts, with the narrative "disordered" as a consequence of the way it had been produced for television broadcast purposes. The second version consisted of a rearrangement of the same sentences according to the principles of Thorndyke's story grammar, with the setting and theme set out clearly at the outset and the various plots that made up the story presented as coherent units in an appropriate narrative order. As a result of this restructuring, say Berry and Clifford, the causes and consequences of the events reported in the stories were made more apparent. In the first experiment, Berry and Clifford presented the items to 36 adults, aged 18 to 39 years, and 20 adolescents, aged 15 to 16 years, from a technical college. They filled out a general knowledge questionnaire and answered detailed questions about each of the three news stories. Recall performance was found to be much better from the modified text than from the original broadcast version. In a subsequent study, 20 college students were allocated equally to original or revised versions of the news stories, and recall focused on the second story only. Once again, recall performance was much better from the rearranged story narrative.

In discussing the results of these experiments, Berry and Clifford draw out and highlights the following points. First, when measured both by cued and spontaneous recall, memory was better for the modified narrative than for the original "disordered" story text. Furthermore, comparisons of better and less well educated people indicated that the better-organized texts may be of particular benefit to less able individuals. Secondly, Berry and Clifford also make the point that in asking how well people understand the stories presented in the news it is essential to examine the details that are remembered and whether they correspond to the central theme of the story. Comparison of groups receiving the original and modified narratives indicated that, with the original version, most subjects could reproduce only about five miscellaneous story details. With the revised version, on the other hand, a majority could give important background information and could also answer questions on points that indicated a grasp of the essential meaning of events. These findings suggest that disrupting the structure of the news texts through giving priority to moving pictures not only leads to recall of fewer points but also impairs understanding of the story.

CONCLUDING REMARKS

The telling of the story has been the focus of this chapter. As with many other features of the news, the way news stories are told tends to follow a well-defined structure that is designed both to facilitate the routinised production of news each day and to enhance audience comprehension of the information being presented. Clarity in writing the news is a skill all journalists try to develop and take pride in. It is regarded within the profession as absolutely essential to good journalism. Technique is acquired and shaped through practise on the job. But as with many other features of broadcast news production, professional intuition could benefit from the input of research. Evidence is accumulating from research on the cognitive impact of broadcast news that suggests that the comprehensibility of standard news narratives could be improved. Research done by cognitive psychologists on learning from narrative materials has discovered that memory and comprehension levels can be significantly influenced by the way information is structured and elaborated within the narrative. Applying their techniques of measuring the effects of narrative structures on learning from extended written discourse to the study of learning from broadcast news materials, cognitive researchers have found that news comprehension can be improved over that measured from normally structured news stories when alternative narrative structures are employed that emphasise more clearly some of the central elements important to the meaning of the story.

The application of discourse-processing paradigms to research on broadcast news comprehension is a recent development, and it is probably too early to put forward practical recommendations on the basis of its early findings. But although this area of investigation still has some way to go, already initial results suggest that standard story-telling formats adopted by broadcast journalism may not be the only or indeed the best ways of presenting the information.

8 Packaging the Programme

Television news programmes are characterised by a variety of structural attributes that are important because they determine the way the news is presented and also because they embody certain intuitive, "professional" assumptions on the part of news editors and producers about audience satisfaction with and learning from news programmes that can be empirically tested. Among these programme factors are the serial ordering of news items and the grouping and placement of news reports according to story category. As we see in this chapter, these physical features of programmes may have profound influences on the amount of information viewers learn from television news broadcasts.

News stories are not presented in a haphazard fashion in television bulletins but are arranged according to certain aesthetic criteria designed to maximise both the professionalism of the production and audience impact. It is essential, of course, to start the show in the right way. Textbooks on news production for television often recommend that the lead story should always be the most significant story of the day. (Green, 1969). Significance, however, may be determined by a variety of factors. As we shall see, lead stories are usually selected from particular topic areas and rarely from others. On days when selection of one news story as the most important proves to be a difficult decision, producers may rely on criteria or values specific to the news profession, such as whether a candidate for the lead is accompanied by film. A good film story makes for a better opening than a good nonvisual story. The film news story is uniquely television's, and producers are usually keen to let the viewer *see* the news, as opposed to merely hearing about it (which can be done equally well on radio).

To some professionals, ending the show properly is as important as beginning it in the right way. One widely held belief is that with all the bad news or serious news that clutters up most of the bulletin, viewers should be sent away with a smile. Therefore, news programmes invariably finish on an interesting and light-hearted note. Once again, careful monitoring of television news content over time has revealed that end stories tend predominantly to be drawn from certain categories of news only (Glasgow University Media Group, 1976).

Between the beginning and the end of the programme comes the centre section, which may contain anything from 8 to 18 additional stories. Although the first story is usually (or should be) the most important of the day, this does not mean that the rest of the programme is structured on a sliding scale of significance, with each successive story designated as less important or newsworthy than the one preceding it.

One professional belief is that news programmes should flow and retain audience interest and attention throughout, rather than start on a high note and gradually and persistently tailing off. In the course of achieving this goal, producers often make naive assumptions about the psychology of the audience. These assumptions embody ideas about how viewers' interest and attention can be sustained and how learning can be aided.

One writer has recommended varying the pace and the emotional tone of the news throughout the programme (Green, 1969). The chief assumption here is that the audience can probably take news about certain topics (e.g., about complex political or economic matters) or pitched at a particular emotional level (e.g., about war, terrorist attacks, death, and destruction) for only so long. It is essential to vary the content and tone to create a wavelike structure of heavier followed by lighter news. The second most important story might therefore be placed not immediately following the lead story but perhaps a little over halfway through the programme.

Another important concept in television news production is that of "packaging." The idea here is that related items should be portrayed or clustered together. Sudden jumps from one type of news to a completely different kind is regarded as bad style. The packaging technique avoids this and is believed by news professionals actually to enhance clarity and comprehension of programme content (Green, 1969; Schlesinger, 1978). Thus one might have a succession of items about international or foreign events in one package, domestic politics in another, industrial and economic matters in another, sports in another, and so on. Mood variations can occur within packages that will not come as a shock to viewers because items in the same package will be from a common subject area.

Serial Position Effects and News Recall. Experimental psychologists have known for many years that the serial position of a stimulus item in a sequence of written or spoken linguistic material that is to be learned can have a powerful effect on the probability of its spontaneous recall. Generally, memory performance is best for those items placed either at the beginning (*primacy effect*) or at the end (*recency effect*) of a sequence, whereas those presented elsewhere are relatively poorly recalled. In view of this, the stereotyped content profiles of television news outlined by researchers such as the Glasgow University Media Group (1976) have important implications for the selective recall of particular types of news more than to other serial position effects that also operate on television news materials during learning. Is there any empirical evidence to show that the placement of one news report relative to others in a bulletin affects its memorability?

In an early study of story-placement effects on recall from a 12-item radio news bulletin, Tannenbaum (1954) instructed subjects to attend to the news material as they would ordinarily when listening to a radio newscast and then tested them for item recall immediately after presentation. A clear pattern of differential recall as a function of item position emerged, with the items near the end recalled best of all (see Fig. 8-1). Recall for different items ranged from a low of about 40% for seventh position to a high of nearly 90% for the last item in the 12-item bulletin. Tannenbaum also reported that in general recall was significantly better for items in the second half of the bulletin than in the first half, although the first and second items were well remembered. However, recall at the very end of the bulletin was markedly better than recall at the very beginning.

In a more recent study of recall from radio news, Stauffer, Frost, and Rybolt (1980) presented samples of college students and adult night-school attendees in Kenya with a single radio news broadcast and tested

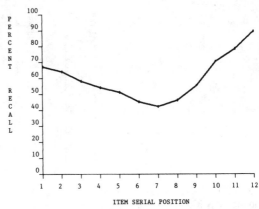

FIG. 8.1 Recall as a function of serial position (Tannenbaum, 1954; Reprinted with permission of the publisher).

memory for its content immediately afterwards in a classroom setting. Stauffer et al. found that recall from this 13-item bulletin was best for the first item, which was remembered by 49% of the entire sample. The least often recalled story was in fifth position and was remembered by 38% of respondents. It is difficult to judge from this study how significant serial position was to recall, in as much as the position of items was confounded with other important presentation factors. The first story, for example, was also the longest and was also summarised at the beginning and the end of the programme. These are the kinds of methodological problems that arise when using "live" broadcast materials that have not been editorially controlled in any way to isolate certain production features (and their possible effects on audience recall) from others.

In an experiment on recall of television news, the author edited together a sequence of 15 brief news headlines recorded previously from actual network TV bulletins (Gunter, 1979). Each item occurred only once in the sequence, and all items were of approximately the same length. One third of the items were presented by a "talking head," another third featured an unseen newsreader narrating over a still photograph, and the remainder consisted of brief sequences of film footage over which an unseen newscaster read a headline. This study was designed to examine the effects of several variables: presentation modality, visual format, and serial position. The news sequence was presented to one group of viewers audio-visually, as on television, and to a second group in soundtrack (audio) only. Results showed that serial position influenced extent of item recall from audio-visual and audio-only presentations. As Figs. 8.2A and 8.2B show, serial learning curves, showing strong primacy and recency effects, were evident following unaided recall of items presented in either modalities. Within the video modality, however, serial position effects interacted with and were to some extent offset by picture-

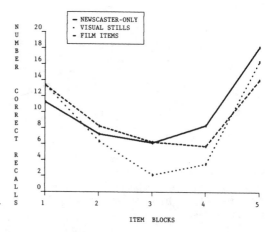

FIG. 8.2A   Recall curves for audio modality (Gunter, 1979).

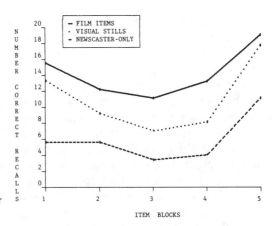

NUMBER CORRECT RECALLS

— FILM ITEMS
· VISUAL STILLS
- NEWSCASTER-ONLY

ITEM BLOCKS

FIG. 8.2B Recall curves for video modality (Gunter, 1979).

content effects. Although a strong serial learning curve emerged for items read by a "talking head" (newscaster-only), this curve was weaker for items accompanied by visual stills or film footage. Thus, on television news, the use of visual illustrations may offset to some extent the otherwise powerful effect of serial position during free recall of programme content.

The practical implications of these findings become clearer when they are considered together with the content-analytic data on network television news output in the United Kingdom (Glasgow University Media Group, 1976). The Glasgow group showed that certain types of news story are much more likely than others to occupy the first three positions in bulletins. Most often stories in these early bulletin positions were about politics, industry, or foreign affairs. A similar pattern occurred over the last three bulletin positions, which were most often occupied by sports, human interest, or science stories. Thus stereotyped newscast content profiles exhibit strong and consistent biases in the serial ordering and treatment of news topics which may in turn have profound effects on the kinds of news events that, are predominantly learned and remembered by audiences, irrespective of their idiosyncratic news interests.

The experimental studies just reported employed fairly artificial programmes and viewing conditions. Do the same serial position effects occur during recall of broadcast news under more naturalistic conditions? Recently, in a survey study of news comprehension operationalised in terms of cued news recall, in which no a priori manipulations of news content were present, Davis and Robinson (1985) reported that story-placement effects do indeed affect broadcast news retention. Respondents in Britain and the US were interviewed after an evening's main network television newscast and were asked questions about the programme's content. Post hoc comparisons were made of retention of information from lead, closing, and middle stories in the bulletin.

201

In contrast to the experimental findings previously described, evidence emerged that lead items were quite poorly remembered on a number of occasions. The authors speculated that this may have been because lead items contained a great deal of extraneous visual and verbal information. Some lead stories were highly complex or abstract and contained technical terms most viewers were unlikely to understand. As we saw in earlier chapters, narrative complexity can have profound effects on memory for textual materials. Furthermore, Davis and Robinson observed that the visuals employed in these items often had little direct relevance to the central point of the story narrative. This again, as we see in the next chapter, is of fundamental importance to memory for broadcast news on television. In sum, there were attributes other than placement that typically characterised lead items in television newscasts that may have contributed significantly to their poor retention.

Closing stories, by way of contrast, were often among the best remembered. This finding was consistent with experimental evidence on news recall (Gunter, 1979; Tannenbaum, 1954). Once again, though, there were confounding factors that complicated the explanation of this finding. Closing items tended predominantly to be human interest stories, which are known to have a strong appeal to viewers (Wober, 1980). It is therefore difficult to know if their high level of remembrance was a function of a recency effect or because of their particular interest value for viewers.

Stories in the middle of the programme did not always exhibit depressed retention, as has been observed in experimental studies. Sometimes these stories were remembered well and sometimes not. Gunter (1979, 1980a) did find, however, that brief news items accompanied by film footage were well recalled even though placed in the middle of a news sequence. Hence, story attributes once again interacted with position factors to mediate retention of story content.

Davis and Robinson reported that brief reports about abstract, remote events were not remembered well when placed in the middle of the programme. Stories having some personal relevance for viewers, on the other hand, were sometimes well remembered despite their brevity and central position in the programme. In particular, stories dealing with the exploits of outstanding individuals (e.g., the Pope visiting Poland) were highly salient. This phenomenon, whereby a unique item stands out from the rest and is especially well remembered, is known in cognitive psychology as the *von Restorff effect*. This effect has important implications for the design of news programmes and for research into comprehension of them. The von Restorff effect not only produces enhanced memory for an outstanding item but also is known to depress recall of items adjacent to the outstanding item. Davis and Robinson (1985) did not report whether this happened in the programmes from which they measured audience memory, but it is a factor that might be worth exploring in the future. The taxonomy of news has been observed to affect not only the serial position of items in a news programme but also the way in which they are grouped together. It is to the effects of news packaging by topic that we now turn our attention.

CLUSTERING EFFECTS AND NEWS RECALL

Two of the most essential qualities for television news programming are clarity and comprehensibility because television reaches a larger and more heterogeneous audience than any other informational medium. Much of the information contained in a newscast is spoken only once during the programme and unlike newsprint cannot be restudied at the leisure of the consumer. News professionals are, it seems, aware of a need for clarity of presentation, but their ignorance of certain basic processes operative during human verbal learning has resulted in the use of production routines that, although designed to make news consumption for the audience easier, are actually self-defeating.

News taxonomy is a very important concept in the production of television newscasts, and it is especially relevant to the problem of clarity. News stories are classified by news people, largely for economy of production treatment, into broad semantic or taxonomic domains—politics, industry, foreign, economics, sports, science, and so forth. In their book *Bad News*, the Glasgow University Media Group (1976) reported findings from a 6-month content analysis of all national network television news output in the United Kingdom that showed that the grouping and distribution of news items in bulletins appear to be strongly determined by these story categories.

One production technique that news people apparently regard as having clarity (and therefore memory?) -enhancing effects is the grouping together of two or more items from the same category of news into taxonomically homogeneous "packages" (Schlesinger, 1978). This is borne out by data on the distribution of news content in TV bulletins in the United Kingdom by the *Bad News* group. One particularly common example of this strategy concerns the dichotomy of news stories into domestic and foreign categories. Thus it is usual practice to have a roundup of foreign news consisting of a series of stories that have the common characteristic of being located outside the United Kingdom. Industrial news concerning pay claims or strikes and sports news are also frequently treated in this way. Also, items on industrial disputes sometimes run in sequence with stories on broader and in actuality unrelated (although semantically often quite similar) economic issues, with implied causal connections between them.

Producers apparently assume that sequencing of bulletin content in this way serves to package together isolated events into more meaningful combinations that can be more readily learned by the audience; but what empirical evidence is there to reinforce this professional intuition? Research done to date has indicated that the packaging strategy does not aid learning and retention of broadcast news, and may even impair it. Indeed, some studies have indicated that the attempt to arrive at simplicity and clarity of presentation by packaging the news thematically may in fact represent one of the fundamental reasons for extensive and rapid forgetting of news information from television bulletins.

Klein (1978) reasoned that a topically organized television newscast would be better remembered and found more interesting by viewers than one in which the stories were ordered with no attention to topics. To test his hypothesis Klein presented groups of college students with either a television newscast in which stories were grouped by subject matter (e.g., politics, economics, crime, etc.), or a bulletin in which items were ordered by their previously independently judged importance, or one in which no specific ordering strategy was employed. A multiple-choice test of memory for programme content given immediately following presentation indicated no significant effects of organization on retention. A set of evaluative semantic differential ratings revealed no effect of production style on interest either.

Klein suggested that a newscast that appears organized to the sender may not appear to be to the receiver. This may be true, but there is another important point often missed by both journalists and academic researchers of mass communications who lack detailed knowledge about experimental cognitive psychology. It is assumed that memory for linguistic materials can be affected by topical or thematic organization of those materials, and certain experimental psychological literature is often cited in support of this assumption. It is important to realise, however, that the topical–organization literature has two strands. There is indeed experimental evidence, with simple verbal materials, that clustering of to-be-learned items by topic can enhance short-term memory performance (Tulving and Pearlstone, 1966). There is an additional, complementary strand of evidence, however, that has indicated repeatedly that under certain learning conditions, clustering topically similar items can interfere with memory for subsequently presented clusters of items from the same topic category. It is important to establish just which of these two kinds of effects are operational when learning from taxonomically or thematically clustered television news bulletins.

The experiments just discussed indicated that serial position effects may be important determinants of memory for bulletin content. Items presented at or near the beginning or at or near the end of a news sequence were much more likely to be recalled than those that occurred elsewhere.

The results of these early studies of item-placement effects also indicated the need for further and more elaborate designs to study organizational influences upon recall of bulletin content. The remaining sections of this chapter discuss research carried out in the last few years by the author to investigate ways in which retention of television news content is related to viewers' categorisation and modes of encoding news materials, and how in turn these latter factors are affected by production attributes of news programmes. This work led to the discovery of powerful content-organization effects on learning over and above the simple serial position effects examined in the last chapter, which have important implications for the production of memorable television news.

INTERFERENCE BETWEEN SIMILAR STORIES

The implications of simple verbal learning research findings on interference between taxonomically similar items for learning from broadcast news have been reinforced by actual studies of broadcast news recall. One of the first observations of inter-item interference during recall of broadcast news was made by Robinson and his colleagues. They reported several studies of memory for television news conducted in the United Kingdom and United States that indicated fairly poor levels either of recall or of comprehension (Robinson, Davis, Sahin & O'Toole, 1980; Robinson, Sahin & Davis, 1982). In particular they found that viewers' understanding of individual stories was often characterised by a phenomenon they called "meltdown," in which elements of one story merged or were confused with elements of another.

The implication that similarities between news stories may affect memory for broadcast news was also made by Stauffer, Frost, and Rybolt (1983). Over four evenings during which they tested people for recall of that evening's network news, items such as the New Hampshire Democratic primary, the Soviet invasion of Afghanistan, the stock reports, and the hostages in Iran appeared each night. These authors suggested that the low recall of evening news they observed might well have occurred in part because these very similar topics were run together and were confused by viewers.

In an experimental study of memory for radio news, Findahl and Hoijer (1985) tested Stockholm residents for immediate retention of a simulated radio broadcast. When examining sources of misunderstanding while testing for news comprehension afterwards, they found that listeners confused information from different items on occasions. This was especially the case with two items dealing with the same type of event, such as items about demonstrations. In one demonstration no police were involved while in the other demonstration they were. Nearly one quarter of the sample mixed details from these two items. Sometimes, confusions occurred even between items that were more loosely connected. Findahl and Hoijer also noted that elements within a story may be transposed. In an item about an oil tanker that ran aground, a few listeners identified a fishing boat, which arrived to rescue the crew, as the vessel that had run aground.

In an attempt to understand more clearly why inter-item interference effects occur, Gunter conducted a series of experiments using an established cognitive psychological procedure originally designed to examine the ways in which people encode verbal information (Gunter, Clifford, & Berry, 1980).

The research reported here focuses on two fundamental empirical questions. Firstly, do individuals differentially categorise and encode television news materials along the taxonomic dimensions that have previously been noted to play an important role in determining the treatment and distribution of news in television bulletins? Secondly, can memory for one news item affect memory for another in the same news bulletin and if so how? In particular, do successively presented (or "packaged") news items from the same taxonomic class interfere with each other when learning and remembering news content? These questions are theoretically as well as practically important because they reflect and extend a long-standing interest among experimental psychologists in the attributes or dimensions along which stimuli are stored in memory.

To enable exploration of these hitherto unasked questions about memory for broadcast news, an experimental paradigm was adopted that previous research had shown to be a sensitive indicator of linguistic categorisation and encoding dimensions and that was also thought to be amenable to the study of memory for television materials. This method, as described by Wickens (1970, 1972) makes the assumption that if a stimulus item is represented in memory by a code similar to that used to represent a preceding stimulus item, *proactive interference* from the earlier code will inhibit correct recall of the current stimulus item. Additional stimulus items of the same type will reduce even further the probability of correct memory performance. If the type of stimulus is changed such that a different type of memory code is employed, a reduction in this interference results. At the point when the initial shift in the nature of the to-be-remembered materials occurs, information recall usually improves considerably. This effect has been termed *release from proactive interference* (PI) and has been cited by Wickens and others as evidence for particular dimensions along which linguistic materials are encoded in memory.

In the typical release-from-PI experiment respondents are given four learning trials. Each trial consists initially of the presentation of the materials that are to be remembered (usually a short list of words) followed by an attention-distracting task that is designed to prevent the learner rehearsing the items in his or her head, and finally a test of recall for the items. The reason for the attention-distracting interval is that this technique is designed to measure the varying strength of encoding of materials at initial presentation across learning trials, uncontaminated by other effects on memory performance such as silent rehearsal of items immediately after they have been coded and before they are recalled.

Respondents are usually divided into two groups, termed *no-shift* and *shift* respectively. In the no-shift condition, materials (i.e., words) from the same semantic or taxonomic category are presented on every trial, whereas in the shift condition taxonomically similar items are presented on the first three trials only and then on the fourth trial the class of material is switched. Typically, recall performance deteriorates for both groups over trials consisting of materials from the same taxonomy, but there is usually a marked improvement in memory performance of the shift group relative to the no-shift group on the fourth trial, following a switch for the former group from material of one sort to that of another. Wickens (1970, 1972) has argued that the amount of recovery in perform-ance (or release from PI) on the fourth trial following a shift in the class of material provides an index of the relative salience or significance of the changed attribute as a dimension in terms of which that material is categorised and encoded into memory.

Generalising from findings obtained in simple verbal learning experi-ments to the context of remembering television news, one would predict substantial forgetting of content to occur across successively presented news items from the same taxonomic class, as a function of taxonomically based, proactively interfering effects of earlier upon later presented items in the news sequence. This technique has been used to demonstrate a large number of semantic (or taxonomic) and nonsemantic (e.g., presentation format) attributes along which linguistic materials are encoded in mem-ory. Although stimulus materials have customarily consisted of relatively simple verbal items such as lists of words, in the current research the release-from-PI technique was elaborated and extended to examine modes of encoding complex meaningful items in the form of television news stories.

Four Experiments on Taxonomic-Clustering Effects

The first study on taxonomic-clustering effects on memory for televised news content looked at recall of news headlines. Gunter, Clifford, and Berry (1980) presented a series of four news-learning trials, each of which consisted of three short television news items or news triads video-recorded several months before from actual network newscasts. The items were carefully selected to control for length and visual format differences as far as possible, and were shown on a small monochrome television monitor to respondents individually. Following each news triad, the respondent worked on a distractor task, in this case a crossword puzzle, for 1 minute and then recalled all the items he or she could from that triad in any order, by writing a short "headline" account of each item. The accuracy of recall was then scored for each triad. Following the fourth news triad, there was a 1-minute period of distractor activity, and then respondents were asked to recall spontaneously as many of the items as possible from all four triads in a test of delayed recall.

As in the traditional paradigm, respondents were divided into two groups: a no-shift group, for whom the news category of the items was held constant over all four learning trials (or news triads) and a shift group, for whom the taxonomy was constant over the first three trials (triads) only and was switched to a different category on the fourth trial (triad). Several different random sequences of the same items were used within this design for each group to minimise idiosyncratic effects related to particular items.

The news materials themselves consisted of items about either political events or sports events, and these were divided evenly among respondents in both groups. Thus, half of the respondents in the no-shift condition received triads of political items over all four learning trials, while half received only sports items. In the shift condition, half of the respondents were switched from political items, which had been presented for the first three learning trials, to sports items on the fourth learning trial, while half were switched in the opposite direction.

As the results summarised in Table 8.1 show, although there was little difference in memory performance for each category of news, recall declined over successive trial, of items from the same taxonomy. During the initial recall phase, when information was tested independently for each learning trial, recall performance deteriorated in the no-shift condition from 80% of (retrieved) information correct on the fourth trial. Following a critical switch in news taxonomy on the fourth trial in the shift condition, however, a substantial improvement in recall performance occurred with 70% of the news information being correctly recalled, signifying an effect that as we noted earlier, is referred to in the technical jargon of this area of cognitive psychology as release from proactive interference. This buildup of interference across learning of thematically or topically similar news items was observed equally for political and sports news, and alleviation of learning impairment occurred to the same extent following each topic shift. In a subsequent replication experiment, Gunter, Berry, and Clifford (1981) reported the same buildup and release of proactive interference effects across and between domestic and foreign political news (see Table 8.2). These learning and recall phenomena appear, on current evidence, to be fairly consistent and reliable, and are not specific to particular categories of news. Wickens (1970, 1972) interpreted release from proactive interference as an indicator of the attributes or dimensions along which linguistic materials are encoded and organized in memory. Consequently, the current findings may signify that viewers encode broad taxonomic features of televised news items along with more specific details of the story narrative and perhaps also organise news events in memory according to these features.

Television news reports may often be quite detailed, and so too, therefore, might be information gain from them. In their first taxonomic-

TABLE 8.1

Mean Proportion of Correct Responses on Each Trial Within Groups As a Function of Taxonomy and Duration of Shift

	Immediate Recall					Delayed Recall				
	Trial Number					Trial Number				
Group	1	2	3	4	M	1	2	3	4	M
No topic shift										
Politics (P)	.89	.71	.61	.42	.66	.65	.49	.37	.23	.44
Sport (S)	.85	.62	.49	.43	.60	.64	.43	.36	.37	.45
M	.87	.67	.55	.43	.63	.65	.46	.37	.30	.45
Topic shift										
P to S	.81	.67	.53	.72	.68	.63	.42	.30	.53	.47
S to P	.83	.67	.56	.65	.61	.68	.48	.29	.60	.51
M	.82	.67	.55	.74	.70	.66	.45	.30	.57	.49

Source: Gunter, Clifford, and Berry, 1980.

TABLE 8.2

Mean Proportion of Correct Responses on Each Trial Within Groups As a Function Taxonomy and Direction of Shift

	Immediate Recall					Delayed Recall				
	Trial Number					Trial Number				
Group	1	2	3	4	M	1	2	3	4	M
No topic shift										
HP	.85	.65	.52	.37	.60	.71	.44	.27	.42	
FP	.85	.56	.48	.42	.58	.65	.38	.33	.29	.41
M	.85	.61	.50	.40	.59	.68	.41	.30	.27	.42
Topic shift										
FP to HP	.90	.61	.46	.73	.68	.67	.35	.24	.52	.46
HP to FP	.79	.61	.50	.69	.65	.67	.42	.33	.59	.50
M	.85	.61	.48	.71	.66	.67	.40	.31	.56	.49

Source: Gunter, Berry, and Clifford, 1981.
Note: HP = home-political news, FP = foreign-political news.

clustering experiment Gunter et al. (1980) tested only brief news-headline recall, which may have primed respondents' awareness of the taxonomic similarities and dissimilarities of news items, thus artificially inducing taxonomically based interference effects. To what extent do losses of information to memory of the same sort occur across taxonomically similar news reports under conditions of detailed retention of content from each item, where the taxonomic nature or similarities of items may be much less salient?

To examine this question, Gunter et al. (1981) attempted a replication of their first experiment on taxonomic clustering, employing a detailed news-learning situation. With all items of constant visual format (news-caster-only presentation), they presented one news story per learning trial. Following an attention-distracting task (crossword puzzle) to mini-mise further rehearsal of item content following initial presentation, respondents received a series of four questions on details of the item. After four such trials, a final delayed cued recall test was given, consisting of eight new and eight repeated questions covering all items shown during the initial phase. The repeated questions covered content previously tested following initial presentation on each learning trial, whereas new questions probed content not previously tested.

Once again, recall declined across taxonomically similar items and improved shifting to a new learning category, and this pattern of responding occurred during the immediate presentation and test phase and during the delayed recall phase (see Table 8.3). Interestingly, al-

TABLE 8.3
Mean Proportion of Correct Responses on Each Trial
Within Groups as a Function of Taxonomy and Direction
of Shift

Group	Immediate Recall					Delayed Recall				
	Trial Number					Trial Number				
	1	2	3	4	M	1	2	3	4	M
No topic shift										
Politics (P)	.81	.69	.47	.44	.60	.72	.44	.41	.25	.46
Industry (I)	.84	.63	.53	.50	.63	.47	.47	.22	.19	.34
M	.83	.66	.50	.47	.62	.59	.45	.31	.22	.39
Topic shift										
P to I	.78	.66	.47	.66	.64	.59	.47	.31	.50	.47
I to P	.81	.66	.53	.69	.67	.66	.38	.19	.53	.44
M	.80	.66	.50	.68	.66	.63	.43	.25	.52	.46

Source: Gunter, Berry, and Clifford, 1981.

TABLE 8.4

Mean Proportion of Correct Responses During Old and
New Delayed Recall as a Function of Groups, Taxonomy
and Trials

| Group | Old | | | | | New | | | | |
| | Trial Number | | | | | Trial Number | | | | |
	1	2	3	4	M	1	2	3	4	M
No topic shift										
Politics (P)	.94	.68	.75	.44	.70	.25	.09	.03	.03	.06
Industry (I)	.88	.82	.38	.38	.61	.03	.06	.03	.00	.03
M	.91	.75	.57	.41	.66	.14	.08	.03	.02	.07
Topic shift										
P to I	.94	.88	.62	.82	.82	.13	.03	.00	.09	.06
I to P	1.00	.75	.38	.88	.75	.16	.0	.00	.09	.06
M	.97	.84	.50	.85	.78	.14	.02	.00	.09	.06

Source: Gunter, Berry, and Clifford, 1981.

though information previously tested during the first phase (i.e., on repeated questions) was remembered much better at delayed testing than previously untested material (i.e., on new questions) the buildup of interference across trials containing items from the same taxonomy and subsequent improvement in memory performance on the trial where the nature of the news was changed were strongly evident for delayed recall on both new and repeated questions (see Table 8.4).

This experiment was designed, however, not simply to demonstrate practical effects on learning and remembering televised news material or organising or structuring that material in one way or another but also to examine the deeper questions of what kinds of memory processes underlie information losses of this sort. That is, do individuals learn equally well information presented in all items on successive learning trials but then experience difficulty *retrieving* later-presented information from memory when preceding content is very similar in nature? Or is the information presented on later trial poorly learned to begin with relative to earlier, similar material, as individuals suffer a breakdown in ability to encode information into memory?

It was for this purpose that respondents were given two types of questions on news item content. Response performance was considerably better an old questions than on new questions, indicating that initial testing facilitated delayed recall. In fact, memory for retested information in the second phase of the experiment was higher even than immediate recall in the first phase, indicating some sort of "reminiscence effect," whereby respondents were able, after a delay, to recall information they had been unable to recall, perhaps because of some sort of block to retrieval, shortly after each item had been presented.[1]

Previous research had shown that short-term recall of simple verbal materials enhanced their further recall after a day, but precisely why this effect occurs has not been conclusively established (Ellis & Montague, 1973). In the current experiment, it seems that initial testing on each learning trial could have facilitated additional rehearsal of tested material, producing in turn interference in learning and/or in recall of information on subsequent trials. This rehearsal effect might be invoked to account for the decline in recall across successive items from the same category, at least on previously tested news content during the delayed test phase. But what about the decline in memory performance on new questions—where the information being probed had not been the object of further active processing incurred through the initial retrieval? Can this effect be interpreted also as due to rehearsal during initial testing? It is possible, for instance, that initial test questions did lead respondents to review the original material, including those aspects not directly relevant to the questions put at the time. What would happen, though, if the effects of additional rehearsal of information afforded by initial testing were eliminated? Would the same decline in memory performance across successive news items from the same story category still occur? To test this, Gunter et al. (1981) carried out a further experiment, using the same design and materials as the previous study, with the exception that no tests of recall for item content were given during the presentation phase. Instead, presentation of one item and a subsequent 1-minute period of crossword puzzle completion were followed immediately by presentation of the next item. When all four items had been shown, there followed a further 2-minutes of distractor activity with the crossword puzzle before a delayed test of recall consisting of 16 questions (4 per item) were given.

Response patterns mirrored those of earlier experiments. Memory performance deteriorated over successive items from the same taxonomic category, with a significant improvement in performance following a shift to a different category (see Table 8.5). However, the buildup and sudden reduction of interference observed in this experiment were particularly interesting because they appeared on a single test of delayed

---

[1]One anomalous result did occur in this experiment for the shift group in receipt of industrial news items (Shift (I)), for which recall performance on Trial 1 during delayed recall on new questions was substantially poorer than for any other group. Given that the same conditions of random allocation of item items to trials for each respondent and random allocation of respondents to no-shift or shift groups existed throughout the experiment, this result is difficult to explain. It may, however, indicate the need to take into consideration individual differences in news preferences and interests of people, which may affect their memory performance on real-life material of this kind.

TABLE 8.5
Mean Proportion of Correct Responses During Delayed
Recall as a Function of Groups, Taxonomy and Trials

Group	Trial Number				
	1	2	3	4	M
No topic shift					
Politics (P)	.75	.50	.38	.29	.48
Industry (I)	.58	.54	.38	.25	.44
M	.67	.52	.38	.27	.46
Topic shift					
P to I	.67	.48	.38	.50	.50
I to P	.58	.54	.42	.58	.53
M	.63	.50	.40	.54	.52

Source: Gunter, Berry, and Clifford, 1981.

recall covering details of all items in the absence of initial testing. As each respondent received a different random order of questions, there was little or no possibility that differential recall across items could have been biased by blocking or serial order of questions. The results therefore strongly implied that information recall from each news item was determined by the number of taxonomically similar items preceding its presentation.

Another interesting finding to emerge from this experiment was that recall score here lay roughly midway between those for the retested and new conditions in the previous experiment. This result suggests that initially tested item information is strengthened thereby, and therefore remembered better after delay, whereas memory for item information that is not tested is harmed by the strengthening given to the tested material. It is possible then that initial testing provides an opportunity for additional or more elaborate rehearsal and storage of information, which is therefore subsequently easier to retrieve.

To sum up, the results from the four taxonomic-clustering experiments reported in this chapter can be interpreted as indicating that news information may be poorly learned or forgotten across a sequence of items from the same story category. This interference can be alleviated by shifting the nature of the news taxonomy at a particular point in the sequence. Although not empirically tested here, if a shift in the news category from the third to fourth learning trial can result in a reduction of interference, alternating between different categories throughout the whole sequence, so that no two successive items are from the same taxonomy, might also have a similar effect, thus preventing the buildup of any taxonomically based interference. That this may be true for learning television news is implied by a study on learning and remembering the content of prose passages that used the same experimental paradigm (Blumenthal & Robbins, 1977). Researchers here found that although substantial information losses occurred across consecutive passages on similar subject matter (e.g., physics or music), no such losses occurred when no two successive passages were from the same topic area.

The main practical implication of this experimentation is that it may be unwise to cluster news items in television bulletins according to taxonomy. This point is important in view of the apparently salient role of news categories in the production of television newscasts, especially in relation to the problem of clarity and comprehensibility of programme content. As noted earlier, producers apparently assume that clustering taxonomically similar news stories seems to package together isolated events into more meaningful combinations that can be more readily learned by the audience. However, the evidence from the psychological research just presented indicates that this reasoning may be incorrect. The attempt to arrive at simplicity and clarity of presentation by packaging the news in this way may in fact impair memory for bulletin content rather than improve it and may contribute in a fundamental way to the rapid forgetting of news information frequently observed among large sections of the audience shortly following exposure to television broadcasts. However, some editors and producers may be reluctant to follow the recommendations to avoid taxonomic packaging of news in television bulletins for one reason (aesthetic or historic-professional) or another, so does experimental research with television news materials offer any other workable solutions? One alternative answer may lie in the use of visualisations.

In television, verbal news items are characterised by features other than taxonomic ones. News broadcasters place much emphasis on presenting a very "visual" news programme to make it more interesting and, in the case of film, to make its content seem more realistic. Research within the release-from-PI framework has shown that with simple linguistic materials, visual context features may also be encoded as salient attributes of to-be-remembered stimuli (Brodie & Lippmann, 1970; Turvey & Egan, 1969). It will be remembered that Gunter (1979, 1980a) showed that brief news items accompanied by film or by stills are better recalled than newscaster-only items. Do these visual format features of news materials also represent encodable dimensions of verbal news reports?

Gunter et al. (1980: Experiment 2) again employed a Wickens-type design, this time with taxonomic category held constant across all items for viewers in both shift and no-shift conditions. Items were differentiated instead according to their visual format characteristics. Two visual categories were used: newscaster-only items consisting of the presenter reading the news directly into camera, and visual-still items in which a still photograph relating to the news event was inserted over the news-caster for between 15 and 20% of the duration of the item. As in the taxonomic-shift experiments, the two categories of items were allocated equally to viewers in the no-shift condition, and visual shifts from news-caster-only to newscaster-plus-still items or vice versa were balanced across viewers in the shift condition. Recall performance declined over taxonomically and visually homogeneous news triads and improved following a visual format shift. However, this shift produced a substantial improvement in memory performance in one direction only, when changing from newscaster-only items to newscaster-plus-stills (see Table 8.6).

The reverse shift resulted in only slight release from PI. According to Wickens (1970, 1972), a symmetrical release effect in both directions is necessary to infer differential encoding along the two critical categories (in this case, visual formats) or stimulus materials. These data suggest that viewers may not differentially categorise and encode news items along gross visual format features to the same degree that they do along taxonomic attributes. However, they also indicate that taxonomically generated interference can nevertheless be alleviated by changes in visual format. Thus visual format variations may be effectively utilised to offset to some extent the information losses that occur in taxonomically homogeneous news packages.

The experiments described previously by Gunter and his colleagues demonstrated interference across topically similar news stories within an

TABLE 8.6
Mean Proportion of Correct Responses Over
Taxonomically Similar News Items as a Function of Visual
Format and Format Shift

Group	Immediate Recall					Delayed Recall				
	News Sequences[1]					News Sequences				
	1	2	3	4	M	1	2	3	4	M
No format shift										
S[2]	.88	.78	.68	.54	.72	.72	.54	.42	.26	.49
N–O[3]	.77	.67	.58	.47	.62	.64	.46	.40	.30	.45
M	.83	.73	.63	.51	.67	.68	.50	.41	.28	.47
Format shift										
S to N–O	.83	.72	.59	.61	.69	.56	.53	.42	.43	.49
N–O to S	.82	.69	.56	.75	.71	.65	.42	.33	.60	.50
M	.83	.71	.58	.68	.70	.61	.48	.38	.52	.50

Source: Gunter, Clifford, and Berry, 1980.
Note: [1]Each news sequence consisted of three news items
[2]S: News items with stills
[3]N–O: Newscaster on camera only

experimental paradigm that involved a highly artificial presentation format. To what extent does this kind of interference occur with news presentation formats approaching in style those normally found in television news broadcasts? More experimental evidence has suggested that interference as such does still occur when topically similar news stories are presented in a more standard fashion.

Berry and Clifford (1985) have reported an experiment in which a television bulletin was prepared in two versions from items prerecorded from an earlier live television broadcast. In one version four out of five items were domestic (U.K.) stories, whereas the middle (third) item was a foreign story. In the other version, a domestic story was surrounded by four foreign stories. Small groups of viewers watched one of these bulletins, after which they filled out a personality questionnaire for about 15 minutes before being tested on depth recall of information contained in the spoken narrative of the news stories. Results showed that information was recalled significantly better from the isolated item than from the surrounding (topically similar) items, thus supporting earlier findings.

CONCLUDING REMARKS

The research discussed in this chapter offers what must by now be regarded as reliable indications about the likelihood of information losses from televised newscasts on the basis of how content is organised within news programmes. On the evidence of content analysis of television news output (e.g., Glasgow University Media Group, 1976) and accounts of professional observations obtained from news personnel concerning the delivery of news (e.g., Golding & Elliott, 1979; Schlesinger, 1978) there is a strong and inherent tendency, it seems, for news editors to package together news stories about similar topics. Frequently, several items from the same topic category are run in quick succession, often also with the implication that they are about related events, even though in reality this may be untrue.

The series of experimental studies of news retention by Berry and Gunter, reported here, have shown that news items from the same topic can be confused by members of the audience, or may be mutually inhibiting at the time of initial presentation and learning. This interference phenomenon been demonstrated to occur not only under the artificial conditions of information presentation dictated by particular experimental paradigms (e.g., Gunter et al., 1980) but also when the news is presented in a more usual fashion (Berry & Clifford, 1985). Furthermore, researchers elsewhere have observed similar interference effects or informational confusion between similar items when viewers are questioned at home after watching a live television newscast (Robinson et al., 1980).

To prevent such information losses, current experimental research evidence points to a recommendation that news editors should try to avoid extensive use of three- or four-item topic clusters. Such packages could be split up and alternated with items from other categories of news. Alternatively, if the topic-related news format is desired for strong professional journalistic reasons, or if jumping around from one news category to another is not aesthetically a comfortable format, another recommendation might be to employ carefully chosen gross visual format changes within such news packages. Experimental evidence indicates that gross visual shifts can alleviate interference and declining memory performance across news items about similar topics (Gunter et al., 1980).

More specific guidelines may become available following further refinements and improvements to existing research methodology. Future research might attempt to define more clearly and comprehensively the range and differentiation of news topics. More accurate measurement of the degree of semantic similarity or distance between two news topics or two news stories, as perceived by audience members (possibly using techniques currently being developed to study the structure and control processes of semantic memory) could lead to more precise predictions about probable levels of interference across stories within a single news programme.

9 Picturing the News

Although the important ingredients of news stories presented in television newscasts are generally those contained in the spoken narrative of the newscaster or reporter, television is nevertheless essentially a visual medium. Many television newsmen hold that the visual channel should always be utilised to its fullest potential, even though it is not clear what exactly this potential is.

There is now an extensive array of visual inputs available to the news professional. News items may consist simply of a newsperson talking directly to camera in the studio. But more often than not the screen is enlivened by the insertion of graphical displays, portraits, or maps over which the newscaster, temporarily absent from the picture, may talk, or which, via the Chromakey device, may be "melted in" behind the newsreader on a simulated screen.

Television is unique among the news media, however, in that it possesses moving pictures. Moving pictures, either on film or, more often these days, on videotape, are used routinely on television news. They are especially favoured because they create the impression of allowing the audience to witness events as they happen (Schlesinger, 1978). The effect of witnessing and vicariously participating in events in this way is to bring about an emotional reaction. It is this ability to generate an emotional reaction to instant news that for some professionals principally distinguishes televised news from any other news medium (Green, 1969). The "talking head" or man-on-camera format, on the other hand, is regarded as very much the second-best presentational mode, and some editors would argue that the latter format may even work to distract the viewer's attention from what is being reported and so interfere with learning (Whale, 1969). How accurate, though, is this naive psychologising of television newsmen? Do visuals such as film or stills enhance news impact and learning? Or does the newsperson's eagerness to use pictures at all costs result in the presentation of much irrelevant and distracting content, which serves only to inhibit information acquisition from the bulletin?

This chapter examines evidence on the efficacy of television to communicate information to audiences. The chapter falls broadly into two sections. In the first section, research is reviewed that has compared television with other media of communication (e.g., radio and print). The second part focuses on television and examines effects of different styles of presentation on information gain from television programmes designed to impart information to viewers.

TELEVISION AND OTHER MEDIA COMPARED

There have been numerous experimental studies since the 1930s that have examined learning from informational media as a function specifically of presentation medium. Many of these studies have been concerned with the relative effectiveness of audio-visual, audio-only, and written media in instructional or educational contexts and have been designed to find out which is the best channel through which to impart information in formal educational settings. In addition to these educationally orientated studies, often using specially prepared instructional materials, there have been a number of experiments that have examined presentation modality effects on learning and recall of news.

Differences in correct information retention from various presentation modalities under experimental conditions have not always been in the same direction, though. Some experimental studies have compared learning from television with that from radio and print, others have compared television with only one of the latter media. One of the earliest comparisons of learning from different broadcast media was a study reported by Goldberg (1950). He looked at retention and appreciation for a group of listeners and viewers of a simulcast—a programme broadcast simultaneously on television and radio. Two groups of college undergraduates were recruited to either listen to the radio version or view the television version of the same broadcast in their own homes. Both groups recorded their reactions to the programme at periodic intervals. Then, a week later, a retention test was administered for all of the material appearing on the show. In the surprise quiz on the content of the programme, the radio group averaged 53% correct answers against a 64% average for the television group. Both groups failed completely on one question, the radio group was ahead on two others, and the television group was ahead on the seven remaining questions.

Barrow and Westley (1959), for example, conducted an experiment to compare the effectiveness of equivalent radio and television versions of "Exploring the News," a series of background-of-the-news programmes for grade-school children. Each version of the programme was shown to randomly allocated classroom groups of 11- to 12-year-olds. Results indicated a superiority of television presentation over radio. Children who saw the television version performed significantly better than a radio group on an immediate recall test of factual knowledge from the programme. Furthermore, the television group continued to score better than the radio group on a delayed test, although the difference was no longer statistically significant.

Williams, Paul, and Ogilvie (1957) compared television, radio, print, and live presentations of a lecture. A sample of over 100 college undergraduates was divided into four groups and received the lecture at the same time in different rooms under one or other of these presentation conditions. A test of knowledge acquisition was given to all groups immediately after the lecture and again 8 months later. Once again, it was found that learning was best for the television group, followed by radio, reading, and finally the live studio lecture group. Television produced significantly better learning than radio, and radio in turn was significantly better than reading. There was no reliable difference between reading and live presentations. Eight months later, retests again showed best retention for the television group, but on this occasion, the studio group had moved up to second place.

Trenaman (1967) compared learning about a variety of different subject materials from television, radio, and print. Programme materials were presented either as television broadcasts, radio broadcasts, or in written transcript from two groups of individuals selected from the general public. Altogether, Trenaman made 11 comparisons between television and other media. In eight of these, the television versions resulted in the higher comprehension score (in seven cases significantly so), and in three cases the other media had the advantage (none significantly so). There were five comparisons between radio and print versions, and in three radio produced between performance (in one case significantly so), whereas in the other two the differences were nonsignificant. Trenaman also found that the extent to which one medium had an advantage over the other varied according to the subject matter of the programme.

These early investigations of learning from different channels of communication indicated that television, in relative terms, could be an effective information medium. More recent experimental research has largely failed to repeat these findings, however, and has consistently reported better learning and retention of information from print than from either television or radio.

Two Canadian studies reported in the mid-1970s showed large losses from all media during immediate, unaided recall of simulated news presentations, and losses were greater from broadcast media than from print. Wilson (1974) constructed two fictitious but plausible news stories in standard inverted-pyramid news styles. That is, the first sentence or two delivered the central point of the story, and successive sentences elaborated on that with further details.

An independent panel of judges was employed to categorise the information contained in each story as *essential* (central to the meaning of the story) or *contributory* (elaborative detail). Short, medium, and long version of each story were then prepared in audio-visual, audio-only, and written form. Over 400 college students were allocated to one or other of these presentation conditions. Afterwards, all respondents were given a free recall test of everything they could remember from each story, which they produced in written accounts.

Points of information judged essential to the stories received two points if recalled fully and accurately, one point if recalled in general, and no points if omitted. Points of information judged contributory were scored one point if recalled fully and accurately, and received no points if recalled otherwise or omitted. The greatest information loss was from radio presentation (77%), second was from television (76%), and the least was from print (72%). There was less loss from short stories (71%) than from medium-length stories (74%) and most from long stories (81%), although the author does not report any interactions between length and presentation modality.

Browne (1978) presented volunteers from two jury panels with either a documentary film that described the legislative process in Oklahoma or a written transcript from the film. Before-after tests revealed significant improvements in knowledge among viewers and readers, but readers gained more than viewers, even though neither group differed significantly from each other on pretesting.

Stauffer, Frost, and Rybolt (1980) examined recall from television, radio, and print news among Kenyan and American college students. In both countries, the experiment consisted of showing an actual television newscast with sound to one group (viewers), presenting the soundtrack only to another group (listeners), and the printed transcript of the narrative to another (readers). Those reading the transcript were allowed to read through the material once at their own pace.

Immediately after news presentation, respondents were asked to make a list of all the stories they could recall by providing a brief description of each item. Following this unaided recall test, respondents completed a four-option multiple-choice test based on the narrative content of the news stories. Both U.S. and Kenyan newscasts contained 14 stories and were about 16 minutes long. Among American and Kenyan samples recall from television and print was similar and significantly higher than from an audio source (see Table 9.1). On combining Kenya and U.S. samples, Stauffer et al. reported that 19% of listeners remembered four stories or fewer compared to only 2% of viewers or readers. Three percent of listeners could recall more than ten stories while 25% of viewers and 27% of readers could do so.

Jacoby, Hoyer, and Zimmer (1981) reported an experimental study with undergraduate students in which they measured comprehension of three news items and three commercial messages following either audio-visual, audio-only, or print presentation. Subjects received either the three news items or the three commercials and afterwards were given a comprehension test consisting of six statements about the three items they had just seen, heard, or read. They had to say whether each statement was true or false. There were four groups in all, created by dividing those receiving the items in print into two subgroups, who either were permitted to read items in their own time or were given 30 seconds to read each item.

Results showed that items conveyed via the print modality were significantly better comprehended than when they were conveyed either via audio-visual or audio-only modalities. Under the print condition, subjects who were allowed to read the items at their own pace fared better than those who had limited exposure. There were no differences in miscomprehension rates between the audio-visual and audio-only modalities. Comparing comprehension of news and advertising, Jacoby et al. found that factual news statements were miscomprehended to a greater extent than were factual advertising statements, while the opposite was true in the case of inferential statements.

Two recent British experiments have provided replicable evidence that print gives rise to better immediate memory of a news narrative than

TABLE 9.1

Mean Recall of News by American and Kenyan Samples as a function of Presentation Modality

	Viewers	Listeners	Readers
Unaided Recall			
Kenya	9.1	6.4	9.0
U.S.	8.5	6.6	8.5
Multiple Choice			
Kenya	12.6	9.6	12.7
U.S.	13.8	12.8	14.5

Source: Stauffer, Frost, and Rybolt, 1980. Reprinted by permission of the publisher.

either television or radio presentations when exposure times are the same across presentation conditions (Furnham & Gunter, 1985; Gunter, Furnham, and Gietson, 1984). The design, materials, and procedures were the same for both experiments.

The news sequence consisted of four items, originally made for television. All items had a common format, consisting originally of televised film reports read by an unseen narrator. Two items depicted violent events—scenes of street clashes between rioters and police in El Salvador and in South Korea,—and two items depicted nonviolent events, about the lifting of trade restrictions by Japan and about a visit to Yugoslavia by the Greek Prime Minister.

In the television condition, the items were presented to subjects over a colour television monitor; in the radio condition, the soundtrack only of each item was played to subjects over an audio-cassette recorder; and in the print condition, transcripts were made from the sound narrative of each item and were read by subjects. Exposure times were the same across conditions. Subjects in the print condition were given 4 minutes to read the news transcript, which was equivalent to the duration of the broadcast versions. Then 15 minutes were allowed to complete the test.

A test of 20 questions (five per item) was devised to probe retention of specific points within each story. Two points were given for each completely correct answer, one point if an answer was just partially correct, and nothing for an incorrect answer or no response.

Gunter et al. (1984) ran 128 male and female sixth-form college students aged 16 to 18 years. To test the robustness and reliability of this experiment, Furnham and Gunter (1985) replicated it with a new and slightly older sample of 68 university undergraduates. Subjects were randomly allocated to television, radio, and print conditions in each experiment.

The results from both experiments are summarised in Table 9.2. In the first experiment, mean recall was significantly better from the print condition than from either the television or radio conditions. There was no reliable difference between the latter two conditions. There were also differences in recall associated with sex of respondent. Males consistently recalled more than females across all modalities, but there was no indication that one sex performed particularly better than the other under any specific modality of presentation.

In the second experiment, differences in mean recall associated with presentation modality partially replicated those of the first study. Mean recall, once again, was best following print presentation. Performance after print was significantly better than that following audio-visual or audio-only presentations. In this second experiment, however, there was a reversal in performance levels for audio-visual and audio-only presentations; mean recall was better this time from the latter modality. Finally,

TABLE 9.2

Recall of News as a Function of Presentation Modality

Presentation Modality	Experiment 1			Experiment 2		
	Males	Females	All	Males	Females	All
Audio-visual	12.1	8.0	10.1	9.9	9.9	9.9
Audio only	10.4	7.1	8.8	13.1	11.6	12.4
Print	13.3	11.6	12.5	15.7	17.0	16.4
All Modalities	11.9	8.9	10.5	12.9	12.8	12.9

Source: Experiment 1: Gunter, Furnham, and Gietson, 1983.
Experiment 2: Furnham and Gunter, 1984.

no sex differences in overall news recall were observed in this study, though females did perform slightly better than males in the print condition, in contrast to their relative levels of performance in this condition in the first experiment.

In summary, these two experiments by Gunter and his colleagues indicate that under controlled laboratory conditions, modality of information presentation can significantly affect information retention, even when narrative content is constant throughout. Reading the news clearly produces better performance than either watching or listening to it, even when exposure times are the same for all modalities.

VISUAL STYLES ON TELEVISION COMPARED

To date the research literature offers widely varying estimations of the value of visual material accompanying the narrative for learning from televised information sequences, although it has been demonstrated that even quite subtle manipulations of presentation format can produce significant perceptual reactions among the audience that may often be beyond the conscious awareness of the viewer. Some of these effects will be examined in the following sections. However, the major focus of this chapter is on learning and remembering television news content. If variations in presentation technique can effect different perceptual-evaluative responses, what effects do they also have on learning? As we shall see, a number of experimental studies with broadcast news and educational or instructional audio-visual materials have indicated that learning and retention of informational content from television programmes can depend often on the way it is visually presented.

Visual format effects and information gain from television presentations have been analysed in naturalistic field settings and under laboratory conditions. Each approach has its own distinct methodological advantages and disadvantages. In field studies, for example, respondents are tested for recall of items from television bulletins they have viewed in their own homes, without any forewarning, so that they do not expect to be tested. Thus, their viewing behaviour is quite natural, and recall scores are likely to reflect how much they normally remember from newscasts. However, it is often difficult when using this kind of study to estimate with any degree of precision the extent to which recall is affected by specific programme attributes. Such estimates are usually possible only on a post-hoc basis and it is therefore difficult to separate the individual effects of any one particular presentation feature from another.

Under laboratory conditions the problem of confounding between production variables can be alleviated or avoided completely through a prior manipulation of the television materials and conditions under which they are viewed. The experimenter can prerecord and reedit materials so as to vary the salience or strength of one programme attribute while holding other features constant. This permits fairly precise measurement of the independent contribution of particular facets of the programme to effective recall of its content. The main problem with the experimental approach, however, is its unnatural setting. Individuals may be placed in a viewing room alone or with small groups of others in a situation that is often far removed from the comfortable living room environment in which they are accustomed to watching TV news. Also, respondents may often be told beforehand that they will be tested on the materials to be shown. Thus, unlike under normal viewing conditions, they will perhaps make a concerted effort to remember as much as possible from a programme—resulting in an exaggeratedly high memory performance. However, even if individuals are trying to learn the materials, memory for items may still vary according to the production treatment they receive. So some indicators can still be obtained about the impact of programme format on information gain. Research on visual production format effects on learning from television news are examined in three parts: (a) the effects of presenter characteristics on audience response and learning; (b) the effects of different accompanying visuals on brief recall of news items; and (c) the effects on in-depth news recall of specific, supportive visual illustrations. In broad terms, because television is a visual medium, all news items in a TV bulletin are presented against some sort of visual background, even if it consists of the newsreader against a plain studio backdrop. However, for most items, visual material is added by news editors to enhance the overall impact of the item or to reinforce particular aspects of the story narrative, such as where the event occurred and who or what was involved. Although the general attentional impact of a news story can be enhanced by accompanying, aesthetically pleasing visual material such as film or still photographs, the specific informational value of these insertions depends on how well they match what is actually being said and which parts of the story they support. Film material, for example, may be nice to look at but often lacks any direct relevance to the narrative and may function only to distort or interfere with learning. Also, visual illustrations designed to reinforce particular parts of a news story may produce better recall of those parts but interfere with recall of other aspects of the same story that may be critical to its overall comprehension.

Effects of Presenter Variables

The focal point of any television newscast is the anchorperson. He or she introduces the programme, reads or introduces the main stories, and is responsible on screen for the smooth running of the show. Since the 1950s, when newscasters first emerged, they have become recognised as one of the most important ingredients of a successful news programme. In many cases they are celebrities in their own right who can command huge salaries on the same scale as show-business personalities. Television stations in the United States these days spend vast sums on research to find out if their current presenters are the right ones for the job, and often looks are given more significance than journalistic ability in selecting a news team (Karpf, 1985). But what is known about the impact of performer characteristics on audience response to the news? In the context of this book, are performer variables crucial to learning and comprehension, and if so, in what ways?

Performer-variable research can be conveniently discussed in two parts. The first area of research has focused upon the presenters themselves and their personal attributes. The second area has been concerned with the way presenters are presented on screen.

Among the major performer characteristics investigated have been the dress, facial expressions, gaze (or eye contact), and sex of the presenter. Although, audience perceptions of a news presenter may be significantly affected by his or her physical appearance, the evidence for effects on learning has been far from consistent. Even so, if audience impressions are affected by presenter attributes, this leaves open the possibility that memory and comprehension of news may also be influenced and that studies conducted so far have failed to use techniques sensitive enough to measure learning effects.

Using a teleprompter, a newsreader these days usually looks straight into camera; eye contact with the viewer is therefore direct. Sometimes, however, newsreaders still use notes when reading the news and occasionally lose eye contact with the audience while looking down at their script. A number of studies have indicated that the impression viewers from about a newsreader may be influenced by the degree of eye contact he or she has with them. It has been found, for example, that straight looking may be seen as less pleasant than looking to the side, while a downward gaze may be perceived as less alert, less interested, and less confident (Tankard, 1971). The latter result, however, was based on judgements of single shots rather than on a continuous performance by a presenter. During a news programme in which notes are used, it may not be so much the fact that eye contact varies, but the extent to which it is directed in a certain way that matters most for audience response. There is some indication that medium eye contact (55% of the time on screen) added more precision to a speaker's delivery than high eye contact (85% of the time on screen) (Baggaley, 1980). In a comparison of a desk-script format (about 70% eye contact) versus a teleprompt format (about 95% eye-contact), a newsreader with script is rated as stronger and more organised (Coldevin, 1979). Coldevin concludes that working with a script appears to provide a more compelling perception of the presenter in that he is seen to be 'working' at his craft rather than merely delivering a monologue' (1979, p. 82). Both the latter two studies call into question many television networks' reliance on maximum eye contact in news delivery. Unfortunately, neither of these studies investigated the effects of eye contact on learning. Results from early studies of eye contact effects found no significant impact on learning when viewers watch television presenters displaying high, medium, or low eye contact (Connolly, 1962; Westley & Mobius, 1960).

Eye contact does not work in isolation to affect audience perceptions of a news presenter. Julian (1977) found that a television newscaster's credibility was enhanced when he wore casual dress, Contrary to other findings, maximum eye contact also enhanced credibility ratings, and, combined with casual dress, newscaster credibility was improved still further. It should be noted, however, that only 16% of total variance in audience evaluations of the newscaster were accounted for by these nonverbal factors. Credibility of the news read by the newscaster was affected even less. Again, learning was not measured.

Although women and men have been used as news presenters since the earliest days of television news broadcasting, until as late as 1970 few women were employed on network news staffs. This began to change during the 1970s as more women were taken on as correspondents and anchors (Singleton & Cook, 1982). This increase in the presence of newswomen on screen stimulated research into the relative effectiveness and audience appeal of male and female presenters. In terms of credibility, studies have generally found no significant differences in audience response to men and women newsreaders (e.g., Stone, 1974; Whitakker & Whitakker, 1976; Hutchinson, 1982). While the claims of audience samples in public opinion surveys indicate that most people find male and female newsreaders equally acceptable and believable, is there any evidence that memory and comprehension of the news vary according to newscaster gender? The answer to this rarely examined question is that it does to some extent. Research with children and adults has indicated that memory for news does vary with the sex of the newscaster and that newscaster gender effects interact with the gender of viewers to produce even more pronounced variations in news retention.

In one demonstration of this with the younger end of the audience, Tan, Raudy, Huff, and Miles (1980) prepared two 15-minute television newscasts identical in every respect except that one was presented by a male and the other by a female newscaster. These newscasts were shown to groups of third- to fifth-grade children who were subsequently asked questions about the relative believability of the two newscasters and about the content of the programme.

Results showed that the male newscaster was generally more effective than the female newscaster in producing retention of newscast material. Furthermore, boys remembered more than girls. Boys and girls varied, however, in their relative levels of recall from male and female newscasters. Whereas boys learned just as much from a female as from a male newscaster, girls learned more from the male. There was a large drop in retention for girls who watched the female newscaster. The results for memory were not matched by believability scores, however. Male and female newsreaders were rated equally on this scale, and there were no differences associated with the gender of viewers.

Tan et al. suggested that children may respond both to the sex of the presenter and the sex-role depicted in the situation. While boys may have considered the role of television newscaster to be appropriate for both males and females, girls may not have perceived that role to be appropriate for a female. Girls may therefore have paid less attention when the female newscaster read the news. This does not explain why there were differences between boys and girls in their learning from a male newscaster when he was perceived equally believable by both sexes. Invoking other research findings, Tan et al. suggest that it could be that there were sex differences in the perceived power of the male newscaster. Perry and Perry (1975) found that "masculine" children of both sexes remembered more of an adult male model's behaviour, whereas "feminine" children responded equally well to both male and female models. It is possible therefore that male newsreaders, though not perceived as more credible, were perceived as more powerful and worthy of attention than were female newsreaders.

In a more recent study, Berry and Clifford (1985) reported differences between males and females in the audience in their recall of television news from alternated and nonalternated male and female presenters. In one condition, young adult viewers were shown six items presented by a female newscaster followed by six items read by a male presenter; in a second condition, male- and female-presented items were alternated.

There was no overall effect of presentation condition, but there was an interaction between condition and the sex of the viewers. Female viewers exhibited poorer memory performance in the alternating condition than in the blocked condition, whereas among male viewers, alternation of female- with male-presented items significantly improved retention. These findings were replicated by Berry and Clifford in a second experiment. It appears therefore that it may not be simply the gender of newsreaders that is important but also the way they are used or presented in a news broadcast.

Audience reactions to a news broadcast may depend on the professionalism with which the news is presented. Normally in news programmes, events run smoothly and mistakes are rare. This is probably just as well, because research has indicated that although audiences may be forgiving of minor errors in presentation, repeated and glaring upsets in the delivery may be met with harsh criticism.

Coldevin (1979) reported that following a period of monitoring news broadcasts in Canada, he had observed a number of different types of errors in news programmes, including slurs in pronunciation, repeated words or phrases, hesitation in responding to an on-camera cue, or looking off to one side of the screen when the shot returns to the studio from a report from elsewhere (e.g., film report). He subsequently conducted an experiment to examine the effects on audience response of the latter "missed cue" error. Results showed that when this type of error occurred once or twice during a programme, viewers' opinions were not soured, but when the newsreader missed his cue more often and took a long time to rectify his mistake, not only the newsreader but also the programme suffered a severe loss of credibility. Unfortunately, memory performance was not measured in this study. Coldevin reported, however, that viewers were conscious of the errors made by the newscaster, which suggests also that they may have been distracted by them and had their memory for information in the news narrative impaired.

In addition to the effects of presenter attributes on audience response to television news, some researchers have also examined characteristics of the way the newscaster is himself (or herself) presented. Studies of camera angle variations and visual setting have indicated that the audience opinions about the presenter and about the programme can be influenced by subtle variations in presentation format.

Camera angles have been found to affect audience impressions of a performer on screen. A high camera angle has been found to reduce the perceived effectiveness, competence, and credibility of a presenter, whereas a low camera angle has the opposite effect (Tiemens, 1970; Mandell & Shaw, 1973). The low-angle shot can be especially effective at strengthening a presenter's performance when used sparingly during the programme (McCain, Chilberg, & Wakshlag, 1977). There is no evidence, however, that camera angle affects factual recall from a newscast (Tiemens, 1970).

The on-screen presentation can also be varied by changing the background against which the newscaster is seated. A relevant pictorial background has been found to increase the newscaster's credibility when compared with plain sets (Baggaley & Duck, 1974, 1976; Coldevin, 1978a, 1978b). The effects of visual background may be more effective with highly professional presenters, however (Baggaley, 1980).

The effectiveness of different visuals in the background behind a newscaster may also depend on the type of information they convey. Visuals designed to establish the location of an event, for example, produce the best impression when displayed in full screen behind the presenter (Coldevin, 1978a). On the other hand, visuals depicting some form of symbolic or schematic representation of the theme of a news item are best located in a corner placement behind one shoulder of the presenter (Coldevin, 1978b).

The placement of background visuals may not only affect audience impressions of the performer and the presentation, but may also influence learning. Metallinos (1980) reported that viewers' perception, retention, and preference for visual images depended on their placement or position on the screen. Viewers were shown single-frame shots of a newscaster with still visuals placed either on the left side or right side of the screen. In tests of memory for these images afterwards, Metallinos found that retention was more accurate when the visuals were placed in the left visual field.

Visuals and Learning in Brief From TV News

Sociological studies of the professional opinions of newspeople concerning how visual format can be utilised most effectively to communicate news information to the audience have indicated that the use of pictorial material is strongly favoured. From his observations of BBC newsmen, Schlesinger (1978) reported that there seems to be a firm belief among many news editors that pictorial accompaniment enhances news impact and information gain. However, empirical studies of news recall from television have not always been as firm in their conclusions as the beliefs of newsmen appear to be regarding the merits of visualisations in programmes.

Early Research.   Early news media research concentrated on the communicativeness of pictures with a spoken script compared with the effectiveness of a "talking head" alone. Results have been equivocal. Jorgenson (1955) found no significant difference in information gain from televised presentations between newscaster-only format and the newscaster speaking over a motion picture film. Further more, he found that viewers liked the newscaster alone more than the film treatment. He did find, however, that film produced considerably more information gain than did the newscaster with still pictures. A subsequent study of learning from television newscasts also failed to find that film produced more information gain than did the newscaster seen alone (Hazard, 1963). Lack of conclusive support for the enhancing effect of picture accompaniment on learning television news materials has been prevalent in studies conducted both in the field and in the laboratory.

Field Studies. In a field experiment examining recall of broadcast news in Israel, Katz, Adoni, and Parness (1977) looked at the extent to which pictures enhanced recall and found that whereas radio listeners forgot more news items than television viewers, individuals who *saw* a television news broadcast performed no better on tests of news retention than individuals who had been asked to only listen to the same programme. But while no gross visualisation effects on overall recall were found, the presence of the visual channel did have selective recall enhancement for particular types of news content. In general, foreign affairs items were less well recalled than items about internal, domestic affairs. However, foreign items were recalled twice as well by individuals who watched that evening's television news as by those who had been asked to listen only (see Table 9.3). Thus, being able to "see" the news enhances recall of news content that has comparatively little relevance to the audience. This finding was supported by Booth (1970), who found that picture accompaniment featured among several presentation factors (including length, frequency of occurrence, and serial position of items) that enhanced recall of news from print and broadcast media for a sample of American news consumers. However, visual format and other presentation enhancement effects were more significant for recall of news for which respondents had little interest. Interesting items were well remembered regardless of presentation style. Unfortunately, Booth did not test recall following single news bulletins, and the main effect of picture accompaniment was not adequately separated from other presentation factors in order to provide a precise measure of its particular influence. Further, there was no control over the number of news programmes on radio or television that had been heard or seen on the test day.

In their Israeli field study, Katz et al. (1977) found differences in rate of recall of items with different styles of presentation. Newscaster-only items were least well remembered both by respondents who viewed the television bulletins and by those who listened only. Items accompanied by stills or by film footage were slightly better recalled, but items including interviews were remembered best of all. However, it is likely that these visual format effects were confounded with other presentation effects, most notably length, which could also have contributed signifi-

TABLE 9.3
Effects of Content and Presentation on Recall

	Content type			Presentation type			
	Domestic	Foreign	Foreign with domestic Implications	Newscaster only	Still pictures	Interview	Film
Total number of items of this type in nine programmes	60	44	44	16	23	11	82
Average number of recalls of items of this type by those who listened only	4.0	1.5	2.7	2.1	3.8	4.4	3.6
Average number of recalls of items of this type by those who viewed and listened	4.4	3.0	4.5	3.0	4.5	7.5	4.1

Source: Katz, Adoni, and Parness, 1977. Reprinted by permission of the publisher.

cantly to variations in rates of item recall. Indeed, Katz et al. found considerable length effects. Items lasting 2 minutes or more were recalled nearly twice as often as items less than 1 minute long by respondents who listened only to the newscasts, and nearly three times as often by respondents who listened to and watched the programmes.

Laboratory Research. In two laboratory studies of visual format effects on retention of televised news headlines, in which item length was fairly constant across items, Gunter (1979, 1980a) reported quite substantial variations in spontaneous recall of items accompanied by film footage or still photographs, or presented by the newscaster against a plain studio background. In these studies, sequence of 15 news-headline items were that had been recorded from actual network television news transmissions several months earlier were edited together.

In the first experiment, 40 respondents received news items in one of two conditions. One group saw the items via a television monitor (video condition); for a second group the TV screen was covered so that only the soundtrack was available (audio condition). Within the video modality, items were differentiated according to visual format into three types:

1. *film items*, in which the newscaster was out of camera shot and read the narrative over a short sequence of film footage;
2. *still-photo items*, in which the newscaster was again out of shot and read the narrative over a still photograph of a figure or scene relating to the news report;
3. *newscaster-only items*, in which the newscaster was in shot for the duration of the item and read the narrative directly into camera.

These items were edited together as five successive triads with fixed within-triad item order—film, then still, then newscaster-only—and so that no two successive items were from the same story category (i.e., politics, foreign, industry, etc.). All items were approximately equal in length, and none was longer than 7 seconds. Table 9.4 shows the actual wording of each news headline used in this experiment. Five sequences of these items were produced, over which the presentation order of the film then still, then newscaster-only triads was varied to control for serial position biases that could have become confounded with visual format effects during recall of specific items.

These results, as illustrated in Table 9.5, showed that overall spontaneous recall of news headlines was better for the video condition than for the audio condition, items accompanied by moving film were better recalled than those accompanied by still photographs, and recall in the latter case was in turn better than that for headlines read by the newscaster on camera. Unfortunately, item content and visual format were confounded

TABLE 9.4

News Headline Narratives

	(V)	(A)
Headlines accompanied by film		
"The McGuire family prefer Belfast and its bad memories to anywhere else."	.75	.65
"When President Amin celebrates, it's everyone's duty to celebrate"	.60	.60
"The Middle East peace talks seem dead; Mr Begin calls some of Egypt's demands preposterous"	.55	.30
"Five people die in the snowstorms in the Highlands"	.65	.25
"Red flu is here, and it could be a killer"	.95	.60
Headlines accompanied by still photographs		
"There's a demand for a £9 million ransom for the kidnapped industrialist, Baron Empin"	.65	.65
"The fears grow for the missing eight-year-old and now another boy is missing"	.45	.30
"Tony Greig says Geoff Boycott's skill is being where fast bowlers aren't"	.35	.10
"Mr Brian Clough returns to Leeds United just to play a cup tie"	.40	.15
"Britain wants to pay back a billion dollars to the IMF"	.85	.80
Headlines presented by the newsreader with no visual accompaniments		
"Mr Michael Foot apologises for Labour MPs' behaviour in the voting lobby"	.25	.55
"The Shetland Islanders have told the Prime Minister they don't want to be governed by the lowland Scots"	.25	.35
"Mrs Thatcher says Britain must not be swamped by immigrants"	.15	.30
"Welsh miners have voted three to one for a productivity deal"	.25	.40
"Left-wing Labour MPs say they'll rebel against all legislation if the Government persists in cutting short the debate on the European elections"	.55	.90

Source: Gunter, 1979.

TABLE 9.5

Percentages of News Headlines Correctly Recalled as a Function of Visual Format and Modality

			Visual Format	
Modality	*Film*	*Stills*	*Newscaster*	*Mean*
			Experiment 1	
Audio-visual	90	54	29	51
Audio only	44	41	50	45
Mean	57	48	40	48
			Experiment 2	
Audio-visual	74	60	35	56
Audio only	50	46	48	48
Mean	62	53	42	52

Source: Gunter, 1979 (Experiment 1)
Gunter, 1980a (Experiment 2)

in this study—that is, items that differed in terms of format also differed in the nature of the events they reported. However, it is comforting to note that no substantial differences, perhaps as a result of intrinsic properties of their narratives, arose between items in the audio-presentation condition to parallel those in the video condition. Nevertheless, averaging over the video and audio treatments, it was found that recall of newscaster-only items was somewhat depressed relative to item recall from the other format categories, and it is notable that all items read by the presenter against a plain studio backdrop tended to cover a fairly narrow range of political-economic issues. It is possible therefore that these items did not have the same impact on respondents as items from the film and still-photo categories, at least in part because of the intrinsic nature of their narrative content.

In a second experiment, the author adopted the same basic design and procedure in an attempt to replicate the results of the previous study, but used a narrower range of news content over which the intrinsic nature of the narrative was less likely to vary. News items here concerned only political and economic issues or events that occurred inside the United Kingdom.

Thirty respondents were presented with 15 headline items; 20 of them received them in sound and vision over a TV monitor, and 10 of them heard the soundtrack with pictures. Once again, within the video modality the items were classified into three types according to visual format. These types may be summarised as follows:

1. *Film items*; (a) Controversial statement made by Conservative Party leader, Margaret Thatcher on immigration; (b) campaign for devolution in Scotland is started; (c) Shetland Islands express opposition to devolution if it means being ruled by Scotland; (d) increase in the number of unemployed is announced; (e) coal production increases following the introduction of a new incentive scheme.

2. *Still photo-items*; (a) Leader of the House of Commons, Mr Michael Foot, apologises for unruly behaviour by Labour MPs; (b) Britain to pay back one billion dollars to the International Monetary Fund; (c) British Leyland announce an increase in their car prices; (d) Increase in Scotch Whisky is announced; (e) on the Stock Market, Sterling goes up against other currencies.

3. *Newscaster-only items*; (a) The Government is defeated in a vote over devaluation of the Green Pound; (b) public support for devolution in Scotland falls; (c) building firms demand that the Government increase prices of homes; (d) an announcement of an increase in food prices is made; (e) Left-wing Labour MPs are angry over direct elections bill.

As Table 9.5 shows, the results of this experiment largely replicated those of the first study. Overall recall was again higher following video presentation than following audio presentation, and within the video condition mean frequency of correct spontaneous recall for news items depended on the nature of their visual format. Items accompanied by film were best recalled, and newscaster-only items were worst recalled, while memory for items accompanied by still photographs falls in-between. Differential recall rates for these groups of items were much less marked in the audio treatment.

These experimental findings indicate that recall of *brief* television news items can be significantly affected by picture accompaniment. Picture items (i.e., those accompanied by film footage or still photographs) were recalled considerably more often than "talking head" items in the video modality. Furthermore, certain types of picture content seemed to facilitate recall more effectively than others, evidenced by the superior memory performance on film-clip items relative to still-photo items, even though differences in recall of the latter two visual categories of news item were not statistically significant.

The fact that no substantial differences in recall rates for the same item-groups occurred when they were presented in soundtrack only weakens the alternative explanation that differential recall of items in the video condition was a function of verbal-narrative content factors rather than of visual format, especially in the replication study where a relatively narrow taxonomic range of news stories was presented anyway.

Visualisation Effects and Brief News Recall: A Psychological Interpretation

It is fairly clear from the two experiments just reported that spontaneous recall of news-headline items may be significantly affected by the visual treatment they receive during presentation. On the surface it appears as if, in the video modality, items accompanied by film footage or still photographs are selectively processed, either prior to or instead of items presented by a newsreader against a plain studio background. But how are these findings to be accounted for in psychological terms? At which stage of learning or remembering does the processing of picture items preempt that of nonpictorial items? Before moving on to examine evidence on visual format effects on in-depth retention of information from news stories, we pause for a while to consider the psychological processes that may possibly be invoked to explain the visualisation effects observed above.

One possibility is that an imagery effect was operating, making the items with picture content easier to remember than newscaster-only items. A number of writers have claimed that imagery is one of the most powerful factors influencing memory for verbal materials (Bower, 1971; Bugelski, 1970; Paivio, 1969, 1971). The necessary and sufficient conditions of picture superiority, however, have not yet been firmly established (Postman, 1978).

The superiority of picture over verbal stimuli is consistent with the conceptual-peg hypothesis formulated by Paivio (1963) to explain the advantage of concrete over abstract stimuli in paired-associate learning. According to this hypothesis, the stimulus term functions as a peg to which its associate is hooked during learning trials and from which it can be retrieved on recall trials. The more likely a stimulus is to arouse imaginal mediators, the more effective it is as a retrieval one (Paivio, 1971).

On this assumption, the advantage of pictorial stimuli is attributable to the fact that they arouse images more directly than corresponding verbal labels. The hypothesis offers essentially a retrieval explanation; that is, a high-imagery item is especially effective as a retrieval cue for the associated member. Generally, the effect of item imagery is more effective on the stimulus side than on the response side of a pair. However, under free-recall conditions, where both sides of a "pair" are recalled, there should be no differential facilitative effect of concreteness favouring either side (Yarmey & Ure, 1971; Yuille & Humphreys, 1970).

It has been argued alternatively that picture superiority in retrieval tasks might be explained in terms of stimulus differentiation rather than in terms of association (Dominowski & Gadlin, 1968; Wicker, 1970; Wicker & Evertson, 1972). This discriminability hypothesis asserts that imagery increases the distinctiveness of items and reduces inter-item interference effects. It is possible that the facilitative effect attributed to imagery, as in the case of the superiority of pictures over words, or of concrete verbal stimuli over abstract verbal stimuli in memory tasks, are due to differential intraverbal interference. Another possibility is that images are generally less susceptible to interference effects than are verbal processes.

A further assumption that is not incompatible with the conceptual-peg hypothesis is one that implies that pictures are encoded less variably than words and that imaginal processes provide a more reliable access route to appropriate responses than do verbal processes. However, another well-supported and well-documented explanation of imagery superiority—the dual-coding hypothesis—has suggested that pictures are more, rather than less, variable encoded, and it is just this availability of an alternative memory code that can serve as a retrieval cue, which accounts for the superiority of pictorial over verbal stimuli in many memory tasks.

To what extent can these imagery hypotheses explain the findings with television news materials? It is likely that the ordering of the news reports presented in the headline-recall study was such as to preclude interference effects between items with common picture content features. It is felt that in order to test adequately the discriminability hypothesis, a series of news reports would be required in which items with similar pictorial attributes occur together in succession. If one assumes that items with picture content would produce less inter-item interference than items that have no picture material, then forgetting should be greater from a sequence of newscaster-only items than from a sequence of film-clip items or still items. However, the news items presented in this experiment were arranged so that two items of the same visual format type never occurred in succession. Consequently, unless the subjects grouped together items from a common format category during encoding or storage of the news sequence, the distinctiveness of imagery hypothesis does not apply because each item was clearly discriminable from those bordering it at presentation. The likelihood of the latter assumption being true was reduced by the observation that subjects did not tend to recall items in groups according to visual format type, which they might have been expected to do if they were also encoding or storing them as such.

Although the discriminability of imagery hypothesis does not apply here, an alternative explanation in terms of the conceptual-peg hypothesis is not ruled out. Once again, though, difficulties arise because of the nature of the test procedure and the information obtained from the subjects in the memory task. All subjects were asked to recall the items they saw, not in terms of any picture information contained in the items but in terms of the verbal content. Although it is possible that the picture content of the film-clip and still items did act as a peg to which the verbal content of the item was attached, so enhancing its retrieval, this experiment cannot offer any direct evidence in support of this hypothesis because no attempt was made to find out whether visual features of the items had been encoded. Research with television news material in Sweden, however, has implied specific cueing properties for visualisations that may serve either to enhance or inhibit recall of bulletin content (Findahl & Hoijer, 1976). Although visual illustrations were not explicitly presented as cues during recall, subtle manipulations of picture content at presentation produced consistent learning effects during verbal content recall. Specifically, those aspects of verbal content supported directly by visual illustrations in the news item were recalled better than they were from newscaster-only presentation of the same report. These results are discussed in greater depth in the Chapter 10 which examines the effects of visual context on detailed retention of news content.

The headline-recall findings can probably best be explained in terms of the dual-coding hypothesis, which states that high imagery and verbal processes will play a mediational role in item retrieval. Thus, during free recall of picture items, the subject presumably will implicitly name (or verbally label) at least some of the pictured items during input. Such items may therefore be stored as imaginal and verbal codes. Assuming that the required verbal response can be retrieved from either code, such dual coding would enhance the probability of item recall because even if one code is forgotten during the retention interval, the other may still be available to permit recall of the nominal item.

Applied to the these findings, the superiority of picture (film-clip or still) items over nonpictorial (newscaster-only) items is seen as a function of the additional channels of information available for coding within the former category. In the newscaster-only items, there are at most two potential codings—verbal and imaginal representations of the verbal text of the item, the latter depending heavily upon the concreteness of the item's verbal content. In fact, a very complex news item about some abstract political or social issue may not give rise to any imaginal representation at all and will thus have only one potential coding—verbal. For picture items (both film-clip and still types), in addition to the above-mentioned codings, there are two possible representations for picture content too—imaginal and verbal labeling.

With as many as four potential memory representations that could serve as implicit retrieval cues, as against only one or two potential representations for the newscaster-only items, the probability is obviously greater that pictorial items will be recalled.

Care must be taken, however, when drawing theoretical or practical implications from experiments on news-headline recall and when attempting to generalise from them to learning with other types of informational television presentations. It is important to emphasise that the recall task used in these studies required only that respondents retrieve brief news headlines, and it is not possible to say on the basis of these experimental findings alone whether picture content would necessarily have this sort of facilitative effect on memory performance where detailed retention of news-story content is tested. In particular, the important question of the mutual relevance and supportiveness of pictorial and narrative components of news items was not directly approached in these experiments Yet this is a fundamental feature of news production that can be expected to be likely to have some influence on learning from items of longer duration. As research evidence discussed in the next section indicates, still or motion picture materials that are only partially relevant or irrelevant to the narrative they accompany may interfere with overall learning from television news.

Cued Recall of Longer News Stories

In their review of educational media research, Chu and Schramm (1967) concluded that the use of visuals will improve learning from audio-visual messages where it contributes to the information contained in the audio-track; otherwise, visual images may actually cause distraction and interfere with learning. A formal embodiment of this position was put forward by Severin (1967, 1968) who hypothesised that presentation of irrelevant cues in either the visual or audio channels will cause a loss of learning from the other channel, but when additional and nonredundant cues are presented in either channel, greater overall learning will take place. Applied to television news broadcasting, this *cue-summation* theory would predict that newsfilm that does not convey information consistent with the story would prove distracting.

In an experimental test of his hypothesis, Severin (1968) found that the degree of irrelevance of cues in one channel to information in the other was particularly important to overall learning, with slightly irrelevant cues often causing more distraction than extremely irrelevant cues. For instance, simultaneously pairing a spoken word with a picture of a different object from the same taxonomic class (e.g. the word *moose* with a picture of a bison) produced poorer recall than when spoken word and picture were of the same object or of objects from different taxonomic classes (e.g., the word *moose* with a picture of a fish). Where newsfilm used in television bulletins to accompany the newscaster's description of an issue may be only partially relevant to the story content, similar interference may also occur while watching news programmes. There may be particular problems in this regard when library film footage is used to back up a story. In a study of educational material, Dwyer (1968) tested three modes of visualisation for their relative effectiveness in an instructional unit on the human heart. His four experimental treatments were: (a) control with no illustrations; (b) simple line drawings of the heart; (c) detailed shaded drawings of the heart; and (d) photographs of a heart model. He used four different kinds of test: (a) a drawing test evaluating learning of specific locations of parts of the heart; (b) and identification test of numbered parts of the heart; (c) a terminology test evaluating knowledge of referents for specific symbols; and (d) a comprehension test measuring understanding of the heart, its parts, and internal workings. The only significant effect occurred following the line-drawing condition, which yielded higher scores on the drawing test. Dwyer suggested that the use of visuals does not necessarily improve learning, and that for his college student sample it may actually have been distracting in this particular instance.

Baggaley (1980) found no significant effects of visual accompaniments on memory for the narrative of a news story. In this experiment six versions of a television news item in the style of an appeal for a fictitious charitable organization were used. There were two newscaster-only versions, one with the presenter directly facing camera and another showing him in profile. Another direct version also showed the presenter looking at notes, while a second profile version included an insert of an observer looking at and nodding in agreement with what the presenter was saying. Two further versions of the direct and profile formats also included sequences of film footage depicting location shots relating to the storyline. Following each version, subjects were administered a questionnaire containing 30 phrases taken from the item's text. Up to four words were omitted from each phrase, and subjects were asked to fill these in. No differences in recall were found between the six presentation conditions, although the effectiveness of this method of testing news recall must be questioned. No indications were given about the types of information tested here, and one must have serious doubts about whether it is realistic to assume that viewers encode and store news-story texts in the fashion tested in this experiment.

In a direct test of the effect of nonredundant film accompaniment on detailed recall of story content in television newscasts, Edwardson, Grooms, and Pringle (1976) showed subjects eight different news items that consisted of actual stories written with some alteration of names and facts so that subjects would not remember the information from previous newscasts or newspaper reports. A male newscaster was recorded on videotape reading the news stories in two versions. In one treatment, four of the stories were also accompanied by film footage, while the others had no film added to them. In the second treatment, the four stories that initially had no film now had film added to them. Meanwhile, the film stories from the first condition were presented on this occasion minus any film footage. Retention of details from each item was tested by a series of multiple-choice questions. A pretest on a separate sample of subjects who saw the film from each item without audio and were then tested for knowledge acquisition indicated that none of the film clips conveyed any of the information contained in the news items. In the experiment proper, no substantial differences emerged between the number of correct responses to questions concerning news materials given with or without film. It should be noted, finally, that the film used with these stories was typical of film footage used in actual news bulletins, and the observed learning effects might therefore be expected to occur also in naturalistic viewing situations.

Gunter (1980b) conducted a similar experimental study in which nine television news stories were presented to 60 college students under three different visual format conditions: newscaster-only presentation, newscaster-plus-film, or newscaster-plus-stills. All nine news stories had originally been broadcast as film reports in television bulletins about 2 years prior to the experiment. Actual stories were rewritten with some alteration of names and facts so that subjects would not remember the information from newscasts or newspapers. A new video-recording was made of a male newscaster reading all nine news stories. He was a member of a college drama group and, following several rehearsals and trial runs through the material, proved a capable and convincing newsreader.

Three versions of each news item were prepared. The first consisted of the newsreader seen in moderate close-up reading the news story against a plain studio background; the second consisted of an initial studio introduction by the newsreader for approximately 10 to 15 seconds, followed by 40 to 45 seconds of film footage, over which the out-of-vision newsreader narrated; and the third consisted of the same studio introduction followed by a series of four still photographs, actually taken from the film footage, over which the newsreader narrated the remainder of the news story. A brief synopsis of each news story, together with a brief description of the picture material included with each, is presented in Table 9.6. Three sequences of news were prepared. In the first sequence, the second, fifth, and seventh stories included film, while the third, sixth, and ninth stories included stills. In the second sequence, the first, fourth, and seventh stories were accompanied by film, and the second, fifth, and eighth by stills. In the third sequence, the third, sixth, and ninth stories had film, and the first, fourth, and seventh stories contained stills. The remaining stories in each sequence were newscaster-only items.

Subjects were run individually and were told that afterwards they would be asked questions about the news sequence they were about to see. Following presentation of the news items, a questionnaire containing 27 randomly ordered multiple-choice items (three per news story) was given

TABLE 9.6
Synopses of News Stories Used in Experiment on Visual
Format and Information Gain

1	A story about missing people in the mountains of Scotland. Pictures showed shots of police with dogs searching the snowbound countryside.
2	A story about a new survival craft to be used in oil rig emergencies. Pictures showed the craft being tested.
3	A story about a strike-bound factory in the north of England. Pictures showed shots of workers coming out of the factory gates.
4	A report about a campaign to get people into shape. Pictures showed a man and a woman jogging in a park.
5	A report on threatened petrol shortages following industrial action by tanker drivers. Pictures showed queues of cars waiting outside garages.
6	A story about renting cars cheaply in London. Pictures showed the cars being hired and driven away.
7	A story concerning the loss of large foreign contracts by a major shipbuilding yard. Pictures showed shots of the dockyards and men at work.
8	A report on fears of a 'flu epidemic. Pictures showed research scientists working on a vaccine and various hospital scenes.
9	A story about a man who won over £91,000 pound sterling on an accumulator bet. Pictures showed the man and his wife inside and outside their home.

Source: Gunter, 1980b.

to the subjects, who were allowed 20 minutes to complete the test. Each correct response was given one point. The percentages of correct answers to each news story for each visual format treatment are shown in Table 9.7.

These findings show that the highest mean percentage of correct responses occurred for newscaster-only items and that poorest performance resulted when news stories were accompanied by stills. Statistical comparisons of visual format treatments indicated, however, that these differences were nonsignificant (ts <1). In the case of each item, two out of three questions probed for retention of narrative content that was read while film or stills were actually being shown in the picture format treatments. The percentage scores on these questions were assessed separately, and the data are shown in Table 9.8.

These data revealed that larger information-gain differences due to visual format occurred on these questions. Statistical comparisons of the latter scores yielded differences at the 10% level of confidence between newscaster-only and newscaster-plus-film treatments ($t = 1.88$, $df = 16$) and between newscaster-only and newscaster-plus stills treatments ($t = 2.08$, $df = 16$). The difference between newscaster-plus-film and newscaster-plus-still treatments did not approach statistical significance (t <1). On the basis of these analyses, the results of this experiment indicated that individuals viewing a televised news story accompanied by film footage or by still pictures gave fewer correct answers to questions about story narrative content than when they viewed the same items presented by the newscaster only against a plain studio background. Whereas these findings were interpreted by the author at the time as suggesting that picture material may impair detailed information assimilation and retention from television news stories "such as those typically

TABLE 9.7
Percentage of Correct Answers as a Function of Visual
Format Treatment

Story	Newscaster only	Newscaster+ stills	Newscaster+ film	Mean % correct
1	72	67	68	69
2	73	67	73	71
3	65	63	65	64
4	56	45	50	50
5	50	37	42	43
6	40	33	37	37
7	37	33	32	34
8	63	60	58	60
9	77	73	70	73
Mean	59	53	55	56

Source: Gunter, 1980b.

TABLE 9.8
Percentage of Correct Answers on Item-Content Running
With Picture Materials

Story	Newscaster only	Newscaster+ stills	Newscaster+ film	Mean % correct
1	75	60	63	66
2	73	55	63	64
3	73	48	50	57
4	63	35	53	50
5	55	25	33	38
6	38	23	25	29
7	30	28	23	27
8	60	55	50	55
9	73	68	55	65
Mean	60	44	46	50

Source: Gunter, 1980b.
Note: Figures for newscaster-only items give scores for content retention during equivalent periods when film or stills were being presented in the picture versions.

found on network newscasts," a more recent reanalysis of these data has produced evidence of an enhancing effect of visual enrichment of news.

In contrast to these findings, more recently Drew and Reese (1984) reported a study with fifth- to eleventh-grade schoolchildren in which memory and comprehension were better for television news items accompanied by film footage than when presented by a "talking head" only. Film had a particularly strong effect on comprehension (as measured by in-depth recall accounts) among eleventh-graders. The authors of this study suggested that perhaps the film's ability to attract and hold attention enhanced learning. They suggested in addition that the visuals may have reinforced the verbal content of the news items, although we are not told the extent to which film and narratives were well matched.

In a further analysis of Gunter's (1980b) findings however, Berry (1983a) found that film material did enhance learning but from a particular part of the item rather than across the item as a whole. Berry (1983a) presented serial learning curves for responses to questions asked by Gunter (1980b) that probed narrative information that coincided with pictures in the film and still-accompaniment treatments, and for responses to questions that probed content during the "talking head" lead-in-phase common to all items in all three experimental conditions. These serial learning curves are reproduced in Fig. 9.1. (a) Lead-in ("talking head" in all conditions) (b) Body of news item

The learning curves for the information in the visual enrichment phase of each item show an apparent impairing effect of stills and film as reported by Gunter in his original paper. Similar curves for the "talking head" lead-in narrative, by contrast, indicate an enhancing effect in the

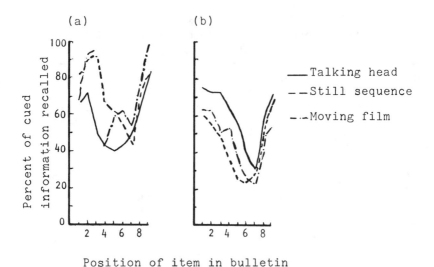

Percent of cued information recalled

Position of item in bulletin

FIG. 9.1 Serial learning curves from Gunter (1980b) (Berry, 1983a; reprinted by permission of the author and publisher).

picture accompaniment conditions. These results, says Berry, are in accord with the findings of other researchers (Findahl, 1971; Renckstorff, 1977; and Edwardson, Grooms & Proudlove, 1981), all of whom reported better-cued recall from visually enriched news stories than from extended "talking head" presentations. Berry also pointed to the fact that the effects of adding film or still-picture content on learning both early and later information were generally more pronounced in the first two thirds of the bulletin than for the last few items. Statistical tests revealed both positive and negative effects to be significant for film and stills conditions.

These further analyses indicated that moving film such as that normally used in television news broadcasts may interfere with the uptake of narrative content *presented at the same time.* Berry suggests that this effect may be a consequence of too much information being presented at once or from a mismatch or incompatability of the learning processes required to deal with simultaneously presented and mutually nonreinforcing or nonrelevant visual and verbal content.

Although it is desirable in theory to match visuals with verbals carefully in order to avoid impairment of learning, in practice this marriage of the two information channels is often less easy to achieve. Loss of information presented alongside film footage in the news is probably unavoidable under the usual conditions and constraints placed on broadcast news producers. One recommendation for news production practice that emerges from the research discussed so far in this chapter, however, is that learning losses may be reduced by minimising unnecessary film

246

accompaniment when important information essential to proper understanding of a news story is to be communicated, especially if the pictures are themselves arousing or distracting. Of course, Berry's (1983a) reanalysis of Gunter's (1980b) data indicated that pictures can enhance learning of certain parts of an item's narrative content. The discovery that later pictures could enhance learning from the "talking head" lead-in phase is an important one inasmuch as the early information is usually that which is most important and central to the story. Another more recent study of the effects of visuals on learning from news stories manipulated the degree of redundancy between pictures and narrative. Reese (1984) found that learning from television news was greater when visuals and script were redundant than when they were not redundant. Excessive or over-redundancy, however, appeared to impede learning.

Reese recorded news stories off-air from television news broadcasts and reedited them to produce several treatment conditions. The stories in their original off-air form were designated as redundant in terms of the relationship between their picture content and narrative content. A nonredundancy condition was created by re-editing the camera shots within each story. Further conditions were created by producing redundant and nonredundant stories with two-line captions representing a complete transcription of the news story.

Reese measured *understanding* and *memory*. The ability of subjects to reproduce the central points of stories was used to operationalise understanding. Central points were based on information contained in the original news script, and open-ended responses were coded according to their correspondence with these points. Then multiple-choice questions were used to operationalise how much each subject remembered from the news.

Results showed that, overall, redundant pictures and words enhanced learning, while there was some evidence that adding redundant print information either had no effect or detracted from learning. Memory for the news was greater in the picture-narrative redundancy condition, and the effect of adding a furture informationally redundant verbal caption was nonsignificant. Overall, story understanding likewise was better following a redundant style of presentation, although it was not substantially improved any further by additional captioning. In the case of one story, adding redundant caption information actually resulted in poorer learning from that item. In summary, the Reese study indicated that viewers can effectively process redundant information through the audio and pictorial channels, but learning drops off when they must also process captioned print information. This additional input would appear to divide attention excessively such that, although the contents of these different channels are redundant, information processing becomes less effective.

A problem with the Reese study, however, concerns the relative redundancy of pictures and words in the original off-air versions of news stories. The author claims that in their original form, the film footage and narrative contents of these items were informationally redundant; but it is often the case on live news broadcasts that film is notoriously out of sync with the spoken narrative in strict informational terms. So although Reese's nonredundant condition may have produced worse memory and comprehension of content than his redundant condition, we do not really know whether the original version produced the best possible performance from viewers. Greater confidence in the match between visuals and narrative can be had when visual illustrations are designed specifically to reinforce the narrative at the production stage. Work done by researchers at the Swedish Broadcasting Corporation, instead of measuring learning-enhancement effects of relatively gross visual format manipulations, has investigated the input of visual illustrations designed to reinforce specific aspects of news stories.

Effects of Narrative Repetition and Reformulation with Visual Illustration

Although in the context of learning from broadcast news there is no unequivocal answer to the question of whether it is always best to use moving film, still photographic, or graphic material, or no visuals as such at all, one factor that has emerged as important when news narratives are accompanied by visuals is the degree of correspondence between picture material and verbal material.[1] Although film has been regarded by news professionals as a natural means of portraying actuality in television bulletins (Altheide, 1976; Schlesinger, 1978), research has shown that where effective communication is the ultimate goal, the impact of still photos, graphics, or schematic drawings can often be just as good (Findahl, 1971; Findahl & Hoijer, 1976), although there is some evidence to support the thesis that film is more appreciated by the audience than other visual modes of presentation (Renckstorf, 1977). From a production standpoint, the use of still or graphic material affords considerably more flexibility and control in the design of individual news items and indeed the bulletin as a whole than the use of film material. Although film is often allowed to dominate production strategy, with the availability or nonavailability of appropriate footage an important factor determining which stories are selected for eventual presentation, stills, graphics, and schematic drawings can be tailored more precisely to fit in with specific

---

[1]What is best from the point of view of learning and understanding needs to be distinguished from what is most attractive to the audience. Conditions that may produce optimal news comprehension and retention may not produce maximal appeal - and this is very important for the ratings and popularity of a news programme.

news storylines that deserve selection on merit for their intrinsic interest, quite apart from their visual potential. Accompanying the greater flexibility afforded by visual stills, however, is the need for considerable care in the way they are applied. An important attribute of memorable news material is the balanced nature of any visual reinforcement therein.

Research in Sweden has implied specific cueing properties for visualisations that may serve equally well either to enhance or inhibit recall of bulletin content, depending on their precise relationship to the storyline of the news items with which they occur (Findahl, 1971; Findahl & Hoijer, 1976). By systematically varying the pictorial accompaniment to some of the narrative content in a standard television bulletin, Findahl showed that recall was best where the narrative was illustrated by pictures that corresponded to the verbal information and poorest with no illustration. No difference was found between film illustrations and stills, although the relevant comparison here was made only for one news item.

The notion that the content of the visual accompaniment to the narrative of a news story is more important than its type was developed further by Findahl and Hoijer (1976). They had previously found that viewers often absorb or retain only fragments of news events, isolated from their contexts. Generally speaking, television audiences were better able to recall the simple, concrete aspects of news items relating to the location and persons involved in the reported events than more abstract relationships surrounding the causes and consequences of events (Findahl & Hoijer, 1972, 1975). This must be regarded as a major problem for news broadcasters and other users of television for informational or instructional purposes, inasmuch as an understanding of the background and causes of events is often a fundamental and necessary aid to comprehension and recall. Findahl and Hoijer also noted, however, that concrete aspects of news items are most likely to be visually illustrated because these features are most readily represented in visual terms. If this is true of news practice, it raises a number of important questions regarding the production of memorable news content.

Findahl and Hoijer (1976) investigated the effects of additional visual information on recall of various aspects of verbal news content. They categorised news events in terms of characteristic journalistic details (i.e., principals, location, cause, consequences) in order to provide a workable typology of item content, each aspect of which could be independently supported by various visual elements, thus permitting systematic examination of the effects of specific kinds of implicit visual cues upon news recall.

They prepared a fictitious but realistic television newscast consisting of 13 items presented by a studio newscaster and illustrated with still photographs and graphics. This programme was shown to over 600 male and female residents of Stockholm, aged between 16 and 65 years, who

participated in small group-viewing sessions. After viewing the programme, the audience answered questions to determine how much they
had learned from it. Five critical items were systematically varied in
terms of visual composition. The fundamental question here was: How
important is the visual component with respect to recall?

In earlier studies, the same researchers found, generally speaking, that
audiences were better able to recall the simple, concrete aspects of news
items relating to the location and principals of the event than more
abstract relationships surrounding the causes and consequences of events
(Findahl & Hoijer, 1972, 1975). This must be regarded as a major
problem for news broadcasters and other users of television for informational or instructional purposes, inasmuch as an understanding of the
background and causes of events is often a fundamental and necessary aid
to comprehension and recall.

In their study of visual-illustration effects on news recall, Findahl and
Hoijer again found that, under visually neutral presentation conditions,
viewers recalled mainly information about the place where the event
occurred (location) and the persons or objects involved (principals), while
causes and consequences information were less well remembered. This
unbalanced mental record of news that the audience acquired is illustrated diagrammatically in Fig. 9.2.

Recall of each aspect of news content could be variously affected
further by manipulation of visual inputs. The following visualisations
were systematically employed to support the verbal content of each of the
five critical items in the fictitious news sequence:

1. maps and captions,
2. still photos,
3. schematic drawings.

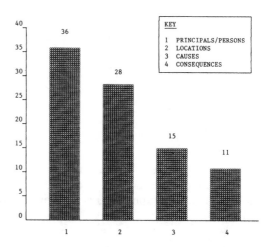

FIG. 9.2 Retention of different aspects of a television news story narrative (Findahl and Hoijer, 1976; reprinted by permission of the authors).

KEY

1 PRINCIPALS/PERSONS
2 LOCATIONS
3 CAUSES
4 CONSEQUENCES

The effects of each of these visual inputs upon learning are now discussed in some detail.

Maps and Captions

Three kinds of treatment of each critical news report were employed here. In the simplest version each item was illustrated with a *map* which labeled the place where the event occurred. This resulted in improved recall of the location of the event but at the same time produced worse recall of information concerning its cause and consequences, thus accentuating the imbalance of memory for item content observed in the basic message condition (newscaster-only presentation). In a *maps-with-symbols* treatment, maps were presented with symbols illustrating who or what was involved in the reported incident. Thus, in one item about an oil tanker running aground, a symbol of a tanker was presented adjacent to the location on the map where the event occurred. This format, which provided additional visual information about principals and location, successfully enhanced recall of both these aspects of content.

In a *superimposed-captions* format, locations and principals information was actually spelled out (e.g., "oil tanker aground"). This visualisation improved recall more than maps with symbols, not only for illustrated aspects but also for nonstressed areas of content such as causes-information. Nevertheless, overall recall was still markedly unbalanced. Further, neither captions summarising causes nor those summarising consequences were able to correct the imbalance in viewers' recall. Thus, although captions can apparently be used to improve viewers' recall of the location of a news event and the people or objects involved, they do not seem to effectively enhance memory for more complex and abstract features of content. One explanation offered by Findahl and Hoijer is that the captions used to convey information about causes and consequences were more complex than those used to illustrate locations and principals and thus required more processing effort. For example, their caption "machine failure puts ship aground" takes longer to read and comprehend that one that reads simply "oil tanker aground." Another problem may be that captions relaying information about the cause of an event did not relate as closely to the map in the background as did captions specifying, for example, its location. Consequently, these two visual (verbal and nonverbal) channels of input could have been mutually interfering and added considerably to the overall processing load of the item.

Still Photos

Photographs of more or less well known figures, famous landmarks, or even remote and totally unfamiliar locations are commonly used types of illustrations in news bulletins. Findahl and Hoijer found that photo-

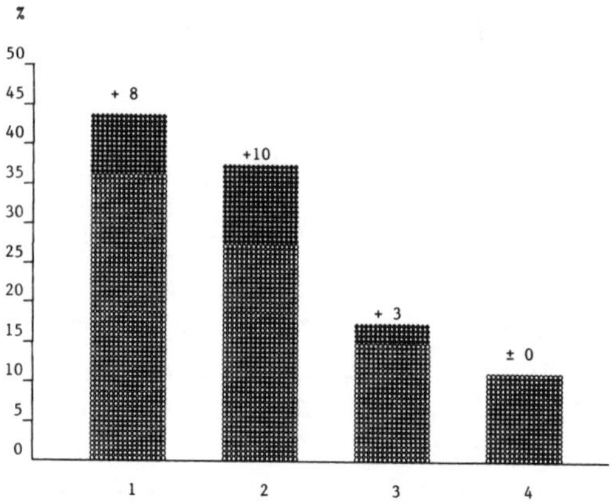

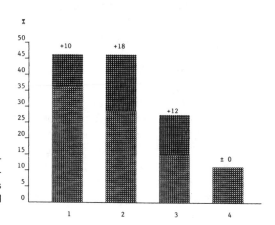

FIG. 9.3A Effects on news recall of still illustrations of different aspects of news stories stills: Place (Findahl and Hoijer, 1976; reprinted by permission of the authors).

FIG. 9.3B Effects on news recall of still illustrations of different aspects of news stories stills: Who/what (Findahl and Hoijer, 1976).

graphic inserts depicting landmarks could either enhance or impair recall, depending on whether the landmark was familiar or unknown to the viewer. Meaningless scenes actually resulted in poorer recall than newscaster-only presentation. Illustrations showing the principal persons or objects involved in the news event facilitated recall of those parts of the verbal news message, together with recall of location and cause of the event. No effect was observed for recall of information about the outcome or consequences of the event. Photographs that clearly demonstrated causal relationships were more difficult to obtain than photos showing where an event occurred and who or what was involved. This difficulty was reflected in the results, where it was found that some cause-illustrations worked well while others impaired recall (see Fig. 9.3).[2]

---

[2]The top darker portion of the columns in fig. 9.3 A–D indicates the improvement in viewers' recall of the items compared to when the item was presented by a "talking head" only.

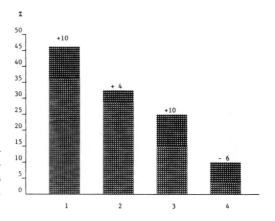

FIG. 9.3C Effects on news re-call of still illustrations of differ-ent aspects of news stories stills: Cause (Findahl and Hoijer, 1976).

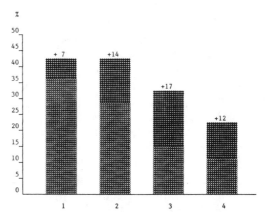

FIG. 9.3D Effects on news re-call of still illustrations of differ-ent aspects of news stories stills: Consequences (Findahl and Hoijer, 1976).

Recall of consequences-information was poorer with cause-illustra-tions than for newscaster-only presentations. Obviously, there is a need to be extremely careful before using still photographs to support visually verbalised causal relationships because of the difficulty of obtaining precisely relevant supportive visual-photographic cues for this abstract verbal information. Interestingly enough, though, visual photographic illustration of consequences—"what happened next"—improved recall over all aspects of news content.

Schematic Drawings

These are original graphic illustrations that are created for the newscast when no other photographic or graphic material is readily available or appropriate to support visually the verbal message of the news item. Although requiring a certain amount of effort on the part of production staff to prepare, these types of visuals have certain inherent informational advantages over other types because they can be designed with greater specificity to fit the verbal content of the news. Preceding evidence has quite clearly indicated the important necessity for a precise match between what is shown visually and what is said verbally if memory for news content is to be enhanced. Furthermore, visual reinforcement of the more difficult-to-illustrate abstract properties of news messages (i.e., causes and effects of events) produces better overall recall of item content than visualisation of concrete components (i.e., locations and principals of events). It is easier to produce accurate visualisations of causes and effects information with schematic drawings than with any other visual inserts because their pictorial content can be planned with greater care and precision than is often possible with still photographs.

Findahl and Hoijer found that viewers' recall of item content showed a direct relationship with which parts of the items were schematically illustrated. Schematic illustration of information concerning the people or objects involved (principals) or the location of a news event enhanced recall for each of those aspects of content relative to newscaster-only presentation of the same items but, at the same time, depressed recall of information concerning the causes and outcomes of the events. Drawings illustrating causes and effects, however, produced improved recall across the whole item, even for those aspects of content not actually visualised. Findahl and Hoijer found that it was easier to produce accurate visual illustrations of verbal content, especially abstract information about the causes and effects of items, with original drawings than with photographic material, and this additional clarity of presentation was reflected in better recall for this condition than when the same items were photographically illustrated. Fig. 9-4A shows the extent to which recall on each

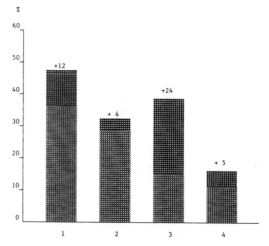

FIG. 9.4A   Effects on news recall of schematic drawings Illustrating causes information (Findahl and Hoijer, 1976; reprinted by permission of the authors). The top darker shaded portion of the columns indicate improvement in viewers' recall of the items compared to when the item was presented by a 'talking head' only

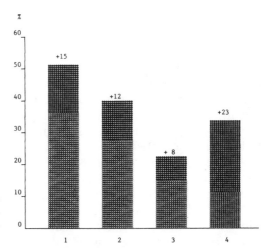

FIG. 9.4B Effects on news recall of schematic drawings illustrating consequences information (Findahl and Hoijer, 1976).

component of item content improved relative to newscaster-only presentation for schematic drawings in which causes were visually illustrated.
Although cause-photos improved recall of principals and locations, they
inhibited recall effects. Cause-drawings however, enhanced recall across
all item components, including effects and to a greater extent than did
still photos.

Fig. 9-4B shows results for effects-illustrations. Effects-drawings produced much better recall of locations but poorer recall of causes than
effects-photos. However, effects information was recalled better when
supported by drawings than by still photos, lending further testament to
the greater clarity and informational value of original schematic illustrations over other forms of visualisation, particularly when abstract verbal
content is visually supported.

PSYCHOLOGICAL INTERPRETATIONS OF
VISUALISATION EFFECTS ON IN-DEPTH RETENTION OF
TV NEWS

Research on memory for brief news-headline items showed that recall of
verbal content can be facilitated by accompanying film or still-photographic material. However, visual illustrations were seen in the last
section not to have the same gross facilitative effects on *in-depth* retention
of verbal content from more extensive news reports. How are the findings
on in-depth learning and its relationship with visual treatment to be
interpreted? Can the hypothesis invoked to account for headline recall
also be applied to explain recall of specific details from news narratives of
longer duration?

255

The dual-code position developed by Paivio (1971) accounts for imagery effects in terms of the differential availability of pictorial or imaginal and verbal codes that are taken to be implicit associations or rearousals of past information inputs. This position has proven sufficiently versatile to account for many image-related phenomena in verbal learning. But it has recently been argued that the dual-coding theory can provide only gross explanations of imagery effects and is not capable of providing deeper levels of analysis required for more specific information tasks (Kieras, 1978).

An alternative propositional-representation position has been formulated, which in its extreme form argues that all knowledge can be expressed in a single, uniform, abstract type of representation, the proposition, and this may provide a more adequate theoretical framework in which to interpret the effects of visual production treatment on in-depth recall of the narrative content of TV newscasts (see Anderson & Bower, 1973; Pylyshyn, 1973; and Simon, 1972), Unlike in the dual-coding position, there is no fundamental distinction between pictorially based and verbally based information as represented in memory. A proposition here is not to be construed as a primarily verbal entity capable of expressing only verbal information. The term is descended from formal (predicate) logic and expresses a network of links or relations between a set of concepts or ideas.

It seems likely, however, that the extreme form of the propositional position is incorrect. There is plenty of evidence to indicate that human memory does retain information about modality of input, and the pictorial events are coded in distinctly pictorial terms (Hopkins, Edwards, & Gavelek, 1971; Kroll, Bee, & Gurski, 1973; Wells, 1973). Nevertheless, propositions can be used to represent pictorial as well as verbal information, and there is no justification for restricting propositional representations to abstract, nonpictorial information (Baylor, 1972; Farley, 1974; Moran, 1974). Thus propositions can express meaningful linguistic and pictorial information effectively, and there is evidence that both kinds of information are stored in human memory. A modified version of the propositional position in the form of a general theory of verbal imagery has been put forward that incorporates the notion of distinct representations of linguistic and picture inputs at the propositional level (Kieras, 1978).

The model has some similarities with the dual-coding theory in as far as both make a distinction between the kinds of information present in memory and both assume that picture (or imaginal) information is more directly related to concrete verbal material than to abstract verbal material. However, there is a significant difference in the explanatory concepts used in these two theoretical perspectives. The dual-code theory is based on a conditioning model in which picture inputs and verbal inputs are stored in separate systems in memory. In contrast, the general model of verbal imagery states that both types of information are stored in the same (propositional) form, which can be equally effective for processing sentence material or visual scenes.

The general model of propositional representation of linguistic and picture materials can be specified further to explain more directly how imagery effects can enhance memory for verbal (narrative) content. A major issue concerns the ease with which visual images can be formed for sentence materials and whether such images are stored in memory and are therefore directly responsible for improving memory of those materials.

One explanation of imagery effects is that memory is better for high-imagery sentences (i.e., those sentences describing events that can easily be pictured) because those sentences are more easily understood. However, research has indicated that imagery effects may operate on memory in ways other than simply enhancing understanding. Moeser (1974) found that when sentences were equated for comprehensibility, the imagery value of a sentence still had a significant effect on memory performance.

Another possibility is that sentences that readily conjure up visual scenes in the minds of individuals can be assigned a context more easily than sentences that do not, leading to better memory performance. In other words, it may be easier to relate new sentence input whose content can also be "pictured" to existing propositional knowledge structures in memory derived from other linguistic or picture inputs, providing an abundance of connections from permanent memory into the new information. This is not to say that highly meaningful abstract sentences about familiar topics such as *higher wage demands will lead to higher unemployment* should not also be assigned a context as easily as more concrete (or easily pictured) sentences; but, as Findahl and Hoijer (1972, 1976) found in their studies of memory for TV news materials, narrative content describing concrete objects and events will, by its very nature, be better remembered. This happens because such material will be related to a larger pool of propositions in the context-assignment process in memory than sentences describing more abstract issues or events.

In the context of coding information from television news programmes, visual illustrations are presumably represented in propositional form along with the verbal narrative content they accompany. Abstract cause-effect relations described in news reports will, however, form fewer connections with other propositional knowledge structures in permanent memory than concrete object-location content. Providing additional "concrete" visual support for the abstract cause-effect components of the narrative should function to enhance the development of propositional connections in the context-assignment process, thus improving memory for this information. This tentative hypothesising is based largely on research with nonnews materials, and there is now a need to test its validity and efficacy for explaining memory for news through direct experimentation on television news materials. Although broadcasters may not themselves be interested in learning about the theoretical underpinnings of human memory performance on complex audio-visually presented narrative content, it is likely that the practical recommendations of researchers in this field can only stand to benefit from a thorough understanding of these processes.

For the moment, the practical recommendations that can be given with reference to production technique and audience recall of TV newscast material, although worth noting, are fairly limited. Balanced recall and proper understanding of news stories seem to depend heavily on careful and selective use of visual illustrations. These should be subordinate to the requirements of the story content rather than predominating over what is said, as is apparently so often the case, especially in the use of film (Schlesinger, 1978). Indeed, the greater control afforded by using still-photographic and specially designed schematic or graphic material when matching visuals to the story text favours the recommendation for more extensive deployment of these kinds of visual inputs in bulletins.

10 Headlines, Pace, and Recaps

HEADLINES AND LEADS

On some television networks, major news broadcasts begin with a sequence of brief news headlines providing an overview of the main stories of the day. Headlines also serve as devices for hooking the audience right at the beginning of the programme. The format of headline presentation is not exactly the same on all networks. On some programmes, for example, the main stories of the day are summarised in brief by the newscaster on camera before he or she gets underway with reading the stories in more detail. On other shows, the headlines may be read out over captions, stills, or short film clips before the newscaster appears on screen. In the United States, for example, some stations use this technique to promote local and network newscasts. Typically, a promo prior to a station break will highlight three or four stories with headlines; then, after the commercial break, fuller details follow in the newscast itself.

Although some thought undoubtedly goes into the selection and wording of news headlines to lead the programme, to what extent is the consideration given to them by journalists and editors concerned with their impact on audience comprehension and retention of the news, in addition to their role in enhancing the appeal of the programme either to viewers or professional peers? This question is important because research done by both communications researchers and experimental psychologists has indicated that the way in which the news is headlined may affect the way it is interpreted and the extent to which it is remembered by the audience.

259

Although headlines and summaries at the opening and close of television news programmes are standard features of news production, little research has been done to investigate their effects on news comprehension. And yet cognitive psychologists have found that memory for texts can be significantly affected by the prior presentation of a short title reflecting their theme or main idea.

Dooling and Lachman (1971) found that presentation of a title immediately before reading a passage produced 18% greater unaided memory for its content than when no title was given. In a follow-up experiment, Dooling and Mullet (1973) compared text-comprehension levels when thematic titles were presented before passages, after passages, or not at all. Results showed that unaided memory performance was best when titles came before passages, indicating that knowledge of the theme of a story aids retention. Presenting a thematic title afterwards produced no better memory than no title at all. According to the authors, this finding indicates that the locus of the thematic title effect is at the initial storage of the material during input. It is possible that prior knowledge of the theme may aid in setting up a retrieval plan that leads to better recall.

Other writers have proposed that headlines or titles help individuals to create contexts that can be used to comprehend texts (Bransford & Johnson, 1972; Kozminsky, 1977). Bransford and Johnson (1972) conducted a series of experiments in which verbal topic headings or picture "summaries" were presented with written or auditory passages. Pictures provided information about the context underlying events described in the passages. It was found that pictorial or verbal headlines presented before passages enhanced comprehension, whereas those presented afterwards were not better than the passages without headlines. In the case of pictures, however, it was important that picture items matched the verbal descriptions of the scene. When they did not, comprehension levels were not improved.

Kozminsky (1977) has proposed that titles or headlines can alter the comprehension of a text by affecting the selection of information from it and the way this information is organised in memory. As we saw in Chapter 3 text comprehension has been assumed to involve an Organizational process that results in the formation of a text base—that is, an overall understanding of what the text is about. This understanding derives not simply from effective processing of information in the text itself but also from its integration with existing knowledge held in long-term memory. The text base can be used as a retrieval schema to reconstruct the text from memory.

Headlines can function as advance organisers, indicating to the individual what the central theme of the text is about and therefore which areas of background knowledge are likely to be relevant to comprehension of its subject matter. Headlines may also bias the way the text is understood by directing the individual's attention towards those elements that were emphasised in the headlines themselves (Niegeman, 1982). Research with broadcast news materials has indicated that the typical emphasis that is placed by journalists on personalities and dramatic ingredients of events, rather than on their causes and meaning, can impair audience comprehension (Findahl & Hoijer, 1972, 1975, 1976). Clearly then, the substance of headlines and summaries in news programmes needs to be carefully considered by journalists and researchers concerned with audiences' memory and understanding of broadcast news.

Tannenbaum (1953) found that newspaper headlines can exert a significant influence on the interpretation of the newspaper stories they summarise. Subsequently, Tannenbaum and Kernick (1954) attempted to investigate experimentally the effect of leads on audience interpretation of radio newscast items. The headline was regarded as one of a number of significant programme variables that may operate to influence the total impression created by the story.

The study had two principal aims. The first was to determine whether, under experimental conditions, different introductory statements or leads give rise to differential interpretation of similar newscast items, and the second was to compare this process between newspaper and radio newscast items.

From more than 20 news stories used in the earlier newspaper-headline study, a 15-item radio newscast script was prepared by a professional newscast writer. This script was then recorded as a radio news broadcast by a professional announcer. Separate recordings were made of the test items using three different leads that had been written for each of two target stories. The first test item was an account of a murder trial (the "trial story") and the second reported a conference of college educators about accelerated college programmes (the "acceleration story").

One introductory statement to the trial story indicated that the defendant was guilty, and one indicated that he was innocent. The third lead indicated neither guilt nor innocence. For the acceleration story, one lead featured the quarter system of acceleration, one featured the trimester system, and one expressed disapproval of acceleration in any form. About 350 introductory psychology undergraduates were recruited to take part in the experiment. They were divided into groups who heard one of the versions of the radio programme.

Although told to listen as they would ordinarily, their attention was drawn to six items, including the two test stories, which "might usually interest the average college student." After the newscast they were immediately questioned on it. Results showed that different introductory statements had a significant effect on listeners' impressions of one of the two test stories. This difference, according to the researchers, might be explained by the fact that opinions were better structured on one story than the other and were therefore less amenable to influence. The results suggest that when listeners' attitudes towards an issue are not strongly formed, opinions can be influenced by subtle message factors such as leads, which can operate to set a frame of reference within which the message is interpreted.

More recently, Bernard and Coldevin (1985) investigated the effects of short, headline-type recaps on the recall of specific information and the gist of the stories in a television news programme. A ten-item programme that included either oral recaps, oral-plus-graphics recaps, or no recaps was viewed by 881 experimental subjects.

It was predicted that recapping would encourage superior retention of recapped story information but would not influence the retention of unrecapped stories. Moreover, recaps were expected to promote better recall of the gist of the stories (i.e., main idea of the story) but to have little effect on memory for specific details. The recap format consisted of a 20-second, four-item recap in either the oral or oral-plus-graphic mode inserted between the end of the commercials and the sign-off. Overall, the recaps added about 4% of the total news presentation time of 7 minutes 45 seconds.

Recaps were found to increase retention of the gist of the stories but did not affect retention of specific details. No differences were found between types of recap. In addition, recaps supplanted rather than supplemented unrecapped items that had been viewed previously.

The authors suggest that this might have been due to retroactive interference effects, whereby recaps represented an intrusion sufficiently similar to the news items themselves as to interfere with the recall of stories previously viewed that were not recapped. It is also worth noting that recaps as used here addressed only general information about items rather than specific details—hence there was an effect on gist retention but not on detailed retention. Another methodological point concerned the test of multiple-choice recognition, which may not have activated appropriate retrieval processes to elicit full recall.

THE PACE AND FLOW OF THE PROGRAMME

Communication in a television news programme is essentially one-way, unlike the two-way communication interaction of face-to-face conversation. Information is presented once (although in some cases, headlines and summary roundups may repeat parts of stories), and the audience member is not given the opportunity to go back through a story in a programme once it has been presented, or to ask clarifying questions.

Because editors seldom if ever have any direct contact with or feedback from their audiences (see Gans, 1979; Schlesinger, 1978), they may have insufficient information or knowledge about the attention, interests, and intellectual capabilities of those who tune into their programmes to tailor the way they present the news to make it optimally comprehensible and relevant to audiences' needs.

Vast quantities of news information are generated every day and provide an overwhelming amount of material from which broadcasters can construct news programmes. News broadcasts, however, are of limited and normally fixed durations. In Britain, for instance, television schedules permit the addition of more airtime for fixed programmes only rarely. The length of a news broadcast therefore restricts the amount of news that can be presented each day.

Time is to television what space is to a newspaper, only television news has much less time than newspapers typically have space. Only so much can be said within a given time period. Measured by wordage alone, a 30-minute television newscast is the equivalent of less than the front page of a serious broadsheet newspaper.

In order to cover as many stories as possible, the news on television tends to report events with extreme brevity, especially as compared with the sort of coverage provided by newspapers. Television news writing has to be concise and to the point. Lengthy reports are not common. In-depth analysis of events does occur on television news bulletins occasionally, but on close examination the volume of information they contain seldom compares with that of a detailed newspaper report.

A crucial difference between newspapers and television is in the degree of control the consumer has over the rate at which news can be taken in. Reading a newspaper is self-paced, whereas the news on television is presented at a rate determined by the producers. It is for this reason that the delivery pace of broadcast news is a very important factor to consider in relation to information acquisition from news programmes by their audiences.

There is growing evidence that comprehension and storage of incoming information is not a rapid process. Simon (1974) reported that the various processes involved in comprehending and storing information usually require a span of time of some 5 to 8 seconds for each new item of information. On this evidence, the rate at which information is typically conveyed in televised communication may often be too fast for a viewer to comprehend all of what is going on, at least for messages of more than a few seconds duration.

Singer (1979) has observed that inherent in the power of television to capture and hold viewers' attention through its constantly changing short sequences of sensory bombardment is its principal limitation as an effective communicator of information. Attention is maintained by rapid shifts of focus, but cognitive processing to any substantial depth of the material it presents is impeded. Before individuals have had time to process the current input, another has already begun. Thus, television generates cognitive overload. In the context of watching television news, trying to comprehend one particular story and engaging in the mental effort necessary to store this material in memory (so that it can be recalled within even a few minutes) may mean that the viewer will necessarily have to miss something else. Indeed, in a bulletin crammed with short news stories, several items may be lost while viewers devote their cognitive information-processing capacities to the task of absorbing and making sense of a particular news story.

NARRATIVE DELIVERY RATE

Experimental studies on the effects of delivery rate in spoken informational sequences have demonstrated that a certain minimum amount of time is required to perceive and encode verbal materials properly, and that as word rate is increased beyond a certain point, the perception time available to the listener becomes inadequate and a rapid deterioration of listening comprehension commences. Although researchers in this field have found that delivery rate of recorded spoken messages can be considerably speeded up (using a special electronic time-compression technique that controls voice pitch regardless of playback speed) without significantly impairing recall, studies have mainly dealt with single-topic messages (Fairbanks, Guttmann, & Miron, 1957; Foulke, 1978; Sticht, 1969).

In news broadcasts, however, a wide range of topics may be covered in rapid succession, and in television news bulletins changes occur not only in the audio narrative but also visually. Does this additional complexity of newscast materials relative to single-topic audio-messages usually studied in compressed-speech experiments mean that the optimal delivery rate of broadcast news can be varied over only a fairly narrow range without damaging comprehension and memory of bulletin content?

Vincent, Ash, and Greenhill (1949) investigated the effects of "fact density" at four levels in a film about the weather made for the U.S. Navy. These researchers concluded that, up to a point, the more facts there are in a film, the more will be learned, but they added the further qualification that as information density continues to increase beyond a certain point, interferences are set up that result in less efficient learning.

Early studies with radio news at the end of the 1940s reported small effects of increased pacing or information density on recall of bulletin content. Harrell, Brown, and Schramm (1949) produced six different fictitious, 12.5-minute radio newscasts. Two contained 20 stories, two had 30 stories, and two had 40 stories. In the 30 and 40-item bulletins, shorter versions of the original 20-story items were included. Memory for bulletin content was tested shortly after presentation via four-option multiple-choice questions. Listeners, who were U.S. Air Force personnel, knew beforehand that they would be tested afterwards.

Results showed that as the number of news items presented over a fixed period of time increased, listeners remembered a progressively smaller proportion of them. Indeed, there was a significant decline in memory performance from the 20-item bulletin to the 30-item bulletin, and then again from 30 items to 40 items. (Correct recall rates were: 20 items—54.5%; 30 items—49.3%; 40 items—45.9%). However, although statistically significant, these differences are not large. In fact, listeners remembered more items, in terms of actual numbers of items recalled, from the 30-item newscast (15 items on average) than from the 20-item newscast (11 items), and more still from the 40-item programme (18 items). In terms of programme appreciation, though, listeners generally preferred the news broadcasts with fewer items.

In another early study, Nelson (1948) tested recall of multiple-topic news materials. Extending the presentation rate from 125 to 225 words per minute produced a slight, although insignificant decline in recall of bulletin content at the upper end of this range. Nelson also found that rate of presentation was related to audience interest in the programme. Over half his sample indicated that slower rates of presentation would cause them to lose interest, even though these versions produced the highest average recall scores. More recently, Smith and McEwan (1974) compiled two 5-minute radio newscasts of exactly 800 words each. One newscast consisted of a detailed single-topic message only, while the other contained 12 different and much briefer news items. A professional newscaster read each message at each of four presentation rates: 160, 190, 220, and 250 words per minute. Delivery rate was found to have a significant effect on recall, and the point at which the onset of detrimental effects occurred depended on the complexity of the programme. Recall began to decline at and above 220 words per minute for the single-topic newscast but at only 190 words per minute for the multiple-topic newscast. The results indicated that a newscaster could vary his or her rate of delivery from 160 to 190 words per minute in multiple-topic newscast situations, and from 160 to 220 words per minute in single-topic commentary-type situations without experiencing detrimental rate effects.

VISUAL DELIVERY RATE

Clearly, audio delivery rates can have important effects on comprehension and recall of broadcast news material, but in the case of television in particular, presentation rate may vary visually as well as auditorily. How important is the effect of rapid visual change on memory for television content?

Educational Television Research

Research on the impact of narrative delivery rate and rate of visual change on information acquisition from television has been conducted on young viewers in connection with educationally oriented programmes, as well as with child and adult audiences with news materials.

Formative research for *Sesame Street* (Palmer, 1969), for example, discovered that preschool children's visual attention was held by fast action and rapid changes of action, as produced by fast editing. Later evaluative research on *Sesame Street* (Lesser, 1974) found that children of all social classes did show gains in learning on a number of measures, compared to pretest scores. However, the researchers did not relate these gains directly to the "attractive" visual style, for example, by using a control programme in which the production was less fast-paced.

Other researchers have found that the extent of children's visual attention does not always correlate well with performance on comprehension tests (Lorch, Anderson, & Levin, 1979). In other words, increased visual attention does not necessarily produce corresponding increases in learning.

Anderson and Lorch (1983) suggested that attention may not be a passive function of attractive production techniques; they argue that it is an active function and that young viewers choose to give attention to particular features because they have learned from experience that these features signal an advance in the sequence of information. Attention is thus seen as "schema driven" by the viewer, not "programme led" by the art of the producer. If this is true, it would appear important to identify which production features are adopted in the formation of the viewers' schema. This means looking more closely at what happens to comprehension and recall when production features such as picture changes take place.

Research discussed earlier indicated the importance of visual illustrations in television news. More especially, from the perspective of learning from the news, it was observed that the relevance of the pictures to the words was important (Findahl & Hoijer, 1976). The question of relevance embodies considerations not just about how to match picture to narrative but also about the degree of correspondence between two different informational structures—visual (film, graphics, stills, etc.) and soundtrack (words, clauses, sentences, etc.). During the course of a news programme or even within a single item, the film shot may change numerous times. What effect does this have on the viewer's ability to absorb the sound narrative?

Millerson (1976) has argued that when the picture changes, "the viewer assesses, interprets and relates the new shot to the previous one." If Millerson's assumption is correct, a shot change imposes extra demands on the viewer's processing capacity, and those demands must be dealt with at the same time as the viewer/listener is processing the verbal information in the soundtrack.

Giltrow (1977) compared two television programmes that dealt with the same information topic but differed in visual style: One use a wide variety of fast-paced film sequences, the other used a studio talk show format. He found that the slower-paced production produced greater cognitive gain than the fast-paced one. Recall of the main ideas and related images and ideas were significantly better, although Giltrow's subjects "preferred" the fast-paced programme when asked to rate both programmes.

The effects of visual presentation speed and of frequency and place-ment of visual changes in television news programmes has been investi-gated in two experimental studies. Schlater (1970) examined the maxi-mum rate of presentation at which relevant visual information could be transmitted in a television newscast before recall was impeded. Simulated newscasts were prepared in which a 4.5-minute narrative was accompa-nied by visual material under a number of rates of presentation. Viewers were tested for comprehension and memory of pictorial information and verbal information from the news message. Memory for picture informa-tion in response to picture cues declined as rate of picture presentation increased, but picture information tested by verbal questions *increased* as rate of picture presentation was increased, and leveled off at about seven visuals per 30 seconds. One explanation for this difference in picture recall between test conditions is that verbal questions formulated about picture content provided additional information to aid memory perform-ance that was not contained in pictorial recall cues. Increasing rate of picture presentation had no substantial effect on viewers' ability to com-prehend and remember the audio-narrative of the television bulletin. However, this is not to say that visual presentation changes are unlikely to affect verbal recall from television newscasts. Schlater admits that much of the picture content presented in this study was informationally redun-dant with respect to the verbal text of the message. Where this is not the case, as is likely in many live news broadcasts, the effects of rate of visual change on memory for story narrative might be more substantial. Further research is needed here before any clearcut statement can be made concerning the effects of presentation rate of information in one channel (e.g., visual) upon recall of information from the other major channel (e.g., audio) in television news programmes.

Davies, Berry, and Clifford (1985) conducted an experiment in which learning was measured from a single television news item, about the

Opening of Parliament in November 1981. In this study, the researchers examined not just the rate of visual change but also manipulated the placement of visual changes vis-a-vis the narrative, and the degree of relevance of pictures to the concurrent verbal text of the item. In its original broadcast form, the news item included a number of cut-away shots used to cover cuts in the film that had very little relevance to the accompanying text and that could thus be used as irrelevant pictures. Parts of the film were edited so that four pairs of sentences from the commentary, each pair linked in topic, were presented with accompanying film that was either relevant (R) or irrelevant (I) to the narrative, and that was cut either between each sentence or within each sentence. Thus the design yielded comparisons between material with picture cuts in the middle of the sentence (RIRI and RRRR) and material without such cuts (RI and RR), and between relevant (RR and RRRR) and irrelevant (RI and RIRI) pictures, as well as between combinations of the two.

Relevance was defined as the subject of the picture being the same as the subject of the accompanying sentence. (Authors' example: "When a sentence pair was dealing with the topic of the Irish State Coach, a 'relevant' (R) picture accompanying the text showed the coach; an 'irrelevant' (I) picture showed some unidentified people on a balcony".)

Davies et al. predicted that irrelevance of pictures and mid-sentence cutting would both impair memory performance. Combining the two, for example, by switching mid-sentence from a relevant to an irrelevant picture would further impede performance, compared with a switch from one relevant picture to another.

Experimental subjects were tested on the eight picture-treatment sentences and on the six remaining sentences in the item. In addition to the four experimental treatment conditions, a fifth condition consisting of the original broadcast version was included. Over 200 individuals took part in the experiment, including adults and children (aged 11–12 years and 14–15 years). Davies et al. found effects of different rates of picture cutting and picture narrative relevance. Furthermore, production techniques did not always have the same effects on learning among adults and children.

Effects of Cutting.   There were certain variations in the effects of mid-sentence picture changes on recall among adults and children. With adults, with all relevant picture material, uncut (RR) material was markedly superior to cut (RRRR), particularly with the first sentence of the pairs. The effects of cutting were weaker where irrelevant pictures were included. The results among 14- and 15-year-olds present a contrast— notably a reversal of the difference between RR and RRRR—with RRRR doing significantly better—and a more marked effect of picture relevance. Where irrelevant picture material was used, uncut material was superior to cut. Thus, among this age group, cutting in mid-sentence appears to be beneficial when all the pictures are relevant and detrimental when the picture switches from relevant to irrelevant. At the same time, however, the worst performance was observed for the relevant picture/uncut treatment which was worse than switches across sentences or within sentences from relevant to irrelevant picture accompaniment. With 11- and 12-year-olds as with older children, the all-relevant material with mid-sentence cuts (RRRR) was superior to the all-relevant material with no cuts (RR), but none of the differences was statistically significant. Other comparisons showed some significant superiorities of uncut material to cut. These occurred on second-sentence material in each pair when comparing mid-sentence cuts to irrelevant material with no mid-sentence cuts, even when second sentences were accompanied for the whole duration (uncut) by irrelevant pictures.

Effects of Irrelevance.   Among adults, comparisons between material with irrelevant pictures and material with relevant pictures (RI vs RR; RIRI vs RRRR) produced no significant differences. However, the switch from relevant to irrelevant material within or between sentences was more likely to produce decrements in performance than comparable relevant-relevant switches. Among 14- and 15-year-olds, between-sentence switches from relevant to irrelevant pictures actually produced better recall than relevant-relevant switches on first- and second-sentence material. However, pairing irrelevance with fast cutting produced worse performance than when the pictures were all relevant. The results suggest a negative effect of picture irrelevance when combined with fast cutting (RIRI) but a positive one when there is no mid-sentence editing (RI). Among 11- and 12-year-olds, the same pattern of scores emerged as with the older children but were less marked. RI produced better recall than RR in most cases but not significantly so. Picture irrelevance appeared to be facilitative when there were no mid-sentence edits (RI) but not when there were mid-sentence edits (RIRI).

Comparisons of the specially edited treatments with the original broadcast version of the news item showed that careful editing did produce better recall sometimes. With the adult sample, recall from the original item was slightly better than from versions that included rapid mid-sentence cuts (RRRR) and (RIRI) but was worse than from between-sentence cuts with relevant picture material (RR). The original version contained eight target sentences, with seven mid-sentence cuts, and irrelevant pictures were used on three occasions. Among the youngest children, the original version produced worst performance of all, whereas among the older children, it actually produced the best performance. There was some inconsistency of results across age groups, therefore.

Davies et al. concluded from their results that standard production techniques, such as shot changes, which are not intended to affect the viewers' understanding of the information in the spoken text nevertheless do seem to do so. A second conclusion was that these production techniques have markedly different effects on different types of viewers. It appears that viewers (in the case from different age groups) are differentially sensitive to unintended production effects and that their cognitive processing of verbal information can be disrupted to different degrees by inappropriately timed picture cuts.

Davies and her colleagues argue that any discussion of the relationship between pictures and text in audio-visual material needs to take account of correspondence not only between picture topic and text topic but also between structural changes in topic: in the case of pictures, changes of shot, in the case of words, syntactic boundaries (such as ends of sentences). Where changes in topic do not correspond, as when the picture changes for no reason in the middle of a sentence, effects on processing may occur. These effects, however, may differ according to viewer characteristics. The finding that adult recall was disrupted by cutting in the middle of a sentence, compared with the same sentences undisrupted by any visual change, bears out the prediction that an unexpected or unmotivated change of shot may disrupt the encoding and hence the recall of the verbal information accompanying it. Interestingly, however, the prediction that irrelevant material would be more disruptive than relevant material was not supported.

The combination of cutting and irrelevance did not produce good results in any group of viewers. Cutting by itself may enhance attention and hence comprehension in children, and it may do the opposite in adults. But if the picture keeps switching from one that is relevant to the text to another that is not, overload and confusion can result for everybody. The detrimental effects of switching from relevant to irrelevant, compared with switching from relevant to relevant pictures, was also seen in the performance decline associated with changes from one picture to an unrelated one, more so than when the change was merely to a different view of the same picture. These results, although not conclusive, further support the hypothesis that some cognitive processing goes on when the pictures change and that some effort to connect the pictures in a meaningful way is being made.

REPETITION AND REFORMULATION EFFECTS

Sahin, Davis, and Robinson (1981) argued that the often observed low rates of viewer comprehension and memory of television news stem to a large extent from the contradiction between the formal aspects of television news transmission and its reception. One important ingredient to which they point in this respect is that television news is presented in a nonrepetitive format that does not permit control or participation by the viewer. The reception of television news is intermittent as viewers tune in and tune out throughout the broadcast.

The format of newspapers, on the other hand, is substantially different from that of television news. Newspapers tend to devote considerably more attention to each story and routinely repeat important aspects of each news item. The newspaper format is therefore more conducive to efficient learning and retention. Moreover, people typically read the newspaper in a leisurely and relaxed manner that allows for rereading and mulling over particular items in the news. By contrast, people typically watch television news while simultaneously engaged in other activities.

Even if viewers are paying fairly consistent attention to the screen, however, the pace of the news may still not be suitable for learning among many viewers.

In television bulletins, news information is presented in a steady stream over which viewers have no control. Unlike the case of reading a newspaper, they do not have the opportunity to go back over a news story again at their own pace to pick up further details from it that they missed first time round.

As we saw in the previous sections, the speed at which information is presented and the overall amount of information presented can have substantial effects on narrative comprehension by the receiver. Although it may be possible to convey more information via accelerated presentation with some audio or audio-visual materials, the complexity and heterogeneous quality of TV news may not lend itself to effective presentation at accelerated rates. The more complex and varied the type of information presented, the lower the optimal speed of presentation for ready assimilation by the audience. One way to offset the information losses that might occur because of inadequate time to process bulletin content effectively on its first presentation is to repeat or reformulate portions of that content at some point in the programme. Two sets of important questions arise here. First, what is the best way to repeat material in a news programme? Or, at what points in the programme relative to the main reports should repetitions occur? Should repetition occur at the beginning of the programme or the end, or perhaps somewhere in the body of the show? Second, which aspects of a news report should be repeated or reformulated to best enhance overall learning?

Repetition of informational material can be "massed" or "distributed." The majority of psychological studies of human learning have operationalised distributed practice as repetition or review of material interspersed within the body of a presentation, and massed practice as a summary occurring at the beginning or more usually at the end of the main body of to-be-learned material—much like the summary of main headlines occurring at the end of a television news bulletin. Experimental psychologists have found these methods to be differentially effective under different learning conditions. Maccoby and Sheffield (1961) found massed practice to be less effective than spaced practice for mastering a sequential learning task, whereas Ash and Jaspen (1953) found spaced practice to be more effective than massed practice in learning military tasks. Further studies by Underwood and Ekstrand (1967) and Rothkopf (1968) have suggested that spaced practice is superior to massed practice in promoting the retention of verbal and motor skills.

Although the evidence on the effect of repetition on learning print material is far from conclusive, most producers of informational television programming hold firmly to the belief that repetition of material will enhance memory for it. But while massed summary treatment seems to be the preferred style of reviewing information in television newscasts, is there any empirical evidence to show that this treatment is the most effective method of structuring a television programme to enhance learning?

The earliest studies on the effects of repeating or summarising information of learning from audio-visual material were conducted by researchers concerned with enhancing the effectiveness of instructional films. Lathrop (1949) and Norford (1949), both from the Instructional Film Research Program at Pennsylvania State College, investigated the effects of introductions (Lathrop) and summaries (Norford) on learning from educational films. Lathrop, for example, tested three films on science or geography topics with and without introductions. Results were equivocal; for one film introductions produced better learning, but for another they had an adverse effect. Norford found minor effects of summaries.

Another researcher from the same institution, Jasper (1950), conducted experiments on the effectiveness of repetition in armed services' instructional films concerning gun breach block assembly and the importance of different rates of delivery (in terms of numbers of words per minute of film). Jasper found that repeated sequences of important processes considerably improved learning.

Another more recent important study in this respect was reported by Coldevin (1975). He examined the overall effects of repetition per se on retention of information from television programming among 12- and 13-year-old schoolchildren and attempted also to isolate the differential effects on learning of three modes of reformulation: spaced, massed, and summary review treatments. A different version of the same 20-minute programme on forest fires was prepared for each review treatment, a simple version with no reformulation was also employed. In the massed review treatment, repetitions of information were distributed within the body of the programme material. A paced review was identical to massed review, with the addition of a 5-second pause between the review statement and the body of the text under review. Finally, summary review consisted of a simple summing up of all repeated material at the end of the programme. Recall scores were substantially greater for all repetition treatments than for the simple treatment, indicating that reviewing material in a programme strengthens information gain from it. However, there were no differences overall between the three review treatments; thus the placement of review segments within the programme appeared to be relatively unimportant to learning. Conflicting results emerged from an earlier study, however, which utilised the same material with an identical sampling age (Coldevin, 1974). Here, superior learning was recorded for the spaced review treatment over both the massed and summary treatments, indicating that the internal temporal distribution of reviews does seem to be crucial to information retention. Coldevin (1975) suggests that the dominance of the spaced review may result from greater internalisation of content and covert practice between repetitions than either of the other two review treatments.

REPETITION EFFECTS WITH BROADCAST NEWS

Following the argument of Sahin et al. (1981) that television news lacks the learning-conductive format of newspapers, Perloff, Wartella, and Becker (1982) reasoned that if television newscasts were constructed so that they resembled the highly informative newspaper style of presentation, viewers might learn more public affairs information from television than they do at present. They focused on two prominent newspaper attributes: (a) redundancy or repetition of information; and (b) the greater time span that is afforded to newspaper readers than television viewers to think through and digest each story. They predicted that learning would be maximised when newscasts repeated and recapped important elements of each news story and slowed down the fast pace of delivery so that there was more time for the audience to assimilate each item.

Perloff et al. designed an experiment in which repetition and speed of presentation of news were manipulated. Repetition was manipulated by the presence or absence of a brief recapping of the main points of the major items in the newscast at the end of the programme. Time for digestion was varied by the pacing of the delivery of the individual items in the newscast. Thus, in one version of the programme a normal 1-second pause occurred between stories, while in another version there were 3.5-second pauses between stories. In all, there were five experimental conditions: (a) recap—long pause between stories; (b) recap—short pause; (c) no recap—long pause; (d) no recap—short pause; and (e) a nonviewing control condition. The bulletin contained ten stories and was viewed by 55 college-student subjects.

Immediately after presentation of the programme, subjects completed a questionnaire that tested their recall of information in the programme. they returned one week later to complete a test of delayed recall. Results revealed a highly significant effect of recapping, whereby news recaps enhanced recall. This effect was observed during both immediate recall and delayed recall one week later. There was, however, no effect of pause length on either immediate or delayed recall. Subjectively, subjects in the recap conditions were more likely than those in no-recap conditions to feel that the newscaster spent more time going over stories in greater detail.

A further important general point of note is that even subjects who viewed the recap versions still recalled only about half the items correctly. Although summarising the main points of the news improves recall to some extent, clearly there is still an awful lot forgotten.

Perloff et al. suggested that recaps should perhaps be used in conjunction with other techniques, such as headline-type summaries of the news at the beginning of the programme or the usual captions, or should be carefully designed to identify and clarify the central point of the story.

EFFECTS OF INFORMATION REFORMULATION WITHIN STORIES

Repetition need not involve simply literal re-presentation of the content. On the contrary, careful reemphasis of vital elements of the basic news message may prove much more effective at enhancing recall of the essential aspects of the reported issue or event. Findahl and Hoijer (1972 1975) investigated the effects of verbally reformulating news messages upon detailed recall of item content. They presented respondents with items under several different conditions in which various portions of the content were repeated within each news report. A fictitious news bulletin was prepared consisting of 13 items. Five of these were independently manipulated under four treatment conditions: repetition of information about the participants or location of an event, repetition of cause information, repetition of consequences information, or repetition of all these aspects of story content. There was also a control condition consisting of the basic news message with no additional verbal information. Retention of story details was measured by means of short open-ended questions that could be answered in one or two words. As Fig.10.1 shows, verbal repetition or reformulation of any part of an item enhanced retention for that part relative to the basic message condition, in which none of the information was repeated. However, this did not necessarily improve overall understanding of the story. If verbal reformulation placed additional emphasis on location and participants of the news event, these facts were retained nearly twice as well as other, more abstract elements of the

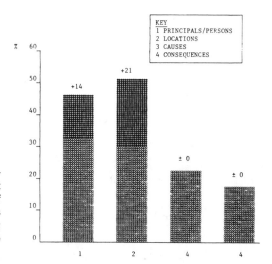

KEY
1 PRINCIPALS/PERSONS
2 LOCATIONS
3 CAUSES
4 CONSEQUENCES

FIG. 10.1A Effects of verbal reformulation of information about persons and location on recall of different aspects of news stories (Findahl and Hoijer 1972, 1975; reprinted by permission of the authors).

story concerning cause and effect relationships (see Fig. 10.1A). However, stressing the latter components not only improved knowledge of causes and consequences but also effected a more general improvement in retention even for those elements (i.e., details of participants and location) that were not explicitly verbally restated (see Fig. 10.1B & 10.1C). Of course, the best results were obtained when information concerning all these aspects of a story were reformulated within the item's verbal narrative (see Fig. 10.1D).[1]

Findahl and Hoijer (1976) also examined the effects on memory for television news of jointly reformulating news texts and manipulating visual accompaniment, and suggested ways in which one mode of additional input may or may not serve to balance the other so as to enhance learning. For example, visually illustrating the location of an event with a map produced an imbalance in memory for item content because, although recall of the illustrated portion of the item was enhanced, other aspects of the story were less well rememberded. Balance was successfully restored, however, when the nonillustrated relational aspects of the item (i.e., cause and consequence information) were verbally reformulated (see Fig. 10.2), but this counterbalancing relationship between additional visual input and verbal repetition does not apparently always lead to improved overall recall on item content. In another treatment, Findahl and Hoijer (1976) used schematic drawings to illustrate the causes and consequences of news events. This improved memory not only for illus-

---

[1]The top darker portion of each bar in Fig. 8.1 A–D indicates the improvement in viewers' recall of the verbally reformulated items compared to a basic non-reformulated version.

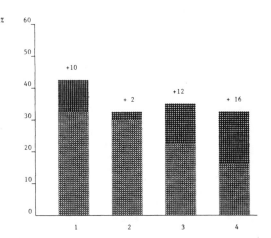

FIG. 10.1B Effects of verbal reformulation of information about causes on recall of different aspects of news stories (Findahl and Hoijer, 1972, 1975).

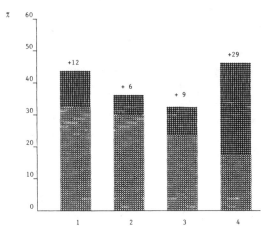

FIG. 10.1C Effects of verbal reformulation of information about consequences on recall of different aspects of news stories (Findahl and Hoijer, 1972, 1975).

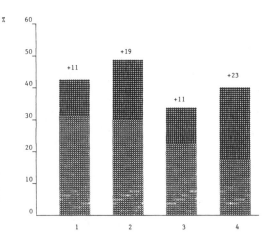

FIG. 10.1D Effects of verbal reformulation of all parts of a news story on recall of its content (Findahl and Hoijer, 1972, 1975).

276

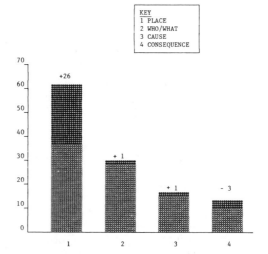

KEY
1 PLACE
2 WHO/WHAT
3 CAUSE
4 CONSEQUENCE

FIG. 10.2A   Basic message and map (Findahl and Hoijer, 1976). Reprinted by permission of the authors.

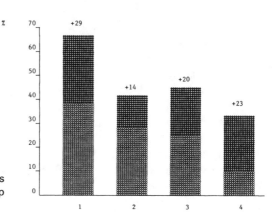

FIG. 10.2B   Repetition of causes and consequences and map (Findahl and Hoijer, 1976).

trated features but also for other aspects of the story. When, in addition to this, however, information about the location and people involved in the event were verbally reformulated within the text, repetition counteracted the effect of the picture material detrimentally and resulted in poorer recall for causes and consequences information.

A similar result was found for visual illustration of the consequences of a news event. Findahl and Hoijer showed that visual illustration of consequences of a news event enhanced recall of all parts of an item, even those not illustrated. However, if, in addition to this, information concerning the location of an event was verbally reformulated, recall performance deteriorated. The most successful condition of all was when the cause or consequences of a news event were visually illustrated *and* verbally reformulated. In this case the respective effects of visual rein-forcement and verbal repetition were additive.

To summarise, the Swedish results reported here indicate that employ-ing visual illustrations with verbal repetition of the narrative can enhance viewers' recall of item content, but that certain combinations of the two work better than others. Under some circumstances, pictures and repeti-tion are mutually beneficial, and under others they are not.

CONCLUDING REMARKS

This chapter has examined a miscellany of production features in news broadcasting and their actual or potential influence on memory and comprehension of programme content. Although it is common practice in television newscasts to begin the programme with headlines of the main stories of the day and to finish with a brief resumé of the "main points of the news," the effects of these features on audience retention and compre-hension have rarely been investigated.

Research done by cognitive psychologists has shown that thematic titles can affect memory for passages of discourse. The nature of this effect depends to a large extent on where the titles are presented relative to the main body of the passage, however. Memory performance is en-hanced when verbal or pictorial topic headlines are presented before a written or auditory passage but not when they come after it. Such findings suggest that headlines may serve as advance organisers of information. They may provide clues about the nature of the detailed information to be presented next and indicate areas of existing knowledge with which the new material may be meaningfully integrated. Headlines or summaries presented afterwards are less effective in this sense because Organiza-tional strategies may be relatively useless when employed retroactively because some if not much of the new information that may have been preserved by schema-driven integration into existing memory structures may already have been lost.

Cognitive research indicates, however, that headlines need to be used with care. There is experimental evidence that headlines may bias the way narratives are understood by directing readers' or listeners' attention to particular elements within the story. It is important therefore that head-lines reinforce central points essential to a proper understanding of the meaning of the story.

Another attribute of news broadcasting that has important implica-tions for learning is the rate at which information is presented. News broadcasts are typically severely limited in the time that is made available to them in the daily programme schedules and therefore not usually able to devote much time to individual news stories. Research has shown that as the density of factual content increases in informational audio-visual material, beyond a certain point, so learning deteriorates (Nelson, 1948; Vincent et al., 1949). It is important to remember also that as the complexity and degree of unfamiliarity with the information increases, so the optimal level of fact density beyond which effective cognitive processing will decline is reduced (Smith & McEwan, 1974).

The deleterious effects of rapid changes of pace in television news programmes may be even more significant when they occur both visually and verbally (Schlater, 1970). Furthermore, a recent experimental study (Davies et al., 1985) of rates of picture changes in television news has indicated that memory for programme content may be especially badly affected when the shot changes in the middle of a sentence and when the pictures are largely irrelevant to what is being said in the narrative.

The pace of the programme is especially important for comprehension when one considers that, unlike with reading a newspaper, audience members have no control over the flow of information in a news broadcast and cannot usually go back over it again at their own leisure. (One could conceive of a situation these days in which viewers could "capture" even broadcast news on videotape and therefore be in a position to play the programme over and over again to check on details they may have missed on its first presentation. U.K. research on how people use their home videos, however, has revealed that few people bother to record the news. Instead, they are much more likely to record films and soap operas [IBA, 1986]) One way of overcoming forgetting or failure to encode the information effectively in the first place may be to reformulate aspects of news stories within the text of the news narrative. This may work quite well provided the cause-effect relationships central to the meaning of a story are the elements given additional emphasis (Findahl & Hoijer, 1972). If pictorial enhancements are also used alongside verbal embellishments as such, the impact on learning can be even more pronounced (Findahl & Hoijer, 1976). Enhancements to the basic news narrative in the form of emphasis on central points within the text or careful use and placement of visual illustrations can improve the informational quality of broadcast news without necessarily slowing the pace and reducing audience interest in the programme, and without the need for a reduction in the number of stories that can be reported in a newscast.

11 Scheduling the News

In the United States, network news on television had its roots in the Monday to Friday, 7:30 to 8:00 p.m. (EST) time period. As news programming expanded, Monday to Friday early evening and Monday to Friday early morning were the two dominant day periods on the news scene for more than 25 years. More recently, however, there has been a significant shift in the distribution of news on television, with additional programmes now being broadcast in previously unscheduled late night and very early morning time periods.

Figure 11.1 shows schematically how the daily distribution of network television news in the United States has changed over the years. In 1950, all network news was broadcast in the early evening on weekdays. By 1955, the pattern of news distribution had already changed dramatically, and over the next 20 years, early evening news constituted on average only about one third of network news output. Since 1980, the amount of news transmitted on the major networks has increased at an unprecedented rate, and early morning and late evening news broadcasts have become predominant.

The hour at which a news programme is broadcast is a major factor in determining its style and character. At different times of the day, the audience may vary in size, composition, mood, interests or tastes, and length of time it has available for watching television. Although there probably is greater heterogeneity of audiences throughout the day these days, with more people out of work, a growing retired population, and

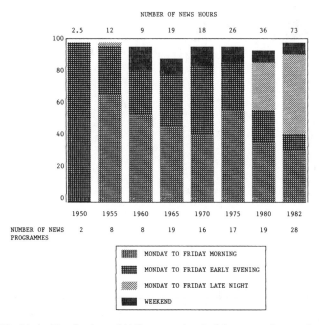

FIG. 11.1 Distribution of U.S. network television news by weekpart and daypart (Nielsen, 1984). Data used by permission of the author

shorter or more flexible working hours, the time at which the news is shown can restrict the potential audience. At midday, for example, there may be relatively more housewives available. During the early evening, the audience is extensively a family audience. In the later evening, the audience consists mainly of adults.

The same individuals may vary in their tastes at different times of the day. In the early morning, the person getting ready for work may have little time to spare for lengthy features. He or she may want the main points of the news delivered in a concise, snappy fashion. All this is not to say that a major news story is only of interest at certain times of day but that the shape and style of the story must be tailored to fit the varying tastes, moods and availability of the audience across the day.

Assumptions have been made by news professionals regarding the character of the audience and different times of the day. From these have developed beliefs about the kinds of programme format that may be best suited for morning, noon, and early or late evening audiences. Most of these assumptions and beliefs are related to strategies designed to produce programmes that will appeal to viewers at different times of the day. Standard audience research data can reveal useful information about the composition of the audience and about the amount of time they usually

282

have available to watch television within different time periods. These are all valuable sources of information and should not be discounted or underestimated. However, there is another source of knowledge, concerning the cognitive information-processing abilities of people at different times of the day, which may also have considerable value for those who manufacture the news. Before turning to a discussion of research bearing on this subject, however, it migh be insightful to consider briefly the kinds of assumptions made about news viewing and news tastes at different times of day by the professionals.

In his book on television news production, American television journalist Maury Green (1969) made a number of suggestions about how to style news broadcasts throughout the day in order to get the best results in terms of audience appeal. These serve as a useful starting point for the present discussion. According to Green, the morning news show requires fast pacing, with lots of hard news packaged in short items. Both lengthy, in-depth items and extensive visual (i.e., film) treatment are not recommended for television news at this time of day.

This is because the morning audience is seen for the most part as one that has other things on its mind, primarily getting ready to go to work. Most people therefore do not have much time to sit in front of the television screen for long spells. At the start of the day viewers in the main need short, snappy items that provide the main points of the news in a quick, lucid fashion. Film is less important in the morning because most people may be too busy to actually watch the screen properly for more than brief spells if they are preparing or eating breakfast, or getting ready to go off to work. Because of its need for fast pacing, the morning news show does not stretch comfortably into a format even as long as half an hour. Few viewers can sit and watch that long. Consequently, they miss either the top of the show or the last half of the news. The assumptions about the time most viewers of early morning television news shows have available are upheld by audience research. In the United Kingdom, for example, a duration of viewing analysis for breakfast television indicated that most viewers of the 6:00 to 9:00 a.m. shows watch for about 15 to 30 minutes; very few watch for longer (Gunter, 1986).

For these longer early morning news programmes, the problem of the transient audience is solved with the so-called "news wheel," in which the same basic news is repeated one or more times, each repeat being updated with fresh developments.

At midday, news is still breaking, although not as rapidly as a few hours earlier. More details are usually available on stories than was so at breakfast time, and so too is more film. Once again, though, the primary consideration must be the nature and mood of the audience. The belief among the professionals is that the midday audience consists largely of women and children. This is not entirely true today. As noted earlier, there are many people out of work or retired, and many more who are either sick, on leave, or working on shifts or flexi-time, including large numbers of adult males, who may also be at home and available to watch television at this time. On the assumption that most viewers are women, however, Green (1969) observed: "At noon these viewers have settled into their day's routine: they are no longer in the midst of the morning rush, they have more time and they are willing to give the news more attention" (p.249). The news, therefore can be presented at a more leisurely pace than in the early morning.

By the early evening, the news audience is the mass audience representative of all the interests of all the people. The entire family may he watching at this time (between 6:00 and 7:30 p.m.). At this time of day, Green observed: "This audience is relaxed at the end of the day's work, ready and willing to sit for an hour or more and get acquainted with the rest of the world and the great events being played out on the stage of mankind. It has both time and inclination to watch lengthy reports as long as they are informative. It seeks the meaning of events which concern its own destiny, and therefore it appreciates analysis which puts the news in perspective. No less than any other audience it appreciates being entertained, but it wants at least a nugget of information in its barrel of news, or it would be watching something other than the news" (p.251).

Later in the evening the audience changes yet again. The late evening viewer is seen as more relaxed, more receptive, more sophisticated than any other viewers. A large section of the audience is perceived as being middle class and more interested in news anyway. Although viewers are tiring at this late hour, they want information provided it is not too heavy. Hence the news show should have a relaxed and casual mood. Circadian rhythms (24-hour rhythms) have been known for some time to exist with respect to human performance on a wide range of tasks. Furthermore, according to some cognitive psychologists, these daily rhythms are substantial enough to be of practical as well as theoretical significance in the study of human cognitive functioning, and may often produce up to a 10% variation in performance during the course of the waking day (Eysenck, 1982).

From the earliest days of experimental research on human memory, findings have shown that performance on tests of short-term memory in the morning is superior to that in the afternoon. Research first noting the effects of time of day on immediate memory for information dates back to Ebbinghaus (1885), who found that he was able to learn lists of nonsense syllables faster at 10:00 or 11:00 than at 18:00. More detailed work was carried out during the early part of this century by educational researchers aiming to provide teachers with guidelines about how best to arrange their school timetables to facilitate learning (Gates, 1916; Winch, 1911, 1912, 1913).

It is only in the last decade or so, however, that experimental psychologists have begun to look seriously and explicitly at time of day as an important independent variable underlying human memory performance on different kinds of learning tasks. As we have seen already in this chapter, the growth in amount of news programming on television since television broadcasts began has been considerable. Not only has the amount of news transmitted by the leading television networks in the United States and United Kingdom expanded significantly but also news nowadays is broadcast at an increasingly greater variety of times of day. In addition to the flagship news programmes broadcast in the early evening (and in the United Kingdom in the late evening), news shows are available around breakfast time, at midday, or in the early afternoon (in the United Kingdom), in the late afternoon (in the United States), and very late at night (again in the United States).

In the United Kingdom, for example, the introduction of breakfast television news and features programming, originally accompanied by a desire on the part of its producers to provide depth to viewers' understanding of the world, provided a fresh impetus to interest in the effects of time of day on memory performance in connection with a real-life learning experience. In this chapter, we examine the research evidence on effects of time of day on learning and remembering, then report on two experiments in which the nature of these effects on memory for television news was investigated.

Perhaps the most extensive body of research on diurnal rhythms and human cognitive performance was reported by Blake (1967, 1971). He asked naval ratings to perform a wide range of tasks at various times of day (08:00. 10:00, 13:00, 15:00, 21:00). He discovered that performance on several of the tasks (including five-choice serial reaction, auditory vigilance, card sorting, letter cancellation, and simple arithmetic) manifested a fairly consistent improvement over the day, with the best level of performance achieved at 21:00. Blake also recorded body temperature on a number of occasions and found that changes in temperature followed the same pattern across the day as did changes in cognitive performance. Body temperature reached a peak between 20:00 and 21:00 and was lowest between 04:00 and 05:00. There was a rapid rise in temperature between 08:00 and 11:00, followed by a more gradual increase over the subsequent several hours and a rapid decline during the late evening and night period. What then, do these findings tell us about time-of-day effects and how they may be explained?

One possible explanation is that body temperature is an indicator of arousal level, and because the optimal level of arousal varies inversely as a function of task difficulty, it follows that for simple tasks, performance should improve as arousal increases across the day, whereas for more difficult tasks, performance suffers with higher arousal later in the day.

The simplicity of this explanation makes it very appealing. Nevertheless, it is almost totally wrong. There is much psychological and physiological evidence that indicates that level of arousal does not in fact increase throughout the day up to late evening. Thayer (1967) found that self-reported activation a peak at just after midday. Other studies have confirmed that self-reported arousal is maximal in the late morning or early afternoon (Clement, Hafer & Vermillion, 1976; Thayer, 1978). In other words people feel that they are at their best in the middle of the day. On a physiological level, measures other than body temperature have indicated that arousal may occur towards the middle of the day rather than towards the end. Klein, Hermann, Kuklinski, & Wegmann (1977) reported that adrenalin secretion reached its peak at approximately midday, and Akerstedt (1977) found that the urinary excretion of both adrenalin and nonadrenalin reached a maximum at about noon, as did subjective ratings of alertness.

The discrepancy between the diurnal rhythm for temperature and those for catecholamines (e.g., adrenalin and nonadrenalin) and self-reported arousal may simply mean that body temperature is an unsatisfactory measure of arousal. Alternatively, there may be two or more arousal systems, with each of the various physiological measures reflecting activity in one of these systems.

Eysenck (1982) has suggested that the most plausible conclusion on the current evidence is that there is a major diurnal rhythm for arousal that peaks at around midday and that can be measured either by self-reported arousal or by catecholamine output. In addition, there may be a minor diurnal rhythm for arousal that is indexed by body temperature; however, it is preferable to regard body temperature as an indirect measure of basic metabolic processes rather than of arousal.

The precise nature of time-of-day effects on learning may vary according to the kind of memory performance being tested. There has been interest in these effects in relation to short-term retention of information (e.g., up to 20 minutes) and long-term retention. For material that is to be tested immediately or fairly soon after presentation, memory performance tends to be better earlier in the day. However, when the test of information retention is delayed for some hours or days after presentation, memory tends to be better for material presented later in the day.

TIME-OF-DAY EFFECTS AND IMMEDIATE MEMORY

Experiments using simple and complex learning materials have indicated that immediate processing of new information deteriorates across the day. Some studies of the effects of time of day on retention have used syntactically unstructured lists of words, while others have tested memory for connected prose or even film materials. In this chapter we look at these kinds of studies and also at two recent experiments on time-of-day effects and memory for televised news.

In experiments using word lists, the words are typically presented one at a time. Recall can be either spoken or written, and reproducing the original order of the words during recall is not usually required. In one study, Hockey, Davies, & Gray (1972) compared the immediate free recall of a single list of 30 nouns presented at 06:30 or at 23:00. Subjects tested in the early morning session recalled on average about 1.8 words more than those tested in the late evening session. Subsequently, Jones, Davies, Hoga, Patrick, and Cumberbatch (1978) reported five studies that compared immediate free recall of word lists in the morning (between 08:00 and 10:30) with that in the afternoon (between 15:00 and 17:00). Of these five studies, one showed a significant morning superiority, two a significant afternoon superiority, and two failed to show any significant effect of time of day. It should, however, be noted that these studies differed from one another in terms of both the modality and the rate of presentation, and that in some cases the numbers of subjects tested were rather small.

Other experiments have shown that time-of-day effects may be particularly significant with learning of complex, real-life informational or instructional materials such as written articles, story narratives, and films. The earliest studies to examine memory for prose as a function of time of day of presentation required subjects to produce their own written accounts of the test passage (Gates, 1916; Laird, 1925).

The original passage was classified according to the major terms or ideas it contained, and a marking scheme was devised to see how many concepts were correctly reproduced. Often, however, the notion of an "idea" was fairly vague, and the scoring procedure(s) probably lacked the objectivity and precision needed for accurate assessment of memory performance.

Gates (1916) tested fairly small groups of subjects at hourly intervals from 08:40 to 17:40. Performance was best at 09:40 and decreased linearly by about 16% to the latest time tested. Laird (1925) had subjects read the whole of a rather short passage, and results were scored in terms of the number of ideas reproduced. Performance was best at 08:00 and worst at 20:00, showing a drop of 30%. In addition, both of these early studies indicated a postlunch "increment" and an increase from 20:00 to the latest time tested in the case of Laird, namely 22:00 or 23:00.

Folkard and Monk (1979) conducted an experiment in which different groups of subjects were presented with a list of 15 nouns at 3-hour intervals from 08:00 to 20:00. Immediate recall for the first few items in the sequence improved from 08:00 to 11:00 (by 0.4 word), then fell (by 1.5 words) from 11:00 to 20:00 in a fairly linear fashion. Immediate recall of the last few items in the sequence varied across the day, showing a W-shaped trend, performance being low at 11:00 and 17:00. In two subsequent experiments, however, the same researchers failed to find any difference in the immediate recall of the most recent items in a sequence between 10:00 and 16:00. Both studies showed a superiority for the earliest items in the sequence (Folkard & Monk, 1979).

While time-of-day effects can affect immediate memory for relatively simple materials such as lists of words, of more interest and relevance to the theme of this book is whether more complicated informational presentations, specifically broadcast news or similar types of material, are learned with differential effectiveness across the day. A series of experiments conducted by Folkard and his colleagues during the late 1970s indicated that time-of-day effects may indeed affect memory for complex materials such as extended and meaningful discourse and for instructional film.

Folkard, Monk, Bradbury, and Rosenthal (1977) studies schoolchildren's immediate memory for information presented in a tape-recorded short story and found that children, aged 12 to 13 years, who heard the story at 09:00 showed better immediate memory for its content than those who heard it at 15:00. The differences associated with time of day observed here were about 10%.

Folkard and Monk (1980) carried out two further experiments that examined time of day and learning from a prose passage and a short instructional film. In the first study, subjects were given 3 minutes to read as much as they could of a 1,500-word scientific magazine article and were then given a multiple-choice test on what they had read. Performance was best at 08:00 and worst at 20:00, exhibiting a drop of 30% across the day.

In their second study, Folkard and Monk examined night nurses' immediate memory for information presented in a 10-minute film sequence either at 20:30 in the evening or at 04:00 in the morning. These times corresponded to the maximum and minimum respectively of the postulated circadian rhythm in basal arousal level, which predicts that immediate memory should be better at 04:00 than at 20:30. Folkard and Monk found a superiority of 04:00 of about 20% for nurses whose circadian rhythm, as indicated by oral temperature, showed relatively little adjustment to night work. For those who had adapted to night work, however, the reverse was true, and memory performance was better in the evening.

TIME-OF-DAY EFFECTS AND DELAYED MEMORY

The precise nature of time-of-day effects has been found to vary according to the type of memory being tested. As we have seen already, when memory for information is tested immediately after it has been presented, performance tends to be better earlier in the day than later on. Researchers have found, however, that if there is a considerable delay between information presentation and test of retention, then performance tends to improve rather than get worse across the day. Once again, the first studies to demonstrate this effect examined memory for relatively simply materials. More recently, though, similar time-of-day-of-presentation effects have been observed with more complex learning material of the sort individuals might be faced with in real life.

Most cognitive researchers have assumed that there is a progressive increase in physiological arousal during most of the working day and have accordingly predicted that short-term retention is best relatively early in the day, whereas long-term retention is greatest following late afternoon or early evening presentations. Baddeley, Hatter, Scott, and Snashell (1970) investigated the effects of time of day on both short-term and long-term retention. They used a technique of surreptitiously repeating the same sequence of digits on every third trial in a memory test involving immediate recall of sequences of nine random digits. The superiority of recall on repeated over nonrepeated trials was assumed to reflect long-term memory. There was the typical morning superiority for short-term retention (i.e., nonrepeated lists), whereas the long-term retention measure indicated a slight but nonsignificant afternoon superiority. It should be noted, however, that the enhancement of long-term retention with time of day and increased arousal has usually been found only after delays of 20 minutes or more, which is much longer than the time intervals considered by Baddeley et al.

In another of the earlier contemporary demonstrations of time-of-day effects on delayed memory performance, Hockey, Davies, and Gray (1972) found significantly less forgetting took place over a 5-hour interval following presentation of world lists at 23:00 compared to presentation at 06:00. Folkard and Monk (1979) measured delayed recall from a single list of 15 words presented at 11:00, 14:00, 17:00, and 20:00. Recall of the first few items in the sequence improved slightly across the day, although the main effect of time of day on overall recall (of all items) was not in itself statistically significant.

In a study referred to earlier, Folkard et al. (1977) tested recall of a story among children following either early morning or midafternoon presentation. As already noted, those who were tested immediately remembered more with the morning presentation. However, children who were tested after a 1-week delay performed better with the afternoon presentation.

Why do these differences between immediate and delayed recall occur as a function of the time of day when to-be-learned material is presented? In an attempt to shed some light on this question, Folkard (1980) reanalysed the data from the 1977 experiment and examined any variations in the aspects of the story recalled. For immediate recall, morning presentation led to equivalent recall of important and trivial story information, whereas afternoon presentation was followed predominantly by recall of the important details. This finding links up well with the notion that attentional selectivity is greater under high arousal (i.e., in the afternoon) (Easterbrook, 1959). Alternatively, the youngsters in the morning session may not have processed the meaning of the story and thus could not be influenced by the importance of the information. Inasmuch as all the children tended to recall mainly important details at the delayed retention test, the implication of the results is that children in the afternoon processed less of the passage than those in the morning session, but what they did process was more thoroughly learned.

TIME OF DAY AND MEMORY FOR TV NEWS

Gunter, Jarrett, and Furnham (1983) carried out an experiment to test the effects of time of day on memory for televised news. At the time of this study, the practical implications of its findings were particularly important following the introduction of early morning or "breakfast" television to Britain, consisting of news and general information programming. One question was whether the audience for these programmes would be likely to remember breakfast-time news on television better or worse than that transmitted at more traditional times later in the day. From an academic standpoint it was of interest to find out if time-of-day effects observed with learning of simple materials would also occur while learning broadcast news.

Eighty adults (42 males and 38 females) took part in this experiment. Sixty-seven were aged 16 to 34 years, 7 were aged to 35 to 49 years, and 6 were over 50. Approximately half were graduates or professionally qualified people, and half were skilled or semi-and unskilled manual and nonmanual workers. These individuals were divided into three groups: Group One (n = 27) was tested at 09:30, Group Two (n = 25) was tested at 13:30, and Group Three (n = 28) was tested at 17:30.

Learning materials consisted of six news items, all of which reported events taking place outside the United Kingdom either in Europe or in the Middle East. These items were:

1. a story about troops parading in Madrid to celebrate Spain's election to NATO.
2. a story about an EEC peace initiative in the Middle East as the Community's president visits Israel.
3. a story about security in the United Nations buffer zone in the Lebanon.
4. a story about French collaboration with the USSR in a forthcoming spaceflight.

5. a story about a state funeral in Turkey for the country's ex-president.

6. a story about an annual May carnival held in Copenhagen, Denmark.

Every item consisted of an opening caption depicting a map and the name of the country from which the story derived, followed by approximately 60 to 70 seconds of film footage over which the unseen newsreader narrated the story. All items were between 70 and 80 seconds long, and the complete news sequence lasted just over 7 minutes. The news materials were played over two colour television monitors to subjects in a classroom setting.

Tests for memory of news content were in four parts:

1. a test of free recall in which subjects had to provide brief written accounts of the main points from each item.

2. a test of recognition of the six countries from which the items came, from a list of 18 countries.

3. a test of minimal cued recall in which the names of the six countries were provided as prompts to recall the main points of each story.

4. a test of detailed cued recall which consisted of 13 questions on specific points mentioned in each news story. Some of the latter questions concerned the people or places involved in a story, whereas others probed for information about the causes or reasons underlying the events reported.

Each group was run in a single session. Subjects were led to believe that they were to take part in a study of programme evaluation. The experiment was described as one that was concerned with measuring public appreciation of television programmes in order to find out which programmes people enjoyed watching most. At no time prior to presentation of the news materials were subjects told that they would be tested on their memory for the content. Subjects were then presented with the news sequence, which they believed was simply the first of many programmes they would have to rate. Then, as soon as this clip had finished, the experimenters handed out the test questionnaire, and subjects were told to begin recalling spontaneously as many items as they could. Five minutes were allowed for free recall. Next, subjects turned to the list of 18 countries and identified those from which news stories had been reported. One minute was allowed for this.

Next, subjects received the names of the six target countries, which were provided as cues for recall of further details about each story, and 5 minutes were given for completion of this task. Finally, a 4-minute test of detailed cued recall followed, in which subjects answered individual questions about particular aspects of each item. The experimenters were careful to ensure that once one section of the questionnaire had been completed, none of the subjects were able to refer back to it again while completing a subsequent section.

The mean scores on each of the four tests of memory performance for each time of day are shown in Table 11.1. With the exception of detailed cued recall of information about places and people, there were significant time-of-day effects on all tests of recall. The general trend throughout was that memory performance decreased across the day: Recall of news was best following presentation in the morning and worst following presentation in the late afternoon. Further analyses revealed significant differences on free recall between 09:30 and 17:30 and between 13:30 and 17:30. On minimal cued recall, detailed cued recall (overall), and detailed cued recall (causes), there were significant differences between 09:30 and 17:30.

While Gunter et al.'s (1983) finding suggested learning advantages for news programmes presented early in the morning, these were observed only for information that was tested straightaway. For content that needs to be retained over a period of time, viewers may, however, perform better on televised news seen later in the day. Certainly, this has been found in previous studies using written and instructional film material. To find out if it was true for learning from the news, Gunter and his colleagues designed an experiment in which recall was tested from tele-

TABLE 11.1
Mean Scores on Six Immediate Memory Performance Measures as a Function of Time of Day of News Presentation.

	Time of presentation			
	09:30	13:30	16:30	F value[1]
Free recall	5.26	4.96	3.57	8.07[a]
Recognition	5.44	5.08	4.71	3.06[c]
Minimal cued recall	4.63	3.82	2.79	5.21[b]
Detailed cued recall				
Causes	1.89	1.44	0.86	5.34[b]
People/places	4.30	3.92	3.18	2.96
Total	6.15	5.36	4.04	4.47[b]

Source: Gunter, Jarrett, and Furnham, 1983.
[1] Degrees of freedom = 2,79.
[a] $p < 0.001$
[b] $p < 0.01$
[c] $p < 0.05$

vised news materials presented to groups of subjects in the morning, early in the afternoon, or late in the afternoon following a delay of 2 hours.

Gunter, Furnham, and Jarrett (1984) ran 90 adults, aged between 18 and 65 years, almost equally divided among males and females, about half of whom were college graduates or professionally qualified people and half of whom were skilled or unskilled manual workers. These individuals were divided randomly into three groups (with the restriction that males and females should comprise about half of each group) who were presented with a television news sequence either at 09:30, 13:30, or 16:30. The materials, all of which reported events occurring outside the United Kingdom, were the same as those used by Gunter et al. in the earlier study. Once again, there were four tests of recall as before: free recall of item content, recognition of countries from which the stories came, general cued recall of story content to country name cues, and detailed cued recall to questions concerning specific points covered by each story. All tests were given about 2 hours after initial presentation. During the intervening period subjects saw excerpts from five other drama, comedy, and light-entertainment programmes.

The mean scores for each test of memory are shown in Table 11.2. Separate detailed cued-recall scores were computed for information recall about the causes of events and about the people or places featured in each story. One-way analyses of variance were computed on these data to examine the strength of time-of-day effects on each type of delayed information recall. There was a significant time-of-day effect only on recognition of the countries where events were located, although patterns of recall on the other tests were consistent in direction with recognition

TABLE 11.2
Mean Scores on Six Delayed Memory Performance Measures as a Function of Time of Day of News Presentation

| | Time of presentation | | | |
	09:30	13:30	16:30	F value[1]
Free recall	2.03	1.80	2.49	1.64
Recognition	3.29	4.39	4.46	8.09[a]
Minimal cued recall	2.94	1.97	2.65	1.11
Depth cued recall				
Causes	0.84	0.88	1.15	1.30
People/places	2.10	2.76	2.81	2.04
Total	2.94	3.64	4.05	1.00

Source: Gunter, Furnham, and Jarrett, 1984.
[1] Degrees of freedom = 2 and 87.
[a] $p < 0.01$

throughout, indicating an improvement in delayed retention across the day. Further statistical analyses revealed significant differences between recognition in the morning (09:30) and early afternoon (13:30) and between morning and late afternoon (16:30). For each comparison, memory performance improved significantly as the day wore on.

INDIVIDUAL DIFFERENCES AND TIME-OF-DAY EFFECTS

Individuals vary in their level of cognitive performance at different times of the day, and there appears to be a valid distinction between people who prefer to work in the morning (morning types) and people who work better in the evening (evening types). The most explored personality dimension in relation to time-of-day effects is introversion-extraversion. Colquhoun (1960) analysed results from 17 vigilance studies carried out at various times of day and discovered that the morning experiments gave a positive correlation between introversion and efficiency, whereas the afternoon experiments gave a negative correlation. This suggested that introverts may be morning types and extraverts evening types.

Blake (1967, 1971) provided an explanation of these findings. He discovered that with introverts, rigid rise in temperature occurred a little earlier in the day than with extraverts. This finding that introverts were phase advanced with respect to the circadian rhythm of arousal suggests that extraverts may be suboptimally aroused in the morning, with introverts being supraoptimally aroused in the afternoon. However, it is somewhat implausible to claim that rather small differences in body temperature between introverts and extraverts are responsible (even indirectly) for large performance differences.

Revelle, Humphreys, Simon, and Gilliland (1980) argued that extraversion should be divided into its two main components of impulsivity and sociability. They discovered in several experiments that interactions between introversion, extraversion, and time of day were due to impulsivity rather than to sociability. Fairly demanding tasks (e.g., analogies, antonyms, and sentence completions) were performed either in the morning (09:00 or 10:00) or in the evening (19:00) and after ingestion of caffeine (an arousing drug) or a placebo.

Caffeine had its greatest beneficial effect on high impulsives (i.e., extraverts) tested in the morning, indicating that extraverts are suboptimally aroused at that time of day. In contrast, the modest effect of caffeine on low impulsives (i.e., introverts) tested in the morning suggested that they were close to optimal arousal level at that time. The opposite pattern of results was obtained at the evening testing session, but the interaction between drug conditions and impulsivity was weak. These data suggest that high impulsives are overaroused in the evening whereas low impulsives are underaroused. Revelle et al. (1980) argued that low impulsives were more aroused than high impulsives in the morning but that the opposite was true in the evening, and they claimed that this was due to a phase difference of several hours between introverts and extraverts in the circadian rhythm of arousal. Eysenck and Folkard (1980) produced partly supportive evidence for this contention. They found a phase difference on body temperature between introverts and extraverts associated specifically with the impulsivity component, though this difference was by no means as great as that reported by Revelle et al.

There was an additional element built into the Gunter et al. (1984) study. Measures of personality were obtained from subjects using the Eysenck Personality Questionnaire (EPQ; Eysenck & Eysenck, 1969, 1975), to take into account individual differences in memory performance at different times of day. One explanation of time-of-day effects has suggested that changes in arousal (usually operationalised in terms of oral temperature) throughout the day (e.g., see Kleitman, 1963; Colquhoun, Blake, & Edwards, 1968) may underlie differences in memory performance. As arousal (or oral temperature) increases across the day, the processing of new information generally becomes less efficient as an optimal level of excitation is exceeded (e.g., Kleinsmith & Kaplan, 1963; Walker & Tate, 1963). This is reflected in a deterioration of immediate memory performance. On the other hand, a higher level of arousal is known to be beneficial to efficient retrieval of consolidated information in memory (Craik & Blankstein, 1975), so that delayed retention may exhibit an improvement as base arousal levels increase (e.g., across the day). Heightened arousal during initial learning has consistently been found to result in superior retention when testing is delayed for at least 15 minutes (see Craik & Blankstein, 1975; and Eysenck, 1976, 1977, for reviews of the literature).

However, not all individuals are alike in arousal levels. Physiological and behavioural evidence has emerged, for example, to show that introverts are functionally more aroused than extraverts. Blake (1967) found that the body temperature of introverts was higher than that of extraverts during the morning and early afternoon, whereas the body temperature of extraverts was higher than that of introverts during the evening. Gale (1969) examined the sensation-seeking tendencies of introverts and extraverts under conditions of mild sensory deprivation and found that the latter made the greater efforts to obtain stimulation, which could indicate a greater need among extraverts to seek external sources of arousal because they are functionally less aroused than are introverts.

If introverts and extraverts are characterised by different functional

TABLE 11.3
Mean Scores on Six Delayed Memory Performance Measures as a Function of
Extraversion and Time of Day of News Presentation

	Free recall	Recognition	General cued recall	Depth cued recall		
				Causes	People/ Places	Total
Morning (09:30)						
Introverts (n = 17)	2.44	3.47	4.18	1.12	2.41	3.53
Extroverts (n = 15)	1.54	3.07	1.43	0.50	1.71	2.21
F-value (1,29)	2.63	<1.00	1.60	2.50	1.53	2.74
Early Afternoon (13:30)						
Introverts (n = 18)	1.64	4.39	2.17	0.94	2.33	3.28
Extroverts (n = 15)	2.00	4.40	1.73	0.80	3.27	4.07
F-value (1,31)	<1.00	<1.00	<1.00	<1.00	2.15	<1.00
Late Afternoon (16:30)						
Introverts (n = 12)	3.58	4.58	3.67	1.25	3.83	5.08
Extroverts (n = 14)	1.55	4.26	1.79	1.07	1.93	4.29
F-value (1,24)	10.38**	<1.00	<1.00	<1.00	6.50*	<1.00

Source: Gunter, Furnham, and Jarrett, 1984.
Note: Degrees of freedom are given in parentheses
*p <0.05
**p <0.01

TABLE 11.4
Mean Scores on Six Delayed Memory Performance Measures as a Function of Neuroticism and Time of Day of News Presentation

	Free recall	Recognition	General cued recall	Depth cued recall		
				Causes	People/ Places	Total
Morning (09:30)						
Stable (n = 15)	1.69	3.38	1.44	0.50	1.88	2.38
Neurotic (n = 16)	2.40	3.20	4.53	1.20	2.33	3.53
F-value (1,29)	<1.00	<1.00	2.09	3.40	<1.00	2.10
Early Afternoon (13:30)						
Stable (n = 18)	1.86	4.22	2.11	0.89	2.61	3.50
Neurotic (n = 15)	1.73	4.60	1.80	0.87	2.93	3.80
F-value (1,31)	<1.00	<1.00	<1.00	<1.00	<1.00	<1.00
Late Afternoon (16:30)						
Stable (n = 12)	2.33	5.00	3.17	1.17	3.17	4.33
Neurotic (n = 14)	2.63	4.00	2.21	1.14	2.50	4.93
F-value (1,24)	<1.00	2.42	1.08	<1.00	<1.00	<1.00

Source: Gunter, Furnham, and Jarrett, 1984.
Note: Degrees of freedom are given in parentheses.

arousal levels, they may also exhibit concomitant variations in memory performance throughout the day. In a modification of Walker's action-decrement theory, Eysenck (1967) hypothesised that with their different basal arousal levels the period of consolidation of new input is longer for introverts than for extraverts, with the consequence that the immediate retention of extraverts exceeds that of introverts, but introverts manifest better delayed retention. In the experiment conducted by Gunter et al. (1984), introverts and extraverts were compared on their delayed retention for television news content at three different times during the day. It was expected that introverts, with their higher basal arousal levels, should perform better than extraverts, especially during the earlier sessions. However, as extraverts' arousal levels approach those of introverts later in the day, their respective memory scores should become more proximal. Table 11.3. shows the mean retention scores on each test for introverts and extraverts as a function of time of day when news was presented. Introverts performed better than extraverts on all tests at all times of day, although significantly so only on free recall and cued recall of personalities and locations of news events. On both of these types of information retrieval, however, significant interactions between personality of the viewer and time of day indicated that personality differences were more pronounced at certain times of the day than others. Direct comparisons of extraverts and introverts' memory performance on these tests indicated that significant differences between them occurred only during the late afternoon session. There were no significant effects of neuroticism on memory performance, nor any significant interactions of neuroticism with time of day (see Table 11.4).

CONCLUDING REMARKS

Currently, in countries such as the United States and United Kingdom there is a choice of news programmes to watch on television throughout the day. Even relatively casual observation of television news programming reveals, however, that there are differences in the kinds of news and styles of presentation adopted in news broadcasts that go out early or late in the day. These stylistic and content differences reflect intuitive assumptions of news professionals about the character and mood of audiences at different times of day. Although there is some awareness from ratings information of the availability of audience in the morning, middle of the day, and evening, this knowledge is not always substantial or accurate. Even less is known or has been investigated empirically about the relative capacities of audiences to absorb news at different times of the day.

And yet, it has long been known by cognitive psychologists that the ability to learn and remember new things varies across the day. This chapter has reported the first experiments to investigate variations in ability to remember television news as a function of the time of day when the news was seen. The results support the classical research findings in this field, which show that immediate retention of material just learned is best early in the day but then gradually deteriorates across the day. In contrast, delayed retention of information learned some time before and consolidated in memory by the time of test tends to improve across the day.

It is from the psychological explanations of these effects that implications for news production emerge. If one accepts the arousal hypothesis, for example, which is supported to some extent by the personality differences in recall observed in these studies, then one would recommend to news producers that they aim to control more carefully the degree of arousal stimulated by their programmes at certain times of the day. In particular, one would recommend control over the use of dramatic styles of presentation later in the day, such as the use of exciting film footage, especially when played alongside or adjacent to complex narrative information with which news audiences may be largely unfamiliar. This is not to say that evening news broadcasts should avoid all film of an exciting nature and restrict themselves rather austerely to "talking head" formats. But research has demonstrated the negative impact of certain kinds of arousing (e.g., violent) film footage on memory for news-story narratives (e.g., Berry & Clifford, 1985; Gunter et al., 1984). In the knowledge that natural levels of arousal in viewers are likely to be higher later in the day, adding to the impact of any programme-induced arousal, steps need to be taken to ensure that information carried in the programme's narrative is somehow "protected" from the deleterious effects of excessive arousal. It may be especially advisable with evening news broadcasts, for example, to present important narrative information before arousing film footage, rather than in parallel with it or immediately following it. In this way, viewers may have the chance to take in complex story meanings before such learning is impaired by arousal effects.

12 Improving Understanding

In this final chapter we consider three groups whose understanding of audiences' understanding of broadcast news needs to be enhanced. These three groups are the audience, the practitioners of news production, and the researchers.

It must by now be evident that learning from television news involves a complex set of psychological processes that vary across audiences and can be influenced by the way the news is told. The extent to which television news enhances audiences' awareness of public events and their understanding of the causes and implications of these events can be fully explained only through careful assessment of audience, medium, and programme factors, and interactions between them.

It must be clear also from the growing research literature (which this book has attempted to review) about production variable effects on memory and comprehension of broadcast news that presentation techniques commonly employed in television news programmes are not always conducive to effective information uptake, and the naive assumptions made about audiences' learning abilities by news professionals are often wholly inaccurate.

In addition to these considerations, another important area of concern that until recently had not begun to be carefully thought through relates to the validity and appropriateness of learning measures used by researchers in mass communications to assess the cognitive impact of the news. In the past few years, however, some writers have begun to examine research methods with a more critical eye, and it has already been observed that mass communications research needs to be clearer in its use and definition of terms such as *memory* and *comprehension* (Kellermann, 1985; Woodall, Davis & Sahin, 1983) and the methods it uses to measure them (Berry, 1983b). Questionable research methods reflect poor theory and a lack of awareness among researchers in the field of the kinds of theoretical models and associated methodological procedures that could more effectively investigate and explain the cognitive effects of the broadcast media. Before turning to discuss the understanding of practitioners and researchers, however, we will begin by giving our attention to audiences for news and summarising the major conclusions of the news comprehension. literature to date.

AUDIENCE FACTORS

For many years sociologically oriented research on the informational effects of mass communications has emphasised the importance of audience factors in relation to information acquisition from the mass media. Differential absorption of mass media messages and growth in knowledge of public affairs observed to occur across different social and educational strata of the population were identified with variations in patterns of media use. Although this may have accounted to some extent for information acquisition from the media, however, it is possible that these demographic-related differences were connected not simply with the use made of the media but also with variations in the cognitive information-processing skills of different population subgroups. These very important psychological variables have not generally been fully or properly considered. Indeed, the sociologically based perspective is equipped neither conceptually nor methodologically to deal with them. Instead, it was commonly assumed that mass media use was motivationally driven; that different mass media or types of media content served various needs or supplied various gratifications for receivers. (e.g., Blumler & Katz, 1974).

However, not all individuals exhibit the same patterns of media use nor the same reasons for using a particular medium (Levy, 1978; Rubin, 1981, 1983, 1984). Thus, some people might deliberately watch the news on television to find out what is going on in the world, whereas others may watch because they like a particular newscaster or simply because they are waiting for the next programme. Within this framework, whether or not the news is learned by audiences depends a great deal on the nature of the audiences and the way these audiences use the media (e.g., Gantz, 1979).

Public affairs knowledge was consistently measured to be greater among those individuals from higher socio-economic and better-educated strata of society (e.g., Robinson, 1967; Tichenor et al., 1970). These types of people typically exhibited patterns of media use that meant that they were regularly exposed to news from a variety of media sources, but especially newspapers and news magazines. In addition, they were usually assumed to be more highly motivated to sustain their knowledge about current affairs than were individuals of lower socio-economic and poorer educational backgrounds (cf. Robinson, 1972).

Although for a long time identified as significant predictors of knowledge gain from the mass media, the predictive value of education and socio-economic background has recently been challenged. There may, for example, be considerable variation in mean learning scores from broadcast news media, even among common (high) ability groups (Berry, 1983b). Berry has argued that a more pertinent variable may be the extent of an individual's general knowledge of current affairs. He reported that background knowledge has been found to correlate highly with information gain from television news bulletins "in the absence of any overlap between the specific knowledge probed in the knowledge test and that in test news bulletins" (p. 363). Because knowledge also correlates with education, it is possible that it may account at least in part if not wholly for the apparent effect of education on learning from broadcast news media. Berry further reported that statistical controls for scores on a current affairs knowledge test reduced to nonsignificance differences between high-and low-ability viewers in their immediate retention of a television news sequence.

As we have already noted, another set of audience factors invoked to account for learning from the media focuses on motivation. The strength and nature of motives for media use have been hypothesised to underlie how much audiences learn and remember. Thus, Booth (1970) observed that interest in the news was the major determinant of how much individuals he interviewed knew about events recently covered by television, radio, and the press. More interested people knew more. Neuman (1976) found that people who said they watched television news for information were able to recall more from a television network's main evening newscast in a telephone interview within an hour or so of the programme than were those who said they watched mainly for entertainment or other noninformational reasons.

The predictive or explanatory efficacy of motivation when operationalised in terms of respondents' self-reports, however, has also been challenged. One crucial point is whether the motivational claims of viewers and listeners actually reflect or have any bearing at all on their cognitive information-processing abilities. Berry (1983b) writes: "Despite the variety of approaches, research hypotheses have again not been closely shaped by behavioural science knowledge about psychological processes in the individual. Researchers have treated motivation in terms either of the intrinsic interest in different broad classes of news topics as inferred from the viewers' social characteristics, or in terms of the type and/or strength of reason for viewing newscasts. Few have made clear whether the supposed effects involved perceptual registration of the input, learning per se, retention or retrieval" (p. 364).

Another important finding from experimental psychology that is relevant to this discussion is that concerning learning without motivation, otherwise known as incidental learning, which may be just as effective as motivated or intentional learning as long as the material is processed at a deep semantic level (Hyde & Jenkins, 1969). Therefore, how much people learn from the news may depend more on the extent to which they analyse its semantic content, regardless of their motives while doing so.

Extremes of interest can of course be important to news acquisition. But if, as seems likely, most news stories have only moderate interest for most viewers and listeners—and this is probably true for most national and international news in network television newscasts—is interest really a significant factor at all? Or is it disguising some other factor or set of factors that are normally neither identified nor measured by researchers? Genova and Greenberg (1979) produced evidence in a knowledge-gap study that interest was only a minor factor in public event awareness in general. Further American research by Neuman (1976) and Gantz (1979), in which motivation and topic interest were invoked to account for levels of learning from television news, in fact indicated that such audience factors at best have only weak or inconsistent effects on news recall. Although Neuman found that memory performance on the same evening's network news was better among those who said they watched to keep informed than among casual viewer when all were given topic-related cues to aid retrieval, spontaneous, unaided recall was unrelated to claimed news viewing motives, and the correlation between a composite recall score and reported motivation was very low. Gantz found that although those who were motivated to obtain information from television news recalled more spontaneously than viewers who were not thus motivated, motivational variables actually accounted for little over 5% of recall variance (Berry, 1983b; Kellermann, 1985).

According to Berry (1983b), although the apparent weakness or absence of clear effects of motivation on learning from the news seems at odds with common sense, it is not inconsistent with psychological theory. Regardless of one's reasons for news consumption, learning and memory may depend more importantly on the way in which the news is cognitively processed. Self-reported motivations may neither predict nor reflect the extent to which the news is cognitively attended to and absorbed by audience members.

Other Audience Factors

Variations in learning from broadcast news have been observed to occur across audiences in relation to audience factors other than those discussed previously. Such factors as age, sex, and personality of viewers and listeners can mediate retention of news. The importance of these kinds of variables, which have been largely ignored and unexplored by mass communications researchers in relation to the informational effects of the media, have emerged more strongly in recent experimental study by psychologically oriented researchers (e.g., Berry & Clifford, 1985; Cairns, 1984; Furnham & Gunter, 1985; Gunter, 1984, 1985; Gunter et al, 1983, 1984a, 1984b)

Survey research in Britain has indicated that males and older people people have greater knowledge of recent news events than females and younger people (Gunter, 1984), and older people were observed to recall more from an evening's news broadcast than younger people when questioned on programme content shortly after transmission (Robinson & Sahin, 1984). The latter age-related difference in news recall was reversed in a similar American study by Stauffer, Frost, and Rybolt (1983).

Experimental research under more controlled conditions of news presentation and viewing has indicated that sex and age differences consistently occur during tests of immediate retention for television news sequences. Often these individual difference factors interact with programme variables to affect memory performance. For example, females have been found to recall news narratives accompanied by violent film footage less well than males (Furnham & Gunter, 1985; Gunter et al., 1984). The packaging of news in different ways can have different effects on male and female viewers' recall of television newscast content. Berry and Clifford (1985) conducted an experiment in which news stories were either blocked by sex of presenter (six consecutive female-presented items followed by six consecutive male-presented items) or were alternated (male-female-male-female). Female viewers did less well in the alternating condition, while males did better under that condition.

Personality factors have long been known by psychologists to influence human cognitive performance. Recent experiments have indicated that personality variables may prove to be effective predictors of memory for broadcast news. In a study concerned primarily with memory for television news as a function of time of day, Gunter et al. (1984a) also examined relationships between memory performance and measures of personality such as extraversion, neuroticism, and psychoticism (Eysenck & Eysenck, 1969, 1975). Psychological theory predicted better delayed retention by introverts than by extraverts. This hypothesis was partially supported, with introverts performing significantly better than extraverts on two out of six measures of retention.

In another study, Gunter and Furnham (1986) examined sex and personality predictors of memory for violent and nonviolent news presented either audio-visually, in audio-only, or in print. Results showed that personality variables were significant predictors of violent news recall within the audio-visual modality. Males recalled violent news better than did females, especially following audio-visual presentation. At the same time, multivariate analyses indicated that introversion, weaker neuroticism, and weaker psychoticism (or tender-mindedness) predicted worse immediate memory for news stories accompanied by violent film footage.

MEDIA FACTORS

Public opinion surveys in the United States and United Kingdom over the years have indicated that television has become the main source of national and international news and that the gap between television and the other two major news media, newspapers and radio, has widened (IBA, 1985; Roper, 1983). People say that the provision of news is one of the most important functions of television and is one of the main reasons why they watch (BBC, 1976a). But despite the apparent significance of television as a news source, how effective is it compared with other media as a communicator of news information? Do people learn more and more easily from television than they do from newspapers, for example?

The answers to these questions are not simple ones. First of all, the amount of information normally carried by television news programmes is much less than that contained in the average daily newspaper. Indeed, most serious newspapers carry more information on their front page than does the narrative of a standard half-hour news show. A second important point is that the act of reading a newspaper is different from that of watching television news. Reading is self-paced, television watching is not. The reader has far greater control over the way she or he takes in the news from a newspaper than from a television newscast. The reader can scan the paper's headlines and then go back more slowly through stories of particular interest. When one is watching the news on television, however, the order of the news and rate at which it is presented are determined by the makers of the programme. There is usually no opportunity for the viewer to slow the programme down or to go back to a story once it has been presented, to check details that may have been missed first time around (unless the viewer was able to video-record the programme, of course). Bearing these two points in mind then, it could well be that even though the public endorses television as its primary news source, people may be able to learn more and more effectively from newspapers. Could the extensive information losses observed among the audiences for broadcast news shortly after transmission therefore occur because television itself is actually a poor medium from which to learn news?

In one study of learning about political issues and events, it was found that newspaper-dependent people knew more about local issues and politics than those who were less newspaper dependent. Newspaper-dependent people were also more likely to think that they understand local affairs, to trust local government officials, and to be knowledgeable about national affairs. The findings for television-dependent people were just the reverse (Becker & Whitney, 1980). As it has already been established that newspapers normally carry a great deal more news information than do television news programmes, it is perhaps not surprising that people who are dependent on print for their news learn more than those who rely on television. However, even when the same news message is presented via television or in print and exposure time in both cases is controlled, reading gives rise to better information apprehension than does viewing (Gunter, Furnham, & Gietson, 1984; Furnham & Gunter, 1985). How is this to be explained?

Research with children's learning from audio-visual and written educational materials has recently shed some light on one reason why reading can give rise to better learning than television viewing even when the basic learning materials are the same. Salomon (1984) reported that children learned less effectively from television than print because they do not try as hard to learn when watching television. It emerged that the children tended to believe that reading required effort but television viewing did not. Consequently, they applied themselves less when watching television and performed badly. When told that television required effort just as much as reading, if learning from the medium was to occur, performance after viewing improved substantially. It seems that a certain level of motivation may indeed be necessary for effective learning from television. The natural tendency of viewers, which may be cultivated by the medium itself among quite young viewers, is to assume that they are experts at watching because they watch regularly. Learning from television, however, just as with learning from any other medium, requires a certain amount of effort on the part of the learner. Recent research on teaching children about television in school has indicated that learning from television news programmes can be improved when young viewers understand more about the way programmes are made and become more active in interpreting for themselves the things they see on the news, rather than simply taking it for granted (Kelly & Gunter, 1984; Kelly, Gunter & Kelley, 1985).

PROGRAMME FACTORS

News broadcasts do not consist simply of series of stories put together in order of decreasing importance. There is generally some underlying aesthetic ideal of how the well-structured programme looks or sounds. News programmes are planned so as to create and then maintain a level of audience interest, and this turn is linked to the goal of maintaining audience size. With this essentially entertainment function in mind, programme concepts therefore incorporate assumptions about content Organization and presentation format that will command the audience's attention. However, some/writers have argued that the practice of adopting styles of news presentation for purposes of holding audience attention purely thorough entertainment value or emotional impact carries with it the inherent danger that the resulting programme will provide transitory satisfaction but only ineffective communication of meaning and memorable information (Robinson, Sahin & Davis, 1982; Sahin, Davis, & Robinson, 1981).

Sociological studies of television newsrooms have shown that news editors have well-formed beliefs and opinions about how news programmes can best be organised and presented to facilitate both emotional impact and the public's ability to absorb their content; this is true even though the professionals themselves tend to be generally ignorant of the audience's real information needs and learning capabilities. In his book *Putting "Reality" Together*, Phillip Schlesinger reports that the people he studied in the BBC's newsroom lacked any objective feedback about the public's attitudes and conceptions concerning the news. Gans (1979) reported a similar lack of feedback about the audience among news professionals working for American television networks.

According to Schlesinger, "Broadcast news is the outcome of standardised production routines; [and] these routines work themselves out within an organizational structure which has no adequate point of contact with the audience for broadcast news, there is no sense in which one can talk of a communication taking place which is truly alive to the needs of the news audience" (1978, p. 106).

Production routines in informational broadcasting are well established and represent formalised processes that professionally competent programme makers are expected to follow in order to manufacture a product that will command acceptance and respect among fellow professionals. Studies of documentary production (Elliott, 1972) and of political television (Tracey, 1978) indicate clearly that the audience is not a focal point or source of conflict for producers. As Schlesinger observed, you do not find people wandering around in a state of existential *angst* wondering whether they are 'communicating' or not. . . . You do, on the other hand, find an intense obsession with the packaging of the broadcast and comparative evaluation of others' goods" (p. 107).

Cognitive psychologists have for many years investigated the ways in which presentation formats and structural attributes of linguistic materials affect our ability to remember things. Students of human learning have now begun to extend the range of stimulus materials tested to include broadcast news. The relationships between specific news programming factors and memory and understanding of transmitted news information represent an elaborate form of information processing and therefore are amenable to investigation by proven psychological methods. Recent studies have uncovered several particularly salient aspects of production technique that greatly affect the extent to and way in which audiences remember broadcast news stories. Characteristics of news stories themselves, such as the kinds of topics they are about and the way in which news events are typically reported, may significantly affect which stories are remembered and the extent to which they are properly understood. Then there are factors relating to the format and structure of the programme, which include the way items are ordered and packaged within a bulletin, whether stories are headlined at the beginning or summarised at the end of the programme, and the use of visual illustrations to support what is read out by the newscaster or reporter. All these features have been found to influence the recall and comprehension of news.

Story Characteristics

One important concept in news production is news taxonomy. News stories may be defined in terms of the taxonomic categories to which they belong. Variations can and have been found in the frequency of occurrence of different news categories in broadcast news. Furthermore, news taxonomy appears to be related to the distribution and placement of items in news bulletins. The Glasgow University Media Group (1976) identified ten major categories of news on United Kingdom television: political, industrial, foreign, economic, crime, home affairs, sports, human interest, disasters, and science. Several of these categories, notably political, foreign, and economic, were further divided into a number of taxonomic subcategories. This important investigation of news profiles revealed that news taxonomy appears to be a major determinant of item selection and placement in television bulletins.

The large majority of items, over the 6-month period of television news output monitored by this research group, were devoted to political affairs, industrial topics, and matters of social and economic management. The proportion of time devoted to sports, human interest, and other non-public affairs coverage, however, was much less. Research has indicated that there may be two types of effect on memory for news related to story category. The first has to do with differences in audience retention of different topics. The second, which we return to later, concerns the important relationship between news taxonomy and the order and placement of news items in television news broadcasts.

In some studies of memory for broadcast news, comparisons have been made of memory for different types of news story. There is some research indication that news editors look for news stories with certain characteristics. Particular sets of attributes have been identified that seem to recur in stories that are selected and treated in a particular fashion (Galtung & Ruge, 1965). Such attributes may be those that the professionals themselves look for in deciding whether a particular issue or event is newsworthy or not. Is there any evidence, however, that stories that qualify as newsworthy in the supposedly professional sense are also the ones that have the greatest impact upon the audience?

At a cognitive level, several studies have indicated that the identification, recall, and understanding of news stories is sometimes related significantly to the news structures of Galtung and Ruge (e.g., Katz et al, 1977; Robinson & Sahin, 1984; Schulz, 1982).

Story categories have been used to infer interest in items among certain members of the audience. And indeed, "news value" attributes such as those specified by or based on the Galtung and Ruge categories have been found to correlate with audience interest in stories (Sparkes & Winter, 1980). If this relationship is robust, then it could carry implications for editorial policy whereby learning from the news might be improved if story selection was guided more closely by topic interests of audiences. Berry (1983b) has argued contrarily that this might not work, however. For example, news interests can vary extensively across audiences (Wober, 1978), and the relation between news recall and interest in the material has not been firmly established (Berry, 1983b).

Nevertheless, substantial differences in recall of different types of news story were reported by Neuman (1976). Fewer than 1% of stories about the U.S. economy and nearly 10% of stories about Vietnam were recalled from network television news broadcasts unaided. Although Vietnam stories occurred more frequently than those about the economy, the discrepancy between levels of recall for these two story classes was five times the difference between their relative frequencies. Furthermore, economic stories were recalled at least seven times less often than the next worst specific category of news (foreign affairs). It is possible, however, that the extremely poor performance for news about the economy could be attributable to consistently unfavourable production treatment. Across the remaining major story categories (excluding commentaries and miscellaneous), variation in unaided recall was much less pronounced.

Story Structures

Another feature of news stories that carries important implications for news memory and comprehension is the way the stories themselves are told. Observational studies of the inner workings of television newsrooms have revealed that news editors tend to employ particular, stereotyped narrative structures with the intention of creating interest and increasing comprehension of news (see Golding & Elliott, 1979). One popular style of story-telling has been referred to as the "inverted pyramid". This style was developed by newspaper journalists but has been adopted by television journalists, too. It puts the major, attention-grabbing facts at the head of the story, secondary facts next, and finally background details at the base of the pyramid. To what extent, though, are routine methods of narrative construction used in broadcast news conducive to effective learning?

In research on learning texts, cognitive psychologists have found that the way information in extended narratives is organised can have a significant effect on how much is remembered. Various cognitive theorists have proposed different structural frameworks that embody specifications concerning how information in narratives can best be organised to enhance learning from them (e.g., Kintsch, 1977; Thorndyke, 1979; van Dijk, 1980).

Several recent news comprehension studies have reported evidence that standard story-telling formats in news broadcasting may not provide the optimal conditions for learning and have offered alternative story frames that have been demonstrated as producing better learning from news broadcast materials under laboratory conditions than did original broadcast versions of the same stories (Berry & Clifford, 1985; Findahl & Hoijer, 1984, 1985; Larsen, 1981).

Story Packaging

One of the most characteristic features of television news is the arrangement of items to form a programme rather than simply a haphazard catalogue of events. Placement analysis reveals the programme as something more than the sum of its individual items. It seems that within certain limits, the placing of items in relation to one another is determined by taxonomy of content (Glasgow University Media Group, 1976). So, for example, in nine-item bulletins studied by the Glasgow group, the categories from which lead stories were most frequently chosen were political and industrial, with an almost equal probability of foreign news. Lead stories seldom, if ever, came from home affairs, sports, human interest, or science categories. Closing items showed a similar pattern in reverse, with bulletins rarely concluding with industrial, political, or foreign news items.

Stories in political categories were generally well distributed throughout the rank order, although at the same time, they took up a larger proportion of lead items than any other category. Items in the industrial category, although one of the largest in U.K. newscasts, tended to be used less often as a source for lead items than either political or foreign news. However, they were not found to be evenly distributed through bulletins, either. They tended to cluster in the first half of the programme and occupied the largest proportion of second- and third-place items.

Close proximity was found between economic and industrial items. Often, items about particular industrial situations were likely to be juxtaposed with items on the general state of the economy, with a resultant strong implication of a casual connection. The bulk of foreign news items were placed in the middle of the programme, usually from fourth to seventh positions. Domestic news, more often than not, was given priority for purposes of presentation, whereas foreign news stories tended to be grouped together because the foreign-domestic distinction is the most fundamental of all. This seldom apparent formula of rank order of news content according to taxonomy has important implications for audience response, particularly in the light of what is known about the effects of serial position and other sequencing factors on recall of verbal materials.

Early and recent research has shown that the position of items in broadcast news programmes can affect their recall (Gunter, 1979; Tannenbaum, 1954). Briefly, items presented at or near the beginning of the programme or at or near the end are most likely to be remembered. The practical implications of such findings become clearer when they are considered together with content-analytic data on network news output. The apparently persistent tendency of editors to place certain types of news story in the first or last two or three positions of a bulletin considerably more often than other types suggests that audiences will be likely to learn and remember specific categories of news topics much more often than others, simply as a function of ordering strategies.

It has also been observed that producers of television news often present stories in homogeneous categories, or packages, according to the news categories to which they belong, in the firm belief that this enhances the overall clarity and memorability of the programme (Schlesinger, 1978). There is evidence that stories from the same topic category can become easily confused by audiences, however, and that this confusion is especially likely to occur when they are run together. Robinson and his colleagues (Robinson et al. 1980, 1982) and Stauffer and his colleagues (1983) have both found that in recalling news from a recent television broadcast, viewers frequently tended to get facts from similar stories mixed up, a phenomenon Robinson has referred to as "meltdown," whereby the story elements of one story merge or are confused with elements of another.

Experimental research by Gunter and his colleagues has indicated more explicitly that it may be unwise to group together news stories about very similar kinds of issues or events. This research has indicated that viewers differentially categorise and encode news items from different news taxonomies and that they have a limited capacity for learning and remembering similar types of material, especially when large amounts of information are presented very rapidly within relatively short periods of time. Under these kinds of learning conditions, which are typical of television news broadcasts, information losses during the encoding and storage of news content may be quite considerable.

Visual Format Effects

Television's potential as a visual medium is exploited in the news in ways that vary from story category to story category. The news is an essentially verbal activity and remains so on television, which relies on news personnel (presenters, correspondents, and reporters) to read this largely written news to the audience. To avoid what is professionally regarded as the monotony of the "talking head"—that is, close-ups of faces talking—a great deal of effort is expended to make bulletins visually interesting. Generally, visual inputs are subordinate to the written text, although film may predominate over other journalistic requirements when the material is exclusive, exceptionally dramatic, or has unusual immediacy.

Film, either with or without commentary, is by far the most important visual input. A central concept in the news production formula is that of "actuality" (Schlesinger, 1978). Moving pictures are for most television newsmen a form of actuality; a medium through which reality can be genuinely and authentically captured and presented. Actuality as such is supposed to enhance news impact and learning. The "talking head" or man-on-camera is very much a second-best presentational mode. In this instance, it has been claimed by certain news editors that the picture adds nothing; and indeed many actually distract the viewer's attention from what is being reported and thus interfere with overall learning (Whale, 1969). Consequently, film is the optimal mode of presentation available to the television news producer.

Although an important part of news presentation, film usage is not homogeneous across all kinds of news. Certain categories of news story have higher levels of film input than others (Glasgow University Media Group, 1976). This variation in frequency of film presence derives from the assumption for some categories of news that journalistic requirements override the programme's "need" for film. Thus, foreign and home affairs news items were found to have frequent film inputs on U.K. network news, while political, industrial, and crime stories had somewhat lower inputs, and, finally, story categories such as sports and economics had relatively few film inputs. However, frequent use of visual stills and graphics as found with the latter two categories to convey scores, statistics, and other information.

Photographs, maps, graphics, and tables also provide a major way to visually break up newscaster-only presentation. Unlike film material, though, which tends to dominate the form of news presentation, stills are typically subordinate to the journalistic structure of the programme. Scores and results of sports events are nearly always presented in this form. Maps are used most frequently in the foreign and disaster news categories, reflecting their value in providing a quick source of illustration for stories otherwise difficult to treat televisually because of access (Glasgow University Media Group, 1976). Clearly, an important consideration for news editors is deciding whether or not to illustrate visually the spoken text of a news story. To recap, studies of television newsrooms have revealed that news editors tend to favour using the visual potential of the medium to the full. Moving pictures are particularly favoured because they create the impression of allowing the audience to witness the news as it actually happens. But to what extent do film and other visual materials enhance impact and learning of television news?

The research literature offers varying estimates of the value of film and other visuals. Some evidence suggests that news stories accompanied by film are better recalled than those accompanied by stills or those simply read by the newscaster on camera (Gunter, 1979, 1980a). Other studies, however, have reported no facilitative effects of film on learning from television news (Edwardson, Grooms, & Pringle, 1976; Gunter, 1980b). The discrepancy between these results probably arises from the fact that the cognitive processes involved are subtle and complex and may be conditional upon the way in which learning is tested. Thus, while film footage may produce better recall of brief headline reports (e.g., Gunter, 1979, 1980a), it may have little influence on learning relative to newscaster-only presentation when viewers are required to recall story content in detail (Edwardson et al., 1976). There is evidence indeed that film footage can interfere with learning from the story narrative (Berry, 1983a).

What does seem to be critically important to learning is the way in which visual accompaniment is used to support the spoken text of television news. The spoken narrative usually carries the essential message of the news item, and any visualisations must be regarded as relatively subordinate and as playing a supporting role to the verbal storyline. It is essential that a fairly precise correspondence exist between the picture material and the verbal material, whether film or other visual inputs are used. Although film has been regarded as a natural means of portraying actuality in television bulletins, research has shown that where effective communication of information is the ultimate goal, the impact of stills and graphics can be just as great. Furthermore, there is no conclusive evidence to support the thesis that film is necessarily more appreciated by the audience than other visual modes of presentation. From a production standpoint, the use of still and graphic material affords considerably more flexibility and control in the design of news items and therefore of the bulletin as a whole than the use of film material. Film is often allowed to dominate production strategy; the availability or nonavailability of appropriate film footage may determine which stories are selected for presentation, as well as emphasising certain features that may not be relevant to the verbal content of the news report. However, as research with specialised instructional audio-visual materials has indicated, slightly irrelevant information in one channel can be more damaging to learning from the other channel than totally irrelevant information (Severin, 1967). This implies that if the film footage chosen from that available in the newsfilm library to accompany a particular news story is only slightly irrelevant to what is actually being said, the negative effect upon overall information gain could be considerable.

Also important for learning from televised news materials is the balanced nature of the visual reinforcement. Swedish researchers have found that viewers are better able to recall concrete facts about the locations of news events or about the persons or objects involved than more abstract relationships associated with the causes and consequences of events from "talking head" presentations (Findahl & Hoijer 1976). However, these writers have also suggested that concrete components of news stories are also more likely to receive visual reinforcement than abstract components because they are more amenable to visual illustration or representation. Their experiments showed, moreover, that visually reinforced concrete story information, while itself well remembered, actually inhibits learning of abstract causes and consequences content. This in turn severely impairs comprehension of the story, which essentially depends on learning about the causes underlying the reported event and what its actual or probable outcome(s) are or will be.

Balanced recall and proper understanding of news stories can therefore be heavily dependent on careful and selective use of visual illustrations in news bulletins, which should be determined by the requirements of story content rather than be allowed to predominate over what is said, as is apparently so often the case, especially where the use of film is involved. Indeed, the greater control afforded by using still-photographic and specially prepared graphical material, when matching visuals to the story test of a news report, favours a recommendation for more extensive deployment of these kinds of visual inputs in television newscasts.

Other Presentation Factors

Besides the ordering and illustration of news stories, there are a number of other presentation factors that can affect news comprehension and retention from broadcast bulletins. It is common practice on many television networks to open the programme with the main news headlines. Sometimes, these one-sentence verbal leads are accompanied by still photographs, visually superimposed headline texts, or even very brief clips of film.

Such headlines serve as devices for grabbing the attention of the audience right from the very start of the programme. However, the way in which the news is headlined can affect the extent to which it is remembered. Experimental psychologists have found that titles can affect story learning (Dooling & Lachman, 1971). Early work with radio newscasts found that leads could influence audience interpretation of broadcast news, too (Tannenbaum & Kernick, 1954).

The nature of headline effects can vary depending precisely on how leads—visual or verbal—are used. There is evidence from cognitive research (e.g., Bransford & McCarrell, 1974) and from the effects of highlighting summaries in educational films (Engquist, 1968) that indicates that recapitulating summaries and explanatory pictures have less effect on the comprehension of spoken text than the same material placed at the beginning of the presentation. Visual leads can thus seem to be able to facilitate the encoding and comprehension of news stories as well as serving as a reminder of the central theme of the story at a later stage after its full presentation.

Another important characteristic of broadcast news is its pace. Television news bulletins, for instance, are usually of fixed duration and only under exceptional circumstances are their transmission times of lengths changed. Clearly, the limited and largely inflexible durations of television newscasts place restrictions on the amount of information they can present.

The number of items in a particular bulletin is not rigidly fixed and may vary from day to day. Generally, though, the mean number of items and the range of events covered tends to increase as the length of the bulletin increases (Glasgow University Media Group, 1976). But although longer television bulletins may contain more news items, the proportion of long-and short-duration items does not seem to vary greatly from one bulletin to the next. Journalistic considerations, such as the need to cover as much ground as possible during the allotted airtime, or the aesthetic need to keep the pace of the programme moving along, ensure a high proportion of items of less than 1 minute. Research in the United Kingdom has indicated that more than half the items on most television news programmes tend to be less than half a minute long (Glasgow University Media Group, 1976). With the need to keep the programme flowing, however, what are the implications of speed of presentation for learning?

Research on speed-of-presentation effects with recorded speech materials has shown that although pace may affect information uptake, it can be increased substantially without interfering too much with learning. However, the impact of pace depends on the nature of the material. Narrative sequences on a single topic can be "time-compressed" quite successfully, but as soon as different topics are presented in quick succession, the optimal delivery rate is soon passed. This means that with multiple topic sequences such as television news bulletins the range over which speed of presentation can be varied without adversely affecting comprehension and information uptake significantly is fairly narrow (Smith & McEwan, 1974). More recently, cognitive researchers have found that frequent visual changes on television news can either enhance or interfere with news apprehension, depending on where relative to changes in story narratives they occur (Davies, Berry, & Clifford, 1985). Thus, there are subtle main effects and interaction effects of production variables on learning from television news, which broadcasters are probably not normally aware of or do not take into account when making their programmes.

One way around the problem of information losses to the audience as a function of the damaging effects of the excessive pace and flow of the programme may be to repeat parts of story narratives during the course of the programme. Thus, if the listener or viewer misses an important element on initial presentation, he or she may be able to pick it up later in the bulletin. Furthermore, reformulation of the main points of the news may help to clarify the meaning of a story consisting of extensive detail about a complex issue or event. Research with radio and television news materials has shown that repetition of story details can improve learning and comprehension, but net improvement in understanding depends crucially on which parts of the story are reformulated. It has been found, for example, that additional emphasis on the abstract causal relationships within news stories enhances recall better than repetition of information about the location of an event or who was involved in it (Findahl & Hoijer, 1972, 1976).

Thus, although producers often employ "main points" summaries at the end of television bulletins, the extent to which they reformulate those aspects of story narratives that produce best overall comprehension and memory of news is arguable.

PRACTITIONERS' UNDERSTANDING OF THEIR AUDIENCES

News practitioners' attitudes and beliefs about their audiences can be ambivalent. Warner (1970) reported that although producers regard the tastes of the audience as being of some importance, there is considerable doubt as to what the audience really wants and a feeling that it is not good professional practice to play up to the needs and requirements of the audience too much. Warner reports a number of quotes from executive producers concerning audience research that provide useful insights into the views that are held by the professionals. One executive was quoted as saying, "We try to (create) . . . a programme for a national American audience based on the assumption they may not have read or heard any other news. We also assume that they are as literate and informed as we on the staff. We don't offend them, even if we simplify our approach. We are watched by millions of people, but that's an abstraction; I sometimes have the feeling nobody is watching. No conception of the audience, except on the smallest possible sampling, namely me, affects my news judgement" (p. 164). An associate producer summed up what is perhaps a typical view held by many producers of TV news: "We don't know the audience and it doesn't matter; we don't tailor the show to the audience" (p. 165).

Indeed, there is some evidence that because of the small numbers of people who are actually involved in the decision-making processes on the news, there tends to develop a relatively homogeneous point of view. News producers make news programmes that will be judged favourably by their peers rather than by the audience. The audience, in fact, is irrelevant in this respect. Warner quotes one network news copy editors who observed, "After working with the show for so long, you can tell what will and will not interest the writers, editors and producers. It's basic journalistic sense . . ." An executive producer claimed, "The other guys here know what I'm after" (p. 159). Constant monitoring of each others' output by the networks also results in the development of a common approach to the selection of news. Although programme formats may vary, the judgmental processes that determine the value of a news story are very similar across networks.

In a later study of journalists in U.S. network television newsrooms, Gans (1979) also found that audiences were seldom if ever considered during the selection and production of news. Gans found that network newsmen he studied had little knowledge about the audience and were not especially interested in receiving feedback from it either. Even if they did have some image, however vague, of the audience, they paid scant attention to it. "Instead, they filmed and wrote for their superiors and for themselves, assuming . . . that what interested them would interest the audience" (Gans, 1979, p. 230).

Although journalists have little direct contact with the audience, they nevertheless seem to construct an image of it, which is not always an accurate reflection of the real thing. For some journalists the average audience member at whom they are aiming may be a married professional person with children. Gans (1979) found that journalists may on initial questioning describe the audience in fairly broad demographic terms but when pressed for detail usually end up elaborating a profile that reflects an up-market audience consisting of people on the same social and educational plane as themselves. In many instances this is probably because when news editors do obtain feedback it comes from family and friends who have the same and social educational backgrounds (i.e., professional and middle class) as themselves. One top producer interviewed by Gans illustrated this point by describing his way of designing the news for people he knew.

> "You do the show for a cell of people—the office staff, the wife and the kids. These are the only known audience. I know we have twenty million viewers, but I don't know who they are, and I don't care. I can't know, so I can't care." (p. 234)

Outside the United States, news practitioners in television newsrooms seem to function according to very similar principles. One chief subeditor on BBC Television News interviewed by Schlesinger said,

> "I'm really writing for myself and the wife. Otherwise you'd think of the 18 million viewers (sic). The wife's my hardest critic, by the way; always saying 'Why did you do that?'" (p. 119)

By and large though, what appears on the news and the way it appears is determined by the codes of practice of a professional subculture whose members believe they have their fingers on the pulse of public tastes and needs for news. This knowledge grows out of professional experience, common sense, and intelligence, and does not depend on nor can it be significantly improved by research feedback from the audience. Another reason why news editors choose to follow professional ideals about the kinds of news network news programmes should report, rather than turning to audience research for guidance, is a belief, embodied in journalistic lore, that many audience members are not particularly interested in the news they now receive, preferring instead gossip about celebrities to those activities, events, and issues deemed to be important by the news editors themselves. Television journalists are also fearful that many viewers would prefer attractive or cheerful "newsreaders" to experienced journalists. In short, they fear that if audience preferences were considered, journalistic news judgment would go by the wayside. Journalistic integrity and standards are best preserved, therefore, by keeping editorial and presentation decision-making processes divorced from the influence of audience research. Newspeople are confident of their own awareness of the news needs of the audience and what audiences can and cannot easily comprehend. To what extent, though, are the professionals in tune with their audiences, especially at the level of what viewers and listeners comprehend?

There is evidence to suggest that journalists and their audiences are poles apart on both levels. At the level of taste, for example, the judgements made by viewers about the news may differ markedly from those made by news editors. Gans (1979) provides an interesting illustration of this:

> When a network audience-research unit presented findings on how a sample of viewers evaluated a set of television news films, the journalists were appalled because the sample liked the films which the journalists deemed to be of low quality, and disliked the "good stories." In fact, the viewers' sample made its choices on the basis of film topics rather than film quality, preferring films about personally relevant topics to those about important national and international news. The journalists were so involved in judging the films from their own perspective, however, that they did not notice that the viewers' sample applied a very different one (p. 232).

More recent observations of Robinson and Sahin (1982) suggest that television news journalists may not have their fingers as close as they themselves believe to the pulse of audience comprehension and knowledge about the news either. When these researchers asked ten BBC news staff members about eight leading stories from the previous week, they averaged 7.9 out of 8 correct answers. In contrast, not one person in a nationally representative sample of 510 people scored that well on the same test items. Only 2% scored six or seven out of eight on the test. This suggests that the average news editor is more knowledgeable than 90 to 95% of the audience. "Moreover, it is difficult for the editors to gauge the capacity of their viewers to understand their stories. They fail to provide the necessary background information to help these viewers comprehend their stories because they assume that most people already know this information" (Robinson & Sahin, 1982, p. 167).

UNDERSTANDING RESEARCH AND ITS USES

There is no doubt that news practitioners regard research and researchers with deep suspicion. What are the reasons behind this, and how can journalists' anxieties be allayed?

Although it has been suggested that one reason for news practitioners' rejection of research is because most journalists come from arts background and have a hard time making sense of numbers and statistics, perhaps a more important reason is that, traditionally, journalists have never really seen the use of audience research for their own profession

(Gans, 1979). The decisions they make every day are based on professional judgment and experience, something with which research can, so they believe, be of very little additional help. Nevertheless, news editors tend to adopt the same patterns of decision making and selection of news stories, and the same methods of presenting stories within their programmes, which often embody assumptions about audience members, their news interests, and their capacities for learning about the news (Schlesinger, 1978).

Another not totally unconnected reason for journalists' rejection of audience research is a reluctance to accept any questioning of their professional ability, integrity, or autonomy. As we see in later sections, this reaction to research is not with good cause, especially in the American context where audience research of one specific kind has been used to justify changes to news formats that undermine the traditional professional values and principles of journalism.

Journalists are wary of research because they are concerned that research findings might be used by senior executives to enlarge audiences by switching to more sensationalism or show-business styles. Thus journalists see research as part of the attempt to attain commercially supportive audiences on the part of television networks and local stations. The so-called "demand model" of broadcasting, which does take audience research into account, emphasises the need for programmes to obtain high ratings, thus making the advertising time within the programme more profitable (Cantor, 1980). Thus the market determines the content of the programme because its audience size is taken to be the only really valid indicator of audience demand.

What the audience wants is defined by what they bother to watch in greatest numbers. The audience consists of individuals who are consumers of programmes, and as such they are a quantifiable commodity that television stations can sell to advertisers on a cost-per-thousand basis. If the audience for a programme rises, it is assumed that this must be the kind of show people currently want to watch. If the audience is on the decline, it is concluded that so too is the need among viewers to see this kind of programme. Much of the research conducted in broadcasting has therefore been concerned principally with audience sizes and how to maximize them.

Operating within the demand model, therefore, the manufacture of news programmes has been guided or even determined by the supposed wants of audiences as defined by the numbers in which they watch. Audience-maximisation strategies have resulted in changes being instigated to programme formats and presenters as well as to the kinds of stories that are reported. Often, changes have resulted in the production of news shows that offer entertainment as well as information, in the belief that this is what attracts the largest audiences and must therefore represent what people really want from news programmes.

As a consequence of this trend, the distinction between news and entertainment has become blurred, and this is seen by many journalists as a threat to their professional autonomy, integrity, and standards. Managerial control has steadily been moving away from news editors to sales executives concerned with doctoring the news to make it "sexier" and more entertaining rather than more purely informative.

In his observations of two American network newsrooms, Gans (1979) found that this fear was not completely unfounded, for while audience researchers did not view themselves as representing business or management, their own careers depended on impressing them. Researchers' interests may genuinely be scientific, but the results of their work are evaluated by executives charged with achieving commercial objectives.

The conflict that ensues between researchers and journalists may be over the priority of commercial versus professional considerations in story selection and style of presentation. Researchers observed at one television network studied by Gans were eager to enlarge the audience by attracting people who disliked the present news programmes or did not watch them at all, but the journalists were prepared to add only those viewers who would accept their news judgement. Gans found that even executives who were exjournalists were suspicious of research and reluctant to threaten the autonomy of news producers on the basis of research evidence.

CLARIFYING COGNITIVE PROCESSES

This book has presented a cognitive information-processing perspective on the analysis of memory and comprehension of broadcast news. It has been argued that this psychological model provides conceptual and methodological frameworks that are highly appropriate for the study of learning from the news. There are many different ways in which learning can occur. Human memory is characterised by a complex array of cognitive structures and processes. These require a different level of conceptualisation and different techniques of measurement from those normally employed in mass communications research on the informational impact of the media, in order to reveal the important and unique role each cognitive entity has to play in the news-learning experience.

Before an adequate assessment of information acquisition from broadcast news can begin, there are several concepts that need to be clearly defined. The first of these is attention to the news. In most cognitive information-processing models the first stage to consider is concerned with attention-related processes. Before information is assimilated it has to be attended to. Attention, as a cognitive process, therefore precedes memory and comprehension of information. Survey data have indicated that individuals are often engaged in other activities while watching and listening to the news, so that they are probably not giving their complete and undivided attention to all news stories that are presented in news broadcasts (Bechtel, Akelpohl, & Akers, 1972; Levy, 1978; Robinson & Sahin, 1982). All the same, it is quite likely that there will be some stories that do receive the focused attention of audience members. To what extent should attention-related processes therefore be considered by communications researchers interested in the impact of broadcast news? It will be argued here that some attention at least should be given by researchers to the attention given by audiences to the news.

Two main kinds of attention-related processes have been identified by recent cognitive theorists. These have been referred to as *bottom-up processing* and *top-down processing*. Bottom-up processing involves information flowing from perceptual features of input information that serve as the focus of attention and lead to larger information units being built. Top-down processing involves the use of general world knowledge to guide attention and to determine the interpretation of low-level perceptual features. Anderson (1980) has noted that in most situations, attention relies on an interaction of both of these types of processing. This is probably true of processing information from broadcast news.

Recent work on cognitive switching strongly suggests one way that processing may be top-down or what is otherwise known as conceptually driven. McCain and Ross (1979) found that viewers of news broadcasts cognitively switched (that is, unitised) news information on the basis of four functional modes: agreeing, disagreeing, thinking, and questioning. They found that viewers exhibited similar cognitive switching patterns under similar processing conditions. As Woodall, Davis, and Sahin (1983) point out, "while the processing modes identified in this research are rather broad, it is very likely that such modes are based on the use of activated knowledge already stored and available. It is also likely that pre-existing knowledge guides, to some extent, which stories in a newscast get paid most focused attention to" (p. 4) Woodall et al. believe that most attention-related research suggests that processing of television news is mostly conceptually driven.

Memory and Comprehension

Studies of the informational impact of broadcast news have often suffered from serious conceptual and methodological shortcomings. Conceptually, there is often confusion between principal concepts such as retention and comprehension. Some researchers talk about news awareness, others about news comprehension, and others about news retention. Often these concepts are not clearly defined or differentiated, and not infrequently have been used almost interchangeably. The fact is, however, that they do not refer to the same cognitive phenomena, and it is important that mass media researchers begin to realise and accept that these processes are not one and the same thing. These cognitive processes need to be distinguished conceptually and operationally. A measure of retention is not necessarily a measure of how well the news was understood.

At a theoretical level, cognitive psychologists have distinguished between memory processes and comprehension processes. Memory processes involve the encoding, storage, and retrieval of new information, while comprehension involves an interaction between incoming information and knowledge already stored in memory. In acquiring news information, therefore, the audience members go beyond simply what is presented to them in a broadcast and place interpretations and draw inferences from that new input by matching it against what they already know about the world (Ortony, 1978). This distinction allows the possibility of remembering things we do not understand and of understanding things we cannot later remember (Woodall et al., 1983).

Researchers of news comprehension have not always defined clearly what it is they are measuring. Comprehension has often been defined simply in terms of memory performance, even though it is actually more than that.

A great deal of the research on the acquisition of information from news broadcasts on television and radio has focused on quantitative estimates of how much information audiences are able to remember after exposure. This emphasis on quantity of news reproduction, however, may miss out on a lot of what goes on cognitively among viewers and listeners when they tune in to the news. Broadcast news stories do not simply relay simple statements that such and such happened. They usually give some, albeit often brief, account of where an event occurred, who was involved, why it happened, and with what consequences. A proper understanding of any news event depends crucially upon effective apprehension of these discrete components of the news story. Thus, more important than simply measuring how much information was retained and can be recollected is the question of what aspects of news stories typically can be reproduced.

Nordenstreng (1972) has argued, for instance, that successful news watching is to be measured in terms of comprehension. Subsequently, Katz, Adoni, and Parness (1977) also emphasised the importance of citizens' understanding of the broader societal and international implications of news stories as well as the literal meanings conveyed by news reports. But empirical work in the field so far has tended to focus to a greater extent simply on how much individuals are able to recall from newscasts.

The fact that memory and comprehension are distinct concepts representing cognitive processes that do not always overlap does not mean, however, that measures of memory performance cannot ever indicate that comprehension has occurred. Berry (1983b) has argued for the use of measures of retention but nevertheless emphasised the need to exercise caution in the design and interpretation of memory tasks and performance in demonstrating that understanding of the news has taken place.

Carefully thought-out questions or cues designed to probe retention of different features of news stories, such as their causes and consequences, may provide acceptable evidence of comprehension. There is an important methodological distinction to be made, however, regarding the relative efficacy of free and cued recall tests to reveal all that a person has absorbed from a news bulletin. In many studies that have been heavily cited as evidence for the failure of information broadcasts to communicate effectively to audiences, retention was tested soon after presentation using the free-recall method. Under this method, viewers and listeners must recall without any help from the experimenter or interviewer all the details he or she can from the programme just seen or heard. An alternative method, cued recall, provides respondents with questions about specific aspects of programmes and the stories they carried. This often reveals that a great deal more was taken in from the programme than was indicated by free recall. Even so, typically a great deal is not remembered, or whatever is recalled following careful probing reveals miscomprehension of story meanings.

Berry (1983b) emphasises, however, that the distinction between the two methods is important, because "the measure can determine the functional relationship between dependent and independent variables. Hence it is basic to a full understanding of the processes involved, and crucial both to broadcasting policy and to theoretical objectives" (p. 359).

On the subject specifically of remembering the news, there is an important distinction made by cognitive psychologists between *episodic* and *semantic* memory that might be conceptually and methodologically very useful and relevant to communications researchers working in this field. Within each of these conceptual entities many further models and accounts of memory processes have been discussed concerning the functioning and interplay of each of these aspects of the human cognitive system.

Episodic memory is an event memory that stores episodes as unique historical traces that consist of target information and the context in which that information was presented or encountered. According to some writers, this event memory includes behavioural and situational details and preserves the temporal order of activity with an event (Carlston, 1980). Semantic memory has been conceptualised as a complex network of interrelationships between words, ideas, and properties of objects or situations. "Such networks represent the mental thesaurus of human cognitive systems, and can be taken as the pre-existing knowledge that an individual brings to a situation" (Woodall et al., 1983, p. 11).

Woodall et al. (1983) invoked the levels-of-processing framework as another that could provide a useful theoretical base on which to build a systematic empirical investigation of learning from broadcast news. This model states that information can be processed at different levels, some of which it defines as deeper or more profound than others. The deeper the level to which information is processed, the more strongly it is learned. The model has not gone uncriticised, however. Some writers have argued that the levels-of-processing approach involves circular reasoning. Although it assumes that different rates of forgetting are due to processing at different levels, at the same time it often works backwards by inferring different levels of cognitive processing from different rates of recall (e.g., Eysenck, 1984).

Some cognitive theorists have provided more developed explanations of why semantic-level processing is deeper and produces better retention (e.g., Anderson & Reder, 1979). In a two-part explanation of semantic processing superiority, these theorists have argued that first of all semantic-level processing provides more opportunity for elaboration of information through network node activation than other levels of processing. Thus input information that is elaborated by way of additional association in an activated network leads to more accessible memory traces. And secondly, semantic-level processing may provide more distinctive memory traces through elaboration, and thus such traces are more easily recallable because they are discriminable different from other stored information. Processing of information at other levels does not seem to provide the distinctiveness that semantic-level processing does.

Most research on retention of broadcast news has focused on recall of episodic information, however. In other words, individuals are often asked to remember facts, events, or episodes that occurred at particular times—during the previous week or on last night's or this evening's network news. This emphasis on temporally defined information primes respondents to search the episodic memory store, and this limits the conclusions that can be made about news comprehension, inasmuch as episodic memory may not be the place where most information from broadcast news is actually stored. Rather, semantic memory could be the principal store.

The notion of semantic memory in the context of processing news information places emphasis on the importance of preexisting knowledge relating to a particular news topic and on knowledge frameworks within which new inputs can be readily processed and absorbed. Media researchers have noticed many times before that memory for news content is significantly related to general knowledge (a feature of semantic memory). In other words, those people who have good general knowledge tend to remember more from the news. One cognitive researcher, Larsen (1981), suggested that watching or listening to the news broadcasts serves a knowledge-updating function. Further, the more specific the knowledge a person has about a particular subject matter, the better still he or she will learn any new information relating to it. In support of this hypothesis, Findahl and Hoijer (1976) found that individuals with high levels of current issue knowledge were able to recall more news programme content than those with low levels of current issue knowledge. And Stauffer, Frost, and Rybolt (1978) found significantly higher scores for literate than for illiterate listeners on free and cued recall of and inferences drawn from the content of a radio news broadcast.

More recently, Berry and Clifford (1985) have reported topic-specific background knowledge is the best predictor of television news recall in an experimental setting. It could therefore be that, in future, mass communications researchers interested in the informational effects of broadcast news may need to develop more sensitive measures of knowledge growth as a function of exposure to different news media.

One further important role research might play—in addition to enhancing practitioners' understanding of audience cognitive information-processing capacities—in the context of learning from broadcast news may be to create educational frameworks through which a better understanding of the practitioners may be cultivated among audiences. One way in which this goal might be achieved is through teaching about television in schools.

CULTIVATING A MORE UNDERSTANDING AUDIENCE

Research has indicated that television news may play an important role in the political socialisation process among young people (Dominick, 1972; Conway, Stevens & Smith, 1975; Atkin & Gantz, 1978). Indeed, television news viewing would seem to be related independently of interest in politics to levels of political knowledge in adolescence (Furnham & Gunter, 1983). Other evidence has emerged that children may learn about their own and other environments from television news (Cairns, 1984; Cairns, Hunter, & Herring, 1980). The extent to which children are able to remember television news, however, depends on their attitude to the news and on the level of sophistication they bring with them to the viewing situation (e.g., Drew & Reeves, 1980; Kelley, Gunter, & Buckle, in press; Kelley, Gunter, & Kelley, 1985). Recent evidence has indicated that when children know more about the background to television news and the way it is produced they also seem better able to learn from it. Research on teaching television in the classroom has indicated that children's comprehension of factual programmes can be substantially improved through a relatively simply practical course (Kelley & Gunter, 1984; Kelley et al., 1985).

In a 6-week course featuring six 40-minute lessons each week, 14- and 15-year-old children were taught about television production techniques, and to evaluate critically the content of television news broadcasts and drama programmes. The course involved analysis of specific broadcasts and the planning, preparation, and production of programmes by the pupils themselves, using video-recording and editing equipment. The children also completed three pieces of written work on discussion topics about different aspects of television.

During one part of the course, the children examined television newscasts, considering the selection of items, presentation format, and news as entertainment or information. The pupils were divided into three groups to form news production teams. Each team had to produce a script, with the members acting as presenters, interviewers, and interviewees, outside broadcasters, sound technicians, camera operators, and floor managers. The three groups performed their scripts one after the other and then completed films were discussed.

Their first essay was an analysis of the news broadcasts. Although they enjoyed making them, they all felt that news production was infinitely more difficult than they had imagined. The production focused their attention on questions of editing, timing, camera work, and performances, as well as on wider issues.

At the end of the course the children were tested and compared with another matched group of the same ages who had not taken the course for their comprehension of drama and news programmes. In the news tests, both groups were shown an edited network television newscast recorded several days earlier from a lunchtime bulletin that none of the children would have seen as they were in school at the time of original transmission. Questions probed recall and comprehension of the news stories in the bulletin. For each question there was a precise answer to be derived from the narrative of the news reports against which the children's responses were matched.

The main finding was that those children who had taken the television literacy course had markedly improved their retention and understanding of news broadcasts, whereas those who did not take the course showed no such improvement. The pupils had, it seems, learned to learn more effectively from television news. This work demonstrates that audiences can be taught successfully at an early age to become more active in watching the news and better at making sense of its content.

REFERENCES

Adoni, H., & Cohen, A. (1978). Television economic news and the social construction of economic reality. *Journal of Communication, 28*, 61–70.

Akerstedt, T. (1977). Inversion of the sleep-wakefulness pattern: Effects on circadian variations in psychophysiological activation. *Ergonomics, 20*, 459–474.

Altheide, D. L. (1976). *Creating reality: How TV news distorts events.* Beverly hills, CA: Sage.

Anderson, D. R., & Lorch, E. P. (1983). Looking at television: Action or reaction? In J. Bryant & D. R. Anderson (Eds.), *Children's understanding of television: Research on attention and comprehension.* New York: Academic Press.

Anderson, D. R., Lorch, E. P., Field, D. E., Collins, P. A., & Nathan, J. G. (in press). Television viewing at home: Age trends in visual attention and time with TV. *Child Development.*

Anderson, D. R., & Smith, R. (1984). Young children's TV viewing: The problem of cognitive continuity. In F. J. Morrison, C. Lord, & D. Keating (Eds.), *Advances in applied developmental psychology* New York: Academic Press.

Anderson, J. R. (1978). Arguments concerning representations for mental imagery. *Psychological Review, 85*, 249–277.

Anderson, J. R. (1979). Further arguments concerning representations for mental imagery: A reply to Hayes-Roth and Pylyshyn. *Psychological Review, 86*, 395–406.

Anderson, J. R. (1980). *Cognitive psychology and its implications.* San Francisco: W. H. Freeman.

Anderson, J. R., & Bower, G. H. (1973). *Human associative memory.* New York: V. H. Winston.

Anderson, J. R., & Paulen, R. (1978). Representation and retention of verbatim information. *Journal of Verbal Learning and Verbal Behaviour, 16*, 439–451.

Anderson, R. C. (1977). The notion of schemata and the educational enterprise: General discussion of the conference. In R. C. Anderson, R. J. Spiro, & W. E. Montague (Eds.), *Schooling and the acquisition of knowledge.* Hillsdale, NJ: Lawrence Erlbaum Associates.

Arenberg, D. (1965). Anticipation interval and age differences in verbal learning. *Journal of Abnormal and Social Psychology, 70*, 419–425.

Ash, P., & Jaspen, N. (1953). *The effects and interactions of rate of development, repetition, participation and room illumination on learning from a rear projected film* (Technical Report SFD 269-7-39). Port Washington, NY: US Special Devices Centre.

Atkin, C., Bowen, L., Nayman, O., & Sheinkopf, K. (1973). Quality versus quantity in televised ads. *Public Opinion Quarterly, 37*, 209–224.

Atkin, C., & Gantz, W. (1978). Television news and political socialisation. *Public Opinion Quarterly, 42*, 183–197.

Atkinson, R. C., & Shiffrin, R. M. (1965). *Mathematical models for memory and learning* (Technical Report No. 79). Palo Alto, CA: Stanford University, Institute for Mathematical Studies in the Social Sciences.

Atkinson, R. C., & Shiffrin, R. M. (1968). Human memory: A proposed system and its control processes. In K. W. Spence & J. T. Spence (Eds.), *The psychology of learning and k motivation: Advances in research and theory. Vol. 2.* New York: Academic Press.

Atkinson, R. C., & Shiffrin, R. M. (1971). The control of short-term memory. *Scientific American, 225*, 82–90.

Atwood, L. E. (1970). How newsmen and readers perceive each others' story preferences. *Journalism Quarterly, 47*, 298–308.

Ausubel, D. P. (1968). *Educational psychology: A cognitive view.* New York: Holt, Rinehart, & Winston.

Baddeley, A. D., Hatter, J. E., Scott, D., & Snashell, A. (1970). Memory and time of day. *Quarterly Journal of Experimental Psychology, 22*, 605–609.

Baggaley, J. P. (1980). *The psychology of the TV image*. Aldershot, England: Saxon House.

Baggaley, J., & Duck, S. W. (1974). Experiments in ETV: Effects of adding background. *Educational Broadcasting International, 7,*

Baggaley, J., & Duck, S. W. (1976). *The dynamics of television*. Farnborough, England: Saxon House.

Bahrick, H. P. (1969). Measurement of memory by prompted recall. *Journal of Experimental Psychology, 79*, 213–219.

Barnes, J. M., & Underwood, B. J. (1959). "Fate" of first-list associations in transfer theory. *Journal of Experimental Psychology, 58*, 97–105.

Baron, R. Baron, P. H., & Miller, N. (1973) The relation between distraction and persuasion. *Psychological Bulletin, 80*, 310–323.

Barrett, M., & Sklar, Z. (1980). *The eye of the storm*. New York: Lippincott & Crowell.

Barrow, L. C., & Westley, B. H. (1959). Comparative teaching effectiveness of radio and television. *Audio-Visual Communications Review, 7*, 14–23.

Bartlett, F. (1932). *Remembering: A study in experimental and social psychology*. New York: The Macmillan Company.

Baylor, G. W. (1972). A treatise on the mind's eye: An empirical investigation of visual mental imagery *Dissertation Abstracts International, 32*, 6024B. (University Microfilms No. 72-12699)

BBC (1971). *Annual review of audience research findings*. London: British Broadcasting Corporation.

BBC (1976a). *Annual review of audience research findings*. London: British Broadcasting Corporation.

BBC (1976b) *The book of broadcasting news*. Report of a study the BBC General Advisory Council, London: British Broadcasting Authority.

BBC (1977). *Annual review of audience research findings*. London: British Broadcasting Corporation.

Beagle-Roos, J., & Gat, I. (1983). Specific impact of radio and television on children's story comprehension. *Journal of Educational Psychology, 75*, 128–137.

Bechtel, R. B., Achelpohl, C., & Akers, R. (1972). Correlates between observed behaviour and questionnaire responses on television viewing. In E. A. Rubinstein, G. A. Comstock, & J. P. Murray (Eds.), *Television and social behaviour: Vol. 4. Television in day-to-day life: Patterns of use*. Washington DC: U.S. Government Printing Office.

Becker, L., McCombs, M., & McLeod, J. (1975). The development of political cognitions. In S. Chaffee (ED.), *Political communication: Issues and strategies for research*. Beverly Hills, CA.: Sage.

Becker, L., Sobowale, I., Casey, W. E. (1979). Newspaper and television dependencies: Effects on evaluations of public officials. *Journal of Broadcasting, 23*, 465–475.

Becker, L., Sobowale, I., Cobbey, R., & Eyal, C. (1978). Debates' effects on voters' understanding of candidates and issues. In G. F. Bishop, R. G. Meadow, & M Jackson-Beeck (Eds.), *The presidential debates: Media, electoral, and policy perspectives*. New York: Praeger.

Becker, L., & Whitney, D. C. (1980). Effects of media dependencies. *Communication Research, 7*, 95–120.

Begg, I., & Clark, J. M. (1975). Contextual imagery in meaning and memory. *Memory and Cognition, 3*, 117–122.

Begg, I., & Paivio, A. (1969). Concreteness and imagery in sentence learning. *Journal of Verbal Learning and Verbal Behaviour, 8*, 821–827.

Belson, W. A. (1967). *The impact of television*. London: Crosby Lockwood & Son Ltd.

Benton, M., & Frazier, P. J. (1976). The agenda-setting function of the mass media at three levels of information. holding. *Communication Research, 3*, 261–274.

Berelson, B., Lazarsfeld, P., & MacPhee, W. (1954). *Voting: A study of opinion formation in a presidential campaign.* Chicago: University of Chicago Press.

Berlyne, D. E. (1960). *Conflict, arousal and curiosity.* New York: McGraw-Hill.

Berlyne, D. E. (1970). Attention as a problem in behaviour theory. In D. I. Mostofsky (Ed.), *Attention: Contemporary theory and analysis.* New York: Appleton-Century-Crofts.

Bernard, R. M., & Coldevin, G. O. (1985). Effects of recap strategies on television news recall and retention. *Journal of Broadcasting and Electronic Media, 29,* 407–419.

Berry, C. (1983a). A dual effect of pictorial enrichment in learning from television news: Gunter's data revisited. *Journal of Educational Television, 9,* 171–174.

Berry, C. (1983b). Learning from television news: A critique of the research. *Journal of Broadcasting, 27,* 359–370.

Berry, C. & Clifford, B. (1985). *Learning from television news: Effects of presentation factors and knowledge on comprehension and memory.* London: North East London Polytechnic, unpublished manuscript.

Berry, C., Gunter, B., & Clifford, B. (1982). Research on television news. *Bulletin of the British Psychological Society, 35,* 301–304.

Bilodeau, E. A. (1967). Experimental interference with primary associates and their subsequent recovery with rest. *Journal of Experimental Psychology, 73,* 328–332.

Bishop, G. F., Meadow, R. G., & Jackson-Beeck, M. (1978). *The presidential debates: Media, electoral and policy perspectives.* New York: Praeger.

Bishop, M., & McMartin, P. (1973). Toward a socio-psychological definition of transitional persons. *Journal of Broadcasting, 17,* 333–344.

Bjorkman, M. (1984). Decision making, risk taking and psychological time: A review of empirical findings and psychological theory. *Scandinavian Journal of Psychology, 25,* 31–49.

Black, J. B., Turner, J. T., & Bower, G. H. (1979). Point of view in narrative comprehension, memory and production. *Journal of Verbal Learning and Verbal Behaviour, 18,* 187–198.

Blake, M. J. F. (1967). Time of day effects on performance in a range of tasks. *Psychonomic Science, 9,* 349–350.

Blake, M. J. F. (1971). Temperament and time of day. In W. P. Colquhoun (Ed.), *Biological rhythms and human behaviour.* London: Academic Press.

Blumenthal, G. B., & Robbins, D. (1977). Delayed release from proactive interference with meaningful material: How much do we remember after reading prose passages? *Journal of Experimental Psychology: Human Learning and Memory, 3,* 754–761.

Blumler, J. G., & Katz, E. (1974). *The uses of mass communications: Current perspectives of gratifications research.* Beverly Hills, CA: Sage.

Blumler, J. G., & McQuail, D. (1968). *Television in Politics: Its uses and influence.* London: Faber and Faber.

Blumler, J. G., & McQuail, D. (1969). *Television in politics: Its uses and influence.* Chicago: University of Chicago Press.

Bogart, L. (1980). Television news as entertainment. In P. Tannenbaum (Ed.), *The entertainment functions of television.* Hillsdale, NJ: Lawrence Erlbaum Associates.

Booth, A. (1970). The recall of news items. *Public Opinion Quarterly, 34,* 604–610.

Bousfield, W. A. (1951). *Frequency and availability measures in language behaviour.* Paper presented at the annual meeting of the American Psychological Association, Chicago.

Bousfield, W. A. (1953). The occurrence of clustering in the recall of randomly arranged associates. *Journal of General Psychology, 49,* 229–240.

Bower, G. H. (1970) Organizational factors in memory. *Cognitive Psychology, 1,* 18–46.

Bower, G. H. (1971). Mental imagery and associative learning. In L. Gregg (Ed.), *Cognition in learning and memory.* New York: Wiley.

Bower, G. H. (1972). Mental imagery and associative learning. In L. W. Gregg (Ed.), *Cognition in learning and memory.* New York: Wiley.

Bower, G. H. (1976). Experiments on story understanding and recall. *Quarterly Journal of Experimental Psychology, 28*, 511–534.

Bower, G. H., Black, J. B., & Turner, T. J. (1979). Scripts in memory for text. *Cognitive Psychology, 11*, 177–220.

Bransford, J. D., & Johnson, M. K. (1972). Contexual prerequisites for understanding: Some investigations of comprehension and recall. *Journal of Verbal Learning and Verbal Behaviour, 11*, 717–726.

Bransford, J. D., & McCarrell, N. S. (1974). A sketch of a cognitive approach to comprehension. In W. Weimer & D. S. Palermo (Eds.), *Cognition and the symbolic processes.* Hillsdale, NJ: Lawrence Erlbaum Associates.

Broadbent, D. E. (1958). *Perception and communication.* New York: Pergamon Press.

Brodie, D., & Lippmann, L. G. (1970). Symbolic and size shifts in short-term memory tasks. *Psychonomic Science, 20*, 361–362.

Brown, J. (1958). Some tests of the decay theory of immediate memory. *Quarterly Journal of Experimental Psychology, 10*, 12–21.

Browne, K. (1978). Comparisons of factual recall from film and print stimuli. *Journalism Quarterly, 55*, 350–353.

Bryant, J., Zillmann, D., Williams, B. R., Reardon, K., & Wolf, M. (1980). *Acquisition of information from educational television programmes as a function of differently paced humourous inserts.* Paper presented at the International Communication Association conference, Acapulco.

Bryant, J., Zillmann, D., Wolf, M., & Reardon, K. (1980). Learning from educational television as a function of differently paced humour: Further evidence.

Budd, R. W., McLean, M. S., & Barnes, A. M. (1966). Regularities in the diffusion of two major news events. *Journalism Quarterly, 43*, 221–230.

Bugelski, B. R. (1970). Words and things and images *American Psychologist, 25*, 1,002–1,012.

Byrd, F. D., Buckhalt, J. A., & Byrd, E. K., (1981). Age differences in WISC-R subtest numbers of children experiencing academic difficulties. *Psychological Reports 48*, 599–604.

Cairns, E. (1984). Television news as a source of knowledge about the violence for children in Ireland: A test of the knowledge-gap hypothesis. *Current Psychological Research and Reviews, 3*, 32–38.

Cairns, E., Hunter, D., & Herring, L. (1980). Young Children's awareness of violence in Northern Ireland: The influence of Northern Irish television in Scotland and Northern Ireland. *British Journal of Social and Clinical Psychology, 19*, 3–6.

Canestrari, R. E. (1968). Age changes in acquisition. In G. A. Tiland (Ed.), *Human aging and behaviour.* New York: Academic Press.

Cantor, M. (1980). *Prime time television: Content and control.* Bevery Hills, CA: Sage

Carlston, D. (1980). Events, inferences and impression formation. In R. Hastie, (Eds.), *Person memory: The cognitive basis of social perceptions.* Hillsdale, NJ: Lawrence Erlbaum Associates.

Chaffee, S. H. McLeod, J. M., & Wackman, D. B. (1973). Family communication patterns and adolescent political participation. In J. Dennis (Ed.), *Socialisation to politics.* New York: Wiley.

Chaffee, S. H., Ward, L. S., & Tipton, L. P. (1970). Mass communication and political socialisation. *Journalism Quarterly, 47*, 647–659.

Chapman, A. J., & Compton, P. (1978). Humorous presentations of material and presentations of humorous material. A review of the humour and memory literature and two experimental studies. In M. M. Gruneberg, P. E. Morris, & R. N. Sykes (Eds.), *Practical aspects of memory.* London: Academic Press.

Chiesi, H. L., Spilich, G. J., & Voss, J. F. (1979). Acquisition of domain-related information in relation to high and low domain knowledge. *Journal of Verbal Learning and Verbal Behaviour, 18*, 257–274.

Chu, G., & Schramm, W. (1967). *Learning from television: What the research says*. Washington, DC: National Association of Educational Broadcasters.

Clarke, P., & Fredin, E. (1978). Newspapers, television and political reasoning. *Public Opinion Quarterly, 42*, 143–160.

Clements, P. R., Hafer, M. D., & Vermillion, M. E. (1976). Psychometric, diurnal and electrophysiological correlates of activation. *Journal of Personality and Social Psychology, 33*, 387–394.

Cohen, A. A., & Bantz, C. (1984). *Social conflicts in TV news: A five-nation comparative study*. Papers presented at the annual meeting of the International Communication Association, San Francisco.

Cohen, A. A., Wigand, R. T., & Harrison, R. P. (1976). The effects of type of event, proximity and repetition on children's attention to and learning from television news. *Communication Research, 3*, 30–36.

Cohen, B. H. (1966). Some-or-none characteristics of coding behaviour. *Journal of Verbal Learning and Verbal Behaviour, 5*, 182–187.

Cohen, G. (1979). Language comprehension in old age. *Cognitive Psychology, 11*, 412–429.

Coldevin, G. (1974, April). *The differential effects of voice-over, superimposition and combined review treatments as production strategies for ETV programming*. Paper presented at the International Conference for Educational Technology, Liverpool, England.

Coldevin, G. (1975). Spaced, massed and summary treatments as review strategies for ITV production. *AV Communication Review, 23*, 289–303.

Coldevin, G. (1978a). Experiments in TV presentation strategies I: Effectiveness of full screen vs. corner screen location establishment background visuals. *Educational Broadcasting International, 11*, 17–18.

Coldevin, G. (1978b) Experiments in TV presentation strategies II: Effectiveness of full screen vs. corner screen 'symbol establishment' background visuals. *Educational Broadcasting International, 11*, 158–159.

Coldevin, G. (1979). The effects of placement, delivery format and missed cues on TV presenter ratings. In J. Baggaley & J. Sharpe (Eds.) (pp. 73–90). *Proceedings of the Second International Conference on Experimental Research in Televised Instruction*. St. Johns: Memorial University of Newfoundland.

Collins, A. M., & Quillian, M. R. (1969). Retrieval time from semantic memory. *Journal of Verbal Learning and Verbal Behaviour, 8*, 240–247.

Collins, W. A. (1979). Children's comprehension of television content. In E. Wartella (Ed.), *Children Communicating: Media and development of thought, speech and understanding*. Beverly Hills, CA: Sage.

Collins, W. A. Wellman, H., Keniston, A. H., & Westby, S. D. (1978). Age-related aspects of comprehensive and inference from a televised dramatic narrative. *Child Development, 49*, 359–399.

Colquhoun, W. P. (1960). Temperament, inspection, efficiency and time of day. *Ergonomics, 3*, 377–378.

Colquhoun, W. P., Blake, M. J. F., & Edwards, R. S. (1968). Experimental studies of shift work I: A comparison of 'rotating' and 'stabilised' 4-hour shift systems. *Ergonomics, 11*, 437–453.

Connolly, C. P. (1962). *An experimental investigation of eye-contact on television*. Unpublished master's MA thesis, Ohio University.

Conway, M. M., Stevens, A. J., & Smith, R. G. (1975). The relation between media use and children's civic awareness. *Journalism Quarterly, 8*, 240–247.

Craik, F. I. M. (1970). The fate of primary memory items in free recall. *Journal of Verbal Learning and Verbal Behaviour, 9*, 143–148.

Craik, F. J. M., & Blankstein, K. (1975). Psychophysiology and human memory. In P. Venables & M. Christie (Eds.), *Research in psychophysiology*. London: Wiley.

Craik, F. I. M., & Lockhart, R. S. (1972). Levels of processing: A framework for memory research. *Journal of Verbal Learning and Verbal Behaviour, 11*, 671–684.

Craik, F. I. M., & Simon, E. (1980). Age differences in memory: The roles of attention and depth of processing. In L. W. Poon, J. L. Fozard, L. S. Cermak, D. Arenberg, & L. W. Thompson (Eds.), *New directions in memory and aging*. Hillsdale, NJ: Lawrence Erlbaum Associates.

Craik, F. I. M., & Tulving, E. (1975). Depth of processing and the retention of words in episodic memory. *Journal of Experimental Psychology: General, 1,* 268–294.

Davidson, R. E. (1976). The role of metaphor and analogy in learning. In J. R. Lewin & V. L. Allen (Eds.), *Cognitive learning in children*. New York: Academic Press.

Davies, A. P., & Apter, M. J. (1980). Humour and its effects on learning in children. In P. E. McGhee & A. J. Chapman (Eds.), *Children's humour*. New York: Wiley.

Davies, M. M., Berry, C., & Clifford, B. (1985). Unkindest cuts? Some effects of picture editing on recall of television news information. *Journal of Educational Television, 11,* 85–98.

Davis, A. (1976). *Television: Here is the news*. London: Severn House Publishers.

Davis, D. K., & Robinson, J. P. (1985). News story attributes and comprehension. In J. P. Robinson & M. R. Levy (Eds.), *The main source: Learning from television news*. Beverly Hills, CA: Sage.

Davis, S. H., & Obrist, W. D. (1966). Age differences in learning and retention of verbal material. *Cornell Journal of Social Relations, 1,* 95–103.

Desroches, H. F., Kaiman, B. D., & Ballard, H. T. (1966). Relationships between age and recall of meaningful material. *Psychological Reports, 18,* 920–922.

Deutschmann, P., & Danielson, W. (1960). Diffusion of knowledge of the major news story. *Journalism Quarterly, 37,* 345–355.

Dhawan, M., & Pellegrino, J. W. (1977). Acoustic and semantic interference effects in words and pictures. *Memory and Cognition, 5,* 340–346.

Dijk, T. van. (1980). *Macrostructures: An interdisciplinary study of global structures in discourse interaction and cognition*. Hillsdale, NJ: Lawrence Erlbaum Associates.

Dijk, T. van. (1983). Discourse analysis: Its development an implication to the structures of news. *Journal of Communication, 33,* 20–43.

Dixon, R. A., Hultsch, D. F., Simon, E. W., & von Eye, A. (1984). Verbal ability and text structure effects on adult age differences in text recall. *Journal of Verbal Learning and Verbal Behaviour, 23,* 569–578.

Dixon, R. A., Simon, E. W., Nowak, C. A., & Hultsch, D. F. (1982). Text recall in adulthood as a function of level of information, input modality and delay interval. *Journal of Gerontology, 37,* 358–364.

Dominick, J. R. (1972). Television and political socialisation. *Educational Broadcasting Review, 6,* 48–56.

Dominick, J. R., Wurtzel, A., & Lometti, G. (1975). Television journalism vs. show business: a content analysis of eyewitness news. *Journalism Quarterly, 52,* 213–218.

Dominowski, R. L., & Gadlin, H. (1968). Imagery and paired-associate learning. *Canadian Journal of Psychology, 22,* 336–348.

Dommermuth, W. P. (1974). How does the medium affect the message? *Journalism Quarterly, 51,* 441–447.

Dooling, D. J., & Lachman, R. (1971). Effect of comprehension in retention of prose. *Journal of Experimental Psychology, 88,* 216–222.

Dooling, D. J., & Mullet, R. L. (1973). Locus of thematic effects in retention of prose. *Journal of Experimental Psychology, 97,* 404–406.

Drew, D., & Reese, S. D. (1984). Children's learning from a television newscast. *Journalism Quarterly, 61,* 83–88.

Drew, D., & Reeves, B. (1980). Learning from a television news story. *Communication Research, 7,* 121–135.

Dwyer F. M. (1968). When visuals are not the message. *Educational Broadcasting Review, 2,* 38–43.

Easterbrook, J. A. (1959). The effect of emotion on cue utilization and the organization of behaviour. *Psychological Review, 66*, 183–201.

Ebbinghaus, H. (1964). *Uber das Gedachtnis: Untersuchungen zur experimentellan Psychologie.* H. A. Ruger & L. E. Bussenius, Trans.) 1913 and reissued by Dover publications, 1964.

Edelstein, A. (1974). The uses of communication in decision making. New York: Praeger.

Edwardson, M., Grooms, D., & Pringle, P. (1976). Visualisation and TV news information gain. *Journal of Broadcasting, 20*, 373–380.

Edwardson, M., Grooms, D., & Proudlove, S. (1981). Television news information gain from interesting video vs. talking heads. *Journal of Broadcasting, 25*, 15–24.

Elliott, P. (1972). *The making of a television series: A case study in the sociology of culture.* London: Constable.

Ellis, J. A., & Montague, W. E. (1973). Effect of recalling on proactive interference in short-term memory. *Journal of Experimental Psychology, 99*, 356–359.

Erbring, L., Goldenberg, E., & Miller, A. (1980). Front-page news and real-world cues: A new look at agenda-setting by the media. *American Journal of Political Science, 24*, 16–49.

Ettema, J. S., & Kline, F. G. (1977). Deficits, differences, and ceilings: Contingent conditions for understanding the knowledge gap. *Communication Research, 4*, 179–202.

Eysenck, H. J., & Eysenck, S. B. G. (1969). *The structure and measurement of personality.* London: Routledge & Kegan Paul.

Eysenck, H. J., & Eysenck, S. B. G. (1975). *Manual for the Eysenck personality questionnaire.* London: Hodder & Stoughton.

Eysenck, M. W. (1976). Arousal, learning and memory. *Psychological Bulletin, 83*, 389–404.

Eysenck, M. W. (1977). *Human memory: Theory, research and individual differences.* Oxford: Pergamon Press.

Eysenck, M. W. (1982). *Attention and arousal: cognition and performance.* Berlin: Springer-Verlag.

Eysenck, M. W. (1984). *A handbook of cognitive psychology.* Hillsdale, NJ: Lawrence Erlbaum Associates.

Eysenck, M. W., & Folkard, S. (1980). Personality, time of day, and caffeine: Some theoretical and conceptual problems in Revelee et al. *Journal of Experimental Psychology: General, 109*, 32–41.

Fairbanks, G., Guttmann, N., & Miron, M. S. (1957). Auditory comprehension in relation to listening rate and selective verbal redundancy. *Journal of Speech and Hearing Disorders, 27*, 23–32.

Fang, I. E. (1968). *Television news: Writing, editing, filming, broadcasting.* New York: Hastings House.

Farley, A. M. (1974). VIPS: A visual imagery and perception system: The results of a protocol analysis. *Dissertation Abstracts International, 35*, 1230B. (University Microfilms No. 74-20494).

Feigenbaum, E. A. (1970). Information processing and memory. In D. A. Norman (Ed.), *Models of human memory.* New York: Academic Press.

Field, D. E., & Anderson, D. R.(in press). Instruction and modality effects on children's television attention and comprehension. *Journal of Educational Psychology.*

Findahl, O. (1971). *The effects of visual illustrations upon perception and retention of news programmes.* Stockholm: Swedish Broadcasting Corporation, Audience and Programme Research Department.

Findahl, O., & Hoijer, B. (1972). *Man as a receiver of information: Repetitions and reformulations in a news programme.* Stockholm: Swedish Broadcasting Corporation, Audience and Programme Research Department.

Findahl, O., & Hoijer, B. (1975a). Effect of additional verbal information in retention of a radio news programme. *Journalism Quarterly, 52*, 493–498.

Findahl, O., & Hoijer, B. (1975b) *Man as a receiver of information: On knowledge, social privilege and the news.* Stockholm: Swedish Broadcasting Corporation, Audience and programme Research Department.

Findahl, O., & Hoijer, B. (1976). *Fragments of reality: An experiment with news and TV visuals.* Stockholm: Swedish Broadcasting Corporation, Audience and Programme Research Department.

Findahl, O., & Hoijer, B. (1984). *Comprehension analysis: A review of the research and an application to radio and television news.* Lund: Studentlitteratur. (English summary available only)

Findahl, O., & Hoijer, B. (1985). *Some characteristics of news memory and comprehension.* Unpublished manuscript.

Folkard, S. (1979). Time of day and level of processing. *Memory and Cognition, 7,* 247–252.

Folkard, S. (1980). A note on time of day effects in school children's immediate and delayed recall of meaningful material—the influence of the importance of the information tested. *British Journal of Psychology, 71,* 95–97.

Folkard, S., & Monk, T. H.,(1978). Time of day effects in immediate and delayed memory. In M. M. Gruneberg, P. E. Morris, & R. N. Sykes (Eds.), *Practical aspects of memory.* London: Academic Press.

Folkard, S., & Monk, T. H. (1979). Time of day and processing strategy in free-recall. *Quarterly Journal of Experimental Psychology, 31,* 461–475.

Folkard, S., & Monk, T. H. (1980). Circadian rhythms in human memory. *British Journal of Psychology, 71,* 295–307.

Folkard, S., Monk, T. H., Bradbury, R., & Rosenthal, J. (1977). Time of day effects in school children's immediate delayed recall of meaningful material. *British Journal of Psychology, 68,* 45–50.

Foulke, E. (1978). Listening comprehension as a function of word rate. *Journal of Communication, 18,* 198–206.

Fowler, R., Hodge, R., Kress, G., & Trew, A. (1979). *Language and control.* London: Routledge & Kegan Paul.

Frederiksen, C. H. (1977). Semantic processing units in understanding text. In R. D. Freedle (Ed.), *Discourse production and comprehension.* Norwood, NJ: Ablex.

Funkhouser, G., & McCombs, M. (1971). The rise and fall of news diffusion. *Public Opinion Quarterly, 35,* 107–113.

Furnham, A., & Gunter, B. (1983). Political knowledge and awareness in adolescents. *Journal of Adolescence, 6,* 373–385.

Furnham, A., & Gunter, B. (1985). Sex, presentation mode, and memory for violent and non-violent news. *Journal of Educational Television, 11,* 99–105.

Gale, A. (1969). "Stimulus hunger"—individuals' differences in operant strategy in a button-pressing task. *Behaviour Research and Therapy, 3,* 265–274.

Galtung, J., & Ruge, M. H. (1965). The structure of foreign news: The presentation of the Congo, Cuba and Cyrpus crises in four foreign newspapers. *Journal of Peace Research, 2,* 64–91.

Gans, H. (1979). *Deciding what's news.* New York: Pantheon.

Gantz, W. (1979). How uses and gratifications affect recall of television news. *Journalism Quarterly, 56,* 115–123.

Gates, A. I. (1916). Diurnal variations in memory and association. *University of California Publications in Psychology, 1,* 323–344.

Genova, B. K., & Greenberg, B. J. (1979). Interests in the news and the knowledge gap. *Public Opinion Quarterly, 43,* 79–91.

Gerbner, G., & Gross, L. (1976). Living with television: the violence profile. *Journal of Communication, 26,* 173–199.

Gerbner, G., Gross, L., Eleey, M. E., Jackson-Beeck, M., Jeffries-Fox, S., & Signorielli, N. (1977). Television violence profile no. 8: The highlights. *Journal of Communication, 27,* 171–180.

Gerbner, G., Gross, L., Jackson-Beeck, M. Jeffries-Fox, S., & Signorielli, N. (1978). Cultural indicators: Violence profile no. 9. *Journal of Communication, 28*, 176–207.

Gerbner, G., Gross, L., Morgan, M., & Signorielli, N. (1980). The "mainstreaming" of America: Violence profile no. 11. *Journal of Communication, 30*, 10–29.

Gerbner, G., Gross, L., Signorielli, N., Morgan, M., & Jackson-Beeck, M. (1979). The demonstration of power: Violence profile no. 10. *Journal of Communication, 29*, 177–196.

Gieber, W. (1964). News is what newspapermen make it. In L.A. Pieter & D. M. White (Eds.), *People, society and mass communications.* New York: The Free Press.

Gieber, W., & Johnson, W. (1961). The City Hall beat. *Journalism Quarterly, 38*, 289–297.

Giltrow, D. (1977). More than meets the eye: discrepancies in cognitive-affective adult student responses to live television production styles. In T. Bates and J. Robinson (Eds.), *Evaluating educational television and radio.* Milton Keynes: Open University Press.

Glanzer, M., & Cunitz, A. R. (1966). Two storage mechanisms in free recall. *Journal of Verbal Learning and Verbal Behaviour, 5*, 351–360.

Glasgow University Media Group(1976). *Bad news.* London: Routledge & Kegan Paul.

Glasgow University Media Group(1980). *More bad news.* London: Routledge & Kegan Paul.

Goldberg, H. D. (1950). Liking and retention of a simulcast. *Public Opinion Quarterly, 14*, 141–142.

Golding, P., & Elliott, P. (1979). *Making the news.* London: Longman.

Goleman, D. (1978). A taxonomy of meditation-specific altered states. *Journal of Altered States of Consciousness, 4* (2), 203–213.

Goodhardt, G. J., Ehrenberg, A. S. C., & Collins, M. A. (1975). *The television audience: Patterns of viewing.* Farnborough, England: Saxon House.

Graber, D. (1984). *Processing the news.* New York: Longman.

Green, M. (1969). *Television news: Anatomy and process.* Belmont, CA: Wadsworth Publishing Company, Inc.

Greenberg, B. S., Brinton, J. E., & Farr, R. S. (1965). Diffusion of news about an anticipated news event. *Journal of Broadcasting, 9*, 129–142.

Greenstein, F. I. (1968). Political socialisation. In *International Encyclopedia of the Social Sciences. Vol. 16.* New York: Macmillan.

Gunter, B. (1979). Recall of television news items: Effects of presentation mode, picture content and serial position. *Journal of Educational Television, 5*, 57–61.

Gunter, B. (1980a). Remembering television news: Effects of picture content. *Journal of General Psychology, 102*, 127–133.

Gunter, B. (1980b). Remembering televised news: Effects of visual format on information gain. *Journal of Educational Television, 6*, 8–11.

Gunter, B., (1983). Forgetting the news. In E. Wartella, D. C. Whitney & S. Windahl (Eds.), *Mass communication review yearbook Vol 4* Beverly Hills, CA: Sage.

Gunter, B. (1984). *News awareness: A British survey.* London: Independent Broadcasting Authority, Research Department Research Paper.

Gunter, B.(1985). News sources and news awareness. A British survey. *Journal of Broadcasting.*

Gunter, B. (1986). *The audience for TV-am.* London: Independent Broadcasting Authority, Special report.

Gunter, B., Berry, C., & Clifford, B. (1981). Release from proactive interference with television news items: Further evidence. *Journal of Experimental Psychology: Human Learning and Memory, 7*, 480–487

Gunter, B., Berry, C., & Clifford, B. (1982). Remembering broadcast news: The implications of experimental research for production technique. *Human Learning, 1*, 13–29.

Gunter, B., Clifford, B., & Berry, C. (1980). Release from proactive interference with television news items: Evidence for encoding dimensions within televised news. *Journal of Experimental Psychology: Human Learning and Memory, 6*, 216–223.

Gunter, B., & Furnham, A. (1986). Sex and personality differences in recall of violent and non-violent news from three presentation modalities. *Personality and Individual Differences, 1,* 829–837.

Gunter, B., Furnham, A., & Gietson, G. (1984). Memory for the news as a function of the channel of communication. *Human Learning, 3,* 265–271.

Gunter, B., Furnham, A., & Jarrett, J. (1984). Personality, time of day and delayed memory for TV news. *Personality and Individual Differences, 5,* 35–39.

Gunter, B., Jarrett, J., & Furnham, A. (1983). Time of day effects on immediate memory for television news. *Human Learning, 2,* 1–7.

Gunter, B., Kelley, P., & Buckle, L.(in press). 'Reading' television in the classroom: More results from the television literacy project. *Journal of Educational Television.*

Gunter, B., Svennevig, M., & Wober, M. (1984). Viewers' experience of television coverage of the 1983 General Election. *Parliamentary Affairs, 37,* 271–282.

Gunter, B., Svennevig, M., & Wober, M.(1986). *Television coverage of the 1983 General Election: Audiences, appreciation and public opinion.* Aldershot, England: Gower.

Haaland, G. A., & Venkatesan, M. (1968). Resistance to persuasive communications: An examination of the distraction hypothesis. *Journal of Personality and Social Psychology, 9,* 167–170.

Hall, S. (1973). A world at one with itself. In S. Cohen & J Young (Eds.), *The manufacture of news.* London: Constable.

Halloran, J. (1970). *The effects of television.* London: Panther Books.

Harrell, T. W., Brown, D. E., & Schramm, W. (1949). Memory in radio listening. *Journal of Applied Psychology, 33,* 265–274.

Harvey, R. F., & Stone, V. A. (1969). Television and newspaper front page coverage of a major news story. *Journal of Broadcasting, 13,* 181–186.

Hastie, R., & Carlston, D. (1980). Theoretical issues in person memory. In R. Hastie et al (Eds.), *Person memory: The cognitive basis of social perception.* Hillsdale, NJ: Lawrence Erlbaum Associates.

Hazard, W. R. (1963). On the impact of television's news. *Journal of Broadcasting, 7,* 43–51.

Hebb, D. O. (1949). *The Organization of behaviour.* New York: Wiley.

Hebb, D. O. (1958). *A textbook of psychology.* Philadelphia: Saunders.

Hebb, D. O. (1961). Distinctive features of learning in the higher animal. In J. F. Delafresnage (Ed.), *Brain mechanisms and learning.* New York: Oxford University Press.

Herrmann, D. J., & Neisser, U. (1978). An inventory of everyday memory experiences. In M. M. Gruneberg, P. E. Morris, & R. N. Sykes (Eds.), *Practical aspects of memory.* London: Academic Press.

Hester, H. (1976). *Foreign news on US television.* Paper presented at the annual conference of the International Association of Mass communication Research Leicester, England.

Hockey, G. R. S., Davies, S., & Gray, M. M. (1972) Forgetting as a function of sleep at different times of day. *Quarterly Journal of Experimental Psychology, 34,* 386–393.

Hopkins, R. H., Edwards, R. E., & Gavelek, J. R. (1971). Presentation modality as an encoding variable in short-term memory. *Journal of Experimental Psychology, 90,* 319–325.

Houston, J. P. (1981). *Fundamentals of learning and memory.* New York: Academic Press.

Howe, M. J. A. (1977). Learning and the acquisition of knowledge by students: Some experimental investigations In M. J. A. Howe (Ed.), *Adult learning: Psychological research and applications.* London: Wiley.

Hulicka, I. M., & Rust, L. D. (1964). Age-related retention deficit as a function of learning. *Journal of Consulting Psychology, 29,* 125–129.

Hulicka, I. M., Sterns, H., & Grossman, J. (1967). Age group comparisons of paired-associate learning as a function of paced and self-paced association and response. *Journal of Gerontology, 22,* 274–280.

Hulicka, I. M., & Weiss, R. L. (1965). Age differences in retention as a function of learning. *Journal of Consulting and Clinical Psychology, 11,* 197–210.

Hultsch, D. F. (1969). Adult age differences in the Organization of free recall. *Developmental Psychology, 1*, 673–678.

Hultsch, D. F. (1971). Adult age differences in free classification and free recall. *Developmental Pscychology, 4*, 338–347.

Hultsch, D. F. (1974). Learning to learn in adulthood. *Journal of Gerontology, 29*, 302–308.

Hunt, E., Lunneberg, L., & Lewis, J. (1975). What does it mean to be high verbal? *Cognitive Psychology, 7*, 194–227.

Hutchinson, K. L. (1982). The effects of newscaster gender and vocal quality on perceptions of homophily and interpersonal attraction. *Journal of Broadcasting, 26*, 457–467.

Hyde, T. S., & Jenkins, J. S. (1969). The differential effects of incidental tasks on the Organization of recall of a list of highly associated words. *Journal of Experimental Psychology, 82*, 472–481.

IBA (1982). *Attitudes to broadcasting.* London: Independent Broadcasting Authority, Research Department Special Report.

IBA (1983). *Attitudes to broadcasting.* London: Independent Broadcasting Authority, Research Department Special Report.

IBA (1985). *Attitudes to broadcasting,* London: Independent Broadcasting Authority, Research Department Research Paper.

IBA (1986). *Attitudes to broadcasting in 1985.* London: Independent Broadcasting Authority.

Insko, C. A., Turnbull, W., & Yandell, B. (1974). Facilitative and inhibitory effects of distractors on attitude change. *Sociometry, 37*, 508–528.

Israel, H., & Robinson, J. P. (1972). Demographic characteristics of viewers of television violence and news programmes. In E. A. Rubinstein, G. A. Comstock, & J. P. Murray (Eds.), *Television and social behaviour; Vol. 4, Television in day-to-day life: Patterns of use.* Washington, DC: U. S. Government Printing Office.

Iyengar, S., Peters, M., & Kinder, D. (1982). Experimental demonstrations of the 'not-so-minimal' consequences of television news programmes. *American Political Science Review, 76*, 848–858.

Jacoby, J., & Hoyer, W. D., (1983). Viewer miscomprehension of televised communication: selected findings. In E. Wartella & D. C. Whitney (Eds.) *Mass communication review yearbook: Vol..* Bevery Hills, CA: Sage.

Jacoby, J., Hoyer, W. D., & Sheluga, D. A. (1980). *Miscomprehension of televised communications.* New York: American Association of Advertising Agencies.

Jaspen, N. (1950). Effects on teaching a perceptual motor skill of experimental film variables: verbalisations, "how it work" participation, succinct treatment. *American Psychologist, 5*, 335–336.

Johnson, N. (1973). Television and politicisation: A test of competing models. *Journalism Quarterly 50*, 447–455.

Johnson N. S., & Mandler J. M. (1980). A tale of two structures: Underlying and surface forms in stories. *Poetics, 9*, 51–86.

Jones, D. M., Davies, D. R., Hoga, K. M., Patrick, J., & Cumberbatch, G. (1978). Short-term memory during the normal working day. In M. M. Gruneberg, P.E. Morris, & R. N. Sykes (Eds.), *Practical aspects of memory.* London: Academic Press.

Jorgenson, F S. (1955). *The relative effectiveness of these methods of television newscasting.* Doctoral dissertation, University of Wisconsin.

Julian, F. D. (1977). *Nonverbal determinants of a television newscaster's credibility: an experimental study.* Unpublished doctoral dissertation, University of Wisconsin, location.

Kaplan, R. M., & Pascoe, G. C. (1977). Humorous lectures and humorous examples: Some effects upon comprehension and retention. *Journal of Educational Psychology, 69*,

Karpf, A. (1985). July 22 News with the miracle ingredient. *The Guardian*, p.13.

Katz, E., Adoni, H., & Parness, P. (1977). Remembering the news: What the picture adds to recall. *Journalism Quarterly, 54*, 231–239.

Katz, E., Blumler, J. G., & Gurevitch, M. (1974). Utilization of mass communication by the individual. In J. G. Blumler & E. Katz (Eds.), *The uses of mass communications: Current perspectives on gratifications research.* Beverly Hills, CA: Sage

Kellermann, K (1985). Memory processes in media effects. *Communication Research, 12,* 83–131.

Kelley, P., Buckle, L., & Gunter, B. (1985). The television literacy project. *Secondary Education Journal, 15,* 21–22.

Kelley, P., & Gunter, B. (1984 October 12). Television literacy. *The Times Educational Supplement,* p.

Kelley, P., Gunter, B., & Kelley, C. (1985). Teaching television in the classroom: Results of a preliminary study. *Journal of Educational Television, 11,* 57–63.

Kieras, D. (1978). Beyond pictures and words: Alternative information processing models for imagery effects in verbal memory, *Psychological Bulletin, 85,* 532–554.

Kintsch, W. (1974). The representation of meaning in memory. Hilldale, NJ: Lawrence Erlbaum Associates.

Kintsch, W. (1977). *Memory and cognition.* New York: Wiley.

Kintsch, W., & van Dijk, T. (1978). Toward a model of text comprehension and production. *Psychological Review, 85,* 363–394.

Klapper, J. (1960). *The effects of mass communication.* New York: The Free Press.

Klein, A. (1978). How telecast's Organization affects viewer retention. *Journalism Quarterly, 55,* 356–359, 411.

Klein, K. E., Hermann, R., Kuklinski, P., Wegmann, H-P (1977). Circadian performance rhythms: Experimental studies in air operations. In R. R, Markie (Ed.), *Vigilance theory, operational performance and physiological correlates.* London: Plenum.

Kleinsmith, L. J., & Kaplan, S. (1963). Paired associate learning as a function of arousal and interpolated interval. *Journal of Experimental Psychology, 65,* 190–193.

Kleitman, N. (1963). *Sleep and wakefulness.* Chicago: Chicago University Press. Kosslyn, S. M. (1980. *Image and mind.* Cambridge, MA. Harvard University Press.

Kosslyn, S. M. (1980) *Image and mind.* Cambridge, MA: Harvard University Press.

Kozminsky, E. (1977). Altering comprehension: The effect of biasing titles on text comprehension. *Memory and Cognition, 5,* 482–490.

Kraus, S. (1962). *The Great debates: Background, perspective effects.* Bloomington: Indiana University Press.

Kraus, S. (1979). *The great debates: Carter vs. Ford, 1976.* Bloomington: Indiana University Press.

Kroll, N. E. A., Bee, J., & Gurski, G. (1973). Release of proactive interference as a result of changing presentation modality. *Journal of Experimental Psychology, 98,* 131–137.

Kuiper, N. A., & Paivio, A. (1977). Incidental recognition memory for concrete and abstract sentences equated for comprehensibility. *Bulletin of the Psychonomic Society, 9,* 247–249.

Laird, D. A. (1925). Relative performance of college students as conditioned by time of day and day of week. *Journal of Experimental Psychology, 8,* 50–63.

Larsen, S. F. (1981). *Knowledge updating: Three papers on news memory, background knowledge and text processing* (Psychological Reports, 6,(4)). Aurhus: University of Aarhus, Institute of Psychology.

Lathorp, L. W. (1949). *An experiment to determine the effectiveness of the film introduction in present instructional sound motion pictures.* Unpublished master's dissertation, Pennylvania State College, City.

Lebowitz, M. (1979). *Reading with a purpose.* Paper presented at the First Annual Conference of the Cognitive Science Society, San Diego, CA.

Lee, R. (1975). Credibility of newspaper and TV news. *Journalism Quarterly, 55,* 282–287.

Lesser, G. (1974). *Children and television: Lessons from Sesame Street.* New York: Random House.

Levy, M. (1977). Experiencing television news. *Journal of Communication, 27*, 112–117.

Levy, M. (1978). The audience experience with television news. *Journalism Monographs* (No. 55).

Linne, O., & Veirup, K. (1974). *Radio producers and their audiences: A confrontation.* Danish Radio Training Department, No. 24.

Loftus, G. R., & Kallman, H. J. (1979). Encoding and use of detail information in picture recognition. *Journal of Experimental Psychology: Human Learning and Memory, 5,* 197–211.

Lorch, E. P., Anderson, D. R., & Levin, S. R. (1979) The relationship of visual attention to children's comprehension of television. *Child Development, 50,* 722–727.

Lumsdaine, A. A., & Gladstone, A. I. (1958). Overt practice and audio-visual embellishments. In M. A. Miy & A. A. Lumsdaine (Eds.,) *Learning from films* New Haven, CT: Yale University Press.

Maccoby, E. E., & Jacklin, C. N. (1974). *The psychology of sex differences.* Stanford, CA: Stanford University Press.

Maccoby, N., & Sheffield, F. D. (1961). Combining practice with demonstration in teaching complex sequences: Summary and interpretations. In A. A. Lumsdaine (Ed.,) *Student response in programmed instruction: A symposium.* Washington, DC: National Academy of Sciences National Research Council.

Madigan, S. A. (1969). Intraserial repetition and coding processes in free recall. *Journal of Verbal Learning and Verbal Behaviour, 8,* 828–835.

Maier, N.R., & Thurber, J.A. (1968). Accuracy of judgements of deception when an interview is watched, heard and read. *Personnel Psychology, 21,* 23–30.

Mandell, L. M., & Shaw, D. C. (1973). Judging people in the news—unconsciously: Effect of camera angle and bodily activity. *Journal of Broadcasting, 17,* 353–362.

Mandler, J. M., & Johnson, N. S. (1977). Rememberance of things parsed: Story structure and recall. *Cognitive Psychology, 9,* 111–151.

Martin, E. (1968). Stimulus meaningfulness and paired-associate transfer: An encoding variability hypothesis. *Psychological Review, 75,* 421–441.

Martin, E. (1972). Stimulus encoding in learning and transfer. In A. W. Melton & E. Martin (Eds.), *Coding processes in human memory.* Washington, DC: Winston.

Mayer, B. J. F. (1977). What is remembered from prose. A function of passage structure. In R. O. Freedle (Ed.), *Discourse production and comprehension.* Norwood, NJ: Ablex.

Mayer, R. E. (1979a). Can advance organisers influence meaningful learning. *Review of Education Research, 49,* 371–383.

Mayer, R. E. (1979b). Twenty years of research on advance organisers: Assimilation theory is still the best predictor of results. *Instructional Science, 8,* 133–167.

McCain, T. A., Chilberg, J., & Wakshlag, J. (1977). The effect of camera angle on source credibility and attention. *Journal of Broadcasting, 21,* 35–46.

McCain, T. A., & Ross, M. G. (1979). Cognitive switching A behavioural trace of human information processing for television newscasts. *Human Communication Research, 5,* 121–129.

McClure, R., & Patterson, T. (1973). *Television news and voter behaviour in the 1972 presidential election.* Unpublished paper, American Political Science Association.

McClure, R., & Patterson T. (1974). Television news and political advertising: The impact of exposure on voter beliefs. *Communication Research, 1,* 3–31.

McClure, R., & Patterson, T. (1976) Print vs. network news. *Journal of Communication, 26,* 23–28.

McCombs, M. (1976). Agenda-setting research: a bibliographic essay. *Political Communication Review, 1,* 1–7.

McCombs, M., & Shaw, D. (1972). The agenda-setting function of mass media. *Public Opinion Quarterly, 36,* 176–187.

McCombs, M., Shaw, D., & Shaw, E. (1972) *The news and public response. Three studies of the agenda-setting power in the press.* Paper presented to the Association for Education in Journalism, Carbondale, Il.

McGeoch, J. A., & MacDonald, W. T. (1931). Meaningful relation and retroactive inhibition. *American Journal of Psychology, 43,* 579–588.

McGhee, P. E. (1980). Toward the integration of entertainment and educational functions of television. The role of humour. In P. H. Tannenbaum (Ed.), *The entertainment functions of television.* Hillsdale, NJ: Lawrence Erlbaum Associates.

McIntyre, C. J. (1954). *Training film evaluation: FB 254—Cold weather uniforms.* (Technical Report SDC 269-7-51). Port Washington, NY: U.S. Naval Special Devices Center.

McLeod, J. M., & McDonald, D. G. (1985). Beyond simple exposure: Media orientations and their impact on political processes. *Communication Research, 12,* 3–33.

Melton, A.W. (1963). Implications of short-term memory for a general theory of memory. *Journal of Verbal Learning and Verbal Behaviour, 2,* 1–21.

Melton, A. W. (1970). The situation with respect to the spacing of repetitions and memory. *Journal of Verbal Learning and Verbal Behaviour, 9,* 596–606.

Melton, A. W., & Irwin, J. M. (1940). The influence of degree of interpolated learning on retroactive inhibition and the overt transfer of specific responses. *American Journal of Psychology, 53,* 173–203.

Meringoff, L.K. (1980). Influence of the medium on children's story apprehension. *Journal of Educational Psychology, 72,* 240–249.

Metallinos, N. (1980, August). Asymmetry of the visual field: Perception, retention and preference of still images. In J Baggaley (Ed.), *Proceedings of the Third International Conference on Experimental Research in Televised Instruction.* St. Johns: Memorial University.

Meudell, P. (1983). The development and dissolution of memory. In A. Mayes (Ed.), *Memory: In animals and humans.* Cambridge, England: Van Nostrand Reinhold.

Meyer, B. F. (1975). *The organisation of prose and its effects on memory.* Amsterdam: North Holland.

Meyer B. F. (1977). What is remembered from prose. A function of passage structure. In R. O. Freedle (Ed.), *Discourse production and comprehension.* Norwood, NJ: Ablex.

Meyer, D. E. (1970). On the representation and retrieval of stored semantic information. *Cognitive Psychology, 1,* 242–300.

Meyer, D. J. F. (1978). *The Organization of prose and its effects on memory.* Haag: Mouton.

Miller, G. A. (1956). The magical number seven, plus or minus two: Some limits on our capacity for processing information. *Psychological Review, 63,* 81–97.

Miller, G. A., Galanter, E., & Pribram, K. H. (1960). *Plans and the structure of behaviour.* New York: Holt.

Millerson, G. (1976). *Effective television production.* Sevenoaks, Kent: Focal Press.

Moeser, S. D. (1974). Memory for meaning and wording in concrete and abstract sentences. *Journal of Verbal Learning and Verbal Behaviour, 13,* 682–697.

Monge, R. H., & Hultsch, D. F. (1971). Paired associate learning as a function of adult age and the length of the anticipation and inspection intervals. *Journal of Gerontology, 26,* 157–162.

Moran, T. P. (1974). The syntactic imagery hypothesis: A production system model. *Dissertation Abstracts International, 35,* 551B–552B (University Microfilms No. 74-14657).

Morris, P. E., & Gale, A. (1974). A correlational study of variables related to imagery. *Perception and Motor Skills, 38,* 659–665.

Murdoch, G. (1973). Political deviance: The press presentation of a militant mass demonstration. Ian S. Cohen & J. Young (Eds.), *The manufacture of news: Deviance, social problems and the mass media.* London: Constable.

Murdock, B. B., Jr. (1962). The serial position effect of free recall. *Journal of Experimental Psychology, 64,* 482–488.

Murdock, B. B. Jr. (1974). *Human memory: Theory and data.* Potomac, MD.: Lawrence Erlbaum Associates.

Murdock, G. (1973). Political deviance: The press presentation of a militant mass demonstration. In S. Cohen & J. Young (Eds.), *The manufacture of news.* London: Constable.

Nelson, H. E. (1948). The effect of variation of rate on the recall by radio listeners of "straight" newscasts. *Speech Monographs, 15,* 173–180.

Neuman, W. R. (1976). Patterns of recall among television news viewers. *Public Opinion Quarterly, 40,* 115–123.

Nickerson, R. S. (1965). Short-term memory for complex meaningful visual configurations: A demonstration of capacity. *Canadian Journal of Psychology, 19,* 155–160.

Niegeman, H. M. (1982). Influences of titles on the recall of instructional texts. In A. Flammer & W. Kintsch (Eds.), *Discourse processing.* Amsterdam: North Holland Publishing Company.

Nielsen, A. C. (1984). Television viewing to network news programming. *Nielsen Television Index.* New York: A. C. Nielsen Company.

Nordenstreng, K. (1972). *Policy of news transmission.* In D. McQuail (Ed.), *Sociology of mass communications.* Harmondsworth: Penguin Books.

Norford, C.A. (1949). *Contribution of film summaries to the effectiveness of instructional sound motion pictures.* Pennsylvania State College, Unpublished masters dissertation, location.

Norman, D. A. (1978). Notes toward a theory of complex learning. In H. M. Lesgold, J. W. Pellergrino, S. D. Fokkema, & R. Glaser (Eds.), *Cognitive psychology and instruction.* New York: Plenum Press.

Norman, D. A., & Rumelhart, D.A. (1975). *Explorations in cognition.* San Francisco: W. H. Freeman.

Oberschall, A. (1973). *Social conflict and social movement.* Englewood Cliffs NJ: Prentice-Hall.

Opinion Research Centre (1972). *News and current affairs.* London: ORC 1047,7.

Ortony, A. (1975). Why metaphors are necessary and not just nice. *Educational Theory, 25,* 43–53.

Ortony, A. (1978). Remembering, understanding, and representation. *Cognitive Science, 2,* 53–69.

Ostgard, E. (1965). Factors influencing the flow of news. *Journal of Peace Research, 1,* 39–63.

Ozier, M. (1980). Individual differences in free recall: When some people remember better than others. In G. H. Bower (Ed.), *The psychology of learning and motivation. Vol.4..* New York: Academic Press.

Paivio, A. (1963). Learning of adjective-noun paired-associates as a function of adjective-noun word order and noun abstractness. *Canadian Journal of Psychology, 17,* 370–379.

Paivio, A. (1969). Mental imagery in associative learning and memory. *Psychological Review, 76,* 241–263.

Paivio, A. (1971). *Imagery and verbal processes.* New York: Holt.

Palmer, E. L. (1969). Research at the Children's Television Workshop. *Educational Broadcasting Review, 3,* 43–48.

Palmgreen, P., & Clarke, P. (1977). Agenda-setting with local and national issues. *Communication Research, 4,* 435–452.

Patterson, T. (1980). *The mass media election.* New York: Praeger.

Patterson, T., & McClure, R. (1976). *The unseeing eye.* New York: G. P. Putnam.

Peled, T., & Katz, E. (1974). Media functions in wartime: The Israel home front in October 1973. In J. G. Blumler & E Katz (Eds.), *The uses of mass communications: Current perspectives on gratifications research.* Beverly Hills, CA: Sage.

Perloff, R., Wartella, E., & Becker, L. (1982). Increasing learning from TV news. *Journalism Quarterly, 59,* 83–86.

Perry, D. G., & Perry, L. C. (1975). Observational learning in children: Effects of sex of model and subject's sex role behaviour. *Journal of Personality and Social Psychology, 31,* 1083–1088.

Peterson, L. R., & Peterson, M. J. (1959). Short-term retention of individual items. *Journal of Experimental Psychology, 58,* 193–198.

Petty, R. E., Ostrom, T. M., & Brock, T. C. (1981). *Cognitive responses in persuasion.* Hillsdale, NJ: Lawrence Erlbaum Associates.

Pezdek, K., & Royer, J. M. (1974). The role of comprehension in learning concrete and abstract sentences. *Journal of Verbal Learning and Verbal Behaviour, 13,* 551–558.

Philipchalk, R.P. (1972). Thematicity, abstractness, and the long-term recall of connected discourse. *Psychonomic Science, 27,* 361–362.

Postman, L. (1978). Picture-word differences in the acquisition and retention of paired associates. *Journal of Experimental Psychology: Human Learning and Memory, 4*(2), 146–157.

Postman, L., & Phillips, L. W. (1965). Short-term temporal changes in free recall. *Quarterly Journal of Experimental Psychology, 17,* 132–138.

Pylyshyn, Z. W. (1973). What the mind's eye tells the mind's brain: A critique of mental imagery. *Psychological Bulletin, 80,* 1–24.

Quarles, R. C (1979). Mass media use and voting behaviour. *Communication Research, 6,* 407–436.

Rawcliffe-King, A., & Dyer, N. (1983). The knowledge-gap reconsidered: Learning from "Ireland: A Television History by Robert Kee." *BBC Annual Review of Research,* London: British Broadcasting Corporation.

Reese, S. D. (1984). Visual-verbal redundancy effects on television news learning. *Journal of Broadcasting, 28,* 79–87.

Reitman, J. S. (1971). Mechanisms of forgetting in short-term memory. *Cognitive Psychology, 2,* 185–195.

Reitman, J. S. (1974). Without surreptitious rehearsal, information in short-term memory decays. *Journal of Verbal Learning and Verbal Behaviour, 13,* 365–377.

Renckstorff, K. (1977). Nachrichtensendungen im Fernsehen eine empirische Studie zur Wirkung unterschiedlicher Darstellung in Fernsehnachrichten. *Media Perspektiven,* 1/77, 27–42.

Restorff, H. von, H. (1933). Uber der Wirkung von Bereichsbildugen im Spurenfeld. *Psychologisch Forschung, 18,* 299–342.

Revelle, W., Humphreys, M. S., Simon, L., & Gilliland, K. (1980). The interactive effect of personality, time of day and caffeine: A test of the arousal model. *Journal of Experimental Psychology: General, 109,* 1–31.

Robinson, J. P. (1967). World affairs information and mass media exposure. *Journalism Quarterly, 44,* 23–40.

Robinson, J. P. (1972). Mass communication and information diffusion. In F. G. Kline & P. J. Tichenor (Eds.), *Current perspectives in mass communication research.* Beverly Hills, CA: Sage.

Robinson, J. P., Davis, D., Sahin, H., & O'Toole, T. (1980, August). *Comprehension of television news: How alert is the audience?* Paper presented to the Association for Education in Journalism, Boston.

Robinson, J. P., & Levy, M. (1985). *The main source: Learning from television news.* Beverly Hills, CA: Sage.

Robinson, J. P., & Sahin, H. (1984). *Audience comprehension of television news: Results from some exploratory research.* London: British Broadcasting Corporation, Broadcasting Research Department.

Robinson, J. P., Sahin, H., & Davis, D. (1982). Television journalists and their audiences. In J. S. Ettema & D. C. Whitney (Eds.), *Individuals in mass media Organizations: creativity and constraint.* Beverly Hills, CA: Sage.

Robinson, M. J. (1975). American political legitimacy in an era of electronic journalism: Reflections on the evening news. In D. Cater & R. Hiller (Eds.), *Television as a social force: New approaches to TV criticism*. New York: Praeger.

Robinson, M. J. (1976). Public affairs television and the growth of political malaise: The case of the "selling of the Pentagon." *American Political Science Review, 70*, 40–432.

Robinson, M. J. (1977). Television and American politics: 1956–1976. *Public Interest, 48*, 3–39.

Robinson, M. J., & Zukin, C. (1976). Television and the Wallace vote in 1968: Are there implications for 1976? *Public Opinion Quarterly, 38*, 445?

Roediger, H. L. (1973). Inhibition in recall from cueing with recall targets. *Journal of Verbal and Verbal Behaviour, 12*, 644–657.

Roediger, H. L. (1974). Inhibiting effects of recall. *Memory and Cognition, 2*, 261–269.

Roper Organization (1983). *Trends in attitudes towards television and other media: A twenty year review*. New York: Television Information Office.

Rosenberg, E. J. (1977). The effect of cueing on recall of unrelated words. *Biological Psychology Bulletin, 5*, 17–28.

Rosengren, K. (1977). Four types of tables. *Journal of Communication, 27*, 67–

Rothkopf. E.A. (1968). Textual constraint as a function of repeated inspection. *Journal of Educational Psychology, 1*, 20–25.

Rubin, A. (1981). A multivariate analysis of "60 minutes" viewing motivations. *Journalism Quarterly, 58*, 529–536.

Rubin, A. (1983). Television uses and gratifications. The interactions of viewing patterns and motivations. *Journal of Broadcasting, 27*, 37–51.

Rubin, A. (1984). Ritualised and instrumental television viewing. *Journal of Communication, 34*, 67–77.

Rubin, A., & Rubin, R. (1982). Older persons' TV viewing patterns and motivations. *Communication Research, 9*, 287–313.

Rumelhart, D. E. (1975). Note on a schema for stories. In D. Laberge & S. J. Samuels (Eds.), *Basic processes in reading*. Hillsdale, NJ: Lawrence Erlbaum Associates.

Rumelhart, D. E., & Ortony, A. (1977). The representation of knowledge in memory. In R. C. Anderson, R. J. Spiro, & W. E. Montague (Eds.), *Schooling and the acquisition of knowledge*. Hillsdale, NJ: Lawrence Erlbaum Associates.

Rundus, D. (1971). Analysis of rehearsal strategies and single level processing. *Journal of Verbal Learning and Verbal Behaviour, 16*, 665–681.

Sahin, H., Davis, D., & Robinson, J. P. (1981). Improving the TV news. *Irish Broadcasting Review*, No. 11 (Summer), 50–55.

Salomon, G. (1979). *Interaction of media, cognition and learning*. San Fransisco: Jossey-Bass.

Salomon, G. (1983). Beyond the formats of television: The effects of student preconceptions on the experience of televiewing. In M. Meyer (Ed.), *Children and the formal features of television*. Munich: K. G. Saur.

Salomon, G. (in press). TV is 'easy' and print is 'tough': The role of perceptions and attributions in the processing of material. *Journal of Educational Psychology*.

Sande, O. (1971). The perception of foreign news. *Journal of Peace Research, 8*, 3–4.

Schank, R. C., & Abelson, R. P. (1977). *Scripts, plans, goals and understanding: An inquiry into human knowledge structures*. Hillsdale, NJ: Lawrence Erlbaum Associates.

Schlater, R. (1970). Effect of speed of presentation on recall of television messages. *Journal of Broadcasting, 14*, 207–214.

Schleicher, M. D., Bryant, J. & Zillmann, D. (1980). Voluntary selective exposure to educational television programmes as a function of differently paced humorous inserts.

Schlesinger, P. (1978). *Putting 'reality' together: BBC news*. London: Constable.

Schramm, W. (1973). *Men, messages and media: A look at human communication*. New York: Harper & Row.

Schulz, W. (1976). *Die konstruktion von Realitat in den Nachrichtenmedien: Analyse der acktuellen Berichterstaltung.* Munich: Kart Alber.

Schulz, W. (1982). News structure and people's awareness of political events. *Gazette, 30,* 139–153.

Schwartz, M. N. K., & Flammer, A. (1982). Text structure and title—Effects on comprehension and recall. *Journal of Verbal Learning and Verbal Behaviour, 20,* 61–66.

Schwartz, S. (1975). Individual differences in cognition: Some relationships between personality and memory. *Journal of Research in Personality, 9,* 217–225.

Severin, W. (1967). The effectiveness of relevant pictures in multiple-channel communications. *AV Communication Review, 15,* 386–401.

Severin, W. (1968). *Cue summation in multiple-channel communication* (Technical Report No. 37) University of Wisconsin, Madison, Wisconsin Research and Development Center for Cognitive Learning.

Shaw, E. (1977). The agenda-setting hypothesis reconsidered: Interpersonal factors. *Gazette, 23,* 230–240.

Shepherd, R. N. (1967). Recognition memory for words, sentences and pictures. *Journal of Verbal Learning and Verbal Behaviour, 6,* 156–163.

Shiffrin, R. M. (1975). Short-term store: The basis for a memory system. In F. Restle, R. M. Shiffrin, N. J. Castellan, H. R. Lindman, & D. D. Pisoni (Eds.), *Cognitive theory: Vol 1.* Hillsdale, NJ: Lawrence Erlbaum Associates.

Shosteck, H. (1974). Factors influencing appeal of TV news personalities. *Journal of Broadcasting, 18,* 63–71.

Simon, H. A. (1972). What is visual imagery? An information processing interpretation. In L. W. Green (Ed.), *Cognition in learning and memory.* New York: Wiley.

Simon, H. A. (1974). How big is a chunk? *Science, 183,* 482–488.

Singer, J. L. (1980). The power and limitations of television: A cognitive-affective analysis. In P. H. Tannenbaum (Ed.), *The entertainment functions of television.* Hillsdale, NJ: Lawrence Erlbaum Associates.

Singer, J. L., & Singer, D. G. (1979). Come back Mister Rogers, Come back. *Psychology Today,*

Singleton, L. A., & Cook, S. L. (1982). Television network news reporting by female correspondents An update. *Journal of Broadcasting, 26,* 487–491.

Smith, E. E., Shoben, E. J., & Rips, L. J. (1974). Structures and process in semantic memory: A factual model for smeantic decision. *Psychological Review, 81,* 214–241.

Smith, J. R., & McEwan, W. J. (1974). Effects of newscast delivery rate on recall and judgement of sources. *Journal of Broadcasting, 18,* 73–83.

Sparkes, V. M., & Winter, J. P. (1980). Public interest in foreign news. *Gazette, 20,* 149–170.

Spence, J. T., & Spence, K. W. (1966). The motivational components of manifest anxiety: Drive and drive stimuli. In C. D. Speilberger (Ed.). *Anxiety and behaviour,* London: Academic Press.

Spilich, G. J., Vesonder, G. T., Chiesi, H. L., & Voss, J. F. (1979). Text processing of domain-related information for individuals with high and low domain knowledge. *Journal of Verbal Learning and Verbal Behaviour, 18,* 275–290.

Stauffer, J., Frost, R., & Rybolt, W. (1978). Literacy, illiteracy and learning from television news. *Communication Research, 5,* 211–232.

Stauffer, J., Frost, R., & Rybolt, W. (1980). Recall and comprehension of radio news in Kenya. *Journalism Quarterly, 57,* 612–617.

Stauffer, J., Frost, R., & Rybolt, W. (1983). The attention factor in recalling network television news. *Journal of Communication, 33,* 29–37.

Stern A. A. (1971, September). Presentation to the Radio-Television News Directors Association, Boston. Unpublished paper, University of California at Berkely, Graduate School of Journalism).

Sticht, T. G. (1969). Comprehension of repeated time-compressed recordings. *Journal of Experimental Education, 37*, 60–62.

Stone, V. A. (1974). Attitudes towards television newswomen. *Journal of Broadcasting, 18*, 50–61.

Stradling, R. (1977). *The political awareness of school leavers.* London: Hansard Society.

Strassner, E. (1975). *Fernschnachrichten: Eine Produktions-Produktund Rezeptionsanalyse.* Tiebingen: Neimeger Verlag.

Svensson, J. (1981). Etermediernas Nyhetssprak 2. Studier over Innehall och Informationsstruktur [News language of the media 2. Studies on content and information structure]. Lundastudier i Nordisk Sprakvetenskap, Serie c, Nr 11 Lund: Walter Ekstrans Bokforlag.

Tan, A., Raudy, J., Huff, C., & Miles, J. (1980). Children's reactions to male and female newscasters: Effectiveness and believability. *Quarterly Journal of Speech, 66*, 201–205.

Tankard, J. W., Jr. (1971). Eye contact research and television announcing. *Journal of Broadcasting, 15*, 83–90.

Tannenbaum, P. H. (1953) The effect of headlines on the interpretation of news items. *Journalism Quarterly, 30*, 189–197.

Tannenbaum, P. H. (1954). Effect of serial position on recall of radio news stories. *Journalism Quarterly, 31*, 319–323.

Tannenbaum, P. H., & Kernick, J. (1954). Effects of newscast item leads upon listener interpretation. *Journalism Quarterly, 31*, 33–37.

Tannenbaum, P. H., & Zillmann, D. (1975). Emotional arousal in the facilitation of aggression through communication. IN L. Berkowitz (Ed.), *Advances in experimental social psychology: Vol. 8*, New York: Academic Press.

Tarpy, R. M., & Mayer, R. E. (1978). *Foundations of learning and memory.* Glenview, IL: Scott, Foresman.

Taylor, S. E. & Crocker, J. (1981). Schematic bases of social information processing. In E. T. Higgins, C. P. Herman, & M. P. Zanna (Eds.), *Social cognition: The Ontario symposium: Vol. 1.* Hillsdale, NJ: Lawrence Erlbaum Associates.

Thayer, R. E. (1967). Measurement of activation through self-report. *Psychological Reports, 20*, 663–678.

Thayer, R. E. (1978) Factor analytic and reliability studies on the activation-deactivation adjective check list. *Psychological Reports, 42*, 747–756.

Thompson, D. M., & Tulving, E. (1970). Associative encoding and retrieval with weak and strong cues. *Journal of Experimental Psychology, 86*, 255–262.

Thorndyke, P. W. (1977). Cognitive structures in comprehension and memory for narrative discourse. *Cognitive Psychology, 9*, 77–110.

Thorndyke, P. W. (1978). Pattern directed processing of knowledge from texts. In D. A. Waterman & F. Hayes-Roth (Eds.), *Pattern directed inference systems.* New York: Academic Press.

Thorndyke, P. W. (1979). Knowledge acquisition from newspaper stories. *Discourse Processes, 2*, 95–112.

Tichenor, P. J., Donohue, G. A., & Olien, C. N. (1970). Mass media flow and differential growth of knowledge. *Public Opinion Quarterly, 34*, 159–170.

Tiemens, R. (1970). Some relationships of camera angle to communicator credibility. *Journal of Broadcasting, 14*, 483–490.

Tracey, M. (1978). *The production of political television.* London: Routledge & Kegan Paul.

Traxler, A. J. (1973). Retroactive and proactive inhibition in young and elderly adults using an unpaced modified free recall test. *Psychological Reports, 32*, 215–222.

Treat, N. J., & Reese, H. W. (1976). Age, pacing, and imagery in paired-associate learning. *Developmental Psychology, 12*, 119–125.

Treisman, A. M. (1969). Strategies and models of selective attention. *Psychological Review, 76*, 282–299.

Trenaman, J. (1967). *Communication and comprehension.* London: Longman.

Trenaman, J., & McQuail, D. (1961). *Television and the political image.* London: Methuen.

Tuchman, G. (1978). *Making news: A study in the construction of reality.* New York: The Free Press.

Tulving, E. (1962). Subjective Organization in free recall of "unrelated" words. *Psychological Review, 69,* 344–354.

Tulving, E. (1968). Theoretical issues in free recall. In T. R. Dixon & D. L. Horton (Eds.), *Verbal behaviour and general behaviour theory.* Englewood Cliffs, NJ: Prentice-Hall.

Tulving, E. (1972). Episodic and semantic memory. In E. Tulving & W. Donaldson (Eds.), *Organization and memory.* New York: Academic Press.

Tulving, E., & Osler, S. (1968). Effectiveness of retrieval cues in memory for words. *Journal of Experimental Psychology, 77,* 593–601.

Tulving, E., & Patterson, R. D. (1968). Functional units and retrieval processes in free recall. *Journal of Experimental Psychology, 77,* 239–248.

Tulving, E., & Pearlstone, Z. (1966). Availability versus accessibility of information in memory for words. *Journal of Verbal Learning and Verbal Behaviour, 5,* 381–391.

Tulving, E., & Thompson, D. M. (1973). Encoding specificity and retrieval processes in episodic memory. *Psychological Review, 50,* 353–373.

Tunstall, J. (1971) *Journalists at work.* London: Constable.

Tunstall, J. (1983). *The media in Britain.* New York: Columbia University Press.

Turvey, M. T., & Egan, J. (1969). Contextual change and release from proactive interference in short-term verbal memory. *Journal of Experimental Psychology, 81,* 396–397.

Underwood, B. J. (1961). An evaluation of the Gibson theory of verbal learning. In C. N. Cofer (Ed.), *Verbal learning and verbal behaviour.* New York: McGraw-Hill.

Underwood, B. J. (1970). A breakdown of the total time law in free recall learning. *Journal of Verbal Learning and Verbal Behaviour, 9,* 573–580.

Underwood, B. J., & Ekstrand, B. R. (1967). Response term integration. *Journal of Verbal Learning and Verbal Behaviour, 6,* 432–438.

Underwood, B. J., Kapelak, S. M., & Malmi, R. A. (1976). Integration of discrete verbal units in recognition memory. *Journal of Experimental Psychology: Human Learning and Memory, 2,* 293–300.

Vincent, R.C., Crow, B. K., & Davis, D. K. (1985, May). *When technology fails: The drama of airline crashes in network television news.* Paper presented to the mass communication division of the International Communication Association conference, Honolulu, Hawaii.

Vincent, W., Ash. P., & Greenhill, L. (1949). *Relationship of length and fact frequency to effectiveness of instructional motion pictures* (Technical Report SDL-267-7-7). Port Washington, NY-U.S. Navy Special devices Center.

Wade, S., & Schremm, W. (1969). The mass media as sources of public affairs, science and health knowledge. *Public Opinion Quarterly, 33,* 197–209.

Wagenaar, W. A. (1978). Recalling messages broadcast to the general public. In M. M. Gurneberg, P. E. Morris, & H. C. Foot (Eds.), *Practical aspects of memory.* New York: Academic Press.

Wagenaar, W. A. & Visser, J. G. (1979). The weather forecast under the weather. *Erogonomics, 22,* 909–917.

Wakshlag J., Day, K. D., & Zillmann, D. (1980). Selective exposure to educational television programmes as a function of differently paced humorous inserts. *Journal of Educational Psychology, 73,* 23–32.

Wakshlag, J., Day, K.O.,& Zillman, D. (1981). Selective exposure to educational television programmes as a function of differently-paced humorous inserts. *Journal of Educational Psychology, 73,* 27–32.

Walker, E. L. (1958). Action-decrement and its relation to learning. *Psychological Review, 65,* 129–142.

Walker, E. L., & Tate, R. D. (1963). Memory storage as a function of arousal and time with homogeneous and Heterogeneous lists. *Journal of Verbal Learning and Verbal Behaviour, 4*(2), 113–119.

Wamsley, G. L., & Pride, R. A. (1972). TV network news: Re-thinking the iceberg problem. *Western Political Quarterly, 25,* 434–450.

Warner, M. (1979). Decision-making in network TV news. In J. Tunstall (Ed.), *Media Sociology.* London: Constable.

Waugh, N. C., & Norman, D. A. (1965). Primary memory. *Psychological Review, 72,* 89–104.

Wells, E. (1973). Words and pictures as distinct encoding categories in short-term memory. *Journal of Experimental Psychology, 97,* 394–396.

Westley, B. H., & Mobius, J. B. (1960). *The effects of "eye contact" in televised instruction.* University of Wisconsin, Madison, unpublished paper,

Whale, J. (1969). *The half-shut eye: Television and politics in Britain and America.* London: Macmillan.

Whitakker, S., & Whitakker, R. (1976). Relative effectiveness of male and female newscasters. *Journal of Broadcasting, 20,*

Wickens, D. D. (1970). Encoding categories of words: An empirical approach to memory. *Psychological Review, 77,* 1–15.

Wickens, D. D. (1972). Characteristics of word encoding. In A. W. Melton & E. Martin (Eds.) *Coding processes in human memory.* New York: Wiley.

Wickens, D. D. Born, D. G., & Allen, C, K. (1963). Proactive inhibition and item-similarityyin short-term memory. *Journal of Verbal Learning and Verbal Behaviour, 2,* 440–445.

Wicker, F. W. (1970). On the locus of picture-word differences in paired-associate learning. *Journal of Verbal Learning and Verbal Behaviour, 9,* 52–57.

Wicker, F. W., & Evertson, C. M. (1972). Prerecall and postrecall imagery ratings with pictorial and verbal stimuli in paired-associate learning. *Journal of Experimental Psychology, 92,* 75–82.

Williams, D. C., Paul, J., & Ogilvy, J. L. (1957). The mass media, learning and retention. *Canadian Journal of Psychology, 11,* 157–163.

Wilson, C. E. (1974). The effect of medium on loss of information. *Journalism Quarterly, 51,* 111–115.

Wimer, R. E. (1960). A supplementary report on age differences in retention over a twenty four hour period. *Journal of Gerontology, 15,* 417–418.

Winch, W. H. (1911). Mental fatigue during the school day as measured by arithmetical reasoning. *British Journal of Psychology, 4,* 315–341.

Winch, W. H. (1912). Mental faitgue in day school children as measured by immediate memory: Parts I and II. *Journal of Educational Psychology, 3,* 18–28, 75–82.

Winch, W. H. (1913). Mental adaptation during the school day as measured by arithemtical reasoning: Parts I and II. *Journal of Educational Psychology, 4,* 17–28, 71–84.

Winocur, G. (1981). Learning and memory deficits in institutionalised and non-institutionalised old people: An analysis of interference effects. In F. I. M. Craik & S. Trehub (Eds.), *Ageing and cognitive processes.*

Wober, J. M. (1978). *The need for news: Audience attitudes towards nine news topics.* London: Independent Broadcasting Authority.

Wober, J. M. (1980). *The need for news: Audience attitudes towards nine news topics.* London: Independent Broadcasting Authority, Special Report.

Wober, J. M., & Gunter, B. (1981). *Recall of TV weather forecast information: An introductory experiment.* London: Independent Broadcasting Authority, Research Department Special Report.

Wood, G., & Underwood, B. J. (1967). Implicit responses and conceptual similarity. *Journal of Verbal Learning and Verbal Behaviour, 6,* 1–10.

Woodall, W. G., Davis, S, & Sahin, H. (1983). From the boob tube to the black box: Television news from an information processing perspective. *Journal of Broadcasting, 27*, 1–23.

Yarmey, A. D., & Ure, G. (1971). Incidental learning, noun imagery-concreteness and direction of associations in paired-associate learning. *Canadian Journal of Psychology, 25*, 91–102.

Yerkes, R. M., & Dodson, J. D. (1908). The relation of strength of stimulus to rapidity of habit-formation. *Journal of Comparative and Neurological Psychology, 18*, 459–482.

Yuille, J. C., & Paivio, A. (1969). Abstractness and the recall of connected discourse. *Journal of Experimental Psychology, 82*, 467–471.

Yuille, J.L., & Humphreys, M. S. (1970). *Free recall and forward and backward recall of paired-associates as a function of noun-concreteness.* Paper presented at a meeting of the Canadian Psychological Association, Winnepeg.

Zelinski, E. M., Gilewski, M. T., & Thompson, L. W. (1980). Do laboratory tests relate to self-assessment of memory ability in the young and old? In L. W. Poon, J. L. Fozard, L. S. Cermak, D. Arenberg, & L. W. Thompson (Eds.), *New directions in memory and aging: Proceedings of the George A. Talland Memorial Conference.* Hillsdale, NJ: Lawrence Erlbaum Associates.

Zillmann, D., & Bryant, J. (1980). Uses and effects of humour in educational television. In J. Baggaley (Ed.), *Proceedings of the Third International Conference on Experimental Research in Televised Instruction.* St Johns: Memorial University. Newfoundland.

Zillmann, D., Williams, B. R., Bryant, J., Boynton, K. R., & Wolf, M. A. (1980). Acquisition of information from educational television programmes as a function of differently paced humorous inserts. *Journal of Educational Psychology, 72.*

Index